Temple of the World

Karnak in the early 1840s.

The Great Hypostyle Hall in Karnak.

MIROSLAV VERNER

Temple of the World

SANCTUARIES, CULTS, AND MYSTERIES OF ANCIENT EGYPT

The American University in Cairo Press
Cairo New York

First published in English in Egypt in 2013 by
The American University in Cairo Press
113 Sharia Kasr el Aini, Cairo, Egypt
www.aucpress.com

First published in Czech in 2010 as *Chrám světa, svatyně, kulty a mysteria starověkého Egypta*
English translation by Anna Bryson-Gustová
Published by arrangement with Charles University in Prague

This book was written within the Program for the Development of Fields of Study at Charles University, No. P 14, "Archaeology of Ancient Egyptian Civilization: Cultural and Political Adaptation of the North African Civilizations in Ancient History (5000 BC–AD 1000)."

Dar el Kutub No. 2252/12
ISBN 978 977 416 563 4

Dar el Kutub Cataloging-in-Publication Data

Verner, Miroslav
Temple of the World: Sanctuaries, Cults, and Mysteries of Ancient Egypt / Miroslav Verner; translated by Anna Bryson-Gustová.—Cairo: The American University in Cairo Press, 2013
p. cm.
ISBN 978 977 416 563 4
1. Egypt—Antiquities
932

1 2 3 4 5 16 15 14 13

Printed in China

CONTENTS

"Do you know, Asclepius, that Egypt is an image of heaven or, to be more precise, that everything governed and moved in heaven came down to Egypt and was transferred there? If truth were told, our land is a Temple of the whole world."

PREFACE

<< Karnak: Obelisks of Thutmose I and Hatshepsut.

In the eyes of the world that surrounded it in its time, and as viewed by later ages, ancient Egypt was a land of gods and grand temples, and the ancient Egyptians one of the most religious peoples in the world. In the early modern era the monumental remains of Egyptian temples, their walls covered with mysterious inscriptions and scenes, evoked wonder, and contributed to the impression of a highly esoteric and spiritually distinctive civilization. Even today visitors often feel a similar sense of awe and mystery, although thanks to Jean-François Champollion, since 1822 we have been able to read the inscriptions and a great many of the enigmas of this magnificent civilization have been solved, although far from all.

Archaeological excavations have shown that over the several millennia of ancient Egypt's existence, innumerable sacred structures were built all over the land—from simple 'dwellings of the god' to immense, architecturally and religiously sophisticated complexes. The number of gods worshiped was also very large; according to one estimate as many as two thousand gods, demigods, and various demons are known from the sources. Their dwellings, even those that were very plain structures made of clay and rushes, were an essential part and even the central point of all but the very smallest human communities. The great majority of these buildings eventually collapsed or disappeared beneath deposits of mud. Only the most important have survived, and even then often not in original form, for their architectural history has usually been complex, involving multiple reconstruction and replacements of older elements, alterations, and extensions. In the case of large and important temples this architectural development expressed the royal ideology of ancient Egypt, according to which each ruler had the duty and desire to accomplish something "not yet achieved in the times of the ancestors."

Archaeological research, which has now been underway for nearly two centuries and in recent years has become ever more thorough and comprehensive, has been contributing greatly to the discovery, understanding, and rescue of many ancient Egyptian temples. The greatest temple complex in Egypt is a good example: excavations and other research in the great temple of Amun in Karnak have been going on for decades, involving among others a large Franco-Egyptian team of archaeologists, epigraphers, architects, and other experts who have been publishing the results of their work in numerous academic articles and splendid monographs. Similarly, studies of ancient Egyptian religion have been coming out in increasing numbers, including detailed monographs on particular gods and religious doctrines. Yet there have been surprisingly few publications that seek to combine the two currents of research—the architectural-archaeological and in some cases epigraphic research on the temples themselves, on the one hand, and scholarship on religious ideas and cults, on the other hand. Moreover, even though research teams in Dendera or Edfu, for example, have been starting to adopt this integrated approach, there is still very little in the way of books designed to present an accessible account to the general public. Popularizing books combining descriptions of temple architecture with some information on religion tend to be of the encyclopedic kind, offering brief summaries of the architectural history of as many temples as possible, plus, in each case, simple plans and a few very telegraphic pieces of information on which god was worshiped in the temple, who built it, and sometimes who excavated it in modern times.

Though scientific and popular in tone, and written by an archaeologist rather than a scholar of religion, this book is intended to offer a rather broader and more thorough view of the subject, and tries to set a selected group of ancient Egyptian temples in a wider historical, religious, and archaeological context. It seeks to bring temples to life, presenting them to the reader not just as catalogues of pylons, courts, hypostyle halls, obelisks, statues, and chapels, but as the settings of many often complicated rituals, as the centers of a priesthood with a highly organized hierarchy and allocation of religious duties, and as the stages for great religious festivals and festivities. It also shows that the temples in ancient Egypt also had a more or less extensive economic infrastructure and assets with their own administration, and that the very largest temples were major power centers deeply involved in the political life of the country.

It is obvious that a book of this kind, in just one volume and written for readers who have an interest in the subject but not a specialist's academic knowledge, cannot possibly claim to be comprehensive. It is focused on a selection of archaeological localities, those with the most important ancient Egyptian temple complexes. These include the places where the oldest Egyptian myths and principal religious teachings on the creation of the world and its order emerged. Even in the case of these selected temple complexes and monuments it has not been possible to go into detail, and so architectural-historical description has been limited to the major features and parts. The chapters concerned with the different religious centers and temples are preceded by an introductory chapter on the basic religious conception and meaning of the temple and its parts, and the categories and duties of the temple staff. The individual chapters are interlarded with several thematic 'excursi,' the last of these giving a brief outline of the overall architectural history of the ancient Egyptian temple. While the number of excavated sites means that there is plenty of material for purposes of comparison, documentation remains incomplete and very unbalanced as regards periods and regions. Therefore, the task of identifying the main trends in the development of different types of temples in ancient Egypt, in general and in their specific features, is still an immensely difficult one. A scholarly monograph on the theme has yet to be written.

ACKNOWLEDGMENTS

The author would like to thank everyone who has assisted in the writing of this book, especially the following individuals and organizations for their kind support and permission to reproduce their photographs and other copyrighted materials: Jolana Malátková for editing the text and for the selection and editing of the illustrations, as well as for the lovely drawings and photographs; Luděk Wellner for drawings of the plans of monuments; Milan Zemina, Jaromír Krejčí, Martin Frouz, Miroslav Bárta, and others for the beautiful photographs that make up the major part of the visual material in the book; Miroslav Ottmar for reproductions of period illustrations and for scanning photographs; Marta Štrachová for scanning photographs; Lucie Jirásková for locating photographs in the photograph archives of the Czech Egyptological Institute of the Faculty of Arts of Charles University in Prague; and Alexandra Hejduková and Iva Vojtková for help in creating the index. Special thanks are also extended to the library of the Strahov Premonstrate Monastery in Prague for permission to photograph its copy of the *Description de l'Égypte* for the archive of the Czech Egyptological Institute.

The author would like to extend his special thanks to Dr. Zahi Hawass, former minister of state for antiquities in Egypt, for his kind permission to take photographs of artifacts in the Egyptian Museum in Cairo, the Luxor Museum, and the Egyptian archaeological sites. Special thanks are also extended to Dr. Dieter Arnold for his permission to use some of his plans of ancient Egyptian temples. The author also gratefully acknowledges other Egyptological colleagues who kindly allowed their illustrations to be reproduced in this book, namely, Dr. F. Arnold, Dr. G. Charloux, Dr. D. Eigner, Professor D. Kessler, Dr. G. Vörös, and W.R. Johnson.

Thanks are also due to Jaroslav M. Pařík, Knight of the Military and Hospitaller Order of Saint Lazarus of Jerusalem, and to Ludvík Hegerlík for their generous sponsorship gift, without which the original Czech edition of this book and its translation into English could not have been published.

In the illustration captions only an abbreviated reference to the origin of the illustrations is given. For a full citation of the reference, consult the Acknowledgments and Bibliography sections.

The view of Karnak that captivated the scholars and soldiers of Napoleon's expedition.

1

The Temple of the World

<< In the ruins of an ancient Egyptian temple (Philae).

In the later nineteenth century, the English traveler and writer Amelia Ann Blanford Edwards (1831–92) embarked for Egypt to see the country and its remarkable monuments. Once in Egypt, she continued her journey in a manner favored by foreign visitors at the time: cruising along the Nile on board a *dahabiya*, an elegant and comfortable river sailing boat. She gave a captivating account of her impressions of the trip in her now classic travelogue entitled *A Thousand Miles up the Nile*, which was first published in London in 1891. At one point in her book Edwards relates that one day she decided to visit the Temple of Karnak. When she entered the temple she was awestruck, and felt as if she were dreaming:

> *To describe all that we saw after leaving the Great Hall would fill a chapter. Huge obelisks of shining granite—some yet erect, some shattered and prostrate; vast length of sculptured walls covered with wondrous battle subjects, sacerdotal processions, and elaborate chronicles of the deeds of Kings; ruined courtyards surrounded by files of headless statues; a sanctuary built all of polished granite, and engraved like a gem; and a second Hall of Pillars dating back to the early days of Thotmes the Third; labyrinths of roofless chambers; mutilated colossi, shattered pylons, fallen columns, unintelligible foundations and hieroglyphic inscriptions without end, were glanced, passed by, and succeeded by fresh wonders . . . . We rode back across the plain, silent and bewildered. Have I not said that it was like a dream?*

The romantically-minded Victorian lady was so enchanted that, at the time, she could find no words to describe the feelings and impressions that Karnak inspired in her. Much has changed since the day that Amelia Edwards walked through Karnak, solitary and in a dream: the fallen columns have been raised again, the ruined pylons re-erected, and the seemingly endless series of scenes and hieroglyphic inscriptions on the walls of the temple chambers have, for the most part, been documented and explained. Furthermore, if Karnak has changed in any other way, it is because the era of solitary travelers is long gone, and now thousands

In the nineteenth century the ruins of the temple complex in Karnak became a destination for European travelers. The Great Hypostyle Hall of the temple of Amun at the turn of the nineteenth century.

of visitors crowd into the temple precincts every day. All the same, despite the hustle and bustle of the tourist industry, many are certainly overcome by the same feelings that consumed Amelia Edwards, all those years ago. To give even more potency to these impressions, the light and shadows play magically before visitors' eyes in the monumental, millennia-old setting of the temple. Visitors are astonished by this gigantic work of human hands of a now long-vanished world. They inevitably are awestruck by the sheer amount of skill, effort, and time that must have been invested in its creation, and the power of the ideas that impelled its creators to break huge pieces of stone from rocks throughout the country, transport them to this place, subject them to their will, and mold them and raise them toward the sky!

Although Karnak was the biggest, dozens and even hundreds of similar—mainly smaller but sometimes very large—temples were built in ancient Egypt. Today, most of them are more or less picturesque ruins. How did they look at the time of their greatest glory? What took place inside them? What did they have in common and how did they differ? What was their purpose? What spiritual legacy, if any, have they left us? I shall try to answer these questions, though due to the scale and complexity of the theme, I cannot possibly provide exhaustive answers. What was the world of the ancient Egyptian temples like?

Abode of the Gods

The institution of the temple, in ancient Egypt most often termed 'abode of the god,' was not the embodiment of just one idea; it was a place where many beliefs and conceptions came together and became mutually entwined, while its deeper meaning was known only to those with special knowledge—those who had been initiated into the mysteries of the transformations and purposes of the gods. Above all, the temple was a symbolic primordial mound—the form that the god-creator took when he emerged from the chaos of the primordial waters and started on his work at the beginning of time and the world. It was an expression of *maat*, the order that the gods had created in the midst of chaos, and it was the point of contact between heaven, earth, and the underworld. It was the seat of God, or the gods, the sacred place where people came to worship the god, to bring him offerings, and to ask for his favor. As time went by, the

Queen Hatshepsut and the goddess Seshat during the ritual of *pedj-shes*, stretching the cord. This ritual accompanied the founding of any temple or other important building. Scene on a quartzite block from the queen's Red Chapel in Karnak.

temple also acquired important political and economic functions, became a center of learning, and served as a place of upbringing and education; judicial cases were heard in front of its entrance gate. Last but not least, it was a place where people sought healing from curative waters, statues, and magical stelae.

Only the king could found a temple. It was his task to build a temple and deliver it to the god, so that the god could abide there. As the earthly incarnation of the sky god Horus (Hor), the king was equal to the gods, and was lord of 'doing things,' that is, rituals. Rituals accompanied a temple's construction from the very start. The founding of a temple, which took several weeks, would begin at the new moon with the ceremony of 'stretching the cord,' which the king was supposed to perform with the help of Seshat, goddess of writing and mathematics, and in the presence of other deities. Scholars believe that in fact the king would usually leave it to a priest to represent him at the founding ritual, and another priest would represent the goddess at the ceremony by wearing her mask or holding her symbol in his hand. The building layout would be marked with ropes and sticks, and its proper orientation to the points of the compass would be determined by the stars or sun. The main axis of the building would run east to west, the course of the sun across the sky.

There then followed the ritual of 'digging the earth,' sometimes expressed in the texts as "digging a trench right down to water, so that the building will be excellent." Evidently the ritual involved digging down to the groundwater, from which the temple was then conceived as emerging like the primordial mound from the primordial waters. The ritual also had a practical purpose, however, since the water level would at the same time define the horizontal line. The trench would then be filled with clean sand symbolizing ritual purity, the sand would soak up the groundwater, and models of work tools, bricks with magical texts, and sacrifices (a goose, the head of a bullock, and the like) would be placed at the corners of the future building. Once the temple had been built, the ritual of the 'opening of the mouth' would be performed in every temple interior so that the rooms would be magically endowed with life and ritually cleansed. At the very end of the process a cult statue of the god would be placed in the innermost shrine, and the temple thus symbolically presented to the god.

When drawing the building plan, designers and builders respected certain principles that were distinctive for ancient Egyptian temples (except in the earliest period when the basic scheme of the temple was still taking shape). Originally poles, reeds, and mud bricks were the

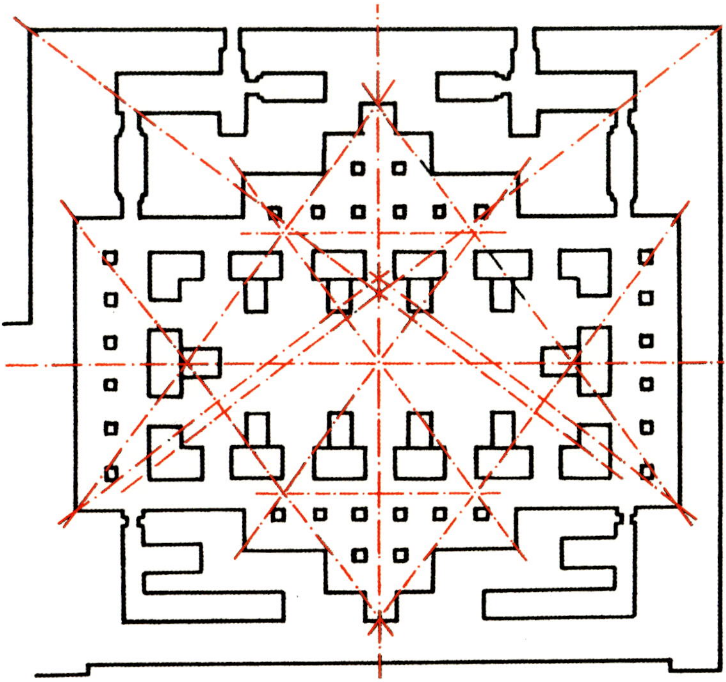

This plan of the temple of the Sphinx in Giza, with its proportions precisely calculated in advance, is an example of ancient Egyptian ideas of harmonious architectural style.

building material, but these were gradually superseded by stone, mainly sandstone or limestone, with other kinds of stone used for individual architectural elements. One frequent feature of the plan is the application of a right-angled triangle with a 3:4:5 ratio of sides, which gave the temple harmonious proportions. The attempt to achieve symmetry and a ratio of 6:2:1 among the length, breadth, and height of the building is also evident. The towers of the pylon, reminiscent of a fortress and guard gate, and the massive, slightly slanted exterior walls separated the temple from its surroundings and emphasized that this was a sacred place, the dwelling of a god. The temple district, which consisted of the temple itself and the administrative and utility buildings associated with it and which was called 'the domain of the god' in the texts, was also separated from the world around it by a massive mud-brick wall. The layers of bricks were not even, but rhythmically undulating, which added stability to the masonry and at the same time evoked the idea of the waves of the primordial waters. The boundary wall thus symbolically protected the mythical primordial mound, the temple, from the omnipresent chaos that was forever threatening the work of the gods.

<< Ramesses III raising a curved sword to behead the defeated enemies of Egypt with one blow. Detail from the decoration of the king's mortuary temple in Medinet Habu.

Religious principles were also expressed in other aspects of the temple's disposition. The approach to the entrance was often formed by an alley of sphinxes, their function being apotropaic—that is, to ward off evil. The two towers of the pylon at the entrance to the temple symbolized the hieroglyphic sign for 'horizon'—consisting of two hills on the horizon between which the sun would rise each morning. In this way, the temple entrance could also be symbolically identified with the womb of the sky goddess Nut, from which the sun was born anew each day. The obelisks in front of the pylon were symbols of the sun god. High poles with banners, also in front of the pylons, were likewise apotropaic in meaning; their sharp gold-covered points were directed upward against the evil that might threaten the temple in the form of clouds and rain, expressions of the chaotic primordial waters. The scenes in relief on the front walls of the pylon towers had similar mythic significance; these showed the king holding defeated and kneeling representatives of enemy nations by the hair and raising a stone mace to smash all their heads with one blow, thus destroying external evil and restoring *maat,* the order of the world.

The courtyard beyond the temple entrance was as far as the public was allowed on special holy occasions. The areas deeper inside the temple were reserved for priests, and the shrine itself only for the king and certain initiated priests and dignitaries. The pillared hall (column hall) beyond the courtyard symbolized the mythical thicket in which life was born and where after his birth the god Hor found a refuge from his pursuer Seth. In the next interior, the 'offering hall,' sacrificial gifts were gathered three times per day in accordance with temple ritual, while behind it, the 'Hall of the Nine' was the dwelling place of the gods who accompanied and protected the principal god, to whom the temple belonged. In the 'Hall of the Barque' there would be a barque resting on a stone base, and in the barque a wooden casket containing a statue known in the texts as 'this noble god.' At times of special festival processions the statue in the barque would set out, on the shoulders of the priests, on a journey around his temple, or sometimes to visit the temples of other gods. The junior priests, known as 'pure,' were allowed access as far as the barque. In the shrine itself a cult statue of the god, known as 'holy,' rested in a sealed and gilded casket inside a larger stone case. Access to this was permitted only to the few who had gone through the initiation ceremonies and had been initiated into the mysteries (see 'Servants of the God,' p. 26).

As a visitor to the temple penetrated ever deeper, he would move from the sun-drenched courtyard into the half-light of the column hall, then into the dim hall of the barque, and finally to the shrine, which was wholly submerged in darkness. As he proceeded he might notice other less immediately obvious changes: toward the interior of the temple the floors of each successive room would be higher and the ceilings lower. In this way the visitor to the cult focus of the temple was encouraged to rid himself of the disturbing influences of the outside world, to concentrate spiritually, and to prepare to meet the god.

In another part of the temple there was a small pool, fed either by groundwater or by a flood water channel, since the flood was believed to spring from the primordial waters. This pool would be used by the priests for their daily ritual purification, but also played a role during some festivals and rites, for example at the Osiris mysteries in Dendera. In some cases, the pool had a special religious meaning; for example, in the Temple of Thoth in Hermopolis it was identified with the mythical lake containing the 'Island of the Flames,' the birthplace of the god Re in the form of a lotus.

The route to the inner shrine was also characterized by appropriate choice of individual architectural elements and decoration of walls in the successive spaces. The choice of type of pillar, for example, had its own religious symbolism. The palm, providing abundant food and shade from the glare of the sun, was the symbol of fertility and peace.

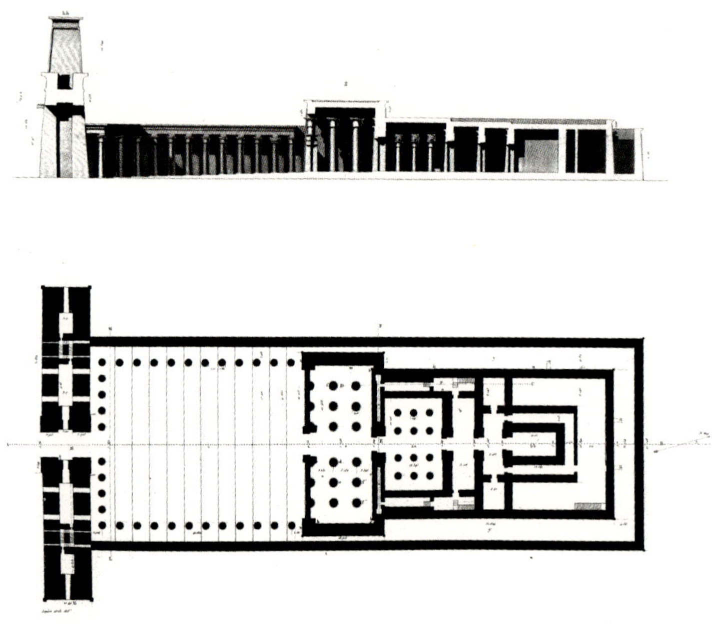

This reconstruction of the ground plan and cross-section of the temple of Horus in Edfu shows the basic architectural arrangement of the ancient Egyptian temple: the gradual progress from larger open spaces through ever smaller interiors, culminating in the sanctuary, sunk in darkness. This arrangement encouraged the visitor to intensify his spiritual concentration as he moved deeper into the temple.

The lotus *(Nymphaea caerulea)*, which has a flower that sinks under the water surface at night and rises again to open in the sun's rays in the morning, symbolized resurrection and played an important role in the solar religion. The evergreen papyrus in a thicket full of birds, fish, butterflies, and other fauna symbolized eternal life. The ceiling of the temple was the vault of heaven with stars and a winged sun.

Polychrome relief decoration (scenes and inscriptions on the walls, ceilings, pillars, and piers) harmoniously complemented the architecture of the temple and defined its religious character. To put it very generally, we can say that the decoration reflected the character of the god worshiped in the temple and the myths and rituals associated with him or her. Another important theme in the decoration was the builder of the temple—the king—his importance for maintaining the order of the world, his personal relationship with the god concerned, and his role as the lord of rituals. The decorative scheme likewise reflected the functions of the different rooms and the specific rituals performed in them. Significant space, especially on the exposed parts of the temple (the entrance gate, enclosure wall, and walls of the courtyard accessible to the public), was reserved for representation of historical events, the depiction and description of major battles, military campaigns, and so on. From the Late Period, the disposition and decoration of the temple was also influenced by the increasing interest of Egyptian society in traditional customs, ancient rituals, and magic, and the temple became even more the place of secret mysteries.

The relief decoration was complemented by statues, whose type and location were governed by certain principles. As has already been noted, the principal cult statue of the god known as 'holy' was placed in the shrine, the holy of holies, while another statue of the god, known as 'this noble god,' rested in the sacred barque and took part in processions and festivals inside and outside the temple. Statues of the relevant gods would be placed in chapels dedicated to other gods, and as time went by the number of statues of the principal god, other gods, kings, and important dignitaries increased, and began to fill other areas of the temple, especially the open courtyard. Stelae, symbols of gods, and various votive gifts accumulated in the temple interiors as well, and so from time to time there was no option but to clear out and bury the superfluous objects somewhere, without the least regard for the gods or gifts, and ideally under the flooring of one of the temple courtyards. The colossal statues of kings found their place in front of the pylon by the entrance gate.

Ramesses II offers the symbol *maat* to the god Amun (broken off from block), thus symbolically expressing his devotion to the god and his determination to consolidate the order of the world established by Amun. Detail of scene on a fragment of a granite block from the temple of Amun in Tanis.

Doing Things

In different places in Egypt the actual worship of gods in the temples was—for the most part—conducted according to the same pattern, and differing only in details. The ancient Egyptians believed that the world of men and the world of the gods were interrelated and closely linked in harmony with *maat*, the order established by the god-creator, which was nonetheless constantly threatened by the forces of chaos. For

Queen Hatshepsut uses perfumed incense to cense a standing statue of Amun-Re, lord of heaven, in front of a chapel containing his sacred barque. Scene on a quartzite block from the queen's Red Chapel in Karnak.

this order to be maintained it was essential to honor and worship the gods on cult principles that the gods themselves had established and continued to watch over through the god of wisdom and knowledge, Thoth. A complex of prescribed religious operations—rituals—ensured the proper conduct of the cult and thus its effectiveness.

Regardless of the character of the god or goddess concerned, the basic ritual of offering took place in the temples three times a day: in the morning, at noon, and in the evening. Its purpose was to obtain the favor of the deity in the spirit of the principle "I am giving so that you will give." The morning ritual was the most important. Preparations for it would start at night, before daybreak, on the orders of the priest on duty, who would observe the movements of the heavenly bodies in the sky from the roof terrace of the temple and determine the precise time. It was necessary to prepare sacrificial gifts, bake bread, and bring fresh vegetables and fruit, beer, meat, and other offerings. A bouquet of freshly picked flowers was essential. The offerings brought to the temple would be taken by a priest, who would then line them up at certain places on altars. The choicest offerings were prepared for the principal god and given to those priests who were allowed to approach the holy of holies.

To approach the shrine, open it, and look at the cult statue of the god and meet him was, in theory, the privilege of the king alone, since he was considered the son of the god, becoming so at his coronation ceremony, which also represented a ritual of initiation into the divine mystery. In fact, given the number of temples throughout the country, the king could personally fulfill this duty only in very rare cases and usually delegated it to high priests as his representatives, and sometimes to other important priests of particular cults. Those permitted to meet the god as representatives of the king had to undergo a special initiation. In rare cases certain high-ranking dignitaries, for example the vizier, might also obtain this initiation, which was known in Egyptian as an 'introduction.' We do not know the details of the initiation ceremony since only general information is provided by the surviving texts—above all, inscriptions preserved in some parts of the Temple of Akh menu in Karnak and on buildings in its immediate vicinity.

Initiation took place in the most intimate part of the temple, at the shrine—the place where the Heaven met the Earth. On his way to initiation the elect individual had first to undergo ritual purification on the boundary between the profane and sacred parts of the temple in the room known as *wabet* ('pure place'). 'Introduction' into the mysteries known as *shetau* would be followed by *akh* ('enlightenment'), and understanding of *maat,* the cosmic order and world of the gods. This led to transformation and culminated in the opening of the casket, 'the opening of the gate of heaven,' and the 'revelation'—the uncovering of the face of the god. Only people who had undergone initiation were then permitted to enter the shrine and perform the prescribed rites.

The inscriptions and scenes that appear on the walls close to the shrine depict a relatively precise picture of the course of the morning temple ritual. First, priests would bring and set down platters of offerings before the shrine, enveloped in its darkness. After they had left the room, an initiated priest, by candle or lamplight, would approach the stone casket containing the second, richly decorated wooden casket, in which the cult statue of the god rested. The aim of the ritual was to honor and sate the god, who had spent the night in the underworld but had just returned at daybreak so that he could unite in the statue with his soul, or more precisely his life force, his *ba*. The Egyptians believed that the gods had a *ba* in heaven, a statue on earth, and a dead body in the underworld. The priest would first sprinkle both caskets with holy water and cense them with incense, and would then break the clay seal on the lid of the wooden casket, slip the bolt on it, and open the casket. After prostrating himself before the face of the god, he would

Bearers of offerings. Detail from the decoration of the tomb of the magnate Ptahhotep in Saqqara, Fifth Dynasty.

stand up and start to worship and glorify the god with formulae of greeting, honor him with more incense, and offer him myrrh, sacred oil, and also the symbol of *maat*—a figurine of a seated goddess with an ostrich feather in her hair. Then he would take the statue of the god out of the casket and place it on clean sand. He would clean first the casket and then the statue, removing the oil and perfume of the previous ceremony. Then he would apply new cosmetics and perfumed oil to the cleaned statue, re-dress it in fresh robes of fine cloth, adorn it with the symbols of power and jewels, and finally put it back in the casket.

There would follow libations, more incense, and the presentation of offerings with recital of the prescribed formulae of offering. The presentation of the gifts was also governed by the fixed principles of the ritual of offering. At the end, the priest would present the god with the symbol of life in the shape of a sandal strap, the *ankh*, and the symbol *ib* in the shape of a heart, in order to ensure the transfer of life force from the food. After the morning toilette, the priest would offer the four lengths of fabric in which the statue had been dressed: white, blue, green, and red. In ordinary temple practice, however, this particular ritual did not take place every day but every few days and at festivals, and so only symbolic strips of the different materials would be offered on a daily basis. On festival occasions the god's various jewels and adornments (necklaces, bracelets, diadems, sacred symbols, and so on) would be taken out of the temple treasury and presented to the god.

Upon completion of the morning ritual, the priest would present the cult statue with five beads, each composed of two different kinds of natron—the symbol of ritual purification—and resin. He would then close the casket again, seal it with clay, and symbolically purify the place once more by sprinkling it with holy water and censing it. At the very end he would perform just one more ritual known as the 'removal of footprints.' This meant that he would walk backwards when leaving the shrine and on his way he would sweep away the footprints he had left in the clean sand strewn on the ground as a symbol of purity and also of the primordial mound the shrine symbolized. If he failed to renew the

Procession of priests carrying the sacred barque of Amun, the king of the gods, on their shoulders. Hatshepsut and her coregent Thutmose III follow the barque. Scene on quartzite block from the queen's Red Chapel in Karnak.

original, untouched state of the sand, the forces of evil would be able to exploit his footprints and reach the shrine.

At noon there would be another, but this time very short, ritual during which the shrine remained closed, no offerings were presented, and the priest simply sprinkled the place with holy water and censed it while verbally honoring the god. It was similar at dusk for the evening ritual; this was just a matter for the priests and was routine in character, the shrine remaining shut and the rite performed only in the surrounding area. After the evening ritual the god sank into the mysterious underworld. The priests took away the offerings and divided them among themselves according to a prescribed key.

In addition to the morning, noon, and evening rituals, a number of other ceremonies would take place in the temple according to an established calendar, some of them conducted in accessible areas with the participation of the public. At least once a week there would be a procession, in which the priests would carry the barque with the statue called 'this noble god' and progress through the temple courtyards and colonnades, visiting the chapels of the other gods belonging to his retinue. The casket and barque were made of wood, richly decorated with gold, and bearing inscriptions, scenes, and divine symbols. The processions did not always necessarily include the barque, and in some cases the statue of the god would travel in a horse-drawn wagon, for example.

The procession would move through the temple on a prescribed route and would be headed by a priest, who magically protected the way, sprinkling holy water and wafting incense to ward off the evil that might threaten even in the temple itself. The procession would halt at certain places. One of these was in the center of the courtyard, where the barque would be temporarily laid on a 'resting place.' This resting place soon acquired the specific architectural form of a pedestal surrounded by pillars supporting a flat roof, like a kind of canopy for the boat expressed in stone. One such 'halting place of the barque' was the celebrated White Chapel of Senwosret I in the Temple of Amun in Karnak. The halting places had practical as well as religious purposes; the procession needed to rest from time to time because some barques were large and heavy, requiring several dozen priests to carry them. The stops were at the same time an opportunity to pay homage to the god. On the journey the statue might provide prophecies, for example, by various movements or tilting of the sacred barque. The procession was not confined within the temple but might also set out beyond its enclosure wall, for example, to visit neighboring or even very distant temples. On the Feast of the Beautiful Union the procession bearing the statue of Hathor would embark by river on a several-day voyage to Edfu.

There was, however, more to life in the temple than the daily rituals and occasional processions with the statue of the god in the sacred barque. It was also the stage for other rituals and festivals, some common to all temples but others differing from temple to temple. One important ritual performed from the Late Period at the New Year at sunrise was 'union with the sun disc.' This was a festival at which statues and cult symbols that had long been out of commission were brought to life: These statues were sometimes used at various ceremonies, but most were not in cult use and lay buried in crypts as if in the underworld. The priestly procession would take them from the crypts, first to the *wabet* area, and then up a staircase to the roof terrace, where they would be reanimated by the first rays of the sun and draw life-giving energy for further cult functioning in the temple. As several inscriptions in the temples in Edfu and Dendera show, the ritual could be conducted not just at New Year but at other times as well. According to Serge Sauneron, the French Egyptologist and great expert on late religious texts, it can be deduced from inscriptions in the temple at Edfu that the 'union with the sun disc' included the ritual of the 'opening of the mouth,' which took place in the 'golden house,' as the location of this ceremony was called. During the ritual the priest would magically bring the statues to life in the same way in which he would bring the mummies of the dead to life in funeral rites. According to the German Egyptologist Jan Assmann, the roots of the 'union with the sun disc' ritual may lie in the ritual originally performed at sunrise on the mummy in front of the tomb.

However much the temple was the stage for rituals and celebrations, it was not the only place where the gods were worshiped. Many people, rich and poor, honored various deities in their homes, where there would be a special place reserved for figurines of a god or at least a small stela with an image of the god and a short inscription. In rich households these might well be important state deities such as Amun, or in Akhenaten's time, Aten. In their own houses, the artists and craftsmen in Deir al-Medina, who worked on the decoration of the tombs in the nearby Valley of the Kings, had small shrines in the form of niches where a figurine of a god would stand. Amenhotep I, the deified founder of this royal cemetery, whom the artists and craftsmen honored as their patron, was particularly popular with them. The poorer people would escape with their cares to protective family gods, to whom they would turn with their pleas for help and favor.

Worship was not reserved only for gods, or deified dead kings, but was also paid to the living king, or his divine attributes. The rulers themselves encouraged this in their own interests, as a way of legitimizing their rule and asserting their authority in the face of other power structures in society. For example, Amenhotep III had scenes illustrating his divine origin incorporated into the decoration of the Temple at Luxor, and Ramesses II had his own deified portrait placed among the three highest state gods of Egypt—Amun, Re, and Ptah—in the cult center of the rock temple at Abu Simbel. The cult of kings continued after their deaths in great funerary temples that they erected in their own lifetimes.

Amenhotep, son of Hapu, represented as a scribe. Gray-black granite. Egyptian Museum, Cairo. Eighteenth Dynasty.

King Scorpion of Dynasty 0 performing the 'digging the earth' ritual on a field surrounded by an irrigation canal. A man standing in front of the king holds a basket of corn. Detail from the decoration on the ruler's limestone mace found in Hierakonpolis.

God's adoratrice Shepenwepet performing the 'driving out of four calves' ritual before Osiris, the lord of life. Detail of decoration from her temple in Medinet Habu.

Sometimes ordinary mortals earned such respect during their lifetimes—although much less often than gods and kings—in a particular place, in which after their deaths they too were deified and became the subject of a cult with the associated cult buildings. One such person was Imhotep, probably the son of King Djoser, who is regarded as the builder of the Step Pyramid. He was venerated as a great sage, especially in the Late Period of ancient Egyptian history. In the same way, a reputation for wisdom, knowledge, and achievement of all kinds led to the deification of Amenhotep, son of Hapu, the architect of the Temple of Amenhotep III and a major figure of the era of the Eighteenth Dynasty. At Elephantine, the district royal administrator Heqaib also enjoyed a popularity that led to the emergence of a local cult.

The veneration of the dead, characteristic of ancient Egypt, occupied an important place among cults. The ancient Egyptians believed in life after death, the survival of the personality, and the immortality of its spiritual essence. To preserve the identity of the dead, however, and to ensure resurrection and eternal life, the dead man's body had to be preserved; this was achieved by funerary, mummification, and offering rituals. An ancient Egyptian's deepest desire was to have his own tomb, the dwelling place of his spirit, built while he was still alive, and after his death to be properly buried and with his eternal life secured there by means of rituals of offering.

The Main Rituals

The ritual described earlier, which took place three times each day in all Egyptian temples, was the most common ritual but not the only one. Rituals connected with often overlapping and intersecting myths, religious festivals, hunting magic, agricultural tasks, or the founding of buildings were numerous. Here we shall give a brief account of a sampling of them.

An important and very ancient group of rituals were those connected with agriculture. At the end of the flood season in the festivals that took place during the month of Khoiak (see p. 38), Egyptians started work on the fields with the old agricultural ritual of 'digging the earth,' the symbolic opening of the earth with a hoe and the sowing of corn. Originally, the ritual was performed by the king himself, as is shown by a scene carved on an early dynastic limestone mace of King Scorpion found in Hierokonpolis. As time went by the ritual became connected with the myth of Osiris. Also probably agricultural in origin was the ritual of the 'erection of the *djed* pillar,' which according to some scholars represented the building of a figure out of sheaves and was supposed to ensure a good harvest. Associated with the myth of Osiris (the *djed* pillar was considered to be the spine of Osiris), this ritual, held at the end of the month of Khoiak, celebrated the resurrection of the god and his victory over his enemies. Likewise originally connected with the harvest was the 'driving out the four calves' ritual. In time, this also came to be associated with the Osiris myth.

Rituals accompanied not just the beginning of work on important buildings, but also their completion, as has been most recently documented by scenes and inscriptions discovered on blocks from the causeway of Sahure's pyramid complex in Abusir.

A whole set of rituals accompanied the journey of the dead to the other world. Funerary ceremonies started with the ritual purification of the dead man, his mummification, and continued with a ritual of offering, a funerary procession escorting the coffin with the mummy to the tomb, and then the ritual carrying of the coffin from place to place inside the tomb. The culmination of the funerary ceremony was the ritual of the 'opening of the mouth,' during which the priest used various instruments (a stone knife in the shape of a swallow's tail, or blades—ideally of meteoric metal, symbolizing the power of the heavens) to touch the different limbs of the mummy, thus symbolically reviving the dead man and preparing him for life in the other world. As has already been noted, this ritual was also performed after the 'birth' of a statue (as the production of these statues was termed in Egyptian inscriptions), showing the great cult significance attached to statues by the ancient Egyptians.

The funeral rites were accompanied by other rituals, some of which are obscure and hard to interpret. The ritual 'dance of *muu*' involved mythical figures of ancestors adorned with high rush hats who were there to lead the deceased away to the other world, but the meaning is not entirely clear, and obscurity also surrounds the 'procession of *tekenu*' that accompanied the burial. Some scholars believe that it involved the removal—on wooden sledges drawn across the sand—of those remains of the body left after mummification but not placed in the canopic jars (that is, blood, pieces of skin, and so on), so that these could be ritually disposed of. Others consider *tekenu* to be a mythical sun bull bearing away the deceased to the other world. The funerary ceremonies ended with a ritual of offering, which would be repeated when people visited the tomb to pay their respects. They would bring the dead man offerings, presenting them to him symbolically through the king, since the king was the only person authorized to perform the ritual and present the offering to the god who would then (as the formula of offering explicitly states) give it to the deceased. Sometimes, however, it was enough just to recite this prescribed

Priests and mourners during the 'opening of the mouth' ritual performed on the mummy of the deceased, who before his burial in his tomb is symbolically taken into the care of the jackal god Anubis, guardian of the cemetery. Detail from a papyrus containing the text of the *Book of the Dead* of the royal scribe Hunefer. Nineteenth Dynasty.

formula starting with the words "a boon which the king gives" for the ritual act to be effective and the spirit of the deceased to be sated.

Another group of rituals, extending into the field of magic, were those concerned with destroying evil. We have already noted that the king often had himself depicted in the symbolic ritual of 'smiting the enemies,' when with one hand he holds the kneeling representatives of foreign nations by the hair and in the other he raises a mace to crush all their heads with one blow. The same purpose—that is, the destruction of enemies—was served by a ritual in which clay figurines bearing the names of hostile tribes would be smashed. Also used to magically avert and overcome evil was the ritual of 'smashing red (that is, burnt clay) vessels' following the ritual of offering, or the funerary ritual, as a

Wooden statuette of a kneeling bound Asian captive, embodiment of the enemies of Egypt, discovered in Raneferef's mortuary temple in Abusir. The statuette may have been part of the royal throne, Fifth Dynasty. Egyptian Museum, Cairo.

way of protecting the deceased from evil in his tomb. The red color of the burnt clay recalled the symbolic color of the god of evil Seth.

Various hunting rituals often provide us with glimpses into the world of the prehistoric society before the unification of Egypt. These too were usually associated with magic and intended to protect the hunter, ensure success in the hunt, a rich food supply, and so on. For example, such rituals accompanied 'harpooning the hippopotamus,' which was a very old, originally royal hunting festival already recorded on clay sealing from the First Dynasty, from the reign of King Den. During the festival, the hunters embarked on small boats on the Nile, repeated eulogies to the harpoon, and finally used it to hunt and kill the hippopotamus. The festival had mythical associations since it was believed that the god of evil Seth, the enemy of the god Horus whose earthly embodiment was the king, took on the form of the

Ramesses III hunting wild bulls in reeds on the edge of the desert. The hunt had a symbolic religious meaning because the wild animals living in the desert embodied the god of evil and ruler of the desert Seth. Detail of decoration on the south tower of the pylon of the king's mortuary temple in Medinet Habu.

hippopotamus. Seth was also ruler of the desert, and so the wild animals of the desert were associated with him. Therefore, the acts of hunting and offering them were ritualized and became part of the basic dogma of the ancient Egyptian state: striving to maintain the order of the world of a given god in eternal struggle with the forces of evil and chaos.

Rituals surrounded the lord of 'doing things,' that is, the king himself, starting with his coronation and ascent to the throne. According to the mythical conception of the ancient Egyptian state, the death of a king ended a historical cycle, and rituals were necessary to get through the critical time of interregnum before a new king could be crowned and enthroned. The royal coronation was essentially an initiation ceremony by which the king was inducted into the world of the gods and initiated into their mysteries. The future king was first ritually purified and dressed, and then two priests—one representing Horus and the other Seth (for the king was regarded as the embodiment of both)—would place the Upper Egyptian White Crown and the Lower Egyptian Red Crown on his head, while reciting the prescribed formulae. He would be presented with the heraldic plants of the two parts of the country: papyrus representing Lower Egypt and *sut* (probably a kind of lily, although scholars are unsure of its precise taxonomic classification) Upper Egypt; in this way the two parts of the realm would be symbolically reunited. There followed a ritual run around the walls, the setting of the royal diadem on the king's forehead, the presentation of the ruler's insignia, and so on. Originally—and ideally—after a king had ruled for thirty years, the *sed* festival would be held (as time went by, however, this happened at much shorter intervals), at which the king would once again show his physical prowess and capacity as a ruler. It is possible that in the earliest times old kings who failed to show these powers were ritually killed.

Servants of the God

Originally, to meet the god in the intimate part of the temple—in the shrine where heaven, earth, and the underworld touched—was a privilege allowed only to the king, who was initiated for the task at his coronation when he himself became a god, Horus, living on earth. The *ba* of the god was ever present in the temple, resting in the cult statue. At dawn the god came from the underworld to join with his *ba* in the temple and in the evening, when the sun set, he would leave it again and go back to the kingdom of death, which was also the place of mystical rebirth where he would prepare himself for further creative and sustaining action. This was why when the king wished to meet the god in confidence and discover his wishes and intentions, he would choose nighttime for the encounter. Also associated with the idea of the temple as a place of the underworld mysteries of death and rebirth was the doctrine increasingly adopted from the New Kingdom onward and given material expression, for example, in the Osireion in Abydos—namely, that the temple was the tomb of Osiris and the place of the mystic union of the sun god with the ruler of the underworld, Osiris.

The growing number of temples and the practical demands on the king led quite early on to the delegation of the royal cult duties to priests who substituted for the king, having been also initiated into the mysteries of the rituals. Whenever the king considered it important, however, he would conduct the ceremony himself, especially at major religious festivals. To perform the ritual offices in his stead in any temple the king would choose the high priest from among respected persons and magnates. At a festival assembly he would formally declare this person to be the high priest of the god honored by that particular temple and also the administrator of his temple, treasury, and granaries. At the end of the festival he would give the chosen individual the insignia of the office of high priest—a seal ring and staff. In his choice of high priest the king would usually take into account not just the needs of the temple and cult but also the political aspects of the appointment, and would therefore consider the political ambitions of the priests and seek to ensure stability and loyalty to the leadership of the state in priestly circles. It is interesting that there existed no unified nomenclature for the office of high priest. Various titles reflecting different historical and religious circumstances are recorded. For example, the title of the high priest of the solar god in Heliopolis was originally *maa wer* ('he who sees the Great One'), that is, the solar god. In the Middle Kingdom there was a shift in the writing and, at the same time, a change in the meaning of the title. Instead of *maa wer* it became *wer maaw* ('greatest of the seers'), that is, greatest of those who observe the movement of the heavenly bodies in the sky. We know that from the Old Kingdom the high priest of Ptah in Memphis had the title 'chief controller of craftsmen.' The high priest in Hermopolis had the title 'greatest of the Five,' which means the four pairs of primordial gods and Thoth. The high priest of Amun had the simple title 'first prophet' (literally, 'first god's servant of Amun').

Nor in ancient Egypt did there exist any special priestly training center or school with students who would automatically become priests or have some advantage when seeking positions as priests. The office of priest required a basic general education, that is, the ability to read and write. Since priests were permitted to marry and have children, it gradually became commonplace for priests to pass their office on to their sons, but the final decision on acceptance into the priestly order (apart from appointment to the office of high priest, as described), was the council of priests of a particular temple. Specific tasks in lower priestly functions required only a small amount of training. The situation was different in the case of specialized and higher priestly offices, which demanded a detailed knowledge of religious texts, rituals, and meditations, while those with access to the shrine and the right to open the 'gate of heaven' also needed religious initiation. In the large temples the priests would not only take care of cult matters but also administered the many and varied branches of the temple economy and estates, managing work in the fields, checking the granaries, the herds of animals, the various craft workshops and stores, keeping accounts, and so on, as is evident from their administrative as well as priestly titles.

Priests in service were required to be physically and ritually clean—each morning and during the day they had to regularly wash themselves in the temple pool. This washing had a significant religious aspect: the water in the pool was considered holy, an outflow of the primordial water in which the god-creator was present. The priests kept their mouths clean by chewing pieces of natron and resin, or by rinsing them with water in which a piece of natron had been dropped. Circumcision was obligatory for men. The removal of hair from the whole body, including the eyebrows, was an important part of personal cleanliness. Sexual abstinence was required just before and during the service.

By ancient Egyptian standards, priestly service on temple estates secured a good material standard of living, but the priests had to observe various kinds of fasts, which differed from region to region and temple to temple. Especially in the later periods, as recorded, for example, by Herodotus, in some places they were not allowed to eat certain kinds of meat or vegetables that were permitted in other places. Eating the flesh of animals considered holy or forbidden in particular places was harshly punished. On the other hand, extant written records show priests banqueting on some occasions, eating and drinking opulently, making merry, and even engaging in debauchery, as is vividly illustrated by scenes in the Erotic Papyrus of Turin.

The priests' basic garb was very simple, composed of just a clean linen loincloth or kilt. Wool was considered unclean and therefore unsuitable. Light sandals woven from papyrus were a privilege, since the common people usually went barefoot. The quality and character of dress varied with the level and type of priestly office. For example the lector-priest wore a sash diagonally across his chest, while the *sem*-priest wore a leopard skin or a cheetah skin thrown over his back and chest and fixed to his shoulders. The high priest of the solar god in Heliopolis, which was the center of astronomical observations, had a robe adorned with stars. Ptah's high priest in Memphis, who was also a *sem*-priest, had a sidelock on his head, a leopard skin across his shoulders, and wore a necklace in the shape of a jackal with human hands.

We can trace, from as far back as the Old Kingdom, the gradual weakening of the king's role in society and the concomitant rise in the importance of gods. As the king's position diminished in power and influence, the temples of the gods flourished, grew richer and more numerous, and engaged a larger number of priests. With the increasing number of priests in the course of time, we witness the development of specialized groups of priests and relevant priestly functions. As time went by, and especially from the Late Period, priests became ever more specialized.

From the Early Dynastic Period the core category of priests was made up of those known as *hem(u) netjer* ('servant(s) of the god'); in later Greek interpretations they were termed *prophetes*. These priests had access to the innermost parts of the temple, which were closed to the public and also to the lower categories of priests, and their work was centered on the shrine. Those who had undergone special initiation had access to the shrine itself and the cult statue of the god.

The priests known as *wab* ('pure') belonged to a lower category of priests, and were relatively numerous. Their function became so identified with the idea of the temple and priestly service that after the acceptance of Christianity and the founding of the Coptic Church, *wab* became the generic word for a priest. They performed only the less important tasks, for example, cleaning and tidying the temple and carrying the barque with the statue of the god in processions. Notably, they had no access to the most important parts of the temple for the cult: the shrine and the space immediately surrounding it.

Between the *wab* priests and the servants of god there was an intermediate priest, *it netjer* ('god's father'), who walked at the head of the processions, sprinkled the way with ritually purified water, and sometimes also carried cult symbols. He would also assist in the ritual purification of people before they entered the most sacred part of the temple, and of the offerings before they were taken to the shrine, as is shown for example by the name 'workshop of the father of the god' used for the room just in front of the entrance to the Temple of Akh menu in Karnak.

Other priests formed a rather heterogeneous but important group. For example, the *sem*-priest in the leopard skin mentioned above had quite a high social standing, and took part in the dressing of the king. At funerary ceremonies he would appear in the 'opening of the mouth' ritual, in which he played the role of a son burying his father. He performed a similar function during the Mysteries of Osiris, in which he represented the king because the king was considered to be the son of Osiris. His title was also part of the titulary of the high priest of Ptah in Memphis.

The *khery hebet* ('lector-priest')—literally, 'he who is under the papyrus scroll' (which means he holds or carries the papyrus scroll)—was highly educated for his time and a generally respected man. He would read out the liturgical texts and religious formulae from the papyrus scroll, and appeared, for example, in funerary and offering rituals; his knowledge may also have made him a respected healer. He was often depicted with a white sash worn diagonally across his breast. The Greeks called these priests *pteroforoi* ('wing-bearers') because of the plumes woven into their hair.

The priests with a good general education, called *hierogrammateis* by the Greeks because of their knowledge of the holy texts, worked in the 'house of life,' which was a part of the Egyptian temple. This was the place where papyrus scrolls containing religious but also secular

Lector-priest, with sash across his breast, reads the text and carries out the ritual of offering. At the other end of the scene another priest holds a broom in his hand and performs the 'removal of the foot-steps' ritual with which the ceremony ended. Detail of offering scene from the mortuary temple of Khentkaus II in Abusir, Fifth Dynasty.

King Ay as a *sem* priest performs the 'opening of the mouth' ritual on the mummy of King Tutankhamun, who after death has already taken on the form of the god Osiris. Detail of decoration from the burial chamber in Tutankhamun's tomb in the Valley of Kings.

texts were compiled, copied, and preserved. Here, future scribes were trained. The houses of life were the centers of learning of their time.

In addition to all these categories, other specialized groups of priests gradually emerged in the temples. These included: the *stolistes,* who would undress, re-dress, and adorn the statue of the god; the *horologos,* who would determine the precise time for the temple rituals by observing the stars, sundials, or water clocks, and who was also the interpreter of the constellations as recorded in temples in the Late Greek and Roman periods; and the *pastoforos,* who carried the receptacle with the statue of the god and was one of the *wab* priests.

There were also priestesses in the temples, although there were far fewer of them than priests. These priestesses were called *hemet netjer,* '(female) servants of the god.' We find mentions of them in the cult of Hathor from as far back as the Old Kingdom, and they appear more rarely in the funerary cult as well. Queens used to be priestesses, for example, of the gods of fertility Tjaspef and Bapfi. Later we encounter them in the cult of Ptah, Min, and Amun and especially of goddesses, such as Mut, Hathor, and others. The title of the priestess, 'god's wife' or 'god's adoratrix,' was associated with the cult of Amun. This was a very important religious and political function, especially in the New Kingdom and the Third Intermediate Period. This category of female priestly titles includes 'god's hand,' which probably has a sexual meaning related to the myth that the god Atum created the first pair of gods by masturbating. Women also participated in ceremonies as singers and dancers.

The running of temples involved not only priests but also lay employees who formed a large proportion of the staff in large and rich temples. They worked on the temple estates as bearers, boatmen, but above all in the fields, pastures, gardens, and stables, in the bakeries, or brewing beer and preparing offerings. The remuneration of the individual priests and employees of the temple depended on their status and also on the resources of the temple. The priests divided the offerings, such as bread, drinks, and meat, among themselves after the god had 'eaten and drunk.'

The priests did not serve in the temple without interruption but were organized—on the basis of an old system taken over from boatmen—into shifts, for which Egyptologists have adopted their Greek designation *phyle* ('watch'). These were named after different parts of the boat, such as 'bow starboard,' 'stern port,' and so on. The phyles were further subdivided, first into four, and later into two subgroups or sections. A similar system was used in construction projects. Quite a precise picture of the organization and alternation of temple staff is provided by papyrus archives from the Fifth and Sixth Dynasties found in the funerary temples of kings Neferirkare and Raneferef in Abusir. For example, Neferirkare's mortuary cult employed as many as two hundred people—priests and lay employees—who alternated in service at monthly intervals.

The Domain of the God

The temple of the god was called *hut netjer** ('the abode of the god') and the term *per-netjer* ('domain of the god') was used to describe its administrative and economic apparatus as well as its estates. The latter term appeared only later, however; unlike the royal mortuary temples, the oldest temples were relatively small and simple structures, served by only a few priests, and economically supported by the royal palace. This was associated with the idea of the role of the king as the living god on earth, securing the order of the world. In the Old Kingdom, the royal mortuary temples were already huge stone structures intended to

* The word *hut* has a very general meaning and is used in various contexts; originally it meant a protected place with an oblong ground plan, surrounded by a wall. There are several other terms for temple, however—for example, *ra-per* and others.

According to Herodotus, the Festival of Banebdjed, the ram god of fertility, in Mendes in Lower Egypt involved the ritual intercourse of a ram and a priestess. Detail of a scene on a plaster mold from the Greco-Roman Period.

ensure that the royal mortuary cult would be maintained forever. The king endowed them with numerous so-called mortuary estates for their material support. The mortuary estates gained further privileges, for example, the exemption of their employees from labor obligations to the state. During the Old Kingdom, however, the situation of the temples of god gradually improved as well. For example, the Fourth Dynasty king Menkaure granted a piece of field by decree to the Temple of Hathor in Tehna and the funerary cult of its priests, and the Sixth Dynasty king Pepi II granted privileges to the Temple of Min in Koptos.

After the reunification of the country at the beginning of the Middle Kingdom, the god Amun became prominent and his cult rapidly increased in importance. The earliest record of his cult dates from the Eleventh Dynasty and relates to 'Amun's domain.' For example, as is attested by the annals of the Twelfth Dynasty king Amenemhet II from Memphis, by this period the temples were starting to obtain a significant share in income from the trading routes and booty from military expeditions. In the New Kingdom, extensive campaigns in western Asia, Nubia, and Libya were bringing a great deal of booty into Egypt, no small part of which was invested in the temples as an expression of gratitude to the gods for victories achieved under their protection. For example, the greatest Egyptian warrior, Thutmose III, assigned 1,288 Asian captives to the Temple of Amun in Karnak. In this period, an extensive program of reconstruction and expansion of old temples and the building of new temples was underway throughout Egypt and in the conquered territories, especially Nubia. It was a tremendously costly project; we can get a clearer idea of the resources involved from extant texts related to the Temple of Montu in Karnak. These show that in the period of the country's greatest development in the mid-Eighteenth Dynasty, King Amenhotep III devoted the following resources to the construction of this temple: 2,865.1 kilograms of gold, 2,290 kilograms of white gold, 425 kilograms of black copper, 384 kilograms of lapis lazuli, 157.6 kilograms of jasper, 98 kilograms of turquoise, 1,310 kilograms of bronze, and 9,460 kilograms of copper.

The stream of wealth flowing into the temples, especially of Amun, was interrupted during the reign of Amenhotep IV–Akhenaten and diverted to Amarna not only for the construction of the new capital, but also for the maintenance of the local temples of Aten. However, the restoration of the old order commenced, under Tutankhamun, shortly after Akhenaten's death.

The Great Harris Papyrus* provides eloquent testimony of the Egyptian temples' property holdings at the end of the New Kingdom. This important document from the Twentieth Dynasty, from the time of Ramesses IV, is concerned with the state of the temple property under Ramesses III, the last great ruler of this epoch of Egyptian history. The table below shows the wealth of the three main Egyptian temples—those of Amun in Karnak, Re in Heliopolis, and Ptah in Memphis—and the privileged position of the Temple of Amun in Karnak.

Temple	Karnak	Heliopolis	Memphis
Staff	81,322	12,963	3,079
Animals	421,362	45,544	10,047
Gardens	433	64	5
Fields (hectares)	591,320	108,973	6,919
Boats	83	3	2
Building sites	46	5	0
Towns	65	103	1

Even after the end of the New Kingdom, in the Third Intermediate Period and the Late Period, the flow of rich gifts from the king and other leading figures continued to individual temples. This tradition was curbed only by Cambyses, the Persian conqueror of Egypt, whose

* The papyrus is named after Anthony Charles Harris (1790–1876), British merchant and collector of Egyptian antiquities.

'respect' for Egyptian religion, cults, and traditions is best illustrated by the report that he allegedly ran the sacred bull Apis, the earthly embodiment of the *ba* of the god Ptah, through with his sword. Reportedly, Cambyses also reduced the supply of sacrificial beasts to the temples by half and completely cut off supplies of some materials, such as construction timber and linen.

The conquest of Egypt by Alexander the Great—despite his respect for Egyptian gods and the warm reception that he received from the priests of Amun in the Siwa Oasis—led from the start to the forcible appropriation of temple land by Greek mercenary soldiers. Alexander's successors, the Ptolemaic kings, nonetheless managed to stabilize political conditions in the country quite quickly and to push through efficient reforms that ensured order. They founded new temples with property distinct from that of the state, and provided an income for the priests by the so-called *syntaxis*, money from the state. On the other hand, the progressive increases in the taxes payable by the temples, and the introduction of labor obligations for some of the lower-ranking temple employees, later led to a growing discontent, which erupted in rebellion around 200 BC.

In late Hellenistic multicultural conditions, Egyptian religious ideas were increasingly subject to foreign influences, while traditional domestic cults gradually declined in importance and were cultivated by ever smaller, introverted communities. Only a small number of priests could read and understand the inscriptions and pictures on the walls of the temples. Many Egyptian religious customs, such as the worship of sacred animals, became the object of open ridicule and expressions of distaste from Romans and other foreigners. Furthermore, the rapid advance of Christianity added active resistance to 'pagan idolatry,' which in many places was expressed in the destruction of statues and relief decorations and the conversion of ancient Egyptian temples into Christian churches. The Edict of Theodosius of 391, which proscribed pagan cults, was the proverbial last straw. The era of the Egyptian temples was over, and one great epoch in the religious history of the world had come to an end.

First Excursus

Ordinary Days and Feast Days

Work in the fields. Detail of the decoration of the tomb of Mena in Qurna. Eighteenth Dynasty.

The Calendar

The onset of the annual inundation of the Nile marked the basic dividing line of the year in ancient Egypt. This cyclical event was the natural starting point for the agricultural year and the civic calendar derived from it. The latter was divided into three seasons: *akhet* ('inundation'), *peret* ('winter'), literally 'coming forth, budding,' and *shemu* (summer, literally 'heat'). Each of these seasons lasted four months, and each month comprised thirty days. The remaining five days, known as epagomenal days, were dedicated to the gods Osiris, Horus, Seth, Isis, and Nebthet. The origins of this calendar go back to the time when learned ancient Egyptians first noticed the heliacal rising of the star Sirius (that is, the appearance of the star above the eastern horizon just before sunrise) after months of absence. According to the Russian Egyptologist Oleg Berlev (1933–2000), this discovery may have occurred in the reign of the first king of the Third Dynasty, Djoser.

>> Limestone block of lintel from the tomb of Hesufkai, overseer of the employees of the Great House (royal residence) and bearer of a number of other titles. In addition to the funerary formula the inscription also contains (in the third and fourth lines from the top) a list of festivals—the New Year, the festival of Thoth, the *wag* festival, and others—when offerings were brought to the tomb of the deceased. Early Sixth Dynasty(?). Abusir.

As the years went by, however, people discovered that the 365-day calendar was starting to depart from the sidereal year,* which was six hours longer. The beginning of the inundation coincided with the (heliacal) rising of Sirius (Egyptian Sopdet, Greek Sothis) roughly once in 1,460 years; this interval is known as the Sothic cycle. The reform of the calendar was not carried out until the Roman period. The names of the months of the civic calendar, etymologically based on the original names of ancient Egyptian festivals, have survived to this day in the Coptic calendar.

Season of Inundation

First Month – Thoth (Egyptian: *Djehuti*)
Second Month – Paopi (Egyptian: *Pa-en-ipet*)
Third Month – Athyr (Egyptian: *Hather*)
Fourth Month – Khoiak (Egyptian: *Ka-her-ka*)

Season of Budding (Winter)

First Month–Tobi (Egyptian: *Ta-abet*)
Second Month – Mekhir (Egyptian: *Pa-en-meher*)
Third Month – Phamenoth (Egyptian: *Pa-en-Imenhetepu*)
Fourth Month – Pharmouthi (Egyptian: *Pa-en-Renenutet*)

Season of Heat (Summer)

First Month – Pakhon (Egyptian: *Pa-en-Khonsu*)
Second Month – Paoni (Egyptian: *Pa-en-inet*)
Third Month – Epep (Egyptian: *Ipip*)
Fourth Month – Mesore (Egyptian: *Mesut-Re*)

* The sidereal year is the period between two successive identical positions of the sun relative to the fixed stars (365.2564 solar days).

Besides the civic calendar there was also a lunar calendar* in ancient Egypt, which probably dated from the period of the unification of Egypt. The lunar calendar was used, for example, in the temple cult, on certain festivals, and so on. One month of this calendar lasted thirty days minus a few hours.

Festivals

So many festivals were celebrated in Egypt over the year, one following close on the heels of another, that it might seem as if there were no time left for ordinary days. The reality was different: not all festivals were equally important and not all were celebrated everywhere in the country. Some were local, others regional or observed in a few adjoining regions. Some of the festivals were quite old and we encounter them in the very earliest written records, while others appeared later, often as late as the Ptolemaic or Roman periods. In many festivals we can see an intermingling of ancient myths, the cults of different gods, and old hunting and agricultural rituals. Funerary festivals were also important, and great significance was attributed to political festivals associated with the royal ideology and basic dogmas of the ancient Egyptian state. In these festivals the king played a major role: just as he was the lord of rituals, he was also the lord of festivals.

* The lunar calendar, based on the moon's cycles, helped determine the time for certain feasts and temple ceremonies, and the priestly duty shifts lasted one month. Some deities were closely linked with the moon, such as Khonsu, 'the Wanderer.' The moon was a powerful partner of the sun god. The moon's rebirth was shrouded in mystery, the deceased hoped to be reborn as the moon, and other beliefs were similarly attached to the lunar cycle.

>> Celebrations of the *opet* festival involved musical and acrobatic performances. Scene on quartzite block from the Red Chapel of Queen Hatshepsut in Karnak.

The ancient Egyptians themselves distinguished between two basic types of festivals: the 'Feasts of Heaven' and the 'Feasts of the Season.' Long lists of festivals were often recorded on the walls of temples. For example, from the great calendar of feasts in Medinet Habu we learn that as many as sixty festivals were celebrated here each year. Rituals were performed in the temples during festivals: offerings were brought to the gods, processions set out for cult sites either on foot or on little boats down the Nile, or there were processions with lamps, banquets, and so on. Behind all the pomp of some festivals and the colorful mummery of others, however, we find one common, unifying idea: veneration and celebration of the gods was meant to maintain the land's prosperity and the order given by the gods, which was constantly threatened by the powers of evil and chaos.

The feasts of heaven

One particularly important 'feast of heaven' was the Rising of Sopdet, a star believed to be the cosmic form of the goddess Isis. This marked the heliacal rising of the star Sirius, after its temporary disappearance from the sky. It meant the arrival of the inundation, but of course differed in time according to the observation point; for example, it happened in Memphis four days after it happened in Thebes.

Feasts of the seasons

There were several calendar feasts in each month. Here we list only those that were widely observed in more than one region, and omitting indication as to which of them were first recorded in written sources.

Season of Inundation

First Month

The month began with the glorious festival of the New Year. The Feast of Thoth, who gave the whole month its name, was also important. Thoth was honored as the god of wisdom and knowledge, as well as the cosmic god of the month and lord of the calendar.

Second Month

The month took its name from the most important festival celebrated at this time, *opet*, during which the god Amun left his main temple in Karnak to visit the Southern Harim, a temple in Luxor. The Memphis festival of 'Ptah Who Is South of His Wall' also took place in this month.

Third Month

Interestingly, the Feast of Hathor, which was held during this month, is not mentioned in records of her chief temple in Dendera, even though the goddess gave her name to the month. It is believed that celebrations of the goddess took place throughout the month and that the month ended with a fertility ritual.

Fourth Month

The great festival of Osiris, known as the time of the Osiris Mysteries, was celebrated during this month. The sorrowful but also festive days, mourning the death of Osiris, started with the originally Memphite feast of Sokar, the god of the dead, when the statue of the god would visit cemeteries in his own barque. Rich offerings were made at the Feast of Sokar.

Season of Budding

First Month

In this month ancient Egyptians celebrated the feast of the snake god Nehebkau, 'He who vouchsafes the *ka*,' in the sense of the *ka* of every god. He was believed to have great influence on the fate of the dead. Other festivals also took place in this month, for example, Wadjet's Going Forth (by boat). The cobra goddess Wadjet was not only a powerful protective goddess; she also represented Lower Egypt and played an important role in several myths.

Second Month

Among other feasts, the Going Forth of Anubis (procession by boat) took place in Thebes.

Third Month

Grain and animals were offered during the Great Feast of Burnt Offerings, which was held on the first day of this month.

Fourth Month

The Lesser Feast of Burnt Offerings was held on the first day of the fourth month. This month also included the Feast of Bastet. Classical authors have given us an account of the merry and even licentious course of this festival in the Late Period in Bubastis, the center of the cult of the cat goddess in the Eastern Delta.

Season of Heat

First Month

This month started with the old festival of Renenutet, the snake goddess of the fields and crops. The climax of this month was the feast of the ithyphallic fertility god Min on the eve of the new moon.

Second Month

The feast of the 'Greening of the Fields' took place in the final third of the second month.

Third Month

Besides the *sadj* feast (feast of the dead) celebrated throughout the whole land, the feast called the 'Excursion of Re' took place in sun temples in the Memphite necropolis.

Fourth Month

Right at the beginning of this month was the feast of the hippopotamus goddess Ipet. On the last day of the month, a special dinner celebrated the end of the month and of the whole year before the five subsequent epagomenal days.

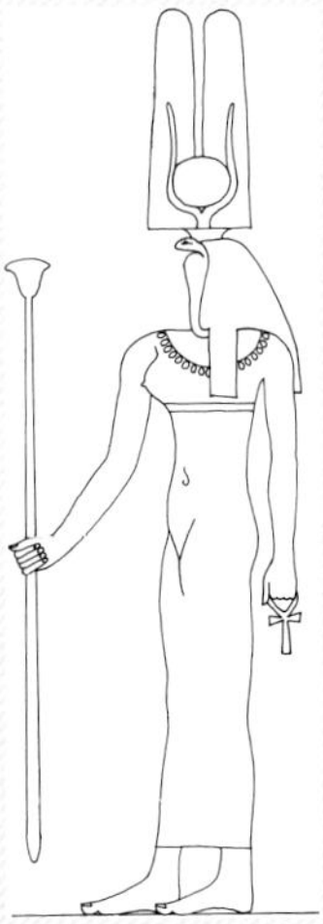

Renenutet, snake goddess of the fields and crops.

At the end of the year during the epagomenal days there were feasts in honor of the five Heliopolis gods, who protected the individual days. In the Ptolemaic Period these became part of the ten-day celebrations known as the 'first feast,' which began on the last day of the last month of the year, that is, the thirtieth of Mesore, and continued beyond the epagomenal days until the end of the fourth day of the first month of the new year.

View of Heliopolis with the pyramids of Giza in the background. Eighteenth-century German engraving.

2

Heliopolis: The City of the Sun

<< Karnak. The materialization of a symbol: the obelisk was regarded as a petrified sunbeam.

The famous Egyptian city of Iunu, known in Greek as Heliopolis ('City of the Sun'), was considered by the historian Herodotus to be the oldest center of learning in Egypt. The visitor who wants to see this site today has to take a complicated route through the winding alleyways of the overpopulated Matariya district in the northeast of Cairo. Some visitors come here just to see an important Christian holy site, the Church of the Holy Family, which stands where, according to legend, the Holy Family rested under a great sycomore—the 'Tree of Our Lady,'—during their flight into Egypt. Heliopolis, on the other hand, is not a popular tourist attraction for it offers no spectacular monuments despite the fact that it was once a city more celebrated than any other. According to ancient myths it was here that the god Atum created the world and later, with Atum presiding, that the court of gods heard the infamous case of fratricide committed by Seth against his brother Osiris. The dispute between Osiris's son Horus and Seth over who was to rule Egypt was resolved in Heliopolis. Here the gods resolved on the foundation of the Egyptian state as the Kingdom of Horus. What little is left of the former glory of Heliopolis presents a rather depressing sight: a partly empty, partly overgrown area shut in on all sides by seedy apartment houses. All that catches an ordinary visitor's eye is an obelisk of red granite, twenty-two meters high, which was erected here four millennia ago on the orders of Senwosret I in honor of the celebrations of the thirtieth anniversary of his ascent to the throne. A second obelisk was still standing here in the twelfth century, according to a report of the Arab historian Abd al-Latif. At the beginning of the 1970s the Egyptian archaeologist Mutawiya Balbush found a fragment of an even older obelisk bearing the name of the first Sixth Dynasty king Teti.

Even for an Egyptologist familiar with all the available historical sources it is very difficult to reconstruct the history of this ancient city, despite the fact that in size it rivaled Thebes and Memphis and its temples and cults still fascinated the learned men of classical antiquity. Schools founded by Plato and Eudoxus flourished here for a long time; the city was visited by the historian Herodotus and later by

Alexander the Great, as well as by the geographer and historian Strabo, in whose time (around the beginning of the Common Era) Heliopolis still stood on a low but prominent hill, surrounded by marshes and a canal. In fact, the tradition of Heliopolis as a center of learning goes back much further, spanning the whole of Egyptian history; two thousand years before Strabo, in the times of the Egyptian Middle

The red-granite obelisk of Senwosret I, twenty-two meters tall, once stood in front of the temple of the sun god. Today it is a solitary reminder of the ancient glory of Heliopolis.

Kingdom, Heliopolis was already regarded as a treasure house of knowledge. An indirect reference to the spiritual importance of Heliopolis is found in the Bible, which relates that the Joseph of the Old Testament was given the daughter of the high priest of Heliopolis to be his wife (Genesis 41:50). According to Arab historians and travelers, obelisks were still seen in Heliopolis in the Middle Ages, while

The remains of Heliopolis are today vanishing under the overpopulated periphery of Cairo.

at the turn of the eighteenth century the French consul in Egypt saw a fallen obelisk and sphinxes, as well as the obelisk that is still standing today. Some Egyptologists now believe that an alley of sphinxes half a kilometer long led from the quay on the canal and the western gate of the holy precinct to the main sun temple in Heliopolis.

The fate of Heliopolis was in many respects even more tragic than that of Memphis (see chapter 3), for the City of the Sun was almost completely robbed of its grand monuments in several successive waves of pillage. Many were removed elsewhere, others destroyed. As early as the New Kingdom, under Ramesses II, obelisks, statues, sphinxes, and other monuments were taken from Heliopolis to Per Ramesse ('City of Ramesses'), the new royal residence and center of government in the Eastern Delta. Later, in the Third Intermediate Period, the removal of Heliopolis' monuments continued; this time they were transferred to another new royal city called Djanet, which in classical antiquity was known as Tanis, and today is called San al-Hagar. Following the conquest of Egypt by Alexander the Great, the remaining monuments were carried off to Alexandria, the newly founded capital not just of Egypt but of Alexander's future world empire. Some monuments ended up even farther from Heliopolis, for example, two obelisks of Thutmose III; today, one of the obelisks stands on the Embankment in London and the other in Central Park in New York.

Archaeologists will probably never be able to determine the original extent and boundaries of Heliopolis or fully investigate the remains of its principal buildings. Today the ruins of the city lie beneath densely populated Cairene districts such as Matariya, Arab al-Hisn, Ain Shams, Abbasiya, and others. Surviving and very fragmentary information from written sources allows us to form only an approximate idea of the topography of the City of the Sun, which, according to the Harris I Papyrus, was surrounded by fields and farms, little lakes, and gardens and orchards.

Heliopolis was the metropolis of the thirteenth Lower Egyptian administrative region and lay not far from Memphis, on the southeastern edge of the Nile Delta. The city was situated close to the easternmost Pelusiac or Bubastite branch of the Nile, known to Egyptians as 'Water of Re' after the god worshiped in Heliopolis. The city was connected to the main course of the Nile and the immediate surroundings of Memphis by a canal approximately thirty-three kilometers long, which ran west from Heliopolis and issued, in the south, into a Nile harbor close to the spot in today's Old Cairo known as the 'Battleground.' Here the Nine Gods, or Ennead of Heliopolis, were worshiped, while not far away, at the mouth of the canal by today's Atar al-Nabi, stood the temple of the god of the Nile Hapy, where great festivals were held at the beginning of the annual inundation.

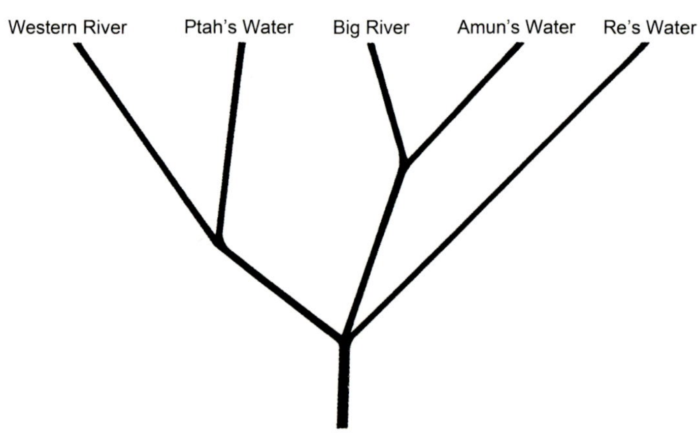

The Nile split at the Delta into five branches, each of which had its own name. The eastern branch was called "Re's Water" because of its proximity to Heliopolis.

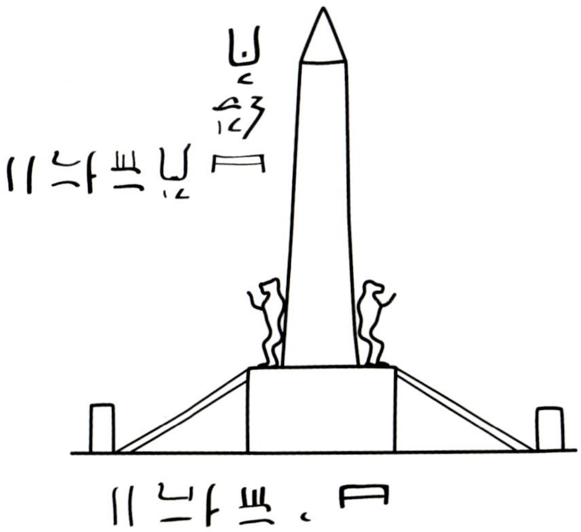

Rock drawing of one of the Heliopolis obelisks, "made by his own hand by the foreman of the works Penamun" in the nearby quarries at Gebel Ahmar. It is clear from the drawing that the obelisk stood on a base, and steps led to its foot where there were statues of baboons adoring the sun god.

Hapy's temple contained an important Nilometer that measured the height of the Nile inundation for the area of Memphis. To the north, the canal opened into the Pelusiac branch of the Nile.

Heliopolis was the starting point for important routes to Sinai and into Palestine. One of these—Re's Road—led along the edge of the desert. On the southern periphery of Heliopolis was the Red Mountain, known today as Gebel Ahmar, with its important quarries yielding a quartzite dark-red to brown in color, which because of the location of the quarries was considered to be the stone of the sun god. A shrine to the goddess Hathor, Lady of the Red Mountain, stood in what today is the district of Manshiyat al-Sadr.

One significant source for the historical topography of Heliopolis is a stela dating from the period of the Twenty-fifth Dynasty, which was discovered in Gebel Barkal in Nubia. We gather—from a text on the stela that describes the campaign of King Piye against Tefnakht, the local ruler in Sais in the northwestern Delta—that the king also visited Heliopolis and the temples of Re-Harakhty and Atum in the city. Some Egyptologists contend that these temples were still separate buildings at that time; others think that they were already connected in a single administrative-economic whole known as the Temple of Re from the Late New Kingdom. According to the oldest texts from the Old Kingdom, part of the temple complex—and the main focus of the solar cult—was the 'sanctuary of the *benben* stone,' where the solar god was worshiped in the form of a stone fetish. Piye visited this sanctuary too and met the god in his shrine. In some much later

Egyptian religious texts the *benben* was compared to Atum's petrified semen. The prevailing view among Egyptologists is that the *benben* was a stone of conical shape; some think it may have been of meteoric origin. In Piye's time, the sanctuary of the *benben* stone was already identified with the shrine of the mythical *benu* bird, regarded as the embodiment of the soul, or *ba*, of the sun god. The *benu* was originally

The royal scribe Hunefer adoring the sacred *benu* bird in the nether world and bringing him offerings. Illustration on a papyrus with the text of the *Book of the Dead*. Nineteenth Dynasty.

represented as a small bird and later as a heron with two long plumes on his head (probably the gray heron, *Ardea cinerea*). Whether the form of the words *benu*, *ba*, and *benben* contributed to this connection is the subject of debate. The *benu* bird, also called 'Coming into being by himself,' later became the symbol of resurrection, eternal life, and long reign. As described in the tradition of antiquity, it always returned like the mythical phoenix after five hundred years (known as the phoenix period or cycle), bringing good fortune and prosperity.

The *benben* stone was not the only fetish worshiped in Heliopolis. The second was the Iun Pillar, which also gave the city its Egyptian name. The fetish was a wooden pillar topped (according to the German Egyptologist Wolfgang Helck) by a bull's skull with horns—the bucranium—which may have been associated with the bull cult that also developed in Heliopolis. The bull, already mentioned in the Pyramid Texts, was known as Merwer (later also as Menwer), and sometimes just as the 'bull of Iunu.' The Greeks called it Mnevis.

Just as Apis in Memphis was considered the earthly embodiment of the *ba* of the god Ptah, Mnevis in Heliopolis was regarded as the embodiment of the *ba* of the god Re. According to Plutarch, it was supposed to be a massive black bull with great testicles, which were the symbol of generative power. So far our earliest evidence for the cult of Mnevis in Heliopolis dates from the reign of Ramesses II, but

Prince Ahmose, the high priest of Heliopolis, bringing offerings of flowers and censing the cult statue of the sacred bull Mnevis, herald of Re. Drawing of the limestone stela from Heliopolis. Nineteenth Dynasty.

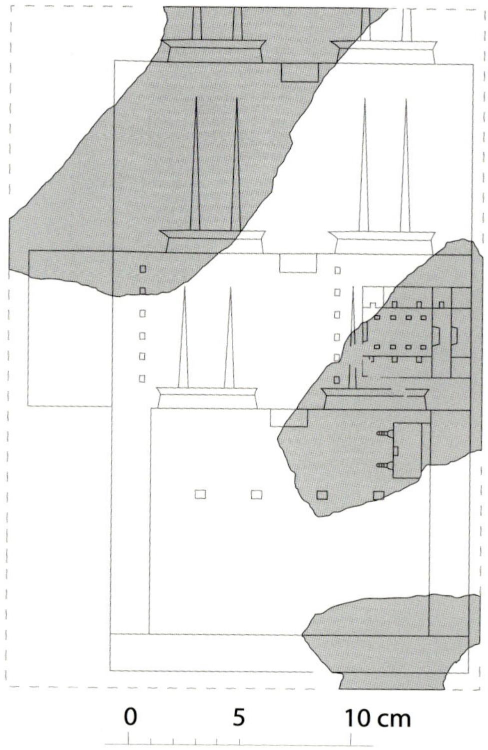

Fragments of a slate tablet from the reign of Senwosret I in the collections of the Egyptian Museum in Turin, showing part of engraving of a plan of the sun temple of Heliopolis, and the reconstruction of the plan as suggested by Ricke. Twelfth Dynasty.

the 'Chapel of the Erected Willow' and the 'House of Atum of the Sycomore'—cult buildings associated with specific rituals—were located in the second courtyard. While it is more probable that this is a plan of the Heliopolis temple of the goddess Hathor, partner of the sun god Re-Harakhty, Ricke did not exclude the possibility that this was the temple of the sun god himself.

However, the most valuable information about Heliopolis and its temples comes from the stela of Piye mentioned earlier. According to the stela, the most important cult place in Heliopolis was the 'High Sand,' the symbolic representation of the primordial mound in the form of which, it was believed, the god Atum emerged from the primordial waters at the creation of the world and on which he then continued his work. An interesting discussion has developed around the 'High Sand' but has not yet led to any firm conclusions. It was stimulated by the results of excavations carried out in Heliopolis shortly after the First World War by the English archaeologist William Mathew Flinders Petrie (1853–1942). He managed to unearth remnants of buildings

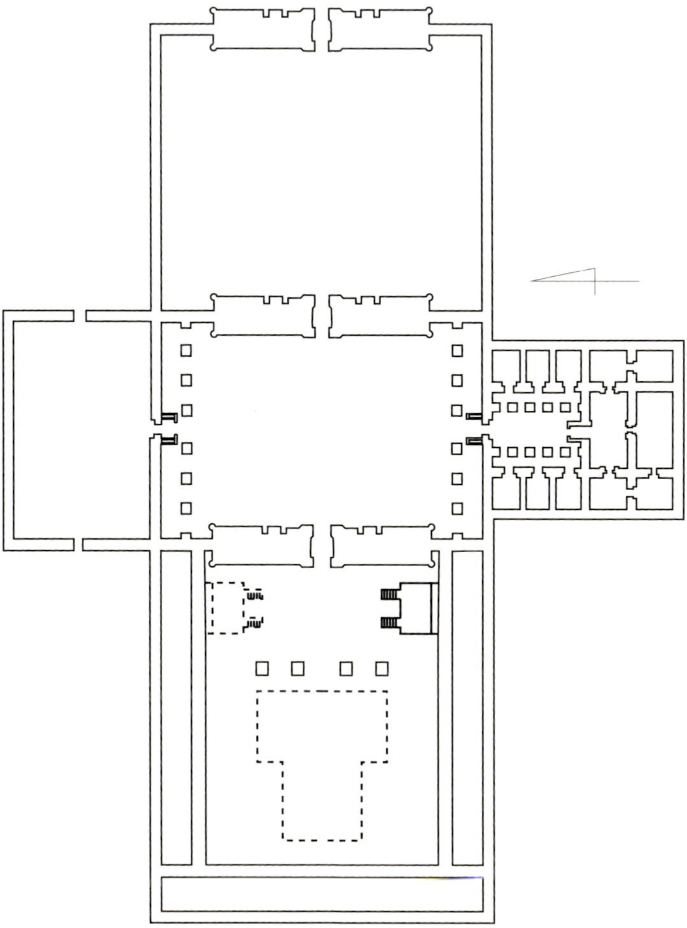

Reconstruction of the ground plan of the sun temple in Heliopolis, as proposed by Herbert Ricke on the basis of the engraving on a slate tablet from the reign of Senwosret I in the collections of the Egyptian Museum in Turin.

encircled by the huge brick wall known as the Great Enclosure. Inside the precincts that he excavated he found a mysterious round artificial mound made of sand and clay.

The mound reaches a height of up to eight meters and its volume is estimated to be a half million cubic meters. The perimeter was secured by a brick wall that was constructed during the New Kingdom period. At the time of Petrie's excavations, the top of the mound was around three and a half meters higher than the base of the obelisk of Senwosret I (already mentioned), which is believed to be standing in its original location. Shortly before Petrie, the Italian archaeologist Ernesto Schiaparelli (1856–1928) had undertaken an excavation of similar scale of the mound area and discovered a "labyrinth of walls," containing fragments of stone slabs adorned with reliefs from a shrine built by the first Third Dynasty king Djoser. Petrie found objects from the Old and Middle Kingdom under the perimeter wall. Schiaparelli had not in fact been the first to dig here. In the mid-nineteenth century the Armenian engineer Joseph Hekekyan, while carrying out survey and probe work for the Egyptian government, had found the massive base of another obelisk about twenty meters south of the obelisk of Senwosret I. Hekekyan's manuscripts and relevant documentation lay for many years unnoticed in the archives of the British Library before being rediscovered by the British archaeologist David Jeffreys.

In the mid-1930s Herbert Ricke, who succeeded Ludwig Borchardt (1863–1938) in the post of director of the Swiss Institute for the History of Egyptian Architecture and Archaeology in Cairo, came up with the theory that the mound discovered by Petrie was the same site referred to as 'High Sand' in the text of Piye's stela. He dated the mound to the Old Kingdom, considered it to have been artificially created, and argued that the temple had originally stood on top of it. Ricke's theory was undermined by research undertaken at the beginning of the 1990s in the northern part of the mound by the Egyptian archaeologists Muhammad Abd al-Gelil and Adel Saadani, who found remnants of masonry containing recycled slabs from Twelfth Dynasty tombs. Ricke's theory is therefore not accepted today, but no other satisfactory explanation of the mound has been put forward. Various

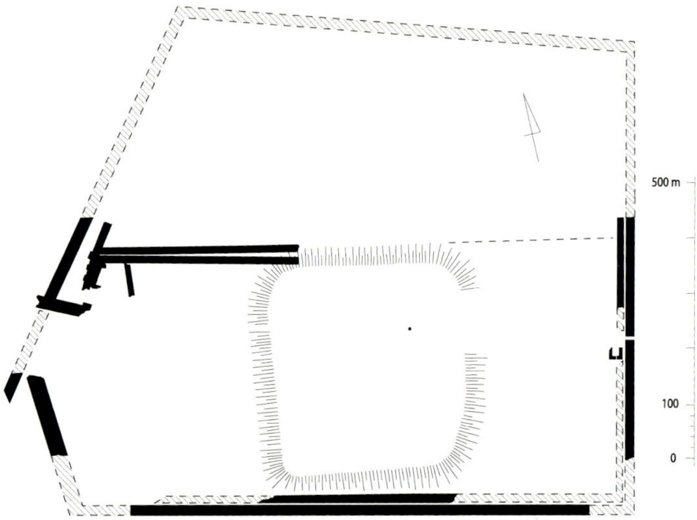

Plan of the Great Enclosure and oval structure in Heliopolis.

The figure depicted on this drawing of a fragment of a relief from Djoser's shrine in Heliopolis is probably Geb, one of the gods of the Heliopolitan Ennead. Egyptian Museum, Turin. Third Dynasty.

datings have been suggested within the very large time period from the Early Dynastic to the Late Period. Petrie himself dated the oval structure to a time just before the New Empire, and believed that it was a Hyksos fortress. The German archaeologist Dietrich Raue, author of what is so far the most thorough study of the history of Heliopolis, leans more toward the later datings (Twenty-sixth to Thirtieth Dynasties). He believes that the mound was the raised platform of a shrine, earlier monuments having been razed to the ground to make way for it, and that the perimeter of the mound was covered with a wall likewise built from the material of the demolished monuments.

The British Egyptologist Stephen Quirke, author of an important monograph on the cult of the sun god Re, has put forward an interesting theory on the basis of analysis of available archaeological and written sources. In his view, the oval mound formed a base on which two temples, facing each other, stood on an east–west axis. The two façades were adorned with pairs of obelisks. Notably, the still standing obelisk of Senwosret I stood by the eastern temple and the obelisk base discovered by Hekekyan was the foundation of one of the obelisks that adorned the western temple's façade. The eastern temple may have been dedicated to Re, and the western temple to Atum. If this theory is correct, this would be a very unusual plan for an Egyptian temple complex built by Senwosret I.

Despite this interesting hypothesis, the question of the original temple of the sun god in Heliopolis remains open. Even if the mound was indeed the modified foundation for the temple built by Senwosret I, materials from other buildings were recycled in its construction and older buildings removed, and so the theory does not throw much light on the problem of the earliest, original temple of the sun god. This

This red-granite column re-erected in the ruins of the temple on Kom al-Hisn in Heliopolis comes from a building of the Nineteenth Dynasty king Merenptah.

original temple, although probably not a grand building, must have come into existence by no later than the beginning of the Third Dynasty, as is indirectly attested by fragments of reliefs from a cult building discovered by Schiaparelli, which might have functionally been connected with the temple. What did this original temple look like? Was its center the shrine of the *benben* stone? Was the original temple so badly damaged during the political and social upheavals of the First Intermediate Period that it had to be replaced by a new one, built by Senwosret I at the beginning of the Twelfth Dynasty?

Unfortunately these questions were not answered by the archaeological excavations undertaken in the years 1976–81 in the locality of Tell al-Hisn, north of the oval mound, by a team of archaeologists from Cairo University led by Abd al-Aziz Saleh. If anything, the questions just mounted up. At Tell al-Hisn the Egyptian team discovered the remains of a temple built in honor of the sun god by Ramesses IV. In its vicinity was a temple from the reign of Ramesses II and chapel of Prince Nebmaatre, son of Ramesses IX. Around the Temple of Ramesses IV the archaeologists unearthed brick granaries, a workshop of some undefined kind, and an extensive estate of dwelling houses, many of them preserved up to a height of about six and a half meters, which means that originally they had two stories. The lack of detectible roads was a puzzle that the Egyptian archaeologists failed to explain satisfactorily. Perhaps this was a compact residential area where narrow passageways were all that was necessary for communications. Also very important was the discovery of a large fortress from the reign of Ramesses III. Much suggests that the remains discovered at Tell al-Hisn are those of a later Ramesside extension to the Temple of Re. This may have included mortuary-cult temples by which the rulers wished to associate themselves with the cult of the sun god.

In addition to the oval mound, the sanctuary of the *benben* stone and the oldest part of Re's temple complex in Heliopolis also remain veiled in mystery. We can only speculate about their location and form, as well as the locations of other buildings mentioned in the written sources. For example, does the term 'Great Sanctuary' refer to the whole of Re's temple complex or just its central part? Were the 'Shrine of the Magnate,' the 'Shrine of the Great One,' the 'Shrine of the Lapwings' (the term 'lapwings' referred to the non-noble population who were in a subordinate position to the ruling elite), or the 'Sanctuary of the Ennead' separate buildings or just parts of the temple complex?

According to some texts, there was another cult site close to the sanctuary of the *benben* stone in Heliopolis. This was known as the 'Hill of Beheading.' Probably there was a crypt containing statues of the gods of the Ennead here. In the middle of this enclosed place stood a sacred tree, with a trunk that was believed to burst each morning to open the way for the rising sun. It was also the place where each day the sun god in the form of a tomcat won his battle with the embodiment of mythical evil, the primeval serpent Apophis.

It is fortunate that Egyptologists do not have to rely only on archaeological excavations and material evidence, and that written records—often found entirely elsewhere—also provide valuable information on Heliopolis. These not only indicate that Heliopolis was already an important city and religious center of the land at the dawn of Egyptian history but—as has been mentioned above—inform us in detail that, at the time of its greatest glory during the New Kingdom, Re's temple complex alone (as reported in the Harris I Papyrus from the reign of Ramesses III), employed 12,963 people, including priests, and owned approximately 44,100 acres of fields, 45,544 cattle, sixty-four orchards and gardens, 103 market towns, five large workshops, and three large boats. This property, vast by the standards of the time and supposed to support the cult of Re as well as the funerary cults of the kings who contributed to it with their donations, was not concentrated just in the Heliopolis area, but scattered in different parts of the country. Re's temple complex was at this period the second largest in Egypt after Amun's temple complex in Karnak.

The importance of the Temple of Re was reflected in the prestige of the office of high priest of Heliopolis, although this is documented in written records only from the Fifth Dynasty, the reign of King Neferirkare onward. The tombs of the high priests of Heliopolis that have been archaeologically identified date from the Sixth Dynasty and are located at a site outside the eastern façade of the Great Enclosure. The high priest usually had the title 'He who sees the Great One [that is, the sun god].' It should be added that at this period dignitaries of the royal court usually occupied high priestly offices, and it is in this milieu that the title is first attested, in the context of the *sed* festival commemorating (whether actually or symbolically) the thirtieth anniversary of the king's ascent to the throne. We also meet the title among the leaders of expeditions into Sinai, and sometimes to the quarries on Red Mountain—expeditions that always set out from Heliopolis. The Middle Kingdom saw an important shift in the meaning of the title: 'He who sees the Great One,' became 'The Greatest of Seers.' 'Seers' meant primarily the priests who observed the stars, because Heliopolis was also the chief astronomical observatory of the country.

There is much to support the idea that Heliopolis was more than just the center of the solar cult and an astronomical observatory. Precise measurements have shown that the pyramids of the Fourth Dynasty kings Khufu and Khafre are arranged in the cemetery in Giza in such a way that their southeast corners touch a line that runs to the obelisk of Senwosret I in Heliopolis. Similarly, the northwest

View of the pyramids of Abusir from the north, from Niuserre's sun temple in Abu Ghurab.

corners of the pyramids of the Fifth Dynasty kings Sahure, Neferirkare, and Raneferef in the cemetery at Abusir all touch a line that runs very close to this same site. It therefore seems reasonable to ask whether these lines—axes, as it were—of the cemeteries in Giza and Abusir were oriented to the *benben* in the sun temple, which at the time may have been considered to be the center of the world of the ancient Egyptians.

Sun Temples

Although archaeologists have not yet been able to thoroughly investigate the oldest cult site in Heliopolis and form a more precise idea of how the original sun temple might have looked, evidence from elsewhere in Egypt helps to define the possibilities. This evidence is provided by the sun temples built during the Fifth Dynasty in the necropolis of Memphis, and to a lesser extent the temples constructed in the period of the new flowering of the solar cult during the Eighteenth Dynasty. Although both groups are termed sun temples, there are marked differences between them. As far as the group of sun temples from the Old Kingdom is concerned, it is quite probable that their builders were actually inspired by the sanctuary of the *benben*

Three-dimensional reconstruction of Userkaf's sun temple in Abusir.

stone in Heliopolis where the god was worshiped through a fetish, then represented in stylized form by the obelisk.

The earliest sun temple in the Memphite necropolis was built by the first king of the Fifth Dynasty, Userkaf, on the northern edge of what is today the pyramid cemetery close to Abusir. A few hundred meters farther north, in a place called Abu Ghurab, lies a second sun temple, which was built by Niuserre, another of the Fifth Dynasty kings. From written records we know that another four kings of this dynasty—Sahure, Neferirkare, Raneferef, and Menkauhor—constructed or embarked on the construction of sun temples.

It is not entirely clear why Userkaf chose this particular place. The German archaeologist Werner Kaiser believed that it was because Abusir was the most southerly point in the Memphite necropolis from which Heliopolis was still visible, but measurements made recently by the Czech archaeological team have shown that this is not the case; in fact Abu Ghurab to the north is the southernmost place from which Heliopolis can be seen. A no less important question is why Userkaf decided to build a sun temple at all: What in the royal mortuary cult had changed so fundamentally as to make this necessary? It is also curious that Userkaf's sun temple is around three kilometers away

The court of Niuserre's sun temple in Abu Ghurab. In the rear part of the court are the remains of a base on which an obelisk once stood.

from his pyramid complex, situated very close to the northeast corner of the enclosure wall of the Step Pyramid in Saqqara. Evidently this choice of site for his tomb was the king's way of associating himself as closely as possible with the builder of the first pyramid in the Memphis necropolis and the founder of the strong Egyptian state, so as to strengthen the legitimacy of his rule. But why then did he build the sun temple so far away and, what is more, in a place not even in sight of Heliopolis? Probably we shall never know.

Userkaf's sun temple was built largely of limestone and was possibly known as 'Re's Storehouse' (the meaning of the name is not entirely clear; it may also be interpreted as 'Re's Fortress' or it might have been inspired by the name of one of the Heliopolis shrines). It consisted of three sections that were architecturally and functionally connected but different in elevation. On the lowest level, at the boundary between the Nile Valley and the desert, was what archaeologists call the 'valley temple,' just like other similar temples in the pyramid complexes. Its builders had evidently found inspiration in the complex of the Bent Pyramid of Snofru in Dahshur. Oriented on a north–south axis, the temple has a large open-pillared court with seven deep niches for statues. A fragment of one of these statues

(Userkaf's head with the crown of Lower Egypt) has even been discovered and is on display in the permanent exhibition of the Egyptian Museum in Cairo. It is surprising that the causeway linking the valley temple with the sun temple itself, which is spread out on a hillock roughly twenty meters high, is not built on the east–west axis of the upper temple as is usual in pyramid complexes of the time, but at an angle to it on a northeast–southwest axis. No convincing explanation for this peculiarity has yet been put forward.

The plan of the upper temple was evidently changed several times during construction, as was demonstrated by the Swiss–German archaeological team led by Herbert Ricke, who excavated it in the mid-1950s. Initially the enclosure wall was square in plan but with rounded corners (perhaps in an effort to imitate a stylized primordial mound). In the middle of the temple stood a low pedestal constructed from mud bricks, which probably supported a wooden pillar rising toward the sky. At least this is how the German Egyptologist Elmar Edel envisioned it on the basis of surviving written records. This column presumably evoked the *iun* fetish venerated in Heliopolis. Later, the upper temple was enlarged; it acquired a rectangular ground plan, oriented east–west, following the course of the sun across the sky. The wooden fetish was replaced in the reign of King Neferirkare by a tall obelisk of red granite.

A few hundred meters to the north, in Abu Ghurab, lies the sun temple of Userkaf's great-grandson Niuserre. It was investigated as early as the end of the nineteenth century by a German expedition under Friedrich Wilhelm von Bissing (1873–1956), although in practice directed by Ludwig Borchardt, who led the archaeological excavation. The temple, named 'Re's delight,' was likewise composed of three basic parts but its plan differed from Userkaf's in many respects. Instead of a valley temple there was a simpler building with a pair of columns that was more suggestive of a great entrance gate. The sun temple was built on a small hill and was accessed by an open causeway. As archaeological research has demonstrated, this temple too, constructed from limestone and several other types of stone, underwent interesting plan changes during building; under the stone temple Borchardt discovered not just ramps for the movement of building material but also the remains of massive brick walls that may have belonged to an earlier building phase. It is possible that this phase fell into the reign of Niuserre's predecessor Raneferef.

Niuserre's sun temple had a rectangular ground plan oriented east–west and divided into two main parts: the front section consisted

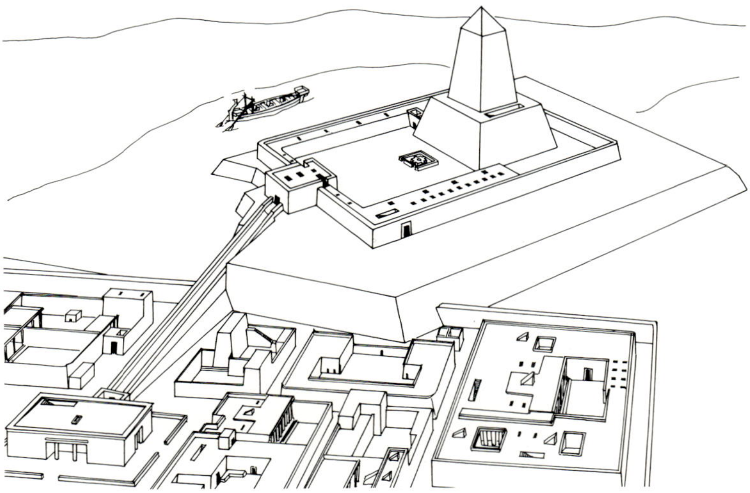

Ludwig Borchardt's reconstruction of Niuserre's solar temple in Abu Ghurab.

of a large open courtyard and the rear section of an obelisk on a base. Along the sides of the court stood large alabaster basins used for the ritual purification of the offerings presented to the sun god on a great alabaster altar at the foot of the obelisk. The altar is a unique work of art composed of five elements in the form of hieroglyphic signs. Four of these imitate the sign *hetep,* meaning 'offering' or 'offering table.' The fifth element imitates the sign *re,* 'sun' or '(sun god) Re.' The whole composition may then be interpreted as 'Re's offering table.' This symbolism in Niuserre's temple may not be a matter of chance, for the sun temple of his brother Raneferef, who died prematurely, was known as 'Re's offering table,' and since only one written mention of it exists in contemporaneous inscriptions it was evidently never completed. Quite possibly, Niuserre exploited the unfinished building and honored his brother's monument by building in the courtyard the great offering table surrounded by a wall pierced by doors in all four directions. Niuserre's sun temple was dominated by the huge obelisk, thirty-six meters high (made of blocks, not monolithic). Its apex—the pyramidion—may have been faced in gold (or gilded copper) sheet. In Egyptian a pyramidion was known as a *benbenet.* Indeed, the two words—the fetish *benben,* and the pyramidion *benbenet*—are both derived from the verb *weben* 'to shine,' which expresses their connection with the sun. The bottom section of the obelisk consists of a square pedestal with slanting sides faced in red granite. This massive base very probably represented a stylized mythical primordial mound. Inside the base and leading to the foot of the obelisk was a passage with walls decorated with scenes in low relief, in which two themes are prominent. One theme is that of the main episodes of the festival of *sed*, the celebrations of the thirtieth anniversary of Niuserre's ascent to the throne. The second is the seasons of the year. The reliefs show all living things—plants and animals—being born and blossoming under the life-giving rays of the sun. The German expedition took the panels with these scenes away with them and today they are among the most remarkable exhibits in the Egyptian Museum in Berlin.

Another component of Niuserre's sun temple was a huge solar barque—a kind of model made of mud bricks. It lay to the south of the temple and was supposed to serve the symbolic voyage of the sun god and his entourage across the heavenly ocean.

The remaining four sun temples have not been located and we know them only from written records by their names: Sahure's was called 'Re's field (of offerings),' Neferirkare's 'Re's favorite place,' and Menkauhor's 'Re's horizon;' as has already been said, Raneferef's 'Re's offering table' may well have been taken over and completed by Niuserre as his own. To judge from the written records the temples of Menkauhor and Sahure functioned for only a short period (or were not completed), but there is a relatively large number of records relating to the Temple of Neferirkare. Several generations of archaeologists have been searching for it, and its discovery would be a great step forward, probably throwing more light on the whole meaning and purpose of sun temples. If we are right in supposing that the pyramid field by Abusir was founded deliberately close to the southernmost point from which Heliopolis was still visible, then the as yet undiscovered sun temples probably lie somewhere between Abu Ghurab and Abu Rawash, where the northernmost pyramid in the Memphis necropolis stands—that of Djedefre.

Although we have not yet managed to find the other sun temples, let alone to answer most of the questions that surround them, a few answers are beginning to take shape. The discovery of the remains of papyrus archives in the nearby pyramid complexes of kings Neferirkare and Raneferef at Abusir has been of great value in this respect. The papyri show that at the period of the height of the solar cult the sun temples were assigned an important role in the mortuary cult of the kings. For example, some types of offering, such as vegetables, meat, certain kinds of baked goods, and so on were first taken to a sun temple, to Re's offering table, and only then to a pyramid complex. The idea then was that these sacrifices had first to be accepted and blessed by the sun god, before the king symbolically received them from Re's table in the other world. This represented a significant shift in the relations between the king and the god in comparison to the preceding period.

The penultimate king of the Fifth Dynasty, Djedkare, did not build a sun temple, but this by no means meant that the solar cult ended in his reign. On the contrary, it continued to flourish, but in the course of the Fifth Dynasty much changed in ideas of the afterlife and the nature of the mortuary cult. From the reign of Niuserre at the latest the cult of the god Osiris, ruler of the kingdom of the dead, was starting to make great headway, and the hitherto privileged position of the sun god Re was eroded. Under Djedkare's successor Unas, the earliest religious inscriptions—known today as the Pyramid Texts—appeared on the walls of the underground chambers of the royal pyramid, and in these texts Osiris already plays at least as important a role as Re, if not greater. There were also changes in the economy and society, although the extent of these changes and their interconnections are the subject of much academic debate, which is unlikely to reach firm conclusions soon. The same applies to the vexed questions of why sun temples came to be built during the Fifth Dynasty, where those not yet discovered lie, and why sun temples were then no longer built during the same dynasty. We have no records of sun shrines from the Middle Kingdom. Only several centuries later, at the beginning of the New Kingdom during the Eighteenth Dynasty, do we once more encounter a boom in the solar cult and sun temples. One specific type of solar shrine at this period was known as 'Re's shadow.'

We are indebted to the German Egyptologist Rainer Stadelmann for deeper understanding of the architectural style and development of 'Re's shadow' temples, and of their religious meaning. Before considering this we should note, however, that there are other types of sun temple dating from the Eighteenth Dynasty, but these have a very specific character and are associated with Akhenaten's religious reform (see chapter 6).

The name 'Re's shadow' is expressed in hieroglyphic script by a combination of two signs, a parasol and the sun, but it would be a mistake to think of the temples concerned as a kind of 'place of shade' where the god paradoxically sheltered from his own rays. Here 'shadow' refers to an integral part of a being, in the case of Re the creative power of the creator god. (A 'shadow' in this sense was also attributed to human beings, part of the personality but independent of the physical body and represented as a human silhouette, sometimes with an eye; in late texts it often means a spirit or even a ghost.)

We are familiar with 'Re's shadow' not only from the surviving remains of such buildings but also from contemporary depiction. We find one in Amarna in the tomb of Hay, administrator of Queen Tiye's *harim*. It is clear from the depiction that one temple of this type had an entrance gate in the form of a pylon, leading into an open court with rows of pillars, statues of King Akhenaten on both sides, and in the center an offering table covered with gifts for the god. Another component of the temple was the 'shrine.' This was an open kiosk on a base with a façade in the form of a pylon; inside the kiosk there was once again an offering table, in this case adorned with the figures of the king and queen bringing the sun god (here the shining sun disc Aten) offerings. The main tract was surrounded by a series of adjoining small courtyards with offerings put on altars.

The earliest surviving archaeological evidence of a 'Re's shadow' temple dates back to roughly three decades before the reign of Akhenaten and Amarna. It is found in the northwest section of the first terrace of the Temple of Queen Hatshepsut in Deir al-Bahri. It consists of an antechamber, with ceiling supported by three pillars, and beyond it an open courtyard with an offering table. There are recesses in the south, west, and north walls of the courtyard. Their rear walls are decorated with representations of the god Re-Harakhty and the queen is depicted sitting at a funerary banquet at the offering table on their side walls. The queen is sharing in the cult and the offerings to the sun god with her funerary banquet. The north recess is extended and turns into a small chapel of the jackal god Anubis, who was associated with mummification rituals, the protection of cemeteries, and the mortuary cult. Unlike in the picture in the Amarna tomb, however, here there is no shrine with kiosk and another offering table; the reason probably lies in the specific overall plan of Hatshepsut's terraced temple.

We find a 'Re's shadow' shrine, although with various architectural modifications, in other royal mortuary buildings (also known as memorial temples or temples of a million years) on the west bank of the Nile in Thebes. For example, we find 'Re's shadow' shrines in the Temple of Sethi I in Qurna—where the Re shrine is relatively well preserved—and in the Temple of Ramesses III in Medinet Habu. It was not simply a feature of royal mortuary temple complexes, however, for we also find cult places of Re in temples of the gods, for example in the Great Temple of Amun in Karnak in the section built by Thutmose III called Akh menu. Here the shrine of Re was located under the roof of the temple and was known as 'The House of Re under the Roof of Amun's Temple.' Later, from the Twentieth Dynasty up to the Ptolemaic Period, this kind of sun shrine was normally built on, rather than under, the roof terrace of temples of the gods in various places in Egypt. Although the 'Re's shadow' shrines and the solar temples in the Memphite Necropolis are separated in time by one millennium, just this brief account shows that they have some basic common features: they are composed of an open court with an offering table and a more elevated shrine (obelisk or raised kiosk), and both types were closely linked to the royal mortuary cult.

The Primordial Mound and the Ennead (Nine Gods)

A peculiarity of the religious thinking of the ancient Egyptians was the capacity, when faced with two different or even directly contradictory ideas, to resolve the dilemma not by adopting one and rejecting the other but by placing the two side by side or sometimes merging them to create something new. This syncretic tendency was present throughout the history of Egyptian religion from the very start, and as time went by it became stronger and more intense. One very good example of this kind of thinking is the earliest set of religious ideas as preserved in the Pyramid Texts from the end of Fifth Dynasty to roughly the middle of the Eighth Dynasty. Analysis of these texts shows that they include not just current or relatively new religious ideas but much earlier ideas as well. In this thematically very heterogeneous and chronologically layered set of texts concerning the fate of the king in the other world, astral and solar notions and beliefs associated with the god Osiris overlap and permeate each other; there are also elements of shamanism. The form of the texts is likewise very variegated, including sayings, hymns, litanies, and so on. Over time new ideas developed and mounted up, and the old ideas were often transformed; other sets of religious texts were compiled and different temples and religious centers created their own doctrines and cults in which the local deity would play the main part. Identifying the development and interrelationships of the roots of many of these religious ideas is usually a very difficult and often tricky, deceptive business. It will be no surprise that in ancient Egypt there existed different theories explaining the creation of the world and that over time they influenced each other. These different theories will be considered in detail in the next section of this book.

As we have seen, Heliopolis was very old—probably the oldest religious center of Egypt—but the possibility of conducting an adequate study is limited due to current conditions. This is why we do not have—and maybe never shall have—firm evidence of the origins of the religious cults here. For the moment, then, we have to try to reconstruct them mainly from later written records. These show that on the basis of ancient myth the local priests developed a religious doctrine about the creation of the world in which the role of creator was assigned to the sun god Atum.

The priests of Heliopolis did not suppose that prior to the creation of the world there was complete nothingness: in the beginning was material being in a state of chaos and timelessness. The god-creator was present within this being. Unsurprisingly, in a country where the artery of life was the Nile with its annual inundations, this being was conceived as taking the form of primordial waters, which the priests called Nun. In rare cases these deified primordial waters are depicted as a man with the head of a frog. According to the Pyramid Texts, it was at Heliopolis that the god-creator Atum emerged from the chaos as a hill or mound and started on his work of creation. This moment they called 'for the first time,' and with it, timelessness ended and time was born. Undoubtedly projected into this idea was the ancient Egyptians' annual experience of the ebb of the waters of the inundation, when the first little island would emerged from the Nile and with the next inundation be submerged again. The god-creator was a transcendent reality for which they found not only this mythical explanation but also a verbal expression: the basis of the name Atum is the verb *tem*, which means 'not to be' and 'to be whole,' which may be freely expanded to 'he who is not and is all,' 'from nothing, all' and so forth.

At the creation the god gave the world order. The chosen land of divine order was Egypt, but it was constantly menaced by the forces of chaos acting from outside and inside the country. The neighboring hostile nations were the embodiment of external evil. Order was known as *maat* and personified by the goddess of the same name, the daughter of Re who was the noonday culminating form of the sun god. The form of the sun god at dawn was called Khepre, and Atum was the setting evening sun. In line with the way that the solar cycle was continually repeated, creation itself was not considered a one-off, completed work. In harmony with the ancient Egyptians' largely cyclical understanding of time, derived from experience of regularly occurring natural phenomena (the rising and setting of the sun, the phases of the moon, the annual Nile inundation, and so on), creation was considered to be

The god Nun raising the barque with the newborn (morning) sun god Khepre in the form of a scarab out of the primeval waters. Above the scarab is a miniature representation of the sky goddess Nut standing on the head of the god Osiris (curled into a circle) and receiving the sun god in the form of a disc in order to let him slide into the circle of Osiris, that is, Osiris's underworld kingdom. Detail of a scene on the sarcophagus of Sethi I from the royal underworld *Book of Gates* from the New Kingdom.

an unfinished, repeating process in which there were critical moments when prayer and ritual were needed if the world was not to collapse and end. Fitting into the logic of this cycle was the idea that some day the collapse would occur, the world would end and sink back into the primordial waters, but only for a primordial mound to emerge out of these again and yet again to start the work of creation.

According to the doctrine of Heliopolis, the first beings to be created were the first two gods, as a biological pair: a male and female element. These reproduced to create further divine couples. Atum created the god Shu and the goddess Tefnut, the first pair of gods, in a peculiar way: by masturbating. He placed his seed in his mouth and then spat out the first god and expectorated the second. This pair then engendered another divine pair, Geb and Nut, who in turn produced two further pairs, Osiris and Isis and Seth and Nebthet. This group of the first gods, including the god-creator, was known as Pesedjet, 'The Nine' (sometimes also the Great Nine) or 'Ennead.' The number nine had a deeper meaning for ancient Egyptians: the number three expressed plurality, nine is the multiple of three times three, and so nine was the highest imaginable plurality, everything that came forth from the god-creator and the first gods, the whole cosmos. Even though the Ennead first appear in written records only as late as the Pyramid Texts, indirect evidence that this group of gods was defined and venerated much earlier is to be found in the fragments of reliefs (mentioned above) discovered by the Italian archaeologist Schiaparelli in Heliopolis. They are from a shrine built there at the beginning of the

<< The god Re-Harakhty with sun disc and uraeus on his head. Behind Re-Harakhty is Atum, the god of the setting sun, seated on a calf. Tomb of Sennedjem in Deir al-Medina, Nineteenth Dynasty.

Shu, the god of the air, separates the god of the earth, Geb, and the goddess of the sky, Nut, over whom the sun god sails in his barque.

>> Each day the sky goddess Nut gives birth to the sun and later swallows it. Wall painting from the tomb of Ramesses VI in the Valley of Kings, Twentieth Dynasty.

Third Dynasty by King Djoser and bear representations of Geb and Seth, gods of the Ennead.

The first gods immediately lend the Ennead a cosmic dimension. The god Shu, relatively rarely mentioned in written records of the earlier period, represented light, brightness, and clear dry air in contrast to the moistness embodied by his partner Tefnut. This aspect of his character meant that he was usually associated with the sun god, whom he was supposed as air to 'hold up,' but was also connected with the moon. Sometimes his name is interpreted as 'he who lifts himself up.' In religious speculations Shu and Tefnut represented the eyes of the sun god Re.

Tefnut embodied dark humidity, which according to the ancient Egyptians was one of the basic elements creating the conditions for the emergence of life. She was often depicted as a lioness or woman with the head of a lioness. This was because of her connection with the myth of the sun's eye, Tefnut-Hathor, which was supposed to have left the god Re, taking the form of an infuriated lioness and escaping south into the desert, from which it took long efforts of persuasion to get her to return so that prosperity and peace should reign again in the land. Tefnut is also often associated with the moon and its phases and in this context her name is sometimes interpreted as 'she who changes her face.'

According to the doctrine of Heliopolis the children of Shu and Tefnut were Geb and Nut. In the earliest known depiction of Geb—on the fragment mentioned above that dates from the reign of Djoser—the god has the form of a seated man with a long wig on his head and a ritual beard fixed to his chin. Later he was often represented as a semi-recumbent, languorous man (this may be connected to a similar-sounding word *geb*, meaning 'to be enfeebled'), but was sometimes depicted with an erect penis. Arching over him is his partner, Nut, the goddess of the sky. As the god of earth, Geb's body is often painted green; in some cases it is covered with burgeoning flora. He was considered the giver of fruits to the earth, from minerals to corn, and also the lord of earthquakes. Geb's symbolic animal was a wild goose. The goddess Nut, represented as an elongated woman serving as the heavenly vault (and sometimes as a standing woman with raised arms holding the sun disc or as a cow studded with stars), had a particularly important position in the solar religion: The sun was born each morning out of her womb, and would then travel across her body before being swallowed again by the goddess in the evening. This was repeated each day. The eternal cycle of birth from and death

into Nut was soon incorporated into the funerary cult and ideas of the afterlife. Nut was symbolically identified with the coffin, often being depicted on its inside walls, and so took the deceased into her embrace. She also became one of the goddesses protecting the canopic jars that contained the viscera removed during mummification.

Nut and Geb were the parents of the remaining two pairs of gods in the Heliopolis Ennead: Osiris and Isis, and Seth and Nebthet. These deities, who together came to be closely connected with a separate important circle of religious beliefs and also the idea of ancient Egyptian statehood, are considered in detail in chapter 8 and the Third Excursus.

Although the gods of the Heliopolitan Ennead were mutually linked and complementary, as time went by they developed separate existences in religious conceptions and narratives as well as merging and overlapping with other gods. For example, in certain contexts the goddess Tefnut took on characteristics of Hathor and Eset. Yet the Heliopolis Ennead was also worshiped as a group, as is evident for example from its shrine at the 'Battleground' (mentioned above) in what today is Old Cairo, and suggested by the fragments from the shrine of Djoser's time discovered by Schiaparelli. The gods of the Ennead, iconically depicted in mummiform, were shown taking part in important religious events, such as the court hearing in the dispute between Horus and Seth, and political occasions, such as the coronation of the king.

The Sun God

For the ancient Egyptians the sun was a very mysterious heavenly body. They were aware of its life-giving power, each day seeing it born in the east, reaching its height in the scorching heat of noon, and dying on the western horizon. For this eternal cycle they could have had none but a mythical explanation. They imagined that the sun was born from the womb of the sky goddess Nut, who then swallowed it up again on the evening of the same day as divine mother, and the next morning she gave birth to it again. At the same time, they imagined the course of the sun as the unending voyage of the sky god across the heavens by day in a barque called *mandjet* and through the underworld at night in a nocturnal barque called *meseketet*. As time went by the story of the sun god began to overlap and blend with other myths, for example, the legend of the *benu* bird, later the phoenix of classical antiquity. The sun god was likewise compared to the lotus flower, and this too was undoubtedly associated with a phenomenon observed in nature: in the morning the lotus flower emerges on the surface and opens, and in the evening it closes and sinks down under the water. Artistic expressions of this particular idea of the birth of the young sun god include the famous wooden polychrome sculpture from the Tutankhamun treasure depicting the king's head in a lotus blossom; the king's life was considered integrally linked to the sun god from birth to death and even after death in his journey in the underworld. The priests progressively molded and elaborated these various different ideas into a complex system concentrated on the fate of the sun god, which was conceived as a great mysterium (mystery in the religious sense), as ancient Egyptian sun hymns literally put it.

In the morning, the sun god is born as Khepre (from the Egyptian *kheper* 'to become, to arise') and in this phase is depicted as a scarab beetle (sacred beetle, *Scarabeus sacer*; Egyptian *kheprer*), who rolls the sun before him as a real beetle rolls his ball of dung. The sun god comes into existence mysteriously and at the same time causes further life to emerge; he is self-created and creator of the rest of the world. The birth of the sun is vividly illustrated by a scene from the later religious texts called the *Book of Gates*, in which the god is represented as a scarab rolling the sun disc, assisted by various gods, including Heka—the personification of magic.

The sun at its noon zenith is Re, mighty source of life-giving power, the true ruler of the universe. This name is often connected with the word *iar* ('to ascend, to be on the rise'). In his voyage across the heavenly ocean, Re is accompanied on his day barque by other gods; among them were Isis, Seth, Horus, Hu, and Sia. After his death, the king joins this entourage. During the passage, Re, along with his companions, has to overcome his deadly enemy, the embodiment of cosmic evil—the primordial serpent Apophis and his accomplices. Thus, each day Re secures the rule of order, truth, and justice over the forces of chaos and evil. In one of his forms, that is, as a shining sun disc known as Aten, the sun god became the starting point for a separate theological conception and subsequently a religious reformation attempted by the Eighteenth Dynasty king Amenhotep IV, Akhenaten (for more detail see chapter 6).

The setting sun, Atum, represents the fulfillment of the god's work. The weary sun god is ending his journey in this world and dying, and the moment arrives, critical for the whole world, when he crosses into the nocturnal ocean, the underworld. At this point he exchanges his day barque for his night barque, pulled by the 'western *ba* spirits' in the form of jackals. The protective serpent Mehen bends around him in

The god Re in the form of a tomcat kills the primal serpent Apophis, his arch enemy and the embodiment of evil. Illustration on a papyrus containing the text of the *Book of the Dead* of the royal scribe Hunefer, Nineteenth Dynasty.

the shape of a cabin or receptacle casket, and here, too, he is accompanied by other gods, headed by Seth the god of war, ready to throw a spear at the serpent Apophis, who rears up on a sandbank seeking to prevent the sun god from continuing his journey. Ritual and liturgy were needed to help overcome this and other perilous moments on the way through the underworld. At midnight a great mystery would occur, for then the sun god would unite with the ruler of the underworld Osiris, giving rise to a 'joined *ba* spirit.' As the introductory passage (after Jan Assmann) from one of the ancient Egyptian religious texts puts it:

Mystery of the underworld,
initiation into the mystery of the kingdom of the dead,
to see the sun setting
in life, in the West,
when it is invoked by the gods
and the Sayings in the underworld.

In this stage of his existence in the underworld the sun is often depicted as a male figure with the head of a ram (in Egyptian *ba* means not just 'soul,' but also 'ram'). It is then in this form that he concludes the night voyage in order to be reborn as Khepre at daybreak—and as the ancient Egyptians would add, "eternally and forever."

The sun god in the middle of his night journey on his barque through the underworld is represented here with the head of a ram. The serpent Mehen, wound around the case, protects the god. Wall painting from the tomb of Sethi I in the Valley of Kings, Nineteenth Dynasty.

Thus the sun god eternally rules the world and keeps it alive with his health-giving light and warmth. He sustains not only this world, but also the next, which can be reached by anyone who passes final judgment and becomes 'justified.' The world of eternal bliss, paradise, was known as the 'Field of Rushes,' where, in the favor of the sun god, the dead enjoyed every kind of abundance. A series of scenes on of the walls of the tomb of Sennedjem in Deir al-Medina is considered an eloquent illustration of this idea of paradise. On the upper part of the wall, above the whole subsequent series of scenes, the sun god is depicted in his barque as Re-Harakhty, 'Re-Hor in the horizon,' being greeted along the sides of the barque by baboons with paws raised in a gesture of adoration (the ancient Egyptians believed that the similar gestures and cries of baboons at sunset were expressions of worship of the god). Below, in several registers, there are scenes representing the deceased. In the first panel Re-Harakhty, accompanied by his wife, is coming before the tribunal of the gods for final judgment. In the next registers he is shown undergoing the ritual of the 'opening of the mouth,' which

In the next world the deceased plows the fields in the same way as in this world, but in paradise they always yield an abundant harvest. Detail from the decoration of the tomb of Sennedjem in Deir al-Medina, Nineteenth Dynasty.

resurrects him into full life in the other world, and finally enjoying its pleasures. We see him and his wife in fields surrounded by an irrigation canal and trees full of fruit, delighting in various labors in the fields that culminate in an abundant harvest. This paradise, as dreamed of and immortalized in his tomb by Sennedjem, could not have existed without the life-giving sun god.

The scenes from the tomb in Deir al-Medina, like scenes from many other tombs and temples all over Egypt and far beyond its southern border in Nubia, show what an important role the sun god played in the life of Egyptians throughout their history. Worshiping him was a part of that role. The view usually presented in the scholarly literature is that the beginnings of the solar cult in Egypt date from the reign of the first king of the Third Dynasty, Djoser. This view is based partly on the first appearance of the name of the god Re in the personal name of a high official of the time—Hesire, which means 'Praised by Re'—partly on some details from the adornment of stelae in the underground part of the Step Pyramid, and on the very form of the Step Pyramid, a tomb considered to be the material representation of the primordial mound—the symbolic place of the creation of the world and the birth of life. In fact, however, we find architectural expressions of the primordial mound much earlier than this period, in the oldest royal tombs from the Early Dynastic Period in Abydos. New research has been unearthing even earlier archaeological and written evidence relating to the solar cult. Its origins appear to go back very deep into the past, as is perhaps indirectly suggested by some remarkable neolithic structures—a cult site with an astronomical observatory or calendarium—discovered in the Egyptian Western Desert. In short, the iconographic details from the stelae in the underground part of the Step Pyramid can no longer be considered the oldest records of the sun cult.

The German Egyptologist Jochem Kahl recently carried out a detailed re-examination of the oldest written records from the Early Dynastic Period and came to several momentous conclusions that have revised the previous view of the first two dynasties and the origins of the solar cult. This period evidently saw an important shift in religious ideas, specifically on the relationship between kingship and religion, and this was reflected, inter alia, by royal names. In the First Dynasty these names expressed a king's physical strength and power as ruler, but in the Second Dynasty names that reflect a king's relationship to the gods start to appear. The second king of the Second Dynasty, whose throne name was Weneg, chose as his Horus name—by which he identified himself with the ruler of the sky, the falcon god Horus—the name Reneb. Egyptologists are not in agreement on its interpretation, for the name might be understood either as Neb-re ('Lord of the sun') or as Re-neb ('Re is (my) lord'). Kahl regards the second interpretation as the correct one in the context of the abovementioned changes taking place during the Second Dynasty.

Acceptance of the interpretation of the name as 'Re is (my) lord' has even more momentous implications than just a shifting back of the first appearance of the name of the god Re to the beginning of the Second Dynasty. If up to that time the king had been considered the absolute authority, the personification of the sky ruler Horus on earth, then the name Reneb now conveys his subordination to Re, with the king becoming a mere deputy and servant of the god on earth. Reneb's successor chose just one name for both his throne name and Horus name, that is, Ninetjer ('He who belongs to the god'). According to Kahl, it is roughly from the same time that we find the first records mentioning *maat*, the divine principle of truth, law, and justice and the order given to the Egyptians by the gods as the foundation of their state. It is no accident that the goddess Maat, the personification of this principle, is the daughter of Re. The king emerges as the guarantee that this divine principle will be upheld on earth.

The solar cult reached its height in the Fourth Dynasty and at the beginning of the Fifth Dynasty, which Egyptologists sometimes

>> Sethi I receiving the *was* scepter, symbol of power, from the god Amun-Re, Lord of the Thrones of the Two Lands. Behind Amun-Re is his divine partner Mut. Detail from decoration of the temple of Amun in Karnak, Nineteenth Dynasty.

inaccurately call the Sun Dynasty or Dynasty of the Sun Kings. One reason for the adoption of the term has been the story of the miraculous birth of the first kings of the Fifth Dynasty—such as Userkaf, Sahure, and Neferirkare—as triplets from the union of the god Re with the wife of the priest of the solar cult in the town of Sakhebu. This story was preserved in the Westcar Papyrus,* which dates from the much later Hyksos Period. It is a famous literary but not historical work, showing retrospective confusion between the solar cult and interesting events at the beginning of the Fifth Dynasty, when very probably twins were born to King Sahure, as indicated by inscriptions found at the beginning of the twenty-first century in Sahure's pyramid complex in Abusir. In the middle of the Fifth Dynasty the solar cult was at its zenith; from the reign of King Niuserre (or according to some scholars, even earlier) the cult of the god Osiris, ruler of the kingdom of the dead, had been gaining ground and the cult of Re was soon to recede somewhat into the background. During the Middle Kingdom, the cult of the originally local Theban god, Amun, came to the fore. The solar cult, however, continued to develop, as is shown by the obelisk of Senwosret I in Heliopolis, which (as we have already noted) is a relic of a probably very atypical temple built in honor of the sun god.

There was another major flowering of the solar cult at the beginning of the New Kingdom. Alongside Ptah and Amun, Re became one of the three most important gods of Egypt. During the relatively brief episode of Akhenaten's religious reform the sun god, in the form of the sun disc Aten, was once again the most important god. In the meantime, Re also acquired new aspects by fusion with other gods, such as Harakhty and especially Amun. However, the syncretic form of the sun god Amun-Re no longer fully corresponded to the original idea of the Heliopolitan Re because Amun-Re was an absolute deity conceived as a universal moral principle, as not just the ruler of men and gods but also their judge. Apart from the solar shrines of the 'Re's shadow' type, the most prominent symbol of the sun cult—the obelisk—became one of the fundamental elements of the temples that the kings of the New Kingdom built to honor various gods, not only Re, throughout the country. Pairs of obelisks adorned pylons, monumental gates, and temple complexes. Unfortunately, the kings at this period often usurped the obelisks of their predecessors. One example might be Ramesses II and his new royal seat of City of Ramesses (Per Ramesse, which became Piramesse). Some obelisks are enormous and are technical achievements that still astonish us today, both from the point

* The papyrus is named after Henry Westcar (1798–1868), the English collector of Egyptian antiquities.

of view of how they were carved from the quarries and of how they were transported and raised at their intended sites. In fact, in these projects the ancient Egyptian master builders came up against the limits of their knowledge and resources, as is shown by the biggest Egyptian obelisk known—Hatshepsut's—which lies to this day in the red-granite quarries near Aswan. It cracked before it was completed, and was left where it was.

While the solar cult experienced a new era of flowering in the New Kingdom, it would be rather misleading to claim that at the religious level this was a matter of a smooth continuity with ideas that had been associated with the sun god during the Old Kingdom. On the contrary, the concept of the solar god changed so strikingly during the New Kingdom that the German Egyptologist Jan Assmann, a recognized expert on ancient Egyptian religion, even speaks of a new solar theology. The sun god was no longer that which animated and permeated everything, but a distant god journeying through the heavens in complete solitude. According to Assmann, what happened was a demythologization of the anthropomorphic concept of the sun cycle in favor of a theological explanation of cosmic phenomena, so that light, in which the sun god is ever present, was understood as life-giving energy. Akhenaten's religious reform was then just a radical variant of this new solar religion.

Passage from the Morning Prayer to Re:

Heaven exults, earth rejoices,
The gods and goddesses celebrate a feast
And give praise to Re-Harakhty,
When they see him appearing in his barque.
He has defeated the rebel in his frenzied assault.
The cabin is in order, around (it) the twisting serpent is in its place,
The uraeus has repelled the rebel.
O, pass through your mother Nut,
My lord Re,
She is reciting to you the illuminations that are in her body.
Eset and Nebthet will lift you up
As you come forth from the thighs
Of your mother Nut.
O, come forth now, Re-Harakhty!
You are coming forth, you have come out and you shine,
You are vindicated in regard to your enemies.

You are giving free passage to the mandjet *barque,*
You drive away your enemies in their frenzied assault,
In an instant it is halted.
You have crushed many enemies . . .
(translated by J. Assmann, *Liturgische Lieder*)

The Great Sphinx, guardian of the cemetery at Giza.

3

Memphis: The White Wall

<< The idyllic countryside with small fields and palms close to Mit Rahina.

Memphis, that famous metropolis of ancient Egypt, is a city of huge temples, obelisks, and colonnades, of avenues of sphinxes, palaces, and administrative buildings. It is also the city in which the luxurious residences of Egyptian magnates and foreign envoys at the court of the pharaohs were built, and a city in which the coronations of the Egyptian kings were once held. At the height of its glory it was home to around a hundred thousand people. Where has it gone, the "city of the pharaohs with seventy gates and walls of iron and copper," as Arab historian Ibn al-Fakih described it? Could it possibly have vanished without trace?

This question was posed at the beginning of the nineteenth century by the first archaeologists to look for the lost city. From the sources available to them they knew that it must be close to Cairo and near the pyramids in Saqqara, but they found it hard to believe that, in the words of Georges Daressy (1864–1938), "the pieces of stone suggesting a large building west of the marshy depression around a hundred meters from the village of Mit Rahina" could be all that remained of a city from which the destiny not only of Egypt but of a large part of the ancient world had been governed for so long. As archaeological excavations got under way, however, they were soon able to answer the question and discover more about the turbulent history of the city. First and foremost, the excavations confirmed that this was indeed the site of Memphis, but they also showed that in the Ptolemaic Period many of its monuments had been moved to the then royal seat of Alexandria, while over the centuries, and up to quite recently, others had been broken up, taken apart, and used for buildings in the surrounding villages and towns, especially in Byzantine and Islamic Old Cairo. What remained had disappeared under layers of Nile mud meters deep.

Meni, the legendary founder of the First Dynasty of Egyptian kings at the turn of the fourth–third millennium BC, could scarcely have found a more convenient place to establish the capital of the newly unified Egypt than the site by what is today the village of Mit Rahina, about thirty kilometers south of Cairo. It was on the boundary between the two geographically distinct parts of the country, that is, the marshy plain of the Nile Delta to the north and the long Nile Valley, enclosed by rocky slopes on both sides and running far to the south. Lower and Upper Egypt also differed markedly in their historical development: the north was culturally more closely connected to the Syro-Palestinian region, while the south, the source of the main impulses for

Palm groves and small fields crisscrossed with irrigation canals give no hint that once the great and famous city of Memphis stood here.

the gradual unification of Egypt, had more affinity with Nubia and the adjoining desert areas. The new capital was intended not just to facilitate government of the whole country but also to reduce the tension between the north and south and balance their different interests. It was no accident that it was later called the Scales of Egypt.

At its foundation the city was given the name of Ineb hejd or 'White Wall' (sometimes also called Inebu hedj, 'White Walls'). This was because initially it was less a town than a fortress surrounded by a massive wall built either of limestone or of plastered and whitened mud bricks. The fortress was probably encircled by a water channel connected with the Nile, which at that time ran approximately three kilometers farther west than it does today. The ancient Greek authors Herodotus and Diodorus mention a massive dam that Meni had built a hundred stadia (a stadion is roughly 180 meters) south of the capital to protect it from the Nile floods. The existence of this dam—and as time went by there must certainly have been more than one—is indirectly confirmed by a much later inscription from the Late Period describing the threat to the city when a dam broke in the southern part of Memphis.

The Nile flood was an unpredictable element: if low it presaged a poor harvest and hunger, but if too high and fierce it brought destruction.

Despite archaeological excavations and surveys of Memphis, which have been going on now for almost two centuries, archaeological evidence of the White Wall has still to be discovered. British archaeologists concluded on the basis of a series of drilling probes that the fortress

probably lay in the northern part of Mit Rahina and that the city had gradually expanded from there to the south and partly to the east. This theory is given further support by the site of the oldest tombs of the elite, which were found not far from here on a rocky promontory on the edge of the desert in north Saqqara, directly opposite the presumed position of the White Wall. When the new capital city was founded, so too was its cemetery, and there was in fact more than one: in addition to the Saqqara cemetery, intended for those of highest social rank, another was established for members of the middle and lower classes on the opposite, east bank of the Nile near present-day Helwan. The First Dynasty kings, however, continued to be buried in the south, in the cemetery of their forefathers of Dynasty Zero at Umm al-Ga'ab by Abydos, close to the town of Tjeny (called Thinis or This in Greek)—likewise not yet reliably located archaeologically—which in the Early Dynastic Period still served as the capital of the country alongside the White Wall. It was only during the Second Dynasty, in the period when Egyptian unity was weakened by resurgent tension between the two historically distinct parts of the

A royal cemetery was established at the beginning of the First Dynasty at Saqqara on the northern edge of the desert plateau. At the beginning of the Third Dynasty, King Netjerikhet had his stepped tomb—the oldest Egyptian pyramid—built a few hundred meters south of this cemetery.

country, that some kings had themselves buried in Saqqara, although others continued to build their tombs in Umm al-Ga'ab.

If we stand today on the raised desert plateau of the Saqqara cemetery and look east into the Nile Valley, there seems to be absolutely nothing to suggest that this was the site of a great ancient city. The whole valley is covered in green palm copses and tidy strips of fields interwoven by water channels. Only the eye of an archaeologist familiar with the basic topographical features of ancient Memphis can find any traces of this city. The palm copses around Mit Rahina afford the not particularly attractive view of partially uncovered buildings here and there, half-destroyed monuments drowning in piles of rubbish, the humble dwellings of the local population, and above all the tourist industry—wave upon wave of visitors in air-conditioned buses rolling up to the souvenir stalls surrounding the museum with the colossal statue of Ramesses II, which is today the main attraction of the once famous city. In the eighteenth century the site of ancient Memphis must have appeared far more idyllic to the members of the scientific and artistic committee accompanying Napoleon's expedition to Egypt!

William Matthew Flinders Petrie, founder of modern Egyptian archaeology.

We still have not established the boundaries and extent of ancient Memphis and do not even know the location of most of its main buildings as recorded in written sources, for example the hall in which the Egyptian kings were crowned. Nonetheless, the glory and wealth of the city is attested not just by ancient authors, but also by already unearthed temples, housing complexes and workshops, and the statues, stelae, and reliefs that we can find in museums and collections throughout the world. The great British archaeologist Petrie, who worked for several years in Memphis, estimated its extent at thirteen kilometers long and six and a half kilometers wide. The member of Napoleon's expedition, the engineer and geographer Edmé François Jomard (1777–1862), who undertook a land survey here in 1799, was more cautious, estimating it at "only" about fifty square kilometers. According to Diodorus of Sicily, who lived at the time of Christ, the perimeter of Memphis, including its necropolis, measured a hundred and fifty stadia. The *Itinerarium Antonini*, an important geographical work of antiquity, claims that the fortress of Babylon, located in what is today Old Cairo, was at the time—the third century AD—halfway along the road between Memphis and Heliopolis (it then measured thirty-three stadia).

Medieval Arab authors such as Abd al-Latif al-Baghdadi and others mostly just repeated the Late Roman data. According to the British archaeologist David Jeffreys, who carried out excavations of Memphis, the northern edge of the city was by present-day Tammuh, about nine kilometers north of Mit Rahina, while its southern edge was by Barshant, around eighteen kilometers south of Mit Rahina.

Yet who knows? Perhaps the Memphis agglomeration was even larger if we take into account the fact that the city developed over centuries, even millennia, in peculiar symbiosis with its cemeteries and the funerary cults on the edge of the desert. While its oldest part lay close to the present-day village of Saqqara, the cemeteries stretched from Abu Rawash to the north through Giza, Zawiyat al-Aryan, Abu Ghurab, Abusir, Saqqara, and Dahshur as far as Meidum, an overall distance of around eighty kilometers. The so-called pyramid towns (the residential quarters of the priests and employees of the pyramid complexes), which were concentrated around the valley temples, were parts of this agglomeration; as were the royal palaces, which perhaps lay close to the pyramid complexes and so far are known only from written sources. The center of this river metropolis, closed in between the edge of the desert and the Nile, shifted over time and not only moved from north to south with the expanding desert necropolis, but

In good weather, the top of the hillock with the ruins of the palace of Apries offers a view of most of the Memphite necropolis on the western horizon, from the pyramids in Abusir all the way to the pyramids in Dahshur.

also expanded to the east with the changing course of the Nile. On the western edge of the early city lay a lake, known in the Ptolemaic Period as Pharaoh's Lake, but this may in fact have been two lakes separated by a sandbank: one lake in the vicinity of the valley Temple of Unas and the other by the present-day village of Abusir. Running through this area there was also a large canal, later called Bahr al-Libeini ('The Libyan River'), which served as a waterway for the builders of the pyramids. If at the beginning of the third millennium BC, during the First Dynasty, the center of the White Wall probably lay in the northern part of the city roughly opposite the present-day village of Abusir, by the end of the third millennium it was found a few kilometers farther south, in Saqqara close to the Valley Temple of Pepi II, king of the Sixth Dynasty and the last great ruler of the Old Kingdom. The very name of Pepi II's pyramid complex, including its valley temple and entrance gate—Men nefer Pepi, 'Pepi's beauty lasts'—is an indirect indication of this. In shortened form it gave the city its name Mennofer—later to be Grecized as Memphis—at the beginning of the second millennium BC.

The present-day topography of Memphis as an archaeological site is characterized by a number of hillocks known as *kom* in Arabic and marshy depressions known as *birka*. *Kom*s are particularly important archaeologically because they hide the ruins of larger ancient monuments. In the northern part of the locality we find the Kom al-'Aziz, Kom al-Tuman, Kom al-Kalb, Kom Defbabi, and Kom al-Nawa. The northern *birka* divides the northern part of the locality from the central section, where the hillocks Kom al-Fakhri, Kom al-Khanazir, Kom al-Arba'in, Kom al Rabi'a, and Kom al-Qal'a surround a central *birka*. The southern *birka* divides off a southern group formed by two hillocks known as Kom al-Helul and Kom al-Sabakha. Only a small part of the central sector of Memphis is attractive to tourists and open to the public; the other parts of the locality are of interest only to archaeologists, although their activities remain rather fragmented and unsystematic because of the sheer size of the area.

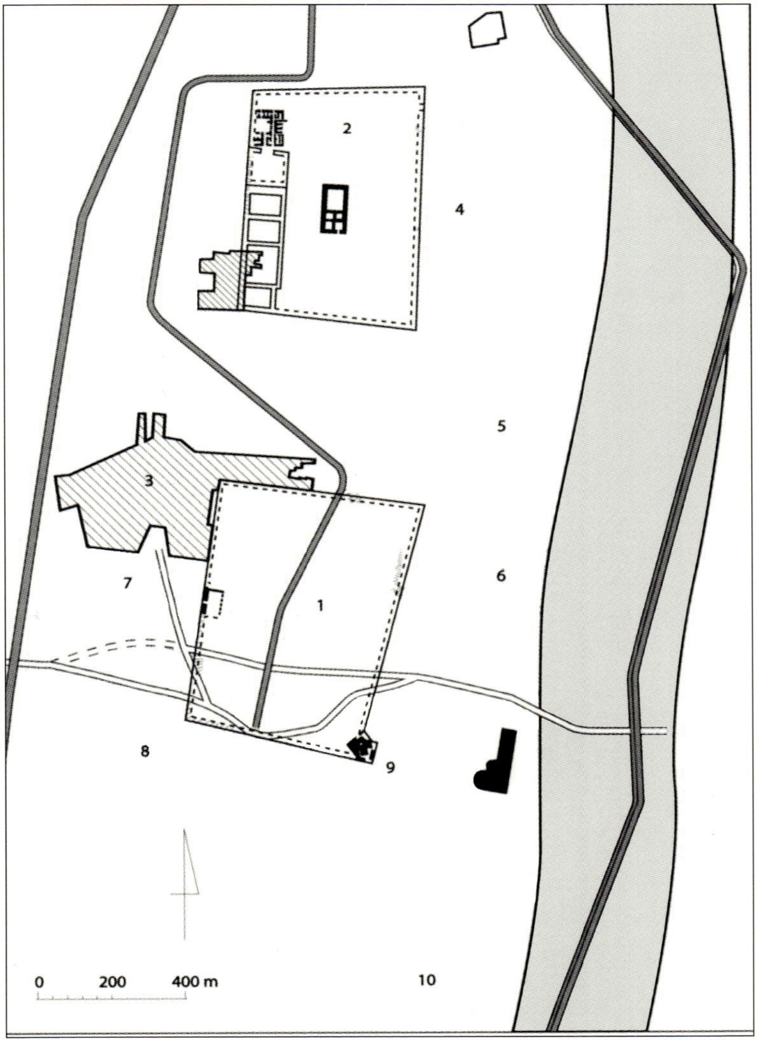

Plan of Memphis showing the main archaeological localities and presumed course of the Nile in the third millennium BC.

1. district of the temple of Ptah
2. Kom al-Tuman and the northern district with the temple of Apries
3. village of Mit Rahina
4. Kom Defbabi
5. Kom al-Nawa
6. Kom al-Arba'in
7. Kom al-Fakhri
8. Kom al-Rabi'a
9. Kom al-Kal'a
10. Kom al-Helul

As has already been noted, modern archaeological research on Memphis began at the turn of the nineteenth century with the surveys carried out by experts from Napoleon's expedition. To them we owe the first more precise plans and maps of Memphis and the surrounding area, as well as pictures of charming village scenes with the ruins of monuments. These pictures evoke an almost idyllic image of the first Egyptological explorations that did not quite correspond to reality, which was far from an idyll, as the fate of the colossal statue of Ramesses II illustrates. It was discovered at the beginning of the nineteenth century and the

Map of Memphis and its surroundings made by French scholars during Napoleon's military expedition to Egypt.

Egyptian khedive later donated it to Great Britain, but because of its size the statue remained in Memphis. The colossus, which was stuck in the mud (the exposed part was significantly damaged by wind erosion), was unearthed in 1820 by two amateur archaeologists—more precisely, they were the kind of adventurers who were common during the early years of Egyptian archaeological explorations. These adventurers—British consular official Charles Sloane (fl. 1820–38) and Giovanni Battista Caviglia (1770–1845), a sea captain from Genoa who collaborated with the British diplomat and collector of Egyptian

Napoleon's scholars unearthing the fist of a colossal statue in the ruins of Memphis.

Detail of a limestone colossus of Ramesses II displayed in the local museum in Mit Rahina.

antiquities, Henry Salt (1780–1827)—took part in excavations of the pyramids and Great Sphinx in Giza. The colossus of Ramesses II, with the figure of the king's daughter standing by his left leg, originally adorned the south gate of the Temple of Ptah and is today the main exhibit at the small local museum in Mit Rahina. Like the Great Sphinx at Giza, the limestone statue, which shortly after its discovery the local people started to call 'the Father of Terror,' is no longer the radiant white that it was in the time of the pharaohs or even at the time when Sloane and Caviglia excavated it. Indeed, today it is ash gray and showing the effects of erosion.

Memphis and its monuments could hardly have escaped the attention of the German archaeological expedition led by Karl Richard Lepsius (1810–84). At the beginning of the 1840s the expedition's engineer and surveyor Otto Erbkam made an archaeological map of Memphis that has lost nothing of its value since then. Shortly afterward another engineer and geodesist, Joseph Hekekyan (1807–75), an Armenian from Constantinople in the service of Khedive Abbas and who also worked for the Geological Society of London, undertook surveying and excavations as part of planning for the construction of canals, roads, and bridges. During this work in 1852 he uncovered the foundation platform on which the colossus stood, and managed to find large pieces of other colossal statues that in most cases lay along the main axes of the Temple of Ptah. In the second half of the nineteenth century and at the beginning of the twentieth century, excavations were carried out in Memphis by a whole series of archaeologists including François Auguste Ferdinand Mariette (1821–81)—the founder of Egyptian archaeology—Gaston Camille Charles Maspero (1846–1916), Daressy, and especially Petrie. With characteristic thoroughness Petrie made a survey of Memphis in 1886 and at Kom al-Qal'a discovered the palace of Merenptah and above all a temple covering around a thousand square meters in which one pillar was still standing. At Kom al-Helul he discovered potters' kilns and at Kom al-Mizanat a quantity of different kinds of stone and metal weights. He was the first to make precise measurements of the western gate of the Temple of Ptah close to Kom al-Fakhri and—as we shall see—did not neglect other parts of Memphis.

The next major phase of excavation of Memphis came with archaeological excavations undertaken in the 1940s and 1950s, in which the Egyptian archaeologists Ahmad Badawi and Mustafa Amir played a significant role. Their work near Kom al-Fakhri included the excavation and study of an important cemetery from the Third Intermediate Period, the discovery of a small Temple of Ptah built by Ramesses II, and buildings connected with the cult of the sacred bull Apis.* In some cases archaeological discoveries in Memphis have been made as a result of major modern construction projects, such as the building of a highway from Saqqara via Mit Rahina to Bedrashen, during which a large cemetery from the First Intermediate Period and the early Middle Kingdom was found near Kom al-Fakhri. It was not only civil engineering projects that led to such finds: the digging of anti-aircraft shelters in 1954 led to the discovery of a beautiful temple to the goddess Hathor at Kom al-Rabi'a. Another important milestone in archaeological excavation of Memphis was the launch in 1982 (on the occasion of the centenary of the founding of the British Egypt Exploration Society) of a project for the identification, documentation, and archaeological study of the monuments of Memphis, which was led by Harry Smith and David Jeffreys. Their work in particular has filled in our picture of ancient Memphis with more precise contours. Let us return, at least in very general terms, to the archaeological topography and to what we know today about Memphis and its monuments.

Kom al-'Aziz on the northern edge of Memphis is still awaiting thorough archaeological research. We have substantially more information from the area of Kom al-Tuman and Kom al-Kalb, thanks to Petrie's excavations. Here he managed to discover a complex of buildings and

* Since 1982, the American Apis House Project, directed by Michael Jones and Angela M. Jones, has continued work on this discovery. The project was conceived by John Dimick, who worked at the site in the years 1954–56.

View of Kom al-Tuman and the ruins of the palace of Apries.

huge enclosure wall (410 × 450 meters, only a little smaller than the precinct of Ptah) made of mud bricks. The term 'Northern Enclosure' (Petrie also used the word 'Camp') has been adopted for this find. Here Petrie found limestone blocks from a pylon erected by the Twelfth Dynasty king Senwosret I with superb relief decorations, including for example a depiction of the sacred palm grove with the tombs of the ancient rulers in the Lower Egyptian town of Buto. Petrie gave the name Palace of Apries to the dominant building of the Northern Enclosure (Apries is the Greek interpretation of the name of the Egyptian ruler Haibre). It dates from the Twenty-sixth Dynasty and today all that is left of it is a mound of brick debris, on top of it a few scattered pieces of the capitals of palmiform limestone columns damaged by innumerable graffiti left by modern visitors. Originally this was a fortified palace with three gates: one facing northward and two facing southward. The palace stood on a fourteen-meter-high raised platform constructed in the caisson method and accessible by a broad ramp. The top of the platform mound, which looms high above the crowns of the surrounding palm groves, is the highest point in the area and on a clear day provides a unique view not only of the northern part of Memphis but above all west over the pyramid fields from Giza to Dahshur.

The central part of Memphis, between Kom al-Fakhri on the west and Kom al-Nawa and Kom al-Arba'in in the east, is occupied by another huge enclosure known as the Enclosure of Ptah, but we have only an approximate idea of the boundaries of the precinct of the Great

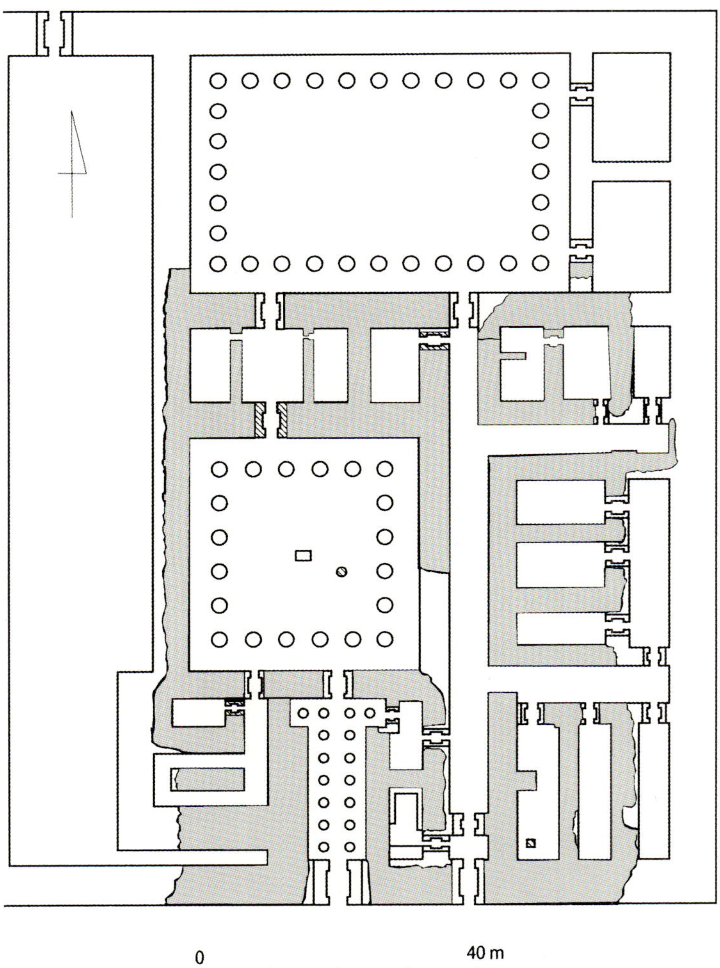

Plan of reconstruction of the palace of Apries; the surviving masonry is shown in solid gray.

Temple of Ptah, since the main section of the temple, including the oldest section, has not yet been located. The sections of this huge, east–west oriented temple complex that have so far been uncovered (and mostly only superficially excavated and investigated) were built during the reign of Ramesses II and later. There are substantive grounds for supposing that the historical center of the temple, which according to tradition was also founded by the legendary King Meni, lie a little farther to the west, in the bowels of Kom al-Fakhri. This theory has been backed by a number of archaeological finds, such as the shards of pottery dating from the Old Kingdom that were discovered at Kom al-Fakhri, not subsequently touched or impaired, or the ramp oriented from the west to the gate in the western wing of the enclosure wall of this part of the temple, which was built under Ramesses II. It is also supported by the fact that the western and eastern wings of this enclosure are not parallel to each other. British archaeologists therefore believe that the line of the western wall almost certainly respected an as yet undiscovered eastern wing of the enclosure wall of the old temple lying under Kom al-Fakhri and ran parallel to that older stretch of wall. In their view the buildings of Ramesses II were a mere extension bridging an evidently considerable gap that existed at the time between the original temple and center of Memphis on one side and on the other side,

<< Cemetery from the First Intermediate Period in the western part of Memphis. In the background beyond the palms is the hill Kom al-Fakhri, with the tomb of the sheikh on the top.

The ruins of the hypostyle hall of Ramesses III in the western part of the temple complex of Ptah are today submerged under groundwater.

to the east, the shifting riverbed of the Nile. Immediate access to the Nile always played a crucial role in the life of the city, and was even more important in the period of the New Kingdom because Memphis had become a major military port and hinterland for campaigns into western Asia.

Future archaeological excavation of the Kom al-Fakhri hill is going to be very difficult, primarily for administrative reasons, since a small village and sheikh's tomb are situated on the top. The research will also be complicated from a technical point of view by the high level of groundwater, which is obvious from the flooded condition of the adjacent parts of buildings from the reign of Ramesses II that have been excavated. But without excavation of Kom al-Fakhri, we will have little chance of throwing light on the earliest history of the Temple of Ptah or indeed Memphis as a whole. The key to the precise localization of the White Wall probably lies here, for the god Ptah, as worshiped in this enormous temple complex, had the attribute 'Ptah South of His Wall.' The general academic consensus is that here 'wall' means the White Wall, and so the attribute is considered to be evidence that the Temple of Ptah was situated south of the fortress. The view is clearly confirmed by the text on a clay sealing discovered by the Czech archaeological team in the pyramid complex of Raneferef in Abusir, where we find the explicit formula 'Ptah South of the White Wall.' It is thus more than likely that the White Wall lay to the north of the oldest Temple of Ptah, which may well have been constructed at the same time. Similarly, on the basis of a recorded epithet of the goddess Neith as 'Neith North of the Wall,' it is deduced that her

Midway between Kom al-Tuman and Kom al-Fakhri.

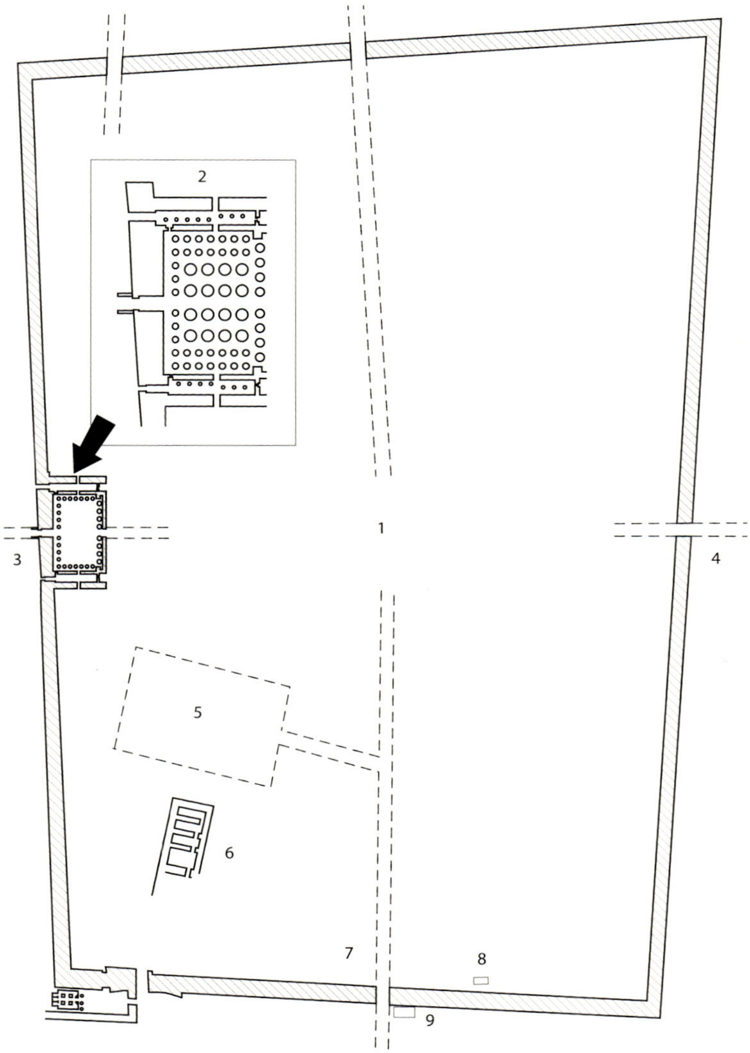

This plan of the temple precinct of Ptah shows just how much of this important monument has not yet been excavated.
1. central part of the temple of Ptah, with what are believed to have been pylons, courts, and columned halls
2. hypostyle hall of Ramesses II
3. western gate of the district of the temple of Ptah
4. eastern gate of the district of the temple of Ptah
5. presumed site of the temple of Apis
6. mummification tables of the Apis bulls
7. southern gate of the district of the temple of Ptah
8. local museum with colossus of Ramesses II
9. sphinx

Memphis temple, which is so far known only from written sources, was situated north of the White Wall.

The immense archaeological importance of the Kom al-Fakhri hill and the great age of the monuments that it probably hides is further suggested by rare objects found close to the western gate in the enclosure wall: an alabaster seated statue of the Fourth Dynasty king Khafre; a diorite seated statue of his successor Menkaure; a granite seated

This limestone stela with representations of ears, hands raised in a gesture of adoration, and the name of Ptah in the middle, which was found in Memphis by W.M.F. Petrie, vividly expresses the supplicant's wish that the god should hear his prayers. New Kingdom.

statue of the Fifth Dynasty king Niuserre; and an alabaster seated statue of his successor Menkauhor. A fragment of an alabaster base probably of a seated statue from the Second or Third Dynasty has also been found here. As was the custom in ancient Egypt, kings gave statues to the temples in order to emphasize their personal relationship to the gods and to combine the cults of these gods with their own.

Last but not least, we can hardly ignore the fact that apart from anything else we know now or may discover about it in the future, the Great Temple of Ptah in Memphis has left one indelible trace in history: the garbled and Grecized form of its name Hwt-ka-Ptah, 'Shrine of Ptah's *ka*,' later rendered as *hikupta,* in its Greek form of 'Aigyptos' gave the whole country its name: Egypt.

The huge enclosure wall of the Temple of Ptah (only a small part of which has been investigated so far) was trapezoid in plan: the southern wall is approximately four hundred meters long and the eastern wall roughly six hundred meters long. The monumental western gate from the reign of Ramesses II gave access to a large columned antechamber, its ceiling supported in the central section by sixteen large columns and on the sides a total of thirty-four smaller columns. East of the antechamber was an open columned court. Excavation of this part of the complex has yielded a great many fragments of architecture and inscriptions, as well as statues of important people, and votive stelae with supplications to Ptah, Sakhmet, and other gods venerated in Memphis. One curious group of these stelae consists of what are known as stelae with ears, graphically emphasizing the supplicants' desire that the god listen to their prayers. A great many monuments were also found in the area of the gate in the south wing of the enclosure wall. Apart from the already mentioned limestone colossus of Ramesses II, these include the left fist of another colossal statue, this time in red granite; today it is part of the collections of the British Museum in London. Also discovered in the vicinity of the gate were statues and fragments of statues of kings Ramesses II, III, and IV, and important personages such as the son of Ramesses and high priest of Ptah, Prince Khamwaset. Some earlier statues were later usurped. For example, the Nineteenth Dynasty king Merenptah appropriated a granite statue of Amenemhet III from the Twelfth Dynasty—which is currently held in the collections of the Egyptian Museum in Berlin—as his own.

Roughly in the middle of the complex bounded by the enclosure wall, archaeologists found the remains of a chapel erected in honor of

The identity of the person represented in this alabaster stela in Mit Rahina is still the subject of academic debate.

Ptah by Amenhotep III, and in the southeast sector of the complex a colossal red-granite statue representing Ramesses II accompanied by his son Khamwaset and daughter Bentanta. The statue spent many years adorning the square by the main railway station in Cairo. Naturally it suffered from the environment of heavy traffic, and so, on 25 August 2006, amid great interest from the domestic and foreign media, it was moved to the store of monuments by the pyramids in Giza. After restoration it is to be exhibited in the future new Grand Egyptian Museum, which is under construction not far away. We know less about another colossal statue discovered in the southeast sector of the complex: an alabaster sphinx whose origin scholars have been debating for many years. According to some researchers, it dates from the Eighteenth Dynasty and belongs to Queen Hatshepsut, while according to others it comes from the Nineteenth Dynasty and belongs to Ramesses II. Also historically significant is a stela from the Late Period on which the Twenty-sixth Dynasty king Haibre enumerates the gifts that he donated to the Temple of Ptah in Memphis.

King Haibre was only one of a long line of pharaohs to give rich donations to the Temple of Ptah in Memphis. Along with the Temple of Amun in Thebes and the Temple of Re in Heliopolis, it was one of the three largest in the country. Its political importance and economic rise was closely related to the status of Memphis as capital city of Egypt. Like the other great temples of the main Egyptian gods, Ptah's temple enjoyed not only various regular privileges but obtained a substantial share of the booty from Egypt's wars of conquest, including captives, as part of royal donations. From a text on the Harris I Papyrus from the time of Ramesses III we learn that in its period of greatest power and wealth during the New Kingdom the Temple of Ptah in Memphis employed 3,079 people including priests, and owned 10,047 farm animals, five orchards, one market town, two boats, and 6,919 acres of land.

Among the monuments discovered in the southwest sector of the complex bounded by the huge enclosure wall, pride of place undoubtedly goes to the building associated with the cult of the sacred bull Apis (for more detail see pp. 124–35), who was regarded as the earthly embodiment of the *ba* of the god Ptah. Right at the beginning of the twentieth century, Petrie, in the course of his excavations in Memphis, had already undertaken probes and found a few alabaster blocks bearing the name of the Twenty-second Dynasty king Sheshonq I, but for many years thereafter Egyptians lost interest in the site, covered as it was by a palm grove. It was not until 1941 that two Egyptian

archaeologists, Ahmad Badawi and Mustafa Amir, managed—despite the economic difficulties of wartime—to obtain a small amount of funding and continue Petrie's unfinished research. The result was the surprise find of the remains of the building in which the sacred bulls after death had been embalmed on great tables carved from a single piece of alabaster and resembling a couch decorated on the sides by figures of lions in low relief. A series of other valuable finds here included an alabaster altar of the Twenty-sixth Dynasty king Nekau II, the diorite statuette of a bull, stelae with depictions of the sacred bull in his shrine, and also a very interesting large alabaster measuring vessel with a volume of seventy-two *henu,* that is, 32.4 liters, dedicated to the 'living bull' Apis by the Persian king Darius I. Possibly Darius wished by the donation to make up for the damage inflicted on the cult of Apis by his predecessor, since according to Herodotus (III, 29) the Persian king Cambyses had stabbed the bull with a dagger and ridiculed the priests, saying that god was not of flesh and blood and could not feel a wound, then accused them of making a fool of him, and had them whipped. The injured bull later died.

Alabaster tables on which dead Apises were mummified in the temple precinct of Ptah.

Detail of the capital of a column from the temple of Hathor at Kom al-Rabi'a in Memphis.

Despite their success, Amir and Badawi did not complete the excavations in the area known as the 'Embalming House of Apis Bulls,' which were later taken up and carried on by a (still ongoing) American archaeological venture known as the Apis House Project.

Inside the south wing of the Ptah enclosure, in the vicinity of Kom al-Rabi'a, many other very important monuments have been found including the chapel of Senwosret I from the Twelfth Dynasty, the tomb of the high priests of Ptah from the Twenty-second Dynasty, and especially the small Temple of Ptah built by Ramesses II and discovered in the 1950s by the American expedition led by Rudolf Anthes (1896–1985), which involved many experts from Egypt and other countries. The walls of the entrance pylon and shrine in the depths of the temple are adorned with inscriptions and scenes of the king bringing offerings to the god Ptah and other deities. The temple had the lofty name of 'Seat of Ramesses Meriamun, may he live, be healthy and prosperous, in the House of Ptah.' Ramesses II built another large temple, dedicated to the goddess Hathor, at Kom al-Rabi'a a little farther to the south. Its entrance likewise consisted of a massive pylon with religious scenes and inscriptions. The limestone columns in the open courtyard of the temple are adorned with superb Hathor capitals in the form of the charming female face of the goddess with cow ears.

In Memphis the goddess was worshiped as 'Hathor Lady of the Southern Sycomore.' What would any museum in the world give to have just one of those capitals in its exhibition! Unfortunately, the temple, which has been only partially excavated and investigated by the Egyptian archaeologist Mahmud al-Said, is in a very dismal state. Groundwater containing aggressive dissolved salts is destroying the structure of the stone and relief decoration. Nor does the rubbish blown here by the wind improve the appearance of the place.

On the hill of Kom al-Qal'a, lying east of Kom al-Rabi'a, Petrie discovered another large temple, which was built by the successor of Ramesses II, Merenptah, in honor of the god Ptah. Finds in the open court of this temple included the reused capitals of limestone lotus columns from the Fifth Dynasty. Where they originally stood is an open archaeological question.

Another building excavated at Kom al-Qal'a was a unique monument: the palace of Merenptah. A fire destroyed the palace after the king's death. For archaeologists it is inspiring as a guide to the possible appearance of earlier, as yet undiscovered royal palaces from the times of the pyramid builders. It was a huge, north–south oriented building on a rectangular ground plan with a massive enclosure wall. It was entered from the north through an exterior columned vestibule leading via an extensive open columned courtyard and so-called inner columned vestibule into the hypostyle—the throne hall. The entrance into the hall is decorated with scenes of the king at the feast of *sed*. Discovered in the hall was the base of a throne on which nine bows and foreigners are depicted, representing the external enemies of Egypt; when seated on his throne the king thus symbolically triumphed over them. The palace also contained the ruler's private rooms, including his bedroom. In and around the palace site at Kom al-Qal'a, a large quantity of antiquities have been found from various periods of Egyptian history: stone blocks from various buildings with remains of relief decoration and inscriptions, as well as statues, stelae, and cult and everyday articles. The finds here include a quartzite head (currently part of the collection of the Egyptian Museum in Cairo), considered to be the likeness of the famous queen Nefertiti. The presence of this piece in this particular location may have been no accident; Jaromír Málek, a British Egyptologist of Czech origin, believes that it was here, not far from the palace of Merenptah, that the Temple of Aten built by Akhenaten once stood.

Even this very sketchy account of the main monuments of Memphis shows not only how huge the city was, but also how patchily and inadequately it has been archaeologically excavated and how little we know about it. The written records alone describe many monuments that archaeologists have not yet managed to locate. For example, Herodotus mentions the beautiful Memphis temple of the goddess Isis, which was probably connected to the cult of the mother of Apis (also related to this cult are representations of Isis with the head of a cow). Archaeological investigation of the southern part of Memphis has progressed not at all since the time of Petrie. It is possible that one of the city's most important harbors was situated here, in the vicinity of Kom al-Sabakha in the place called in Egyptian Heri nefer. The main harbor of Memphis was known as Peru nefer and played an important role (mentioned above) in Egyptian military campaigns from the New Kingdom onward. Since the time of the founding of the city, the riverbed of the Nile has shifted eastward by about three kilometers, and this has ultimately presented archaeologists with a quite insuperable problem, for today the area is covered by the town of Bedrashen, home to more than a hundred thousand inhabitants. The list of unanswered questions is dismayingly long. Where is the oldest part of Memphis, the White Wall, and what did it look like? Where is the oldest Temple of Ptah? Where in the temple was the hall where the coronations of the Egyptian kings took place? Where is the Temple of Sethi I that was called 'Beneficial Sethi Beloved by Ptah in the House of Ptah,' and according to some opinions could have resembled the Great Hypostyle Hall in the Temple of Amun in Karnak? Where should we look for the temples built by Ramesses II to Re or Thoth? Or the Temple of Siamun called 'Amun Lord of Lapis Lazuli'? Where are the buildings of state administration from the Old Kingdom and later periods, the royal palaces, the residences of the viziers? Where were the city workshops, the quarters for foreigners—Asians, inhabitants of the Aegean Islands, or even (according to Petrie), Indians too—and ambassadors to the Egyptian court who built shrines here to their own gods? This list could continue for a long time.

Ptah: Idea, Word, World

Ptah is one of the most important Egyptian gods and his name appears in the personal names of magnates from earliest times. The fact is rather at odds with the absence of representations of Ptah in the royal pyramid complexes of the Old Kingdom. His cult, as evidenced by a depiction of the god on an alabaster vessel from the First Dynasty found by Petrie in Tarkhan, started to make great headway from the beginning of the Early Dynastic Period at the latest. It is assumed that the rapid rise in the importance of Ptah and his cult was partly to be attributed to his status as the local god of the new

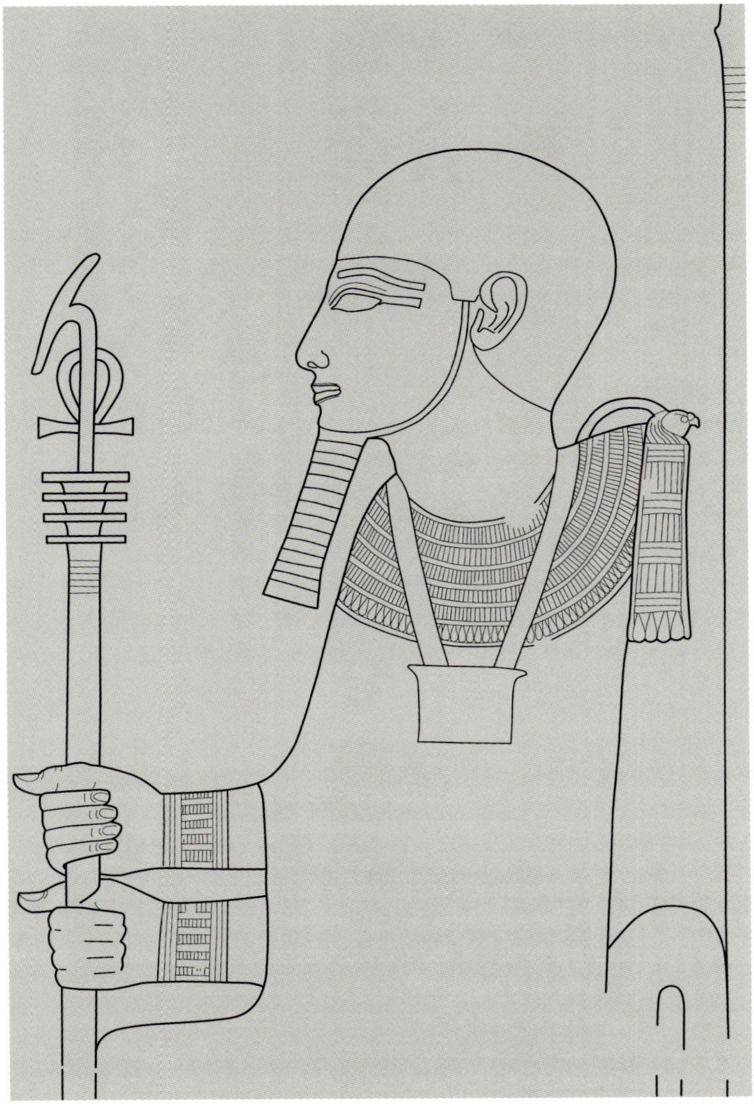

Characteristic representation of the god Ptah. In front of him the god holds the symbols *was* ('power'), *djed* ('duration'), and *ankh* ('life'); his chest is adorned by a broad necklace and pectoral with counterweight. Detail from the decoration of the temple of Sethi I in Abydos.

capital of Egypt. Here he was probably at first the patron primarily of the large concentrations of artists and artisans involved in the building projects in the capital and its newly founded necropolis. This is also suggested by the original title of the high priest of Ptah, which was 'chief controller of craftsmen.' In fact it might be more accurate in the context of the original conception of this title to use the word 'stonemasons' rather than 'craftsmen,' because the hieroglyphic sign for this term is a tool for drilling stone vessels. In any case, the origin of the god's name itself is frequently traced to ancient Semitic languages and associated with the verb 'cut' or 'drill.' In the Greek interpretation Ptah was identified with Hephaistos, the Greek god of metalworking.

Ptah was usually represented as a man, who was standing upright, veiled in a tight-fitting cloak (sometimes people speak of the figure as mummiform), and with two fists placed on his breast in which he holds the symbols *was* (power), *djed* (stability, durability), and *ankh* (life). Ptah wears a tight-fitting skullcap, leaving his ears uncovered. The cap and sometimes the whole figure is usually painted blue, leading the German Egyptologist Wolfgang Helck to theorize that the cult of Ptah enjoyed special favor among makers of colored faience. The god has the long ritual beard fixed by straps to the cap, and on his breast a pectoral (a large piece of jewelry) with counterweights on his back. He is very often shown standing in an open cabin or cabinet with arched roof.

According to the local tradition and religious doctrine elaborated by the Memphite priests, Ptah was considered the creator of the world. Some scholars have proposed that the elevation of Ptah to the status of creator was the expression of a certain intellectual tension and rivalry between priestly circles in Memphis and nearby Heliopolis, the center of the solar religion. According to the Memphite teaching Ptah created the world by thinking (in Egyptian *shai*, which

The barque of Sokar.

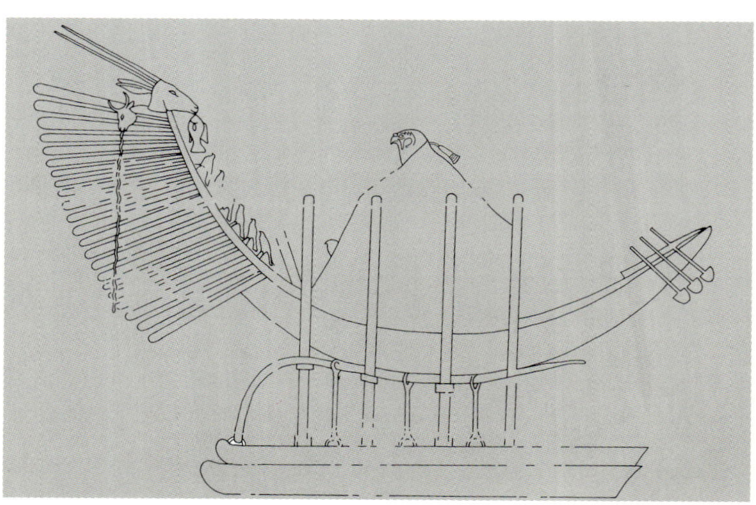

meant the expression of thought, which was itself believed by Egyptians to arise in the heart) expressed in words (speech, in Egyptian *hu*) mediated by the tongue. Also attributed to Ptah is the creation of the ritual of the 'opening of the mouth.' Epithets like 'Ptah Great of Strength' and 'Ptah Lord of Truth (order)' were often attached to his name. Ptah's creative abilities were augmented by the potency and physical prowess of the sacred bull Apis, the earthly embodiment of Ptah's *ba*.

Fully in the spirit of the Egyptian tendency toward syncretism, Ptah in Memphis was soon identified with another, possibly even older local god called Tatjenen—'Raised-up Earth.' Tatjenen was an earth god expressing the originally local concept of the mound that emerged from the mythic primordial waters at the beginning of the world and from which life was born. Tatjenen was worshiped as the god of the earth and ruler of its gifts: minerals, ores, and precious stones. In funerary ideas he was sometimes regarded as the ruler of the underworld and represented as a rearing snake spitting flame. Ptah-Tatjenen was likewise often depicted as a man with ram's horns and a sun disc on his head, and venerated as the primordial creator god.

By now it will scarcely surprise the reader that as early as the Old Kingdom Ptah merged with yet another god, Sokar, venerated in the Memphite necropolis in the form of a falcon. The latter is most frequently represented in a movable cabinet set on Sokar's specific barque *henu* with a high raised prow adorned with the head of an oryx antelope. According to some written records, from the earliest times Sokar had his own shrine in Memphis, and his festival in the third month of the season of inundation was the biggest in the Memphite necropolis. We know that the rituals of 'driving out the four calves' and 'digging the earth' were important elements of this feast, and so it is not impossible that Sokar was originally connected with a fertility cult rather than specifically with the Memphite necropolis. Later, during the New Kingdom, the hybrid funerary god Ptah-Sokar merged with Osiris, ruler of the kingdom of the dead. Ptah-Sokar-Osiris was represented in essentially the same way as Osiris. Statuettes of the god, standing on a base in which a cavity was sometimes carved out to enable a papyrus scroll with the text of the *Book of the Dead* to be inserted (while a small statuette of a seated falcon could be fixed to the base in front of the standing god), became common parts of funerary equipment, especially from the end of the New Kingdom.

>> Bronze seated statuette of the deified Imhotep from the Late Period. The sage's name is recorded both on the unrolled papyrus that Imhotep holds on his lap and on the pedestal of the statuette.

The lion goddess Sakhmet, the 'Mighty,' Ptah's partner, suckling King Niuserre. Detail from the decoration of the king's mortuary temple in Abusir.

Ptah came to be connected with two other gods from the New Kingdom onward—the goddess Sakhmet and the god Nefertem—with whom he formed the so-called Memphite Triad. This was an artificial theological construct, which was intended among other things to connect the chief local gods with an emphasis on the male and female principle augmented by the element of the child. Sakhmet, the 'Mighty,' was a lion goddess venerated especially in Thebes. Although in Memphis she appeared as Ptah's partner, Sakhmet was also considered the daughter of the sun god Re, as his glowing eye. Sakhmet was a goddess of two faces: a terrifying lioness that could wreak frenzied killing and destruction, but equally a warm maternal goddess, a powerful sorceress and protectress from evil and illness (incidentally the title 'Priest of Sakhmet' was also the sign for a physician). Nefertem's name may be interpreted two ways: 'Atum is perfect' or 'Entirely perfect.' He was most often represented as a lotus flower and regarded as the god of scents and perfumes. In addition, however, Nefertem played an important part in the solar religion, in which he was regarded as 'lotus blossom by the nose of Re' and in later theological speculation was associated with the creation of the world.

The cult of Ptah spread beyond the boundaries of Memphis and gradually extended to other parts of Egypt, eventually reaching far into Nubia to the south. Thebes became another important center of his cult from the New Kingdom onward and in Nubia he was worshiped in Gerf Hussein and Abu Simbel. In the Late and especially the Ptolemaic Period the cult of Ptah became linked with the cult of the sage Imhotep, probably the builder of the Step Pyramid, who was considered the son of Ptah. Roughly from the Twenty-sixth Dynasty, from the reign of Ahmose II (in Greek Amasis), Imhotep became a full-value god. The Greeks identified him with Asclepius. Imhotep was considered not just a sage and great healer, but also credited with authorship of learned treatises. The statue in his shrine, where illnesses were treated including with the help of dreams, was an important oracle, especially for women anxious to know whether and when they would conceive. In the theology of the cult of ibises and falcons Thoth represented the night aspect and Imhotep the day aspect of divinity. The Temple of Imhotep, known in Greek as the Asclepeion, was situated in Saqqara by the northern cliffs. In the early Christian period Imhotep was identified with the Biblical Joseph. This has led some archaeologists to look for his tomb in the vicinity of the causeway to the pyramid of Teti, in a place that the local inhabitants call Sign Youssef, or 'Joseph's prison.' Other archaeologists are inclined to the view that the Asclepeion and tomb of Imhotep could lie close to the Serapeum (Greek Serapeion). In the Ptolemaic Period the cult of Imhotep spread throughout Egypt; for example, Ptolemy V built a temple to him at Philae.

The Monument of Memphite Theology

What is known as the Monument of Memphite Theology is one of the key pieces of evidence relating to the history of Egyptian religion. It is a basalt stela from Memphis acquired in 1805 by the British Museum in London. The hieroglyphic text is seriously damaged, especially its central section, because for many years the stela served as a millstone. Despite attracting the attention of several generations of

Egyptologists, this important written monument is still surrounded by a number of unanswered archaeological, philological, and historical questions. Its origin is not entirely clear, although it is very probable that it indeed originally came from Memphis. Where in Memphis did it stand? Was it in the Great Temple of Ptah, the earliest part of which has still not been located? That is possible, but there were other temples dedicated to Ptah in Memphis. Another question is whether this was really a later copy of an originally very ancient document, that is, the dating of the text itself and not simply of the monument.

It is evident from the inscription that the stela dates from the Twenty-fifth Dynasty, the reign of the Nubian king of Egypt Shabaqo. The inscription further clarifies:

> *This writing was copied out anew by His Majesty in the house [meaning temple] of his father 'Ptah Who is South of His Wall,' for His Majesty found it to be a work of the ancestors which was worm-eaten, so that it could not be understood from beginning to end [i.e., it was not preserved in its entirety]. His Majesty had it written down again, so that it is more beautiful than it was before.*

It appears from the introductory passage that the text was originally written on a papyrus that had become worm-eaten, which is an indirect reference to its antiquity. It was almost a century before the inscription on the stela was actually published, but on publication it was intensively studied by leading Egyptologists and experts on Egyptian religion and language: the American James Henry Breasted (1865–1935), and especially the two distinguished German philologists Adolf Erman (1845–1937) and Kurt Sethe (1869–1934).

Erman concluded on the basis of linguistic analysis of the text that it was indeed a copy of a very old document written in the time of the Old Kingdom. He saw what he considered clear connections with the Pyramid Texts, for example, but at the same time noticed heterogeneous linguistic elements and certain irregularities. In his view the text was composite, made up of a number of different parts. He thought that the section on the creation of the world by the god Ptah was key, while the other parts were secondarily attached passages from the myth of the god Osiris.

Sethe agreed with Erman's view that the original of the text was very ancient; however, he dated it as even older, from the Early Dynastic Period. Unlike Erman, he believed that the text was a single, not a composite, work. He came up with a very interesting explanation for

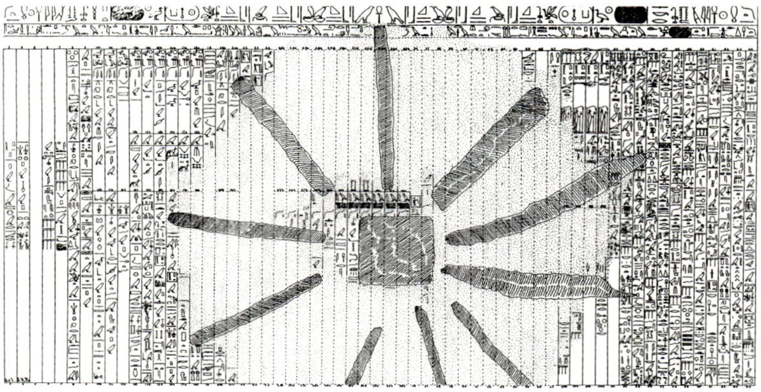

H.J. Breasted's transcription of the text of the Memphis doctrine on the Stela of Shabako, discovered at the beginning of the nineteenth century, probably in Memphis. Today on display in the British Museum in London.

the linguistic incongruities, seeing them as proof that the text contained dramatic passages resembling, for example, the quotations from the Bible in Christian mystery plays. Sethe also argued that apart from the dramatic passages the text had political aspects as well as theological content. Overall he argued that the text had been conceived as a ritual text, but it was hard to say what kind of ritual was involved. With appeal to the fact that the core of the text is a song glorifying Ptah, the German Egyptologist and recognized authority on Old Kingdom texts Hartwig Altenmüller believed that it was probably a ritual in honor of Ptah, and more particularly a ritual relating to a statue of Ptah, because the song is comparable with the hymns of the rituals of statues composed into the Pyramid Texts and the ceremony of the 'opening of the mouth.'

The German Egyptologists Kurt Sethe (left) and Adolf Erman made major contributions to the understanding of the Egyptian language and ancient Egyptian written documents.

The divergence in Erman's and Sethe's understanding of some key passages of the text is already evident in their interpretations of the introduction to the theological discourse in which Ptah is presented as the fundamental all-embracing god. According to Erman, the text reads "the gods, which have arisen from Ptah," while Sethe translates the same passage as "the gods, which have acquired form in Ptah." In the next section of the text Ptah is described as the creator of the world, who created the first primordial gods associated with the genesis of the world (Atum, Nun, Naunet, Nefertem, and others) out of himself, and through them continued in his work of creation. Also described as an expression of Ptah we find Tatjenen, 'The Raised-up Earth,' through whom Ptah is connected to the ancient myth of the primordial mound (encountered in both the Heliopolitan and the Hermopolitan teachings). The key idea of the text is that Ptah created by means of the heart and tongue. The ancient Egyptians believed the heart to be the seat of reason as well as emotion, so what is conveyed here is that Ptah created on the basis of his thoughts, and by means of words (the word, the sentence, was also a creative principle) articulated by the tongue. In the text we read:

> *Thus heart and tongue rule over all the limbs in accordance with the teaching that it [the heart, or: he, Ptah] is in every body and it [the tongue, or: he, Ptah] is in every mouth of all gods, all men, all cattle, all creeping things, and [all] that lives—because the heart thinks of whatever it wishes and the tongue commands whatever it wishes.* (Sethe, *Dramatische Texte,* 55 (54))

It should be noted that the idea of Ptah's creation of the world by means of the word is not one that we meet for the first time in this particular religious text, since it appears earlier in the Coffin Texts from the Middle Kingdom. Nor was the ability to create through thought and word attributed to Ptah only; we also find this power attributed to the Nile god Hapy. Some scholars believe that the origin of this religious idea is to be found not in Memphis, but in Heliopolis.

Leaving aside the question of origins, there is a clear political message in the next passage of the text, which emphasizes that Atum did not create the Ennead of the Oldest Gods; Ptah created it through speech.

> *His [Ptah's] Ennead is before him like his teeth and lips, these are Atum's semen and hands. For the Ennead of Atum came into being through his semen and his fingers. But the Ennead is [in fact] the teeth and lips in this*

mouth which pronounces the name of every thing, from which Shu and Tefnut came forth, and which gave birth to the Ennead.

The text is not speaking of two different Enneads of gods, but of how the one Ennead came into being. According to the Heliopolitan doctrine the primordial god Atum had created the first gods in an unnatural way, by masturbation, while according to the Memphite teaching Ptah created them using thought and word. The passage reflects the tension between the Memphite and Heliopolitan doctrines; here the Memphite is raised above the Heliopolitan not only in religious terms, but also politically.

The next passage quoted here also has a political dimension. It speaks of the creation of the gods, their shrines, and the regions into which the country was administratively subdivided:

He created the gods, he made the towns, he founded the regions [nomes], he set the gods in their places of worship, he settled their offerings [offerings due to them], he set up their shrine, he made their body [meaning statue] according to their wishes. Thus the gods entered into their bodies of every wood, every precious stone, every clay and every other thing that grows on him [Ptah-Tatjenen], in which they received their form. (Sethe, *Dramatische Texte,* 68 (59))

In this passage Ptah is presented not just as the creator of the gods and their cults but also of the Egyptian towns and regions (nomes), the Egyptian state, and its administrative and religious order.

The completion of Ptah's work of creation is expressed thus:

It happened that it was said: He who created everything [Hermann Junker's reading; Sethe gives "He who created Atum"] and created the gods. For he is Tatjenen, who created the gods. All things arose from him, for food, for offerings to the gods, for all good things. So it was established and known that his power is greater than [other] gods. Ptah too was satisfied, after he had made all things and all divine words. (Sethe, *Dramatische Texte,* 66 (58))

In conclusion, it should be emphasized that the Memphite teaching on the creation of the world represents a qualitatively higher level of religious thinking. It is strikingly abstract, working with concepts like thought, intelligence, creative power, and so on. Thought is shifting from the mythological to the theological level, and philosophical and political aspects are appearing in it. This testifies to the high intellectual standard in certain Egyptian priestly circles, in which concepts were developed that were later to influence Judaic and Christian theology. The abstract and intellectual character of the text of the Monument of Memphite Theology is, indeed, what has recently prompted doubts about the dating of that text. Researchers studying Egyptian religion are now reluctant to accept Erman's and Sethe's views on its great antiquity relative to the stela itself. They now consider it a late document, composed during the New Kingdom or even in Shabaqo's time, interpreting the introductory reference to transcription from an old damaged papyrus as simply a device to suggest venerability and so increase respect. If the text was actually created in Shabaqo's time, then it is possible that this Nubian ruler of Egypt was pursuing domestic political goals by deliberately elevating the god Ptah and Memphis, the ancient center of the Egyptian state. Perhaps he wanted to win the sympathy of Egyptians by encouraging self-confidence at a period when the prestige of the country had declined.

The Bull Hapi

According to the ideas of the ancient Egyptians, the bull Hapi, in Greek Apis, was the earthly embodiment of the 'life force,' or *ba*, of the god Ptah. This was no ordinary bull. Herodotus explains:

> *Now this Apis, or Epaphus, is the calf of a cow, which is never afterwards able to bear young. The Egyptians say that fire comes down from heaven upon the cow, which thereupon conceives Apis. The calf which is so called has the following marks: He is black, with a square spot of white upon his forehead, and on his back the figure of an eagle; the hairs in his tail are double, and there is a beetle upon his tongue.* (III, 28)

Apis, although the most famous, was not the only sacred bull revered by the ancient Egyptians. In Heliopolis there was a cult of the bull Merwer (in Greek Mnevis), regarded as the earthly embodiment of the *ba* of the sun god, and in Armant a cult of the bull Bekh (in Greek Buchis), considered the earthly embodiment of the *ba* of the god Montu. Imposing in its size, power, and fertility, the bull had been an object of admiration and honor among Egyptians since prehistoric times. The pharaoh himself even identified with the bull, one of his titles being 'powerful bull,' and one of the important symbols of his rulership being a bull tail affixed to his belt at the back. There are references to the cult of Apis, closely connected with the royal cult, in the very earliest Egyptian religious inscriptions, the Pyramid Texts.

During his lifetime the sacred bull Apis resided in Memphis in the southwest part of the Ptah Temple district. The shrine of Apis with his statue 'Temple of the Living Hapi' (in Greek the 'Apieion') was located there. The shrine was approached through a columned court dating from the reign of Psammetik I, which also led to the shrine of the cow—Apis's mother—entitled 'Isis, mother of Apis.' The whole Apis complex, which also included storehouses and a stable for the cows of Apis's harem, was probably what the Greeks meant by the *sekos*. Only a small part of this complex has yet been excavated and studied, and so once again we must fall back on what Herodotus tells us.

> *When Psammetichus had thus become sole monarch of Egypt, he built the southern gateway of the Temple of Hephaestus in Memphis, and also a court for Apis, in which Apis is kept whenever he makes his appearance in Egypt. This court is opposite the gateway of Psammetichus, and is surrounded with a colonnade and adorned with a multitude of figures. Instead of pillars, the colonnade rests upon colossal statues, twelve cubits in height.* (II, 53)

Bronze statuette of the sacred Apis bull from the Late Period. The bull's head is adorned by a sun disc with uraeus.

At the beginning of 1941, Mustafa Amir, a young Egyptian archaeologist and inspector of monuments located in Memphis, obtained a small sum of money for research and under the occasional supervision of his older and more experienced colleague Ahmad Badawi he began to conduct excavations in the palm thickets southeast of Kom al-Fakhri. Luck smiled on him on the second day of his excavation and he made an important discovery: a big table, two meters broad and four meters long, in the form of a bed carved from a single block of alabaster. It had decorative reliefs of lions along its sides but there was no inscription on them. The top side of the bed was slightly sloping, with a small channel for the drainage of liquid, which led into a large circular vessel also made of alabaster. Four alabaster altars were discovered by the west side of the bed, one of them the gift of the Twenty-sixth Dynasty king Nekau "to the beloved Usir-Hapi (Osiris-Apis), living forever as Re." During probes not far from here some years before, Petrie had found a number of blocks bearing the cartouche of the Twenty-second Dynasty king Sheshonq I.

Amir had found the table on which the sacred bulls were embalmed after their deaths, and at the same time archaeologically localized the complex of buildings and facilities used for the mummification of the bulls and preparations for their burial. It is believed that these facilities were parts of Apis's earthly residence, the abovementioned court *(sekos)*, which probably formed a separate section of the whole district of buildings making up the Temple of Ptah. We know from written sources that the Apis Court also had a 'window of appearance' of the kind known from royal palaces and buildings. Evidently on some special occasions, such as festivals, people other than his priests and keepers could get a sight of the sacred bull. There is no need to emphasize that an Apis bull enjoyed a pampered existence during his lifetime. His keepers took care of him by regularly washing, purifying, and feeding him. He had his own harem of cows. Similar honor was shown to Apis's mother, the cow who had given birth to him and was then considered the embodiment of the goddess Isis. It is clear from some records that Apis would appear in the role of oracle when prophecies were made.

The sacred bull had his own priests to maintain his cult, but we have no detailed information about this cult. We can assume that a new Apis was ceremonially led to enthronement and crowned (in Egyptological literature the Apises, like the rulers, are listed in line starting with the oldest recorded Apis I, who lived during the reign of the Eighteenth Dynasty king Amenhotep III), and that his veneration

Detail of head of a lion from the decoration of one of the mummification tables of the Apis bulls in Mit Rahina.

involved several basic ritual acts known in general terms from the temple cult. The cult of Apis, closely linked with the royal cult from the Late Period, did not come to a final end until the Roman Period, in the late fourth century following Emperor Theodosius's edict abolishing pagan cults.

After his death, the sacred bull was identified with Osiris, ruler of the kingdom of the dead, and so became Osiris-Apis (Osorapis). In later periods, especially in Hellenistic Egypt with its tendency to theological speculation, the duration of Apis's life and rule, the so-called Apis Period, was linked with the cycle of the moon. This led to the supposition that Apis was ritually drowned after twenty-five years of rule, but original documents giving precise chronological data on the birth, enthronement, and death of individual Apis bulls have shown this idea to be false.

Some basic information on the funeral ceremonies that followed the death of Apis are provided by a demotic text on a papyrus (no. 27) dating from the Twenty-sixth Dynasty, which is now in the Kunsthistorisches Museum in Vienna. The text was translated and published

On a fragment of a relief from Niuserre's sun temple in Abu Ghurab we see the sacred bull Apis in his sanctuary, approached by two men—a guard and a lector-priest. The inscription indicates that this is the eastern gate of the sanctuary. Fifth Dynasty.

at the beginning of the 1920s by the leading German expert on demotic, Wilhelm Spiegelberg (1870–1930).

The dead Apis was transported to a place known as a *wabet,* part of which the Egyptian archaeologist Amir managed to excavate. The root of the word *wabet,* translated as 'workshop' or 'place of mummification,' includes the expression *wab,* meaning 'pure and clean.' Apis's corpse was cleaned, purified, and underwent the process of mummification in the *wabet.* This took seventy days (in symbolic parallel to the temporary disappearance and then reappearance—resurrection—of the star Sirius, the cosmic embodiment of Osiris's partner the goddess Isis) and proceeded in the same way as for a dead king. On the pharaoh's order, people from all over Egypt contributed to the costs of the materials used in the mummification (cloth, wine, oil, myrrh, and so on). The pharaoh himself would provide Apis's granite sarcophagus and stone canopic jars, and the funeral equipment (jewels, cases, and other such things) would be paid for by magnates as well as by the pharaoh. On completion of the work and ceremonies in the *wabet* the funeral procession bearing Apis's mummy would set out—along with wailings and lamentations—to the shore of the Pharaoh's Lake, which lay between Memphis and its cemetery

Hypothetical reconstruction of the dromos that once connected Memphis with the Serapeum.

by what today is Saqqara. Further rites would be conducted in a purification tent on the lake's shore.

The funeral procession would cross the lake on boats and continue along the sacred road up to the Serapeum once the rituals were completed. In the Late and Ptolemaic Periods this road was lined on both sides by limestone sphinxes with human heads. The procession was headed by Apis's mummy dragged on sledges, with the priests of Ptah (it is remarkable that Apis's funeral rites were performed by Ptah's priests, not his own) walking immediately behind it. The procession halted only when it reached the area in front of the Serapeum, where other related mortuary-cult buildings stood. There, further rituals would take place, which involved not only the priests but also distinguished personages: dignitaries, officials, invited guests, and so forth. With the pharaoh's agreement some distinguished guests were permitted to place their votive stelae bearing inscriptions with various prayers and requests to Apis in the underground catacombs. The inscriptions offer us important historical data relating to the individual Apises, such as the dates of their birth and death, ascent to the throne, and so on. Sacred bulls are often depicted on these typically relatively small limestone stelae, as in some cases are the petitioners who had them made. Around twelve hundred of these stelae have been found but today the apertures in the walls of the catacombs, where they were once seated, are all empty. The stelae are scattered in different collections throughout the world, with the Paris Louvre boasting the greatest number, thanks to Auguste Mariette, the discoverer of the Serapeum.

Select dignitaries and priests were permitted to set their small stelae with prayers to Osiris-Apis in the walls of the catacombs of the Serapeum.

Before Apis's mummy was taken to its tomb in the underground section, a dwarf would perform a ritual dance and the priests would perform the ritual of the 'opening of the mouth' at the completion of the funeral rites at a place known as the Golden House; it is not known whether this was located in the superstructure or underground part of the Serapeum. Finally, a limited number of people accompanied Apis's mummy to its last resting place and installed it in the huge granite sarcophagus. The sarcophagus, which might weigh as much as eighty tons, was then sealed and the objects of funeral equipment laid around it: stone vessels, canopic jars with the viscera of Apis removed during mummification, *ushabtis* (figurines of Apis's servants in the next world), and so on. The canopic jars sometimes had lids in the form of a bull head; *ushabtis* were sometimes found with bull heads. Finally, the niche in which the sarcophagus lay was walled up and, on departing, the last priest sealed the entrance to the underground catacombs. These were supposed to remain closed until the funeral of the next Apis, who began his rule seventy days after the burial of his predecessor.

The Serapeum

The famous Serapeum (Greek: Serapeion) of Saqqara, the cemetery of the sacred Apis bulls that lies on the northwestern edge of the huge necropolis here, was formed of a complex of above-ground and underground buildings approached by an avenue of sphinxes, called a 'dromos' in the documents from the Ptolemaic Period. The Serapeum was not just the cemetery of the Apises but the center of a large sector of the necropolis devoted to a series of animal cemeteries that came under its management. This sector was divided into the 'northern escarpment of the Serapeum' and the 'southern escarpment of the Serapeum' on the basis of position on one side or the other of the dromos.

The above-ground part of the Serapeum consisted of a complex of cult buildings. Almost none have survived except for a few fragments of architecture. A few dozen meters in front of the entrance to the catacombs, the Thirtieth Dynasty king Nakhtnebef II built the Eastern Temple, which is accessed by a staircase adorned with sphinxes. It was constructed on the site of an earlier Nineteenth Dynasty temple with an Apis statue and offering table. A royal palace adjoined the Eastern Temple on the south. Immediately over the entrance to the catacombs stood the

Plan of the final section of the dromos and eastern temple in front of the entrance to the catacombs of the Serapeum.
1. eastern temple of Nakhtnebef II
2. hemicycle
3. palace district
4. district of the *pastoforium*
5. gate and lion statues of Nakhtnebef II
6. Greek temple of Serapis
7. Egyptian sanctuary with the Apis statue
8. dromos with Dionysian and Egyptian statues

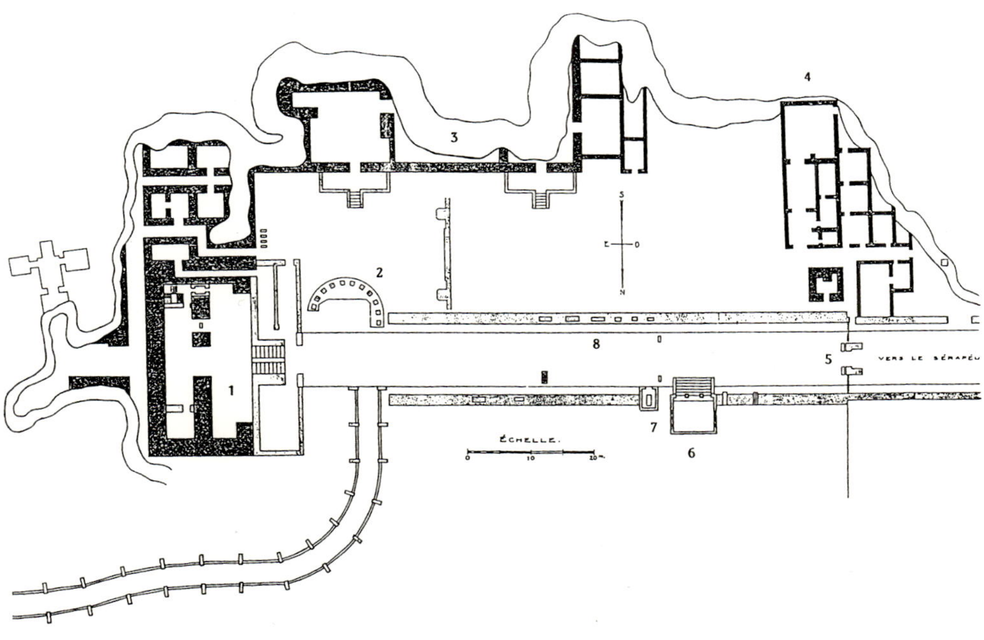

Temple of Osiris-Apis (Osorapis). A chapel with a polychrome limestone statue of Apis—which is now held in the the Louvre—stood on the north side of the temple's entrance. Unfortunately, thorough archaeological excavation of these important buildings has never been carried out. Wind-blown sand now covers the parts of them once unearthed by Mariette; all that can be seen, half protruding from the sand, is the so-called hemicycle, a semicircular building with remnants of statues of Greek poets and learned men (Homer, Pindar, Protagoras, Hesiod, Heraclitus, and others) dating from the reign of Ptolemy I or II. Today most of the tourists hardly notice it as they hurry past it to the more attractive Mastaba of Ti. Just like the buildings above ground, the underground parts of the Serapeum have yet to reveal all their secrets. We do not even know exactly when the Serapeum was founded.

The oldest known burial of a sacred bull in the Saqqara Serapeum, Apis I, is from the Eighteenth Dynasty, the reign of Amenhotep III, while the last securely dated Apis is Apis LVII, who lived during the reign of Ptolemy VIII Euergetes II. This scarcely means, however, that the whole series of sacred bulls from the first to the fifty-seventh has been fully and safely identified from contemporary written sources or that the series necessarily ended with Apis LVII. Far from it. A number of the historically recorded Apises do not yet have archaeologically identified tombs in the Serapeum and are known only from written records. Nor can we say with any precision how many bulls were buried even in the catacombs discovered so far, because while some sarcophagi lay in their own deep niches carved into the sides of the passages, others may have lain only in the passages. The challenge for archaeologists is not then only to find evidence relating to the missing Apises, but to also determine where possibly older as well as more recent burials are located. They may lie in undiscovered catacombs of the Serapeum or, quite possibly, somewhere else in the Saqqara necropolis, as indicated by eighteenth-century European travelers' reports.

The French archaeologist Auguste Mariette discovered the Saqqara Serapeum in 1851 and started to excavate it. He had originally been sent to Egypt to find and purchase rare manuscripts for the museum in the Louvre, but after arriving in Egypt he became far more fascinated with ancient Egyptian architectural monuments and thus began his own excavations. At one point, while exploring the necropolis in Saqqara, Mariette noticed half-buried limestone sphinxes and remembered the classical geographer Strabo's (ca. 63 BC–ca. AD 21) mention of an avenue of sphinxes leading to the Serapeum in his *Geography*. He started excavations immediately (before obtaining official permission),

Hemicycle with statues of learned Greek men shortly after excavation.

which uncovered relics that confirmed Strabo's claims and led to the discovery of the Avenue of Sphinxes linking Memphis with Saqqara and the Serapeum. We know today that Mariette was not in fact the first person to penetrate into the Serapeum in modern times; a number of European travelers had done so before him. The avenue ascended from the shore of Pharaoh's Lake (the title 'Pharaoh's' means that this was essentially a public lake) separating Memphis from its cemetery, cut through the older precincts of the pyramid complex of the Sixth Dynasty king Teti, then led into the courtyard of the Temple of Osiris-Apis before ending in the Temple of the Serapeum, under which was the entrance to the underground passages carved into the rock.

Mariette was not particularly scrupulous in his excavations in the Serapeum. His aim was to find spectacular monuments rather than produce thorough archaeological documentation. He employed hundreds of laborers and when he encountered some serious obstacle he had no qualms about using explosives to remove it. The great majority of the sacred bull burials he discovered had already been breached and plundered, but he managed to find a few that were intact. In one funeral chamber he discovered two adorned wooden coffins of bulls buried in the sixteenth and thirtieth years of the reign of Ramesses II.

François Auguste Ferdinand Mariette Pasha.

In addition to the coffins and canopic jars there were *ushabti*s, amulets, and also figurines in wooden cabinets decorated with scenes of the king and his son, Prince Khamwaset, bringing offerings to Apis. After death both sacred bulls had been divided into small pieces; these pieces were then wrapped in cloth bandages, prompting the theory that their flesh had been consumed before mummification. Herodotus (II, 41), however, reports that the Egyptians sometimes buried dead animals in the ground, leaving only their horns protruding, and waited until the flesh had rotted away before digging up the bones and burying them. Mariette found yet another intact burial involving a wooden coffin. The inscriptions on the jewelry, and especially the male gold mask in the coffin, convinced Mariette that this was the burial of Prince Khamwaset, who had been the high priest of Ptah and whose connection to the Memphite necropolis and the funerary monuments of his royal ancestors had been stronger than simply that of the official responsibility of the position. Later it was found that the coffin contained decomposed bull rather than human remains.

Although Mariette rather retrospectively obtained permission from Khedive Abbas to excavate the Serapeum, the two men were not on the best of terms. Abbas was notorious for sometimes treating precious archaeological monuments as his own personal property and sometimes handed them out to influential foreign guests. It is therefore no wonder that Mariette tried to transport everything he could get his hands on out of Egypt to France as fast as possible. In the end, this amounted to a full 230 big chests, the contents of which are today the pride of the Louvre.

Grand as it was, the Serapeum was not the only cemetery of sacred animals in the Saqqara necropolis. In the Late and Ptolemaic Periods it progressively became the center of a much bigger complex of cemeteries of other sacred animals and their associated temples and cult buildings. The complex even became a kind of religious-cult center for all of Egypt. Its discovery is associated with the name of the English archaeologist Walter Bryan Emery (1903–71), who was excavating Early Dynastic graves in a rocky outcrop in north Saqqara when he happened on underground passages full of ibis burials. The British team also found cemeteries of falcons, baboons, and even a cemetery of mothers of Apis, known as the Iseum, during subsequent excavations. On the eastern edge of the Saqqara necropolis, but close to the avenue connecting Memphis with the Serapeum, a French archaeological team headed by Alain Zivie succeeded in discovering a big cemetery of sacred cats—the Bubasteion. This is unlikely to be the last such find. From written sources of the period we know that cemeteries of other sacred animals, such as cows and bulls (children of Apis), are located in Saqqara, and perhaps not only in Saqqara. Recent archaeological finds suggest that some of these cemeteries may also be located in the Czech archaeological concession in Abusir.

In the catacombs of the Serapeum at Saqqara.

View of the rock reef in Saqqara, which was part of the Bubasteion and in which in the Late Period there were catacombs with a cemetery of sacred cats. Tombs of important dignitaries had earlier been built into the same rock outcrop during the New Kingdom.

Currently, the Serapeum is in a very dilapidated state and closed to the public. Mariette indirectly set off the chain of events that has led to this dismal situation by having a simple excavation hut built on a small hillock above the entrance to the underground galleries. When the excavations were completed, this 'Mariette House' remained and became an integral feature and even a kind of navigation point of the Saqqara cemetery. It was used for a variety of purposes. At one time, a large Bedouin tent café for tourists was erected here. Today there is stabling for camels beside it. The sewage probably seeped right down to the catacombs, which are carved out of the hardened clay sediments known in Arabic as *tafla*. The Egyptian experts are now carrying out costly and demanding reconstruction work in the catacombs.

In conclusion, we should note that the Serapeum in Saqqara should not be confused with the other shrines also known as Serapeum, which, as a result of the development of the cult of the Hellenistic Serapis (see chapter 12), were built in various parts of Egypt, in Alexandria, Fayoum, Hermopolis, and elsewhere. Serapis was a syncretic deity created on the orders of Ptolemy I with the aim of bringing together the spiritual worlds of the Egyptians and Greeks to the benefit of the empire. With the spread of the cult of Serapis in the Hellenistic milieu in the eastern Mediterranean, Serapeums appeared even outside the territory of Egypt.

Cults of Animals

One great peculiarity of ancient Egypt, which often surprised and disgusted foreign visitors and led them to express contempt for the local society, was the veneration of animals. Visitors' feelings of astonishment were intensified by the fact that in many other respects the educated elite of Egyptian society was respected and admired. Things are not always as they seem to be to visitors, however, and so it was with the worship and cults of animals, which was a deep and many-layered religious phenomenon rather than some primitive aberration.

Animals were not worshiped as such, but just as the bearer of a specific divine aspect, the *ba*, of a particular god. According to the ancient Egyptians the *ba*, the divine power of a god, could enter into an animal just as readily as it could move into the stone statue of the god or a faience amulet in the shape of the god's symbol. This idea is expressed in an often-cited text from the Myth of the Heavenly Cow.

> *The* ba *of Shu is air,*
> *the* ba *of time is rain,*
> *the* ba *of darkness is night,*
> *the* ba *of Osiris is the ram of Mendes,*
> *the* ba *of Sobek are crocodiles,*
> *the* ba *of each god is in snakes,*
> *the* ba *of Apophis is in the eastern mound,*
> *whereas the* ba *of Re works through the whole world.*
> (Hornung, *Der ägyptische Mythos von der Himmelskuh,* 47)

The great expert on ancient Egyptian animal cults, Theodor Hopfner (1886–1946), was a professor at the Prague German University in the period between the world wars. He classified sacred animals into three groups: those that are lifelong embodiments of a god, are kept in temples and distinguished from other members of their species by specific marks; those that belong to a divine species of animal, but are not divine in themselves, but sacred; and selected sacred animals kept as fetishes to please a god.

It should be stressed that the fine but nonetheless fundamental theological nuances in the concept of the *ba* and the difference between a divine or sacred animal were comprehensible to the priests and the educated, but probably not to simple uneducated people, who were very unlikely to have made such distinctions in their personal piety and religious practice.

The veneration of animals had origins going back deep into prehistoric times, but acquired greater intensity in the Late Period. Some Egyptologists believe that this may have been a result of the political weakening of Egypt, the growing number and importance of foreigners in the country, and Egyptian society's efforts to cope with the new situation by 'fundamentalization' and a search for its own cultural

Detail of the head of the mummy of a cat wrapped in linen bandages. The head is carefully modeled in the bandages and the face mask of the animal is outlined with black paint. Late Period.

roots and models in the glorious eras of the past. At the same time, one interesting aspect of this process was the growing interest in magic and in mysterious and complex speculative intellectual constructions. The animal cults spread rapidly throughout the country, grand cult buildings were erected, and large animal cemeteries were founded.

Remains of animal cemeteries have been discovered archaeologically in roughly 120 places all over Egypt, from Alexandria to Aswan and even deep into Nubia. The number of buried animals, which were sometimes mummified very precisely, wrapped in cloth bandages, and painted (for example, into the form of a cat), but in most cases just buried, is enormous. Approximately a hundred thousand have been found so far; it is obvious that there must have been millions of animal burials. The range of venerated and buried animals identified is also extremely diverse. For example, in the Hermopolitan cemetery of animals at Tuna al-Gebel, the largest group of burials consists of ibises, and sometimes their eggs, but we also find burials of different species of falcon, cranes, owls, eagles, kingfishers, storks, geese, and many other kinds of birds, as well as cats, dogs, baboons, sheep, cattle, crocodiles, gazelles, and more.

The largest complex of animal cemeteries and cult buildings was established in north Saqqara, in the area around the Serapeum and the Royal Lake. Apart from the Apis bulls and their mothers, there were also falcons, ibises, owls, baboons, dogs, cats, sheep, goats, gazelles, antelopes, fish, snakes, lizards, and even scarab beetles buried here. A picture of activity at the cemeteries, especially the Apis cult and the life of the community of the Serapeum, emerges from the numerous written sources (papyri, ostraka, and so on), one of the most important being what is known as the Serapeum Archive from the mid-second century BC. Its key figure is Ptolemy, son of Glaukias. This material is supplemented by the archive (published by the British scholar J.D. Ray) of the learned scribe Hor, originally from Lower Egypt, where he did a great deal for the local Hermaion (the Greek term for a cult compound of ibises) and was then appointed to serve in the more important Hermaion in Saqqara.

The running of these cemeteries and local cults of animals, linked to the royal cult and the many festivals that took place here, demanded considerable organization and funds. The entire animal cult complex, which was part of the larger area of the Memphite necropolis known as Ankh tawy ('Two Lands Live'), was divided up into districts with individual animal cemeteries and the buildings associated with them. Heading the whole complex was a priest with the rank of 'servant of the god,' and the specific title 'controller of compounds of Ta dehnet in Ankh tawy'; Ta dehnet was the name of the rock outcrop where the cemeteries lay. The complex included the shrine of Isis—the Iseum—and an associated underground cemetery of cows, known as the 'House of Rest of Isis, Mother of Apis.' Isis was also known as the 'Lady of the Valley' that led from the Lake of Abusir and separated north Saqqara from South Abusir. On the north side of the Avenue of Sphinxes, close to the Lake of Abusir, there was a cemetery of ibises known as the Hermaion, with a chapel to Osiris-Ibis and rock galleries. By the Lake of Abusir there was a 'chapel of the birthplace of Thoth-Ibis' and an adjoining ibis farm known as the Ibiotropheion. Galleries containing a cemetery of falcons are carved into the rock outcrop from the north. The mummies of the birds were usually placed in jars set one next to the other along the walls as in a honeycomb.

On the southeast edge of the rocky outcrop was the Anubeion, a district with a cemetery of dogs and jackals and the shrine of the jackal god of the dead 'Anubis, he who is upon his mountain.' South of the Anubeion there was a cemetery of cats known in Egyptian as 'Compound of Bastet, Lady of Ankh tawy' and in Greek as the Bubasteion. Here at the beginning of the 1980s a French archaeological expedition found thousands of cat burials in the rock galleries, some even in little wooden coffins. The great majority were slapdash burials in pieces of cloth bandages, and sometimes only small, roughly carved wooden cat figurines were wound in the bandages, but there were some luxurious burials with painstakingly crossed bandages, a realistically modeled cat head, and a carefully drawn mask in black dye. In the central gallery, which is a kind of chapel, a great cat head is carved into the rock. It is a pity that despite a few marginal discoveries, archaeologists have not yet managed to discover the other big and famous cat cemetery, which was located in the center of the cult of the cat goddess Bastet in Per Bastet ('House of Bastet'), near modern Zagazig in the Eastern Delta.

The cemeteries of other animals in north Saqqara are known only from written records and have not yet been archaeologically confirmed and located; one such example is the hypogeum (a set of underground galleries) containing earlier burials of cows, which were considered to be mothers of Apises. The cemetery of Apis's children, which the sacred bull begot on the cows of his harem, has likewise not been located, nor has the shrine of the lion goddess Sakhmet within which lions were kept and also buried. Lions were considered kings of all animals and bearers of the sun god's *ba*, and they appeared at ceremonial occasions such as the ascent of the king to the throne, festival rituals conducted at the New Year, and so on. According to written records the lion shrine was an enclosed district that may have been situated on the edge of the Lake of Abusir, where in the Ptolemaic Period there was also a kind of zoo.

The forlorn remains of the temple of Hathor lie undeservedly unnoticed by visitors to Memphis.

Khamwaset

Khamwaset, son of the famous Nineteenth Dynasty king Ramesses II and queen Esetnofret, was the high priest of the Temple of Ptah in Memphis and in this capacity also cared for the Serapeum. He showed great interest in the funerary monuments of his royal ancestors in the

Ramesses II and his son, Prince Khamwaset, bringing offerings to Osiris-Apis.

Memphis necropolis, particularly the pyramids. Fragments of inscriptions concerning reconstruction work carried out on his orders have been found in many of these monuments.

One indication that Khamwaset was a very extraordinary figure in Egyptian history whose fame endured for ages is the fact that in the Late Period he was made the main character of a work of literature, the fairy tale "Setne Khamwaset" (*setne* is a mutilation of the priestly title *sem*). He is described in this story as a priest and magician, who is seeking Thoth's—the Egyptian god of knowledge—book of wisdom; this book was thought to provide its owner with unlimited power.

His tomb has not yet been found, but it is thought that it may lie close to the Serapeum. As has already been mentioned, Mariette believed, on the basis of inscriptions referring to Khamwaset on some funerary objects, that he had found Khamwaset's tomb in the underground part of the Serapeum; this later turned out to be a hasty and mistaken conclusion. In the 1990s Japanese archaeologists found the remains of Khamwaset's mortuary chapel, but not his tomb, on a rock promontory west of the Serapeum. The chapel was built on a site that Khamwaset could not have chosen by chance: from this spot there is a superb view over the whole Memphite necropolis, from the pyramids in Giza to the pyramids in Dahshur. Khamwaset's tomb continues to be shrouded in mystery.

The remains of the temple of Thoth in Hermopolis.

4

Hermopolis: The City of the Eight

<< Capital of a column from the early Christian basilica in Hermopolis.

On the west bank of the Nile, about forty kilometers south of Minya, the metropolis of Middle Egypt, lies a site that is rarely visited by tourists but archaeologically very important—Ashmunayn. Its modern Arab name is derived from the Coptic 'Shmoun,' which is in turn derived from the Egyptian 'Khemenu' ('City of the Eight'). This unusual name refers to the Eight (in Greek the 'Ogdoad')—that is, four pairs of frog and snake primordial gods, who were worshiped here from earliest times. The cult of Thoth, however, also put down roots here as far back as the Old Kingdom; in time it came to overshadow the Ogdoad. The Greeks identified Thoth with Hermes, and so in Greek the city's name was Hermopolis, or more precisely Hermopolis Magna ('Great Hermopolis') as distinguished from Hermopolis Parva ('Small Hermopolis'), where Tell Bakliya stands today in northeastern Egypt.

In ancient Egypt the city of the Ogdoad or the city of Hermes was also known as Wenu ('[City of] the Hare'), because it was the administrative center of the fifteenth Upper Egyptian nome, where the hare goddess Wenet was venerated. Another god to enjoy great honor in Hermopolis was Shepsi (the 'Superb One'), a local god with a number of solar and lunar aspects. The desert route to the oasis of Bahariya led west from the city. Hermopolis lies in the center of the land, and so in times of disunity the internal political frontier of spheres of influence often ran through it. This was true, for example, in the First Intermediate Period between the rulers of Nennisut (Herakleopolis Magna) and Waset (Thebes); during the Second Intermediate Period between the Hyksos rulers and the southern, independent part of the country headed by the nomarchs of Waset; and finally in the Third Intermediate Period between the north, controlled by the kings, and the south, controlled by the high priests of Amun. At the end of the Third Intermediate Period the local ruler Namlot even made Herakleopolis Magna independent for a short time and laid claim to a royal title.

Hermopolis was not directly on the Nile but about two kilometers west of it, and was linked to the river by an artificial canal. Another

The ruins of Hermopolis spread out over an area of several dozen hectares.

canal connected the city with its cemetery, situated at a place that is today called Tuna al-Gebel. Although during the twentieth century alone a whole series of Egyptian and foreign archaeologists undertook research in Hermopolis, as yet only a small part of the extensive ruins of the ancient city have been excavated. The remains of the city—temples, colonnades, and other once grand buildings—lie beneath heaps of ceramic shards and ruins overgrown with bushes and grasses that are obviously and uninvitingly the home of snakes and other dangerous wildlife.

We owe much of our archaeological information about Hermopolis to two foreign archaeological expeditions. The first, a German expedition led by Günther Röder (1881–1966), worked here at the end of the 1920s and beginning of the 1930s; they were followed by archaeologists from the British Museum in London. Material archaeological finds are not of course our only evidence of the history of the famous city. There are written records, for example, that in the First Intermediate Period there was a shrine to Thoth in Hermopolis. As yet the oldest archaeologically confirmed building here is a temple built in the Twelfth Dynasty by Amenemhet II and dedicated not to Thoth but to Amun; today all that remains of it are fragments of the pylon and hypostyle hall. On the other hand there can be no doubt that a succession of temples were built to Thoth in Hermopolis at different times, as well as one to his divine female partner Nehmetawy. There was also a temple to the four pairs of Hermopolitan primordial gods, the Ogdoad that gave the city its name. From a text in the Papyrus Harris I we learn, for example, that Ramesses III built monuments in

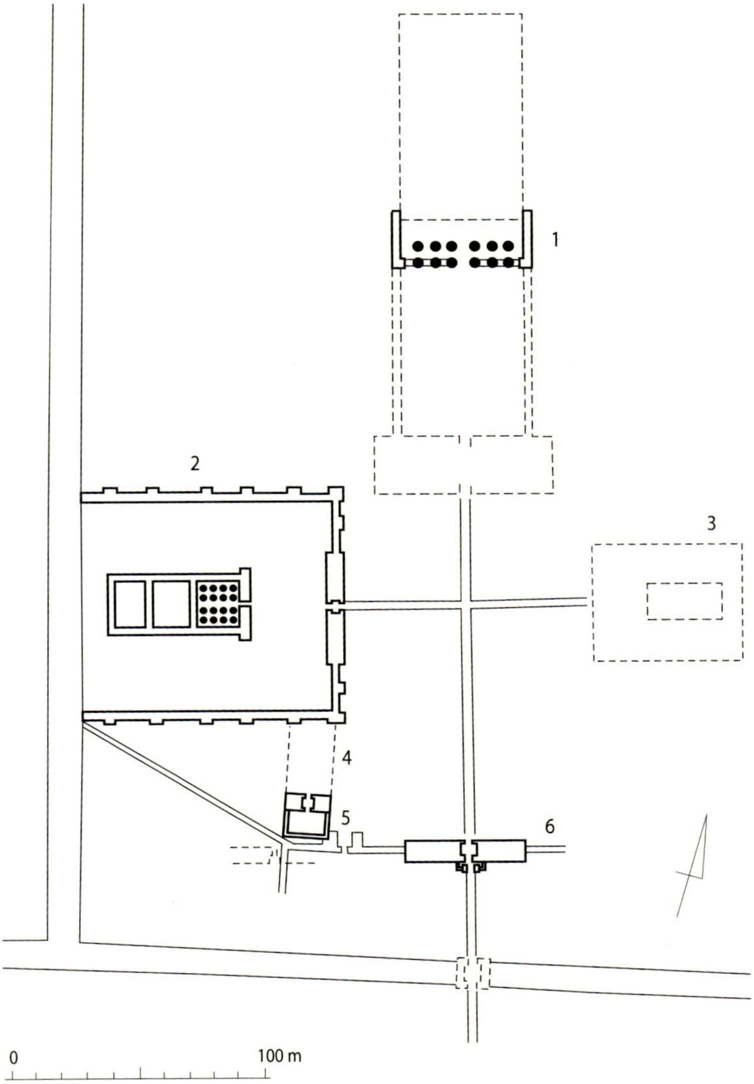

Plan of the temple district in Hermopolis.
1. Temple of Thoth
2. Temple of Amun
3. Temple of Nehmetawy
4. primeval hill and temple of the Ogdoad
5. gate of Amenemhet II
6. pylon of Ramesses II

honor of Thoth in Hermopolis, and from later written records that the biggest Roman temple in traditional Egyptian style was built here by the emperor Domitian.

<< This colossal red-granite statue of a baboon originally adorned the entrance to the temple of Thoth.

The sacred district (with remains of a few temples) later enclosed by a massive, fifteen-meter-thick wall of mud bricks that was built in the Thirtieth Dynasty by Nakhtnebef I, was situated in the center of the city and entered from the south. A new Temple of Thoth was founded in the district during the New Kingdom; it was built by a series of kings including Hatshepsut, Amenhotep III, Haremheb, and Ramesses II. The temple was replaced by a new one during Nakhtnebef I's reign; its decoration was finally completed as late as the reign of Philip Arrhidaeus, the feeble-minded stepbrother of Alexander the Great. This Temple of Thoth was for the greater part destroyed shortly before the start of the Christian era, although its huge pronaos was still standing in 1826. A pair of colossal red-granite baboon statues—Thoth's sacred animal—dating from the reign of Amenhotep III are still standing today. Originally, there were six such statues that adorned the main entrance to the temple.

View of Antinoopolis, a town founded near Hermopolis by the emperor Hadrian in honor of his companion Antinoüs.

South of the district that contained the temples of Thoth lay another district, likewise enclosed by a brick wall. Here Röder's team discovered a temple dedicated to Amun and Ptah. Two colossal red-granite seated statues of Ramesses II adorned the entrance to this building known as the Southern Temple. The temple was later renovated on the orders of Emperor Nero.

In the Ptolemaic and Roman Periods there was a large paved area where festivals and processions were held in the center of the city. The dominating building to the south of this area was the Komasterion

A number of columns from the Christian basilica are still standing. They had been taken from earlier Roman buildings.

('House of Processions'), and to the east of it the Bastion, a building that served as a treasury or storehouse. Adjacent to the Komasterion on the west was the Tetrastylon with statues on huge columns, and the Nymphaion, and there was also an avenue of sphinxes here. Near the Komasterion was the intersection of the two most important roads of Hermopolis. One was the dromos of Hermes running north–south (its full name was 'Paved Dromos of Hermes, Thrice-Great God') and the other was the east–west Antinoopolitan road leading on the east to the Nile ferry that carried passengers across to the celebrated Antinoopolis (by the modern village of Sheikh Abada), founded by the emperor Hadrian in honor of his drowned lover Antinoüs.

An Egyptian archaeological expedition from Alexandria University found the remains of a large fifth-century basilica at Kom al-Kanisa ('Church Hill'); some of its pillars still stand at the original site. The basilica was built using materials from dismantled Ptolemaic-era buildings, in particular the shrine of the royal cults of Ptolemy III Euergetes I and Berenice II. This shrine is one of the few classical Ptolemaic temples outside Alexandria whose foundations have survived to the present. The basilica has red-granite columns and limestone Corinthian capitals from early Roman second- and third-century buildings. The remains of a few other buildings, which were constructed in a purely Greek style and later almost completely destroyed, were found in the vicinity. The devastation and recycling of monuments has been a particularly prominent feature of the history of Hermopolis. The Nineteenth Dynasty kings, especially Ramesses II, used stone blocks from Akhenaten's buildings in nearby Amarna on the opposite bank of the Nile in order to build temples in Hermopolis. And as the fate of the Temple of Alexander shows, the monuments of Hermopolis were still serving the people of the surrounding villages as quarries for building materials in the nineteenth century.

Continuing on from the main artery of Hermopolis (that is, the dromos of Hermes), a road roughly six kilometers long led to the city cemetery near what is today the village of Tuna al-Gebel. The boundary stela of Akhenaten in the rocks above the cemetery shows that the official territory of Akhenaten's new royal city reached as far as here. The cemetery, which originated in the Eighteenth Dynasty, continued to be used until the Roman Period. In its south section there was once a lake where ibises—the sacred birds of Thoth—were bred.

Plan of the catacombs with cemetery of sacred animals in Tuna al-Gebel.
1. Gallery D
2. Gallery C
3. house of priests
4. Temple of Osiris-baboon

Ibises, as well as baboons—another of Thoth's sacred animals—were also buried here from the Twenty-sixth Dynasty in four underground catacombs or galleries designated by archaeologists with the letters A, B, C, and D. From the Ptolemaic Period crocodiles, rams, falcons, and other animals and birds were buried with them.

Bronze figures of ibis and baboon, the sacred animals of Thoth.

The funerary temple district in Tuna al-Gebel has been the site of German archaeological explorations led by Dieter Kessler since 1979. This is a complex of above-ground buildings that also includes underground burial galleries and cult places. The Mortuary Temple of Thoth (more precisely Osiris-Thoth), which held embalming tables for sacred animals, was sited over the entrance to underground Gallery C. Petitions addressed to Thoth were also placed in this temple. In Gallery C there is an underground cult room, with the archaeological designation G-C-C-2, which was sparingly illuminated by a shaft in the ceiling. Here the priests conducted morning and evening ceremonies. This room contained a red-granite statue of a striding ibis (in this context 'striding' means 'moving,' as opposed to 'nesting,' which means 'resting') and a red-granite statue of a striding baboon. Kessler believes that these were representations of Thoth-Ibis and Thoth-Baboon, the gods of the city, Hermopolitan gods, who were the executive forms of the supra-regional Thoth enthroned in the celestial Hermopolis, to whom the epithet 'twice great,' and sometimes 'thrice great,' refers. In

Saqya, the device by which water in Tuna al-Gebel was pumped from a well into the channels in the enclosures where sacred animals were kept.

other words, what we have here is a certain duality: a cosmic Thoth but also a local Hermopolitan Thoth, the earthly guardian of the king, his administration, and the inhabitants of the city. In the underground section numerous ostraka and papyri with Greek and Aramaic texts were discovered.

A road connected the Mortuary Temple of Thoth with the so-called Great Temple, which held water troughs for the sacred animals in its rear section. These were supplied with water from a well by means of a large wooden wheel (in Arabic a *saqya*), which is still to be seen here.

In the northern part of the cemetery there are tombs from the Ptolemaic and Roman Periods, some of them very grand and historically valuable. The most famous and beautiful of these was built by the high priest of Thoth Petosiris, who conceived it as a family tomb as well as his own resting place. The building resembles a small Egyptian temple, its façade adorned by four columns. A limestone offering table with protrusions—what is known as a horned altar—

So-called horned altar in front of the tomb of Petosiris at Tuna al-Gebel.

stands in front of the building's entrance. The walls of the entrance vestibule are covered with inscriptions and scenes that have various secular themes, such as the preparation of grease, the weighing of metal, and so on, in an artistic style that combines Greek and Egyptian elements. Some figures, however, are depicted in a purely Greek style. In the next room, its ceiling supported by four pillars, the walls are decorated with inscriptions and scenes in the same style as the vestibule, but in addition to secular subjects, such as agricultural works or family pictures, we also find religious themes. These comprise various Egyptian gods, Egyptian religious symbols, the bringing of offerings, texts from the *Book of the Dead*, and so on. Another purely Egyptian element is the false door. The tomb soon became a place of pilgrimage for Greeks, who venerated Petosiris as a sage and protector. Pilgrimages to his tomb continued right up to the fourth century AD. Today, the attention of visitors is also drawn to the tomb of Isidora, who lived in the second century in the reign of Antonius Pius and drowned in the Nile. Her tomb became a kind of chapel for the cult of the drowned girl.

The Hermopolitan Ogdoad

As previously mentioned, Hermopolis was originally the place of the cult of four pairs of primordial gods; each pair comprised a frog (the male element) and a snake (the female element). These primordial gods, expressing the state of things at the beginning of the world, were the basis for the local religious teaching on the creation of the world. Pairs were formed by: Nun (the primordial water) and Naunet; Heh (infinite space) and Hehet; Keku (darkness) and Kekuit; and Tenemu (hiddenness) and Tenemuit. Amun and Amaunet, who conveyed the same meaning as the latter couple, replaced them during the New Kingdom. Although the oldest written records of the Ogdoad come later, from the Coffin Texts, its veneration in the Old Kingdom is indirectly documented not only by the name of the city but also the title of the Hermopolitan high priest known as the 'Great One of the Five.' The figure 'five' in the title refers to the four pairs of the Ogdoad along with Thoth—whose main cult center was in Hermopolis—as a fifth element.

According to the Hermopolitan doctrine, first there was a chaos expressed by the four pairs of primordial gods; at the beginning of time an 'Island of the Flames,' on which the sun god started his work of creation, emerged out of this chaos. The Island of the Flames (mentioned in the very earliest religious inscriptions, the Pyramid Texts) was the place not only of the creation of the world but of rebirth and eternal life. According to later theological speculations the island lay in the 'Lake of the Knife' (although sometimes this also refers to a sacred small lake in the Hermopolite temple district) on the eastern horizon. This was the place where, every day, the sun god had to take care that his barque did not run aground in the shallows as it sailed up to cross the celestial ocean, for if it did run aground it would cause the end of the world. Here, he also had to defeat his numerous enemies, who were led by the primordial serpent Apophis and Apophis's accomplices in the form of seventy-seven asses, on a daily basis. Over time the Island of the Flames and Lake of Knives came to be used interchangeably in the religious texts, and also to be used to refer to the cemetery in Hermopolis.

The shrine of the primordial gods the Ogdoad was probably located in the southeast part of the sacred district. During the New Kingdom and at the height of the cult of Amun, the Hermopolitan Ogdoad was integrated into Theban religious teaching. It was then considered an expression or form of the god Amun in the shape of the primordial serpent Kematef ('He who has fulfilled his time'). The Temple of Kematef at Medinet Habu, in what was then western Thebes, also contained the tomb of the Ogdoad. On the Feast of the Decade, Amun (that is, a procession of priests with a statue of the god) would regularly set forth from his temple in Karnak to meet his primal ancestors in a mythical holy place, Djeme, a mound in Medinet Habu on the western bank of the Nile in Thebes, and so be restored and draw new strength.

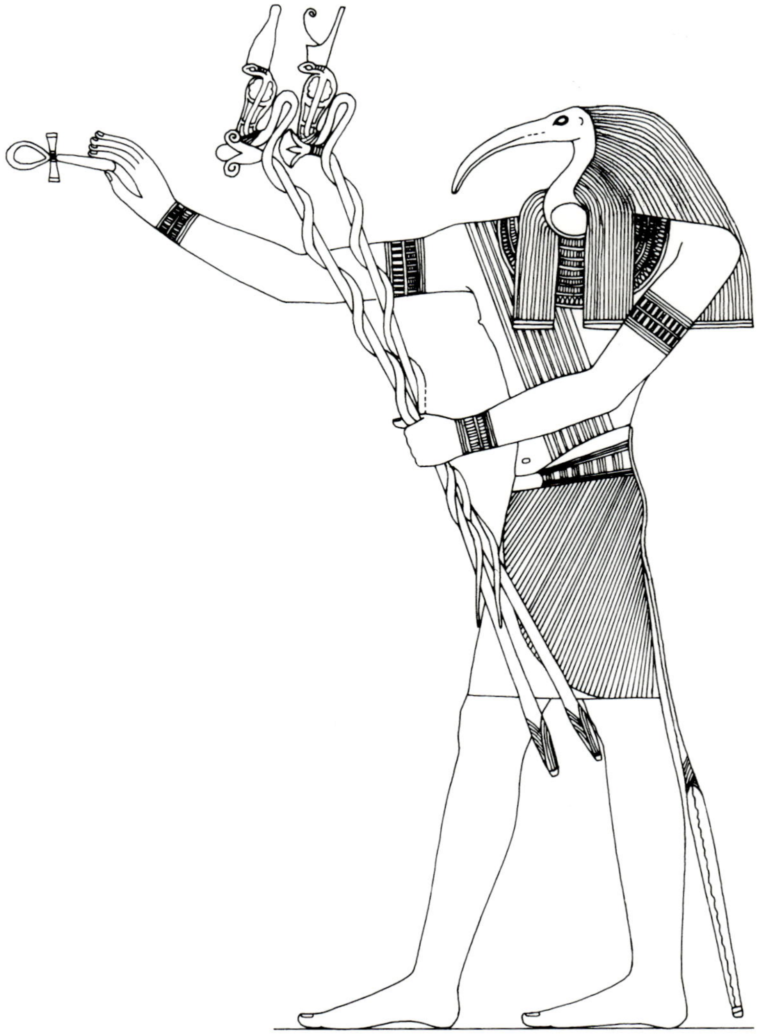

The god Thoth represented as a man with the head of an ibis. He holds the symbolic scepters of Upper and Lower Egypt in his left hand, and the *ankh*, the symbol of life, in his right hand.

Thoth and His Way

The title of the high priest of Hermopolis indirectly shows that the god Thoth was venerated in Hermopolis alongside the Ogdoad from as early as the Old Kingdom. The etymology of the name Thoth is unclear and the subject of dispute among archaeologists. According to some it means 'He of Djehut,' although we do not know precisely where Djehut lies. It is thought that it may be a place in the fifteenth Lower Egyptian nome, which has in its sign a standard bearing an ibis, regarded as the embodiment of the *ba* of Thoth. Another interpretation derives the name from *dehty* ('guide' [of the gods]). The baboon was another embodiment of the *ba* of Thoth, and so the god was most often represented as a man with the head of an ibis, or as a baboon or a man with a baboon head. In the Late, Ptolemaic, and Roman Periods the Thoth of the city was distinguished from the supra-regional, cosmic Thoth and his forms.

Thoth, already mentioned in the Pyramid Texts, was a very important god with a wide range of powers. He was considered the god of knowledge and wisdom, the discoverer of writing and counting, the lord of time, and the administrator of the calendar and rituals. In the form of the moon he had a cosmic dimension as partner of the sun god. According to one religious speculation Thoth even hatched out of a primeval egg at the creation of the world. He took part in the coronation of the king, whom together with Horus he purified with water in the ritual of the 'royal baptism.' He accompanied the king from cradle to tomb and thereafter, on his journey into the next world. We can encounter Thoth in temples in scenes of theogamy, where he introduces the mystery of the divine wedding. He is also present at the final judgments, where he inspects the heart of the deceased for its honesty and justice and records the result. His close connection with the king has a deeper mythological background: in the quarrel between Horus and Seth he took the side of Horus, whom the king was considered to embody. For this reason an important position among the gods was reserved for him. He was also incorporated into other religious teachings, including the Memphite, in which he was regarded as the tongue of Ptah.

The reasons why Thoth was connected with the moon are not entirely clear. This link may originate in the cult of the falcon god at Sekhem (Greek: Letopolis), today Ausim. The right eye of the falcon god was the sun and the left the moon. At the same time he was called 'Lord of Both Eyes' and 'Eyeless' and took care of the alternation of

>> Depiction of nine seated baboons with different names on the wall of Petosiris's tomb in Tuna al-Gebel.

day and night. His right eye was identified with Horus and his left eye with Thoth. As the god of the moon, from the New Kingdom onward, Thoth was connected with another moon god, Khonsu. Thoth's divine partner was Nehmetawy ('She who protects the robbed') and their son was Hornefer.

Thoth played an important role in the lives of people as well as gods. Apart from the aspects and functions already noted, he was considered a powerful magician and protector. For example, Thoth was invoked for protection against snake bites and scorpion stings. On the nineteenth day of the first month of the season of inundation one of the most important festivals in the calendar was held in honor of Thoth. It was followed by the Mortuary Feast *wag*, and by *tekhy*, the Feast of Intoxication. According to Plutarch, friends would come together on the Feast of Thoth and banquet, eat sweet food like figs and honey, and glorify the goddess Maat.

The cult of Thoth was honored not only in Hermopolis, but also in many temples throughout Egypt, in Heliopolis, Memphis, Abydos, Dendera, Karnak, Edfu, and Philae. Veneration of this god is also attested by burials of ibises in fired clay vessels discovered even in such remote places as the oasis of Bahariya. As has already been mentioned, the high priest of Thoth had the title 'Great One of the Five,' and sometimes also 'Administrator of the Two Thrones,' and then, only from the beginning of the New Kingdom, 'First Prophet of Thoth.' The Greeks identified Thoth with Hermes. He is referred to from the third century as Hermes Trismegistus, that is, Hermes Thrice Great. In the Late Egyptian written sources from the Twenty-second Dynasty, Thoth appears with the title Twice Great, and only in one late document from Tuna al-Gebel as Thrice Great (tripling in Egyptian expressed the superlative, and so meant 'the greatest').

Hermes Trismegistus

Starting in the Late Period a new and important trend developed in Egyptian thought: there was a renaissance of ancient cults and rituals, the transcription and development of old teachings, and a search for knowledge and inspiration in the distant past. The aim was a recovery of national pride at a time when a once powerful land that had dominated the whole ancient Near East was being shaken by the raids of foreign conquerors and taking its humiliation hard. Texts on death and resurrection, like the *Book of the Night*, the *Book of the Transition to Eternity*, and others, were supposed to offer new

inspiration. Fascination with questions about the meaning of life, death, and resurrection, and interest in the cultivation of wisdom, naturally led to an increase in the popularity of the god of knowledge and the lord of the mysteries of rituals, Thoth, to whom the authorship of many writings was attributed. In some, for example the *Book of Thoth*, he was the main character. Unfortunately, only fragments of the book have survived.

In late demotic texts, dialogues appear between Thoth—he who knows—and his pupil—he who wishes to find out. The pantheist idea of *hen kai pan* (that is, God is 'one and all') runs like a thread through the dialogues between Hermes, Asclepius, Amun, and Thoth. In these texts, Thoth progressively initiated his pupil into all the secrets of the divine wisdom, and at the end of the initiation the pupil gives a eulogy to his teacher. It is not quite clear where the initiation took place and how long it took, but when it was over, the pupil would go to give thanks to Thoth in his temple in Hermopolis.

In the multicultural environment of the late Roman world, and with the rise of Christianity, the old cults started to wither and die and the remaining priests tended ever more to a symbolic understanding of their doctrines. It is possible, as David Frankfurter argues, that at this period the Egyptian priests carried on their activities in smaller groups, which met in people's homes, and kept the old cults and mysteries alive. These were conditions favorable to the development of Hermetism, a doctrine that had its focus in the wise Thoth Thrice Great, Hermes Trismegistus, who came to be regarded not just as the founder of philosophy, but also as a mage, the father of astrology and alchemy, and a great teacher also known as 'He who knows the mysteries.'

In the early modern age, scholars considered Hermetism to be the quintessence of Egyptian knowledge and wisdom because we encounter other Egyptian gods like Isis, Horus, Kamutef, and others in the Hermetic writings. Later, the interpretation changed radically; the conventional view in the nineteenth and twentieth centuries was that this Hermetism was a Greek and Hellenistic idea derived from Platonism and merely adorned with Egyptian elements. Following the discovery of Coptic texts in Nag Hammadi in Upper Egypt in 1954, however, the theory of the Egyptian origin of Hermetism was reinstated. Its authors are now considered to have been Hellenized Egyptian priests who disseminated their theological conceptions via the Hermetic texts.

The earliest Hermetic writings (generally termed the Corpus Hermeticum) dealing with religio-philosophical but also astrological, alchemical, and medical questions and referring to Hermes Trismegistus, date right back (according to some scholars) to the very beginning of the Ptolemaic Period, that is, the beginning of the third century BC. They appeared successively—first the astrological texts, and a little later the religio-philosophical ones. Plutarch reported on them first, and Clement of Alexandria mentioned forty-two of them. Among the most famous religio-philosophical Hermetic writings is a set of tracts known in Greek, after the first tract, as Poimandres; Hermes's Speech to Asclepius and others are also important. Some Hermetic writings were known to Saint Augustine, who considered Hermetism and Christianity to be incompatible even though Hermes understood God as the creator.

The Copto-gnostic writings discovered at Nag Hammadi, which contain previously unknown Hermetica, have been of great value for the study and deeper understanding of Hermetic writings. They include the "Account of the Eighth and Ninth Heaven" (Codex from Nag Hammadi IX, Treatise 6), according to which truth and the discernment of God cannot be taught or learned easily because the acquisition of this knowledge required rigorous moral and intellectual qualifications. The seeker must live piously, act in accordance with divine laws, and fear God; only in this way can he raise himself to the Ogdoad, which leads to truth and wisdom. Today the Hermetic texts are the subject of quite extensive international research and there is already a large academic literature on them.

In the view of Czech researcher Radek Chlup, Hermetism was born in the cultured circles of Alexandrian society, which, with the influence of Hellenism, had lost their direct connection to their original religious roots. It was thus a specific product of the cultural conditions in the Roman Empire in an era of emergent cosmopolitanism and the creation of a multicultural society that reacted to these deep social changes in a way other than Christianity. Hermetism differed from gnosis and the gnostic view of the world in being more realistic and positive.

The following extract from the beginning of *A Sacred Discourse of Hermes* shows the Egyptian influences—in this case the Heliopolitan doctrine—and the form into which it was recast.

> *[1] God is the glory of all things, as also are the divine and the divine nature.*
> *God, as well as mind and nature and matter, is the beginning of all*

things that are
since he is wisdom meant to show them forth.
The divine is also a beginning, and it is nature and energy and necessity and completion and renewal.
In the deep there was boundless darkness and water and fine intelligent spirit, all existing by divine power in chaos.
Then a holy light was sent forth, and elements solidified [out of liquid essence].
And all the gods [divide the parts] of germinal nature.
(Copenhaver translation)

Apart from religio-philosophic syncretism, however, yet another current of thought developed in the Egyptian society of the Late Roman period, one that was fascinated by the mysteries of transformation and renewal. The first alchemists appeared, searching for the secrets of minerals, precious stones, and metals, but most of all they were interested in gold. The alchemists of late antiquity, and indeed those of the medieval and early modern ages, were considerably influenced by Egyptian religious ideas; Egypt has rightly been considered the cradle of alchemy. However, earlier modern scholars considered that the Egyptian influence related only to 'technical' alchemy and that 'philosophical' alchemy had its origins in Greece. More recently, the work of Egyptologists examining this issue, particularly the French scholars François Daumas (1915–84) and Philippe Derchain, based on the study of original ancient Egyptian sources such as the demotic papyri or inscriptions from a temple in Dendera, has done much to illuminate the great Egyptian influence on alchemy. After all, the famous third-century alchemist Zosimus, who came from Akhmim in Upper Egypt and gained his alchemical knowledge in Memphis, claimed that the Egyptian priests were guardians of alchemical knowledge. One frequently cited and important written source associated with Hermetism and alchemists is *The Emerald Tablet*, in which we read:

And just as all things proceed from the One
mediated by the One, so all things
are born from this one thing by adaptation.

Its Father is the Sun
and its Mother is the Moon.
The Wind carries it in its belly.

Its nurse is the earth.

It is the father of every miraculous work
in the whole world. Its power is perfect
if it is converted into earth.
Separate the earth from the fire
and the subtle from the gross,
softly and with great prudence.

Ascend from earth to heaven
and descend again from heaven to earth,
and unite together the power
of things superior and inferior.

In this way you will acquire the glory
of the whole world
and all darkness will leave you.
This is the power of all powers,
for it conquers everything subtle
and penetrates everything solid.

Thus is the world created. From this,
and in this way, wonders are made.

For this reason I am called
Hermes Trismegistus, for I possess
the three parts of wisdom of the whole world.

(Roberts, *My Heart My Mother*, 221)

Antinoüs: Tragedy and Glory

Opposite Hermopolis, on the east bank of the Nile close to the modern village of Sheikh Abada, lie the ruins of Antinoopolis, an important archaeological site with origins reaching back to the Early Dynastic period. During the Nineteenth Dynasty, Ramesses II built a temple to Amun and the gods of Heliopolis in Antinoopolis; he used columns and blocks with reliefs (*talatats*) from the demolished monuments in nearby Amarna, which were built by the 'heretic' king Akhenaten. Roughly fourteen centuries later the Roman emperor Hadrian had a beautiful city built here with a temple to Isis and Serapis, an amphitheater, a hippodrome, an arch of triumph, and colonnades. Behind this decision was an unfortunate accident that has made its mark on history.

The emperor Hadrian (117–38) was a great admirer of Greek culture and also liked to travel. While on a visit to Eleusina in western Attica he was initiated into the so-called Eleusinian mysteries, in which he underwent a symbolic death and resurrection leading to spiritual transformation. On another journey in 124, he arrived in Bythinia, where he probably met a beautiful boy named Antinoüs, who was about fourteen years old at the time of their meeting. In 130 Antinoüs accompanied the emperor and his wife, the empress Vibia Sabia, and other courtiers on a journey to Egypt, where the emperor visited, among other sights, the library in Alexandria and the Temple of Serapis in nearby Canopus, which was famous for its therapy using 'curative' dreams.

Hadrian and his entourage then embarked on a voyage along the Nile. Unfortunately, a tragedy occurred at Hermopolis—Antinoüs drowned. In the emperor's biography, the *Scriptores Historiae Augustae,* we read that Hadrian wept for his darling like a woman and the misfortune was surrounded by many rumors. According to some, Antinoüs sacrificed himself for the emperor.

The circumstances of the death of Antinoüs remain obscure. As pointed out by G. Bickerstaffe, it could have been suicide, a voluntary sacrifice, an unfortunate accident, or a game that got out of hand. It cannot be excluded that the young man voluntarily underwent a ritual death, sacrificing himself for the emperor. In that case we can only speculate whether he wanted to secure a good harvest by his death or to restore the health of the ailing Hadrian. Who knows, perhaps Antinoüs wanted to escape a 'pathetic' fate and assure himself of eternal youth and immortality.

After Antinoüs' death his soul became a star and he was proclaimed a god. On 30 October 130 Hadrian founded the city of Antinoopolis, which was subsequently beautified, by Hadrian's order, with grand buildings. It is interesting that the city was founded in the Egyptian month of Khoiak, when all Egyptians were celebrating the mystery of the death and glorious resurrection of Osiris. The emergence of a new god—Osirantinoüs—suggests that the death of Antinoüs was perceived by Egyptian society in an Osirian context. The cult of the new god soon spread from Antinoopolis to nearby Hermopolis, farther still to distant Alexandria, and even outside Egypt.

In Antinoopolis the emperor made another important decision: He ordered the building of a strategic road that became known as the

Via Nova Hadriana. The highway started from Antinoopolis and ran northeast toward the Red Sea. Close to the Red Sea, by the later Roman fortress of Abu Sha'r, it wound to the south, linking up the Egyptian Red Sea ports and ending at the most southerly of them, Berenice, which lies roughly on the same latitude as Aswan (previously only a caravan route connected these two towns).

View of the temple in Luxor at the turn of the 18th–19th century.

5

The Kingdom of Amun

Hundred-gated Thebes

<< 'Proto-Doric' fluted columns are among those to be found in Karnak.

During the Old Kingdom and in the heyday of the pyramid builders, Waset (Greek: Thebes) was just an insignificant provincial town in the fourth Upper Egyptian nome; it was administered from Armant on the east bank of the Nile a little farther south. It only rose to importance with the reunification of Egypt following the political and economic decline of Egypt in the First Intermediate Period. The fourth Upper Egyptian nome played a key role in the reunification, leading an ultimately successful military struggle against its enemies in the northern part of the country, who were headed by rulers from Nennisut (Greek: Herakleopolis Magna). The last kings of the Eleventh Dynasty and founders of the Middle Kingdom ruled an Egypt already reunited but did not abandon their regional seat and continued to reign from Thebes and to eventually be buried there. This pattern was interrupted by the first king of the Twelfth Dynasty, Amenemhet I, who left Thebes and sought to govern the state in an administratively and militarily more effective way by founding a new capital city, Itjtawy, close to the boundary between the southern and northern parts of the country. In the later years of this dynasty, however, political and economic decline set in once more and eventually led to the Second Intermediate Period, when the northern part of the country fell under the foreign rule of the Hyksos. It was once again the rulers of the fourth Upper Egyptian nome who placed themselves at the head of the struggle for reunification—in this case, resistance to the Semitic invaders—and eventually achieved victory.

Reunified, Egypt found itself on the threshold of its greatest era of political and cultural flowering, the New Kingdom, and this time its political center was Thebes, although Memphis was the main administrative and, at certain periods, royal seat of the country. Thebes became not only the political but also the religious center of Egypt, for in the second reunification of the country—as with the first—the Theban rulers achieved victory under the banner of their local god Amun. During the Middle Kingdom Amun had already been merged with Re, the powerful sun god of Heliopolis, in a new form: Amun-Re (Amenre). Amun-Re came to be regarded as the first among the gods, 'The King of the Gods.' When the rulers of the New Kingdom enriched the whole country with the immense booty from their wars of conquest, the greater part of the spoils went into the treasuries of Amun as an expression of thanks. Amun's main temple in Thebes, today Karnak, experienced an unprecedented

Thutmose III kneeling before Amun-Re and making a libation while the king of the gods holds out the symbol of life, the *ankh*, for him to inhale. Detail of decoration on obelisk of Thutmose III in Karnak.

flowering as each king tried to outdo his predecessors in the grandeur of his gifts to Amun, with new buildings or at least new statues or obelisks in the god's honor. In the period of Amun's greatest fame and economic power, at the turn of the Eighteenth Dynasty, the estate of Amun in Thebes boasted 81,322 priests and employees; 421,362 cattle, sheep, goats, and pigs; 591,320 acres of fields; 433

View of the temple of Amun in Karnak from the south. The Great Hypostyle Hall is visible in the background.

gardens; a fleet of eighty-three boats, and much more. Amun's temple in Karnak could glory with all the more reason in the title 'Most Esteemed of Places,' which it had borne since the Twelfth Dynasty. Amun's domain in Thebes consisted of more than just the main temple in Karnak; indeed, the god was venerated in Thebes in a number of other huge temples. On the east bank of the Nile the most important of these was the temple in Luxor, located about two and a half kilometers from Karnak, while on the west bank there were a whole series of what were known as 'temples of millions of years,' built successively by Hatshepsut, Amenhotep III, Sethi I, Ramesses II, Ramesses III, and other kings. The temples were linked

Gebel Barkal during the visit of a Prussian scientific expedition in the 1840s.

together by numerous rituals and important festivals held in honor of Amun.

However imposing, the Theban complex was just part, if the most important part, of the huge spiritual imperium of Amun. As we shall see, temples in honor of Amun, or Amun-Re as the highest state god, were built throughout the country and in conquered territories in Nubia far to the south, and even in some oases in the Western Desert. Only at the end of the New Kingdom did the power of the Egyptian state, and with it the might of Amun, start to decline. Paradoxically, the situation in Nubia was reversed, for as Egyptian central power declined, the local rulers with their seat in Napata consolidated their authority over Nubia, and with it the cult of Amun, which eventually centered on the Temple of Amun at the foot of Gebel Barkal, the 'Pure Mountain,' founded during the Eighteenth Dynasty by Thutmose III. The rulers of Napata even gained control of Egypt in the Late Period and founded the Twenty-fifth Dynasty. They were zealous in their honor for Amun, as is clear from the numerous monuments they built to him in Karnak and many other sites in Egypt. The cult of Amun continued there into the Ptolemaic Period, but by this time the Greeks were identifying Amun with Zeus. Our last record of the active cult of Amun dates from the end of the second century AD.

The King of the Gods

The origins and initial meaning of the cult of the god Amun have been the subject of debate among Egyptologists for a long time. Amun's name in translation means 'Hidden One'; he was therefore an invisible, hidden god. We find him making appearances—rarely—with his divine partner Amaunet in the oldest religious inscriptions from the Old Kingdom: the Pyramid Texts. The German Egyptologist Kurt Sethe believed that Amun was originally a Hermopolitan god whose cult moved farther south to Thebes at the beginning of the Middle Kingdom; this view has not won general acceptance. The French Egyptologist Étienne Marie-Félix Drioton (1889–1961) considered Amun to have started out as a minor god of wind, originally worshiped by Nile boatmen in an area of Middle Egypt. Daumas, by contrast, argued that Amun was the original local god of Thebes. However, one problem with this theory is that our earliest evidence for the cult of Amun in Thebes comes from the mid-Eleventh Dynasty.

Amun, 'The King of the Gods,' who was honored with many other lofty epithets, was most often represented in human form. His body was usually colored blue to signify that he is a god of the sky. He wears a crown adorned with two plumes, and sometimes also (as Amun-Re) a sun disc. He sometimes holds the insignia of kingly power: a crook and whip (flagellum). In addition, he was a god-creator and is therefore sometimes depicted in ithyphallic form as the god Min. In this form he also appears as the continually reborn Kamutef ('Bull of his mother'), that is, he who has impregnated his mother who then gives birth to him. In the Temple of Luxor he appears as Amenemopet ('Amun in the *harim*').

Amun's sacred animal, the earthly incarnation of his *ba,* was a ram with horns curved inward toward his head, embodying the fertility and creative power of the god. A banner bearing a ram's head, called the 'noble staff,' symbolized Amun's *ka,* which was another spiritual aspect of the god sometimes translated as 'double' or 'soul.' Amun's other sacred animal was the goose, indirectly symbolizing the primeval egg from which life originally hatched according to one of the Egyptian creation myths. In the Ptolemaic and Roman Periods the eagle, originally a symbol of the god Zeus, with whom Amun became identified, was yet another animal linked to Amun. In the famous

The ram, symbol of fertility, was Amun's sacred animal. Detail from the ram avenue in the temple precinct of Amun in Karnak.

Temple of the Oracle of Amun in the Siwa Oasis, the god was worshiped in the form of an omphalos (an object of unknown but perhaps oval shape); this was also the case in a Napatan temple in Nubia.

The high priest of Amun did not have a specific title, unlike the Heliopolitan high priest, who was 'the highest of the seers,' or the Memphite high priest, who was 'the highest of the masters of the craftsmen.' He was simply known as 'the first prophet (that is, servant of the god) of Amun.' In the huge Temple of Karnak the high priests of Amun were then designated first, second, and third prophets of Amun, and so on. Queen Hatshepsut had particularly close ties with the priests of Amun and was particularly grateful for their political support; under her rule Amun's first servant acquired the title 'foremost of the gods of Upper and Lower Egypt.' Eventually the high priests of Amun also became military commanders. The high point of their power came in the second half of the Nineteenth Dynasty, when, during the reign of Ramesses IV, the high priest proclaimed himself king, controlling Upper Egypt and Nubia while the pharaoh governed Lower Egypt from his capital in Memphis. Subsequently, during the Third Intermediate Period, the power of the high priest of Amun started to wane.

Priestesses, who worshiped the god and sanctified him with music or ritual dance, took part in the cult of Amun alongside the priests. From the New Kingdom onward priestesses were women of high social standing, women from the royal family and even the king's wife, such as Nefertari, the consort of Ahmose. These royal women came to regard themselves as socially the equals of the kings and—like the kings'—their names were even written in cartouches. They had the title 'Divine Wife of Amun' or 'Divine Adoratrice of Amun,' and were sometimes also called 'The Hand of God,' in reference to the old Heliopolitan myth of the creation of the world by an act of divine masturbation and to Amun as the god of fertility.

Morning Prayer to Amun-Re-Harakhty

Praise to you, Lord of Eternity,
Amun, love-awakening bull,
Lofty might, Lord of Thebes,
Ruler, creator of heaven and earth . . .

When you are in the sky, manifest as a sun disc,
And your beauties shine on the two lands,
Then the gods appear and praise you [literally: they jump around before you in praise].
Mankind is awaking to invoke your beauty;
The animals dance before you on their edge of the desert.
Asians invoking you throw themselves to the ground in mountainous parts.
(Assmann, *Ägyptische Hymnen*)

It is interesting to compare this extract with the *Great Hymn of Praise to Aten* (see chapter 6, "Dazzling Aten").

'The Most Esteemed of Places'

On 27 January 1799 the French soldiers of Napoleon's expeditionary corps, under the command of General Louis Charles Antoine Desaix (1768–1800), were pursuing the Mamluk troops when they came in sight of Karnak and Luxor. They stopped in amazement, so impressed at the ravishing panorama of temple ruins that after a moment they spontaneously burst out in applause and cries of admiration. Today the tourists from all over the world who flood Karnak and Luxor in ever greater numbers feel much the same way, often standing in incredulous wonder at the quantity of superb monuments, or struggling to get their bearings, guidebook in hand, among the avenues of sphinxes, monumental gates, temples, chapels, hypostyle halls, colonnades, colossal statues, obelisks, walls covered with innumerable scenes and inscriptions, and other antiquities. It is all but impossible to take it all in on a single visit, for you can spend weeks just in Karnak, from dawn to dusk every day, always finding something new, inter-

The ruins of the temple of Amun in Karnak, as Denon hastily sketched them on a brief visit.

esting, and beautiful. Neither the passage of thousands of years, nor the Roman emperors who had select monuments removed to adorn Rome or Constantinople, nor the local people with their centuries-old habit of using the local temples as easily accessible quarries for building material, nor the 'archaeologists' who in the first phase of the development of Egyptology ruthlessly pillaged the monuments here on behalf of leading European museums and rich collectors, have dimmed the essential grandeur of the Karnak temple complex. This is not surprising, for Karnak is the greatest ancient temple complex on earth.

Applied to Karnak, the term 'temple complex' probably does not adequately convey the sheer number of monuments concentrated here. The term covers a whole three temple enclosures: the largest is that of Amun, which lies in the middle, with the enclosure of Mut on its south side and the enclosure of Montu on its north side—not to mention the huge Temple of Aten discovered here but as yet little excavated—and many other larger or smaller sacred buildings in its environs. Furthermore, the sacred buildings were surrounded by sec-

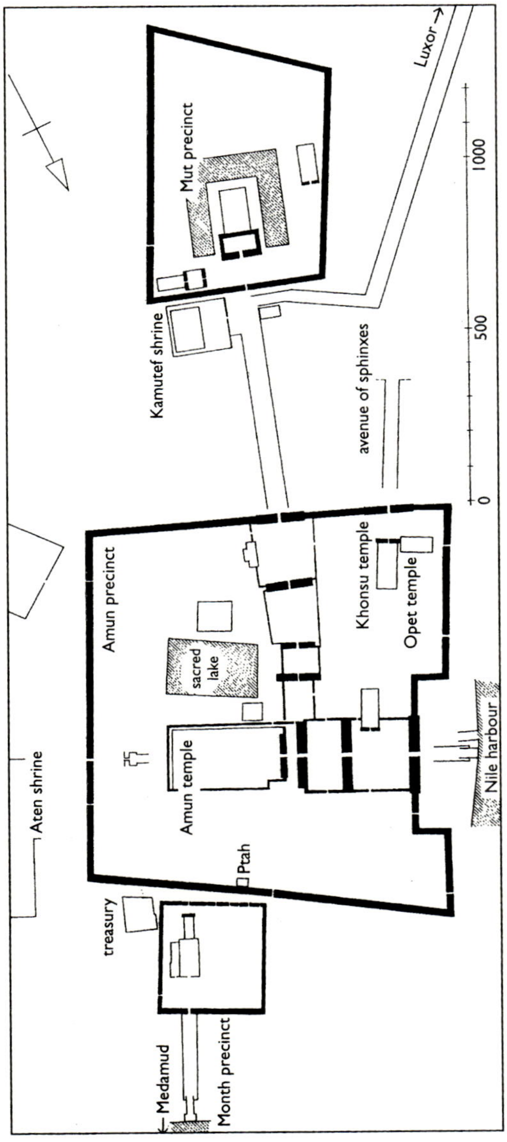

Plan of the three temple precincts in Karnak: Amun's (in the middle), Mut's (bottom), and Montu's (top).

ular structures—workshops, stores, and so forth—which were part of the administrative and economic side of temple life and are mostly still awaiting thorough archaeological research.

In the two hundred years since Egyptologists and archaeologists started their excavations here, the monuments of Karnak have been the subject of many scholarly monographs, smaller studies and articles, and also popular books, which all together would fill a library. Numerous Egyptian and foreign research teams have worked or are still working in the Amun enclosure, undertaking archaeological, epigraphic, documentation, reconstruction, and restoration work. The Centre franco-égyptien pour les études des temples de Karnak, which is dedicated solely to research and restoration of the monuments here, has been in existence since 1967. Its publications, whether specialist studies or major editions of epigraphic and architectural documentation of parts of the Kar-

View of the sacred lake and eastern part of the temple of Amun in Karnak.

nak temple complex, are of a high standard corresponding to the importance of this unique site.

The sheer scale of Karnak and the research conducted here makes it simply impossible to cover all of Karnak, with full descriptions and interpretations of its main monuments, in the few pages available here. Still, we shall do the best we can, presenting a simplified overall view of the Karnak temple complex, including key moments in its architectural development. We have also chosen to focus on a few of the main monuments to highlight their religious and historical importance as well as the events associated with their modern archaeological investigation.

The Temple Precinct of Amun

The temple precinct of Amun lies just a few hundred meters east of the Nile and extends over a site roughly 550 × 480 meters. It was originally connected to the river by a canal and the 'Way of the Rams,' as the ancient Egyptians called it, which is an avenue more than fifty meters in length running between twenty symmetrically arranged pairs of sandstone sphinxes with lion bodies and ram heads—the guardians of entry into the domain of Amun. The Avenue of Sphinxes was originally built by Ramesses II, but later usurped by Pinudjem

The 'Way of the Rams,' the avenue adorned with ram-headed sphinxes leading to Pylon I of the temple of Amun in Karnak.

I. As this and many similar cases show, the ancient Egyptian kings had no great scruples when it came to appropriating the monuments of their predecessors in the cause of their own greater personal glory. Another avenue of sphinxes, about 350 meters long, connected Amun's precinct with Mut's. Surprisingly, there seems not to have been any visible roadway between Amun's precinct and Montu's. North–south in orientation, Montu's temple precinct was accessible from the north via its own avenue, formed of thirty pairs of sphinxes with human heads.

The main entrance to the Temple of Amun is through the first pylon on the approach from the Nile, but to start our account of this very complex monument here (although conventional in tourist guides to Karnak) would be rather misleading. In this historical-archaeological account it is much more appropriate to start from the interior of the temple, from its oldest part, and follow its architectural development, expansion, and the motives behind changes to the building. In this context we need to draw attention to two important facts in advance. First, the temple expanded in two directions: east to west, at right angles to the flow of the Nile and in obedience to the course of the sun across the sky; and north to south as dictated

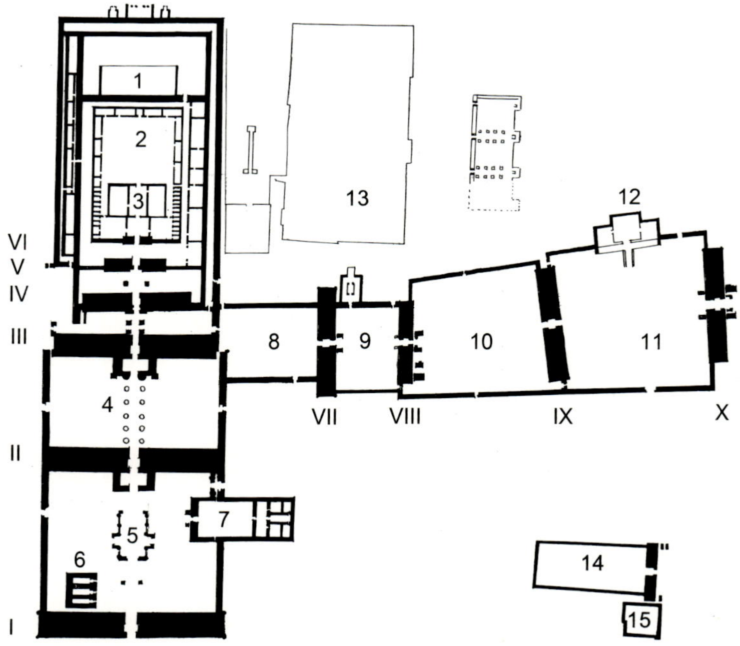

Schematic orientation plan of the principal parts of the temple of Amun in Karnak. The pylons are denoted by Roman numerals and other important buildings by Arabic numerals.
Pylons I–X
Buildings:
1. Akh menu
2. Middle Kingdom court with remains of the temple of Senwosret I
3. hall of the barque
4. Great Hypostyle Hall
5. court with the kiosk of Taharqa in the middle
6. sanctuary of Sethi II, resting place for sacred barques
7. temple of Ramesses III
8. first court
9. second court
10. third court
11. fourth court
12. Jubilee temple of Amenhotep II
13. sacred lake
14. temple of Khonsu
15. temple of Ipet

by the close link between Amun's temple in Karnak and his 'Southern Harim,' his temple in Luxor. Second, the great majority of the buildings in Amun's temple complex are made of sandstone, brought for the most part from quarries in Gebel Silsila in southern Egypt. Only a few smaller buildings—such as the White Chapel and the Red Chapel—and some architectonic elements—such as obelisks and statues—were constructed from other kinds of stone. The building materials originally also included wood and mud bricks, which were used for construction of the enclosure wall, among other things.

Archaeologists have identified the site where the oldest part of the Temple of Amun once stood. It is the open space covered in fine gravel that is today known as the 'court from the Middle Kingdom.' Unfortunately, the site tells us little about the origins of the temple and the circumstances of its foundation. So far our earliest archaeological evidence about Amun's temple in Karnak consists of the roughly 1.5-meter-high shaft of a small octagonal sandstone column that bears a hieroglyphic text from the reign of the Eleventh Dynasty king Intef II Wahankh. It is thought that the temple may have originated in the Old Kingdom, but our earliest architectural-archaeological piece of evidence dates only from the early Middle Kingdom, and this evidence is too slight to allow reliable reconstruction of the appearance of the temple even at that time.

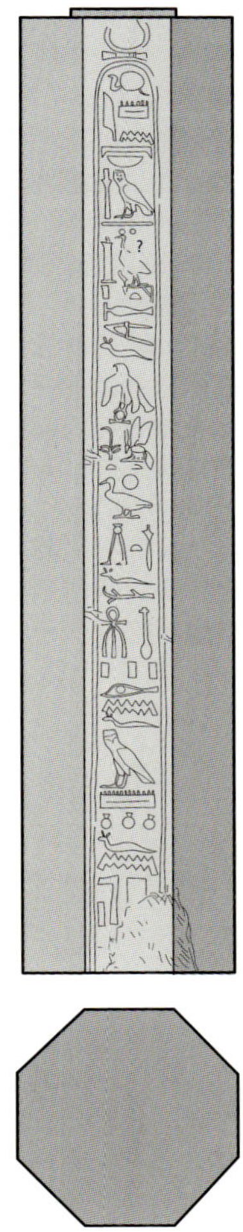

This polygonal column with inscription of the Eleventh Dynasty king Wahankh is our earliest architectural evidence from the temple of Amun in Karnak.

The archaeological exploration of the court thus far suggests that on this site the Twelfth Dynasty king Senwosret I built a temple that was hemmed in on its north, east, and south sides by storage chambers, and enclosed by a mud-brick wall. In the center of the temple stood a naos (a cabinet containing the cult statue of the god Amun) on an alabaster base, and the temple façade was probably adorned with columns that featured royal Osirian (mummiform) statues. This reconstruction of Senwosret I's building is purely hypothetical, however, as is the idea that it was surrounded by a grove and that one particular chapel—or rather a kiosk made of fine white limestone (a favorite building material that for the ancient Egyptians evoked ritual purity)—originally stood in its precincts. We know that this chapel, accessed by a staircase ramp on each side and with a ceiling supported by twenty-four pillars, was built on the occasion of the king's jubilee and served during processions as a temporary resting place for the sacred barque containing the statue of Amun. The walls of the chapel are adorned with inscriptions and scenes in fine low relief; some are historically very important and provide information about the administrative regions of Egypt at that time and their boundaries. This chapel was later dismantled and its components used in construction of the foundations of Pylon III. The French archaeologist and architect Henri Chevrier (1897–1974) found the blocks from the chapel in the damaged pylon and managed to reassemble the monument. As a result, visitors to Karnak can admire it in the Open Air Museum in the northwestern part of Amun's tem-

Senwosret I. Polychromed limestone, Twelfth Dynasty. Luxor Museum.

ple enclosure. Originally the chapel was called 'Extolled Are the Two Crowns of Horus,' but archaeologists have nicknamed it the 'White Chapel.'

There was to be no significant enlargement and development of the Temple of Amun for the next half millennium. This came only at the beginning of the New Kingdom in the Eighteenth Dynasty,

The White Chapel of Senwosret I.

specifically under the reign of Thutmose I, who was a powerful king and one of the greatest Egyptian conquerors of foreign lands. His architect Ineni, also the author of the king's rock tomb in the Valley of the Kings on the opposite bank of the Nile, supervised the building works in Karnak and in an inscription in his own tomb recounts this with pride.

> *I oversaw the grand monuments that he [the king] ordered to be made in Karnak; the construction of a hall equipped with columns, on each side of it the erection of great pylons of limestone from Inu, and by the double gate of the temple the raising of lofty poles of cedar wood with tops covered in white gold; I oversaw the building of . . . covered with white gold; I oversaw the raising of the great gate [called] 'Amun is he that is of mighty power,' the great door of which is made of Asian copper and on it is a picture of Min created from gold; I oversaw the raising of two great obelisks of granite by the double gate of the temple.*
> (Barguet, *Le temple d'Amon-Re à Karnak*, 88)

In other words, in front of the eastern side of the Temple of Amun, the architect Ineni, on the orders of Thutmose I, built the first two sandstone, limestone-faced pylons that are today archaeologically numbered IV and V, and so founded the tract of buildings arranged in an east–west direction in Amun's Karnak enclosure. (It is believed that the older temple dating from the Middle Kingdom was also adorned with pylons.) Ineni erected two tall obelisks of red granite, almost twenty-two meters high, in front of Pylon IV. He then built a limestone columned (hypostyle) hall, originally with a wooden ceiling, in the space between the two pylons, which acquired the name 'Splendid Hall of Papyrus Columns.' Altogether this fulfilled the intention of creating a worthy setting for the king's symbolic reconfirmation in office by the priests of Amun in the hall on the occasion of his jubilee.

The ambitious daughter of Thutmose I and the wife of Thutmose II, Hatshepsut, ignored her underage nephew's claims after her husband's death. Although her nephew was the male heir and future Thutmose III, Hatshepsut took the throne for herself with the help

Queen Hatshepsut burning incense to Amun-Re represented in ithyphallic form. Detail of decoration of the queen's Red Chapel in Karnak.

of the priests of Amun, and decided to provide the Temple of Amun with a new chapel in which the barque of Amun might rest. The material to build it, dark-red quartzite, was brought from the quarries at Gebel Ahmar ('Red Mountain'), far away in the northern part of the country near Heliopolis. The walls of this chapel, built in the space between the original Temple of Amun from the Twelfth Dynasty (still standing at the time) and Pylon V, are decorated with superb, precisely worked scenes and inscriptions in deep relief expressing the queen's loyalty to Amun and also the god's favor to the queen. For example, on the exterior south wall of the chapel there are scenes of a procession on the *opet* festival leaving Karnak for the nearby temple in Luxor, and on the exterior north wall scenes of the return of the procession to the Karnak temple. It is not without interest that in these scenes the queen is depicted not as a woman but as a man. Like the White Chapel, this relatively small but superb building, originally called 'Favorite Place of Amun' and today known as the 'Red Chapel,' was later dismantled and its masonry reused in other buildings (for example Pylon III). The queen's warm relations with the Temple of Amun were further demonstrated by the fact that she had a palace built here, probably north of Pylon IV, where she resided on her visits to the temple.

Like the White Chapel, French archaeologists reassembled the Red Chapel; today it can be admired in the Karnak Open Air Museum. This was not the limit of Hatshepsut's contributions to Karnak. Between Pylons IV and V, on the site of Thutmose I's 'Spendid Hall of Papyrus Columns,' she had two enormous red-granite obelisks erected, over thirty meters tall. Their transport on boats from the quarries of Aswan is depicted on the wall of Hatshepsut's mortuary temple in Deir al-Bahri. South of Pylon IV—and so not on what had hitherto been the main, east–west axis—she had a large new pylon constructed (today Pylon VIII), probably replacing an earlier mud-brick structure. This was intended to mark the southern boundary of Amun's Karnak domain and at the same time to be the main starting point on the route of the processions heading for Amun's temple in Luxor, known as 'Southern Harim.' A large number of statues of Amenhotep I, Thutmose III, and Amenhotep II were set up over the course of time in front of the façade of this pylon.

In the reign of Thutmose III the eastern part of the temple precinct of Amun underwent extensive reconstruction. An older building from the reign of Hatshepsut (Thutmose had already built

>>These red-granite pillars of Thutmose III in the temple of Amun in Karnak are adorned with lilies and papyrus, the symbolic plants of Upper and Lower Egypt.

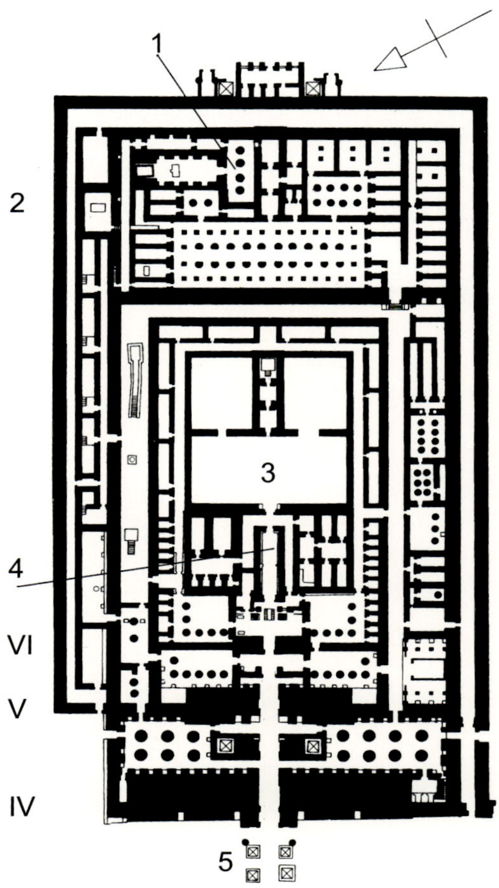

Eastern part of the temple of Amun in Karnak:
1. Botanic Garden
2. Akh menu
3. Temple of Senwosret I
4. Hall of the Barque
5. obelisks of Hatshepsut and Thutmose III
6. pylons VI, V and IV

there before her) was demolished and replaced by a wonderful architectural work called Akh menu ('Blessed through Monuments'), referring to Thutmose III. In the remaining part of the freed space the king put up another limestone pylon (now known as Pylon VI), bearing historical inscriptions of great value to us today with a list of conquered towns (including Megiddo) in Palestine and Syria. The Red Chapel did not escape what seems to have been a policy of obliterating Hatshepsut's monuments; Thutmose III replaced it with one of his own. In the space behind the pylon he had two red-granite pillars set up bearing the floral symbols of Upper and Lower Egypt: the lily and the papyrus. Also to be found here are the first and second 'Hall of the Records,' with inscriptions relating to the Asian

campaigns of Thutmose III. It was here that Tutankhamun later had two colossal reddish sandstone statues set up to express his rejection of the cult of Aten and his return to the worship of Amun; one of them represents Amun and the other Amun's divine partner Amaunet. A further alteration to this cult center packed with monuments was made a thousand years later by the Greek ruler Philip Arrhidaeus when he built a red-granite shrine in which a smaller sacred barque with a cult statue of Amun rested on a base on the

The temple of Akh menu, 'Blessed through Monuments' (referring to the builder Thutmose III), was the cult center of Amun's temple complex in Karnak.

site of Hatshepsut's Red Chapel. The building was a faithful copy of a shrine built by Thutmose III in the same material.

Akh menu copies, to a considerable extent, the older building from the reign of Thutmose I that once stood on the site. It differs from the buildings in the main, east–west tract of the temple complex of Amun at Karnak by having a main axis that runs north-south, that is, at a right angle to the overall axis of the tract. The entrance from the west, close to the southwest corner of Akh menu, was originally adorned by two colossal statues of Thutmose III in the ceremonial dress used at the *sed* festival. The nine rooms arranged in a row along the southern side of Akh menu immediately beyond the entrance were known as the 'workshop of the god's father' and are believed to be where people and the offerings they brought were ritually purified and blessed. The most important part of Akh menu is the 'Festival Hall,' its central section conceived in the shape of a great festival tent supported by two rows of columns with peculiar bell-shaped capitals. A series of pillars surrounds this central section, called 'that which is in the middle,' on all four sides.

According to Paul Barguet, who devoted great efforts to the excavation of the temple precinct of Amun in Karnak, the northern section of Akh menu was solar in character while the southern section was chthonic, that is, associated with the earth and the underworld. In many places, what are now unfortunately only remnants of inscriptions and scenes on the walls show that Akh menu was a place of important and mysterious rituals. The first phase of these rituals took place in the southeastern part of the building, in the Sokar Hall, which had a ceiling supported by polygonal columns. Sokar, a mummiform god of the dead with a falcon head and originally the guardian of the Memphite necropolis, played the chief role in the ceremonies. The ceremonies were held at the New Year, at the beginning of the Nile flood, and involved the mystical union of the king with the sun god Re and the renewal of the king's ruling potency.

Other ceremonies took place in the northeastern section of Akh menu, where some Egyptologists believe that the statues of the kings were ritually brought to life in the setting of burgeoning flora depicted on the walls of one of the smaller columned halls. Today this hall has been nicknamed 'the botanical garden.' We find fauna and flora that were exotic for Egyptians of the time, and which had been encountered by the Egyptian armies during the military campaigns of Thutmose III in western Asia, represented on the walls here. For example, they include faithful depictions of birds (the sea eagle, rock pigeon, and others), flowers (such as chrysanthemums), and fruits (pomegranates and pears), which had previously been unknown to Egyptians; however, there are also depictions of some plants from Arabia and Eritrea. Some scholars believe that the fauna and flora represented were parts of a garden that once existed in the Karnak precinct and may have been situated close to the sacred pool established by Thutmose III on the south side of the Temple of Amun. The French Egyptologists Sydney Aufrère, Jean-Claude Golvin, and Jean-Claude Goyon, co-authors of the major three-volume publication on ancient Egyptian monuments entitled *L'Égypte restituée*—which contains brilliant drawn reconstructions of selected monuments—share this opinion. These experts also believe that beside the botanical garden there may have been an aviary, from which geese,

The polychromed limestone columns with bell-shaped capitals from the Festival Hall in Akh menu are particularly interesting.

Detail from the relief decoration of the Botanical Garden in Akh menu showing birds, plants, and fruits encountered by the Egyptians on Thutmose III's military campaigns into western Asia.

vultures, ibises, and buzzards would have been released at the New Year ceremonies renewing and confirming the power of the king. South of the pool (at the place where benches have now been set up for visitors attending sound-and-light shows) were the dwellings of the priests of Amun.

According to Barguet, Akh menu was where the priests of Amun were initiated into the mysteries of Amun. This is a view shared by Jean-Marie Kruchten, who believes that the rooms immediately behind the entrance, the site of the 'workshop of the god's father,' were where selected priests of Amun were initiated into rituals about which we have fragmentary evidence from a number of inscriptions on stone blocks that were originally parts of buildings close to the procession route between the southwestern edge of Akh menu and Pylon V. According to these inscriptions, known as the "Karnak Records of the Priests of Amun," the initiation ceremony culminated in the mystery of revelation, the meeting with the cult statue

Hatshepsut during the *opet* festival walking behind Amun's sacred barque, which is borne on the shoulders of priests. Detail of decoration of the Red Chapel in Karnak.

of Amun in the shrine, in which according to the ideas of the ancient Egyptians heaven and earth merged into one.

The southern section of Akh menu contained the 'Ancestors Hall.' The names of kings who had shared in the building of the Temple of Amun up to the time of Thutmose III were recorded here on stone panels. The panels with inscriptions, known as the 'King List of Karnak,' and a valuable historical source, were removed from the temple in somewhat dramatic circumstances and are today in the collections of the Louvre in Paris. The French engineer, draftsman, and eccentric archaeologist Achille Constant Théodor Émile Prisse d'Avennes (1807–79) stole the panels. He devastated the hall itself in what was effectively the looting of the tablets. On the other hand, Egyptology is undeniably indebted to him for a great deal of excellent drawn documentation of important Egyptian monuments, some of which no longer exist in the form Prisse d'Avennes recorded. His career is vivid testimony to the conditions that still prevailed in mid-nineteenth-century Egypt and Egyptology. When he discovered the list of kings in Karnak in 1845, he had no scruples about violating the 1835 Egyptian decree on the protection of monuments by secretly removing the list, packing it into chests, and preparing it for export to France. The local governor heard about it, but d'Avennes simply bribed the man, managed to load the chests onto a boat, and with the tacit approval of the French consul convey them to France. The behavior of Prisse d'Avennes was certainly deplorable, but he was convinced that he was saving the monuments from others who might have destroyed them. Despite the decree on the protection of monuments, there was no museum or safe storage space in Egypt and above all there was no real will on the part of state officials to save Egyptian antiquities.

It is believed that statues of the kings named in the list were also placed in the hall of ancestors and that on certain occasions the priests would bring them out on litters in processions. The names on the panels and the statues enabled the old kings to take a symbolic part in the festival ceremonies.

The genius loci of the Festival Hall, its distinctive and powerful spiritual atmosphere, endured for thousands of years. In the Christian period it served as a church and in 1925 the figures of saints on the columns were still easy to make out, although today these paintings have faded almost entirely. Coptic inscriptions have been preserved here too. Like Akh menu, other buildings in the Karnak complex, for example the temples of Khonsu and Ipet, were used for Christian religious purposes in the early Christian period.

Thutmose III had a stone enclosure wall built around the Temple of Amun including Akh menu. East of Akh menu a shrine to Amun-Re built by Hatshepsut adjoined this wall, and had a façade turned to the rising sun. East of this shrine, in the space between the Temple of Amun and the later eastern gate of the precinct of Amun, Ramesses II built a smaller temple called 'Temple of Ramesses beloved by Amun who hears the prayers at the upper gate of the House of Amun.' The building of the temple was overseen by Amun's first servant of god, the high priest Bakenkhonsu, who also had obelisks raised here since this was also a place of worship of the rising sun. Barguet thinks that a cult statue of a specific form of Amun called 'Amun Who Hears the Prayers' was a major feature of this temple, and that people would come here with pleas for intercession and aid.

Thutmose III also turned his attention to the extension of the Temple of Amun's southern tract, where he built Pylon VII and erected two colossal red-granite statues in front of it. He additionally appropriated Pylon VIII, having the name of his predecessor Hatshepsut erased from it; later Sethi I added his name to the pylon.

King Amenhotep III, who proclaimed himself the sun god and adopted the title 'Dazzling Sun Disc of All Lands,' had a passion for luxury and ostentation bordering on megalomania. He was one of the

<< The Colossi of Memnon.

most ambitious monument builders in the history of ancient Egypt, as is clear, for example, from his Temple of Millions of Years on the west bank of the Nile in Thebes. Today, the ruins of this temple—which was comparable to the whole temple complex of Amun in Karnak in terms of the amount of ground it occupied—are dominated by the majestic royal statues known as the Colossi of Memnon.

Amenhotep III entrusted his chief architect, Amenhotep son of Hapu, with the task of building monuments in Karnak to honor the god Amun in a way worthy of the king's greatness and power. These monuments consisted first and foremost of two immense pylons intended to advance and redefine the boundaries of the domain of Amun on both its axial orientations. The new pylon at the western end was at the time the biggest ever built (today Pylon III). For its construction, stones from a total of fifteen earlier, smaller, demolished buildings were used, including the White Chapel of Senwosret I and Hatshepsut's Red Chapel. The new pylon to the south (today designated Pylon X) together with a new entrance gate into Amun's temple precinct was intended to be thirty-five meters high, but the builders failed to finish it during the reign of Amenhotep III. Two royal colossal statues carved from reddish quartzite adorn its façade. Among Amenhotep III's other buildings in the Temple of Amun we should at least mention the large red-granite statue of a sacred scarab, dedicated to the sun god Khepre. The beetle statue on an oval base was placed by the sacred pool, which was fed by water from the Nile by an underground channel and served for ritual purification of the priests. On the base the king is depicted kneeling and making an offering to Aten.

The dramatic reign of Amenhotep III's son Akhenaten, who attempted to abolish the cult of Amun and other gods and introduce the worship of a single deity, Aten, is described in more detail later in this book (see chapter 6). Here we should just note that the temple complex of Amun was not unaffected by the lead-up to this extraordinary reform and its consequences. Akhenaten had a number of temples to Aten built in Karnak in the initial years of his reign, before his final break with the priests of Amun. One of these, Gem pa Aten ('Aten is found'), lay east of Amun's temple. The precise sites of the others, which were called Rudj menu ('Enduring in monuments'), Teni menu ('Exalted in monuments'), and Hut benben ('Mansion of the *benben* stone') are matters of academic controversy. Although its precise layout is still unknown to us, Akhenaten's temple Gem-pa-Aten in Karnak was huge. One important part of it was an open courtyard adorned with statues of Akhenaten and Nefer-

titi in the exaggeratedly expressive early Amarna style. Akhenaten's *sed* festival was a major theme of the decorations of the temple.

The local priesthood could hardly have welcomed Akhenaten's militant building projects in the very center of the cult of Amun. Indeed they may well have been the proverbial last straw, causing patience to be finally abandoned on both sides. As it turned out, however, Akhenaten's new religion did not long outlive its founder and prophet. His successor, Tutankhamun (if we leave aside the rather mysterious Smenkhkare), humbly returned to the worship of Amun and had a colossal statue of the god and his partner Amaunet raised in the Temple of Karnak in the god's honor. Akhenaten's former general Haremheb, who ruled as the last king of the Eighteenth Dynasty, completed the restoration of the old order long afterward. With the brusque forcefulness of a military man, Haremheb had Aten's temples in Karnak demolished and used the materials from them, including Akhenaten's statues, for his own building projects. Haremheb replaced the brick ninth pylon of Amenhotep III with a stone one and expanded the southern tract by completing another (Pylon X). He also started on the building of a new pylon (Pylon II) on the western boundary of the complex. It was planned to be even larger than the pylon built by Amenhotep III (Pylon III), which lay on the same axis behind it. This Pylon (II) was completed by Haremheb's successor Ramesses I.

Not long afterward, an amazing work of architecture was added to the precinct of Amun in Karnak. This was the celebrated Great Hypostyle Hall. Amelia Edwards, the English admirer of Egypt mentioned earlier, offered a view with which few would disagree.

> *How often has it been written, and how often must it be repeated, that the Great Hall at Karnak is the noblest architectural work ever designed and executed by human hands?... The Pyramids are more stupendous. The Colosseum covers more ground. The Parthenon is more beautiful. Yet in nobility of conception, in vastness of detail, in majesty of the highest order, the Hall of Pillars exceeds them every one.* (Edwards, *A Thousand Miles*, 151)

Ramesses I ruled for just two years. His son and successor Sethi I decided to change the large open space—roughly 200 × 100 cubits (around 102 × 53 meters)—between pylons II and III into a huge stone papyrus swamp, regarded by the ancient Egyptians as the symbolic place of the birth of life. The hall was given the name 'Exultant is Sethi Merenptah in the House of Amun,' and today it is known as the Great Hypostyle or Great Columned Hall. The Swiss architect

<< Granite statue of a scarab, the symbol of the morning form of the sun god Khepre. Amenhotep III, represented on the base of the statue under the symbol of the winged sun, is bringing an offering to the sun god.

and archaeologist Gerhard Haeny, on the basis of written records and building analysis, considers that Sethi I conceived it as his Temple of Millions of Years, but it had not been finished when he died, and was thus completed by his son and heir Ramesses II.

<< At the time when the Prussian expedition led by Lepsius visited the temple of Amun in Karnak, the Great Hypostyle Hall looked rather different from today.

The Great Hypostyle Hall is filled with 134 papyrus columns made of sandstone and placed in sixteen rows. These are not monoliths but were assembled from sections (drums). Along the sides of the procession route running east–west through the hall the columns are taller (making this a building of basilica type) and their capitals resemble open bunches of papyrus leaves, while the other columns are lower and have closed capitals. The columns supported lintels on which stone ceiling panels rested; some have shifted as a

The windows in the Great Hypostyle Hall of the temple of Amun in Karnak were carved out of sandstone monoliths.

result of earthquakes. The roof terrace has two levels, corresponding to the two different heights of the columns in the hall. The builders placed slanted stone slabs pierced by a series of narrow apertures between the two levels, which allowed a restricted amount of light into the hall, thereby creating a mysterious twilight in which the statues of the gods that stood here in various places would also have been submerged.

<< View through one of the corridors of the Great Hypostyle Hall in the Temple of Amun in Karnak.

As its architectural design suggests, the Great Hypostyle Hall played an important role in the ceremonies conducted in the Temple of Amun in Karnak. On major festivals, such as the renewal of the king's power at the New Year, a procession of priests bearing Amun's sacred barque would pass through the hall, filling it with the muffled echoes of liturgical chants and prayers glorifying the greatness of the god Amun-Re, who mystically emerged from the papyrus swamp here, started on his work of creation, and delegated his rule over Egypt to the king. Other gods worshiped in Karnak and represented by statues and images on the columns and walls of the hall also symbolically participated in the ceremonies.

The walls of the hall, columns, architraves, and the underside of the ceiling panels—except for the slabs that were pierced to let in light—were covered with polychrome inscriptions and scenes in

The stability of the Karnak temple complex had been threatened by the annual Nile floods for a long time.

sunken relief. These represent Sethi I and his son Ramesses II, who completed the hall, participating in rites and bringing offerings to Amun and other gods. Here we find scenes of the procession with sacred barques, the god of knowledge Thoth depicted with the head of an ibis recording the millions of royal jubilees, the ram god-creator Khnum modeling the royal child on a potter's wheel, Sethi I in the embrace of Amun-Re's ithyphallic form Amun-Re-Kamutef, and much else. The exterior walls of the Great Hypostyle Hall are also covered in decoration. For example, on the northern exterior wall there are historically informative scenes and inscriptions depicting the victories of Sethi I in Palestine and Syria, battles with the Bedouin, the conquest of Yenoam, and other episodes. Documentation and thorough study and publication of the hall and its relief scenes and inscriptions is the purpose of the long-term American Great Hypostyle Project, which is also devoted to conservation research because the decoration is damaged in many places; in some cases even the greatest possible restoration efforts will be unable to save it. The research is bringing us findings that are sometimes surprising, demonstrating how details were subject to secondary alteration and parts of scenes were sometimes even completely reworked.

On the exterior south wall of the Great Hypostyle Hall there are inscriptions and scenes relating to the battle of Qadesh between the Egyptians and Hittites and other military campaigns led by Ramesses II in western Asia. The Battle of Qadesh, which took place in 1286 BC, is also depicted on other monuments erected by Ramesses II, for example, in Abydos, Luxor, and Abu Simbel. Ramesses is always presented as the victor in these images, but the reality was different: In fact, the battle started with a surprise Hittite attack that threw the Egyptian army into disarray and ended inconclusively. This military draw was to open the way to an eventual peace treaty between the Egyptian and Hittite empires in 1270 BC, which defined the empires' respective spheres of interest in the ancient Near East. The treaty was never violated and in practice lapsed only with the fall of the Hittite Empire under the assault of the Sea Peoples around 1200 BC.

In addition to the text of the peace treaty, another important historical document was found among inscriptions in this courtyard. It was carved into the eastern wall to honor the victorious campaign of King Merenptah, son and successor of Ramesses II, in Palestine and Syria. The text is a copy of the so-called Israel Stela—the only ancient Egyptian document to mention Israel. The original stela, now kept in the Egyptian Museum in Cairo, was found in Merenptah's mortuary temple in western Thebes.

In modern times an unfortunate accident in the Great Hypostyle Hall in Karnak eventually led to an important archaeological find. On 3 October 1898 eleven columns in the northern part of the hall collapsed as a result of long-term waterlogging under their bases (the hall's foundations are not in fact very solid). According to James Breasted, an American archaeologist, the problem also arose from the misguided decision of the Egyptian Antiquities Service, run by the French, not to try to prevent water penetrating into the temple precinct during the annual inundations, at which time water buffalo were even wallowing in some parts of the temple. Fortunately, none of the two rows of taller columns in the middle of the hall collapsed. During the subsequent rescue and reconstruction works, led by the French architect and archaeologist Georges Legrain (1865–1917) in the years 1903–1905, a huge quantity of antiquities—the famous Karnak Cachette—was discovered under the paving of the courtyard abutting the Great Hypostyle Hall from the south. In 1883, Auguste Mariette had already found blocks bearing reliefs under the floor here during probes, but the new find exceeded all expectations. An almost incredible number of antiquities of various kinds were uncovered: statues of different sizes and fragments of statues, stelae, vessels, offering tables, obelisks, stone blocks, and architectonic elements from various buildings. Some objects were of stone or wood but the largest number (approximately 17,000) were bronze, among them many votive figurines of the god Osiris.

The cache included almost a hundred royal statues made with different kinds of stone and in various sizes, from the earliest kings of the Early Dynastic Period to the most recent from the Twenty-sixth Dynasty. The kings most often represented were Thutmose III and Akhenaten. There were 330 non-royal statues and eight statues of different gods. The statues of kings and other mortals were in most cases the personal donations of the subjects to the temple, made to honor Amun and in the hope of enjoying his continuing favor. As far as the earliest kings are concerned, however, the finding of their statues in Karnak does not mean that the temple or cult of Amun existed here in their time, for these statues were later donations. There is no reason to suppose that the deposit of the statues of gods in the cache was an expression of dishonor or rejection. Evidently, the temple had become overcrowded with statuary and other objects, and in the reign of Ptolemy III or IV (the period from which the latest antiquities in the cache come) there was a major clean-out. Everything that was obstructing the operation of the cult was simply placed in a trench dug in the floor of the courtyard. It is very possible, indeed probable, that other caches exist in other places in the Karnak temple precincts. This theory is backed by a similar find in the nearby Temple of Amun in Luxor.

It would be erroneous to think that the building of the Great Hypostyle Hall and the reign of Ramesses II was the final act in the golden age of the Temple of Amun in Karnak and in grand building projects there. All the same, political and economic conditions in Egypt started to change and the precinct of Amun was not immune to the consequences. Egyptian imperial vigor was in decline and with it the supply of rich booty, and under Ramesses III, the second king of the Twentieth Dynasty, the Egyptians had to face the great threat posed by the so-called Sea Peoples, who had emerged as if from nowhere, swept away the Hittite Empire, and were now poised to descend upon Egypt. Ramesses III was not unprepared; he went out ahead of his army to forestall the invaders, and managed to throw back the enemy forces and defeat them. It was an achievement that he did not neglect to emphasize in inscriptions and scenes on the walls of his grand Temple of Millions of Years in Medinet Habu, but he turned out to be the last great political figure of the New Kingdom. At the end of the New Kingdom, Egypt was so enfeebled that the government of the country fell apart into two relatively peacefully coexisting parts: the north remained in the hands of the king with his royal seat in Tanis, while the south, in practice, came to be ruled by the high priest of Amun in Karnak. The building activities of the Twenty-first Dynasty kings in Karnak show the mutual respect between the two parts. Sheshonq I (the biblical

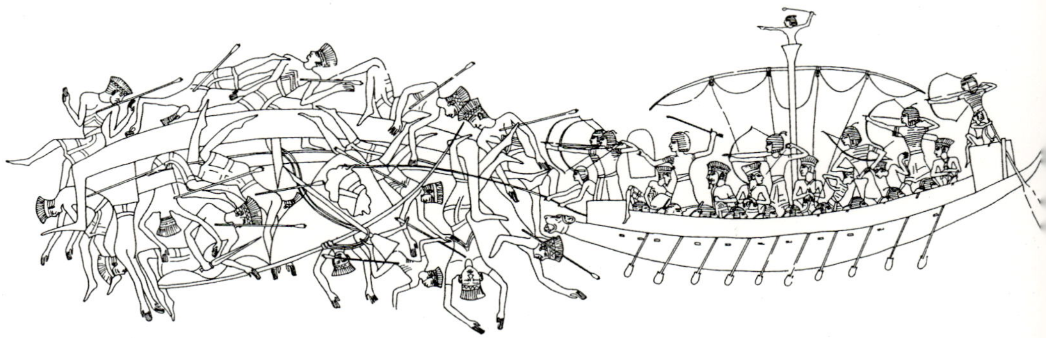

Ramesses III in battle with the Sea Peoples. Detail from relief decoration of the king's mortuary temple in Medinet Habu.

Shishak, 1 Kings 14:25–26), the first king of the Twenty-second Dynasty, resolved to expand the Temple of Amun in a western direction by adding a new courtyard and a new pylon that in size—each tower 113 × 15 meters—would surpass all the preceding pylons in Karnak. The main, and today the only, entrance into the Temple Enclosure of Amun in Karnak is between the towers of this pylon, which is currently designated as Pylon I. As it turned out, Sheshonq I failed to complete the pylon, and a further attempt to do so by the Thirtieth Dynasty king Nakhtnebef I more than six hundred years later likewise failed. Even so, at nearly forty meters high, Pylon I is very impressive.

View of the northern part of the Way of Rams and the unfinished northern tower of Pylon I in the Temple of Amun in Karnak.

<< Colossal statue of Ramesses II. Between his legs stands the much smaller carved representation of his daughter Bentanta.

In the middle of the new courtyard between Pylons I and II, Taharqa, an Ethiopian king of the Twenty-fifth Dynasty, had a kiosk with high papyrus columns erected to serve as a halting place during processions for the sacred barque of Amun. Only one of the kiosk's columns is still standing today; its loneliness and grandeur inspired the German poet Rainer Maria Rilke, who in his poem "In Karnak War's" ('In Karnak It Was') famously imagined this column as holding up "die Ägyptens Nacht" ('the night of Egypt'). The building of Taharqa's kiosk involved the removal of the older avenue of ram-headed sphinxes built under Ramesses II and in Taharqa's time hemming the approach to Pylon II. The displaced sphinxes were then piously arranged along the sides of the courtyard. In front of Pylon II, its façade originally adorned by high wooden poles with banners, there also stood a pair of colossal statues of Ramesses II. Today only one remains, having been repeatedly usurped by later kings. It represents Ramesses II and his daughter Bentanta.

Two earlier buildings also found themselves in the new courtyard. Both were originally intended to be way stations for the sacred barques of the Theban Triad of Amun, Mut, and Khonsu. One is Sethi II's 'Sublime Temple of Millions of Years' with three chapels for the barques of the three gods in the northwestern corner of the courtyard. The other is the Temple of Ramesses III, which runs through the southern side of the courtyard. The courtyard is accessible not only from the west by Pylon I, but also from the south, just beside the Temple of Ramesses III, where a historical text is carved into the gate. The text, "Chronicle of Prince Osorkon," is about the son of the Twenty-second Dynasty king Takelot II; it concerns the prince's successful suppression of a revolt in Thebes in the eleventh year of his father's reign and the measures that the prince later took to benefit the cults of the local divinities and the temple estates.

In the reign of Nakhtnebef I another major building project, in fact the last of the truly grandiose, was undertaken at Karnak. A huge enclosure wall on a trapezoid plan was built around the whole Temple of Amun and several other associated buildings that will be described later. The wall was constructed from mud bricks, as was the custom in similar cases in ancient Egypt. The individual rows of bricks were laid in undulating lines to increase the stability of the wall, which was thirteen meters thick and twenty-five meters high once it was completed. The undulating masonry represented the waves of the primordial waters from which the whole temple complex had symbolically emerged. The wall was connected with Pylon

I on the west and Pylon X on the south and was also equipped with several other gates. The most famous of these is Bab al-Amara, which lies in the southern stretch of the enclosure wall close to the southwestern corner. Processions went out of the Temple of Amun in Karnak through this gate, and then continued first along the avenue of ram-headed sphinxes and then an avenue of sphinxes

The decoration of the gate in the southeastern part of the temple of Amun in Karnak, known in Arabic as the Bab al-Amara, was not completed until the Ptolemaic period.

with human heads to the Luxor temple, Amun's Southern Harim. The gate was at first plain, and only adorned with inscriptions and religious scenes later, in the reigns of Ptolemy III Euergetes and Ptolemy IV Philopator.

For the moment we shall not pass through the gate of Bab al-Amara and take the road to the temple in Luxor, but instead will remain in the Precinct of Amun in Karnak because there is a whole series of other sacred buildings here. We shall mention three, at least briefly: the Temple of Khonsu, the Temple of Ipet, and the Temple of Ptah. One good reason for doing so is that some of their features prefigure the later architectural development of ancient Egyptian temples (see Final Excursus).

The Temple of Khonsu

Khonsu, also known as the 'Wanderer' and depicted as a young god with a sidelock of youth and a sickle moon and full moon on his head, was the son of Amun and Mut. Khonsu represented moonlight and was connected with the underworld in ancient Egyptian theological constructions, while his father Amun in his solar form of Amun-Re represented daylight. Khonsu assisted his father Amun-Re in the latter's regeneration when he sank into the underworld as Amun-Osiris at the end of the day and began the night cycle of his mystical metamorphosis. It is therefore not at all surprising that in Karnak, in the southwestern sector of the Precinct of Amun, Ramesses III should have built a temple to Khonsu, and that this was later altered and embellished in decoration by a whole series of other kings right up to the Roman Caesar Augustus. This series of rulers included the high priests of Amun Herihor and Pinudjem I. Very thorough study of the decoration of the temple shrine—a red-granite cabinet—has shown it was actually made earlier, on the orders of Amenhotep III, and was later usurped by Ramesses II. This gives grounds for thinking that the new temple was built on a site of an earlier, smaller temple to Khonsu.

The temple, which had the full title 'Temple of Khonsu in Thebes Neferhotep' and is sometimes considered the prototype of the later temples of the Ptolemaic and Roman Periods, is roughly north–south in orientation. It was accessible from the south through a propylon built in the reign of Ptolemy III Euergetes. The approach then led along an avenue of ram-headed sphinxes to another pylon, fronted by four poles with banners. This was the entrance to the temple itself, which comprised a courtyard surrounded on three sides by two rows of papyrus columns, beyond it a transverse hall with eight papyrus columns, a hall of the sacred barque, and a hypostyle with four columns. On the floor of the hypostyle stood a relatively small statue of a seated baboon, the sacred animal of the god Thoth with whom Khonsu was sometimes associated. Two smaller halls surrounded the red-granite shrine in the farthest part of the temple,

Khonsu, 'the Wanderer,' son of Amun and Mut, with the symbol of the moon (as sickle and full moon) on his head and the insignia of power, duration, and life in his hands.

the hypostyle and the hall of the barque: one hall contained a single column, the other two columns. East of the barque hall lies the *wabet* ('pure place'), and a flight of steps leading to the roof terrace with a kiosk in which the ritual of 'union with the solar disc' took place at the New Year.

The temple of Khonsu, which is one of the best preserved in Amun's temple district in Karnak, had a major influence on the design of later Ptolemaic temples.

A gray granite statue of Khonsu roughly two and a half meters tall was discovered under the floor of the inner shrine. Tutankhamun gave the statue to the temple and so it bears his likeness; today the statue is on display in the Egyptian Museum in Cairo. The god with his sidelock wears a diadem with a uraeus and his youthful face contrasts with the long ritual beard on his chin. On his chest the god has a heavy gold necklace and in his hands, crossed on his breast, he holds the scepter, flagellum, and *djed* symbol.

The Temple of Khonsu—which is said to be the least visited temple in Karnak today—was originally an important halting place for the procession from Amun's Karnak temple to his *harim* in Luxor, as is witnessed by scenes and inscriptions dating from the reign of Ramesses II in the columned courtyard. The procession would stop here to honor, cense, and glorify the sacred barques bearing receptacles containing the statues of Amun, Mut, and Khonsu. The main barque, Amun's, known as 'Of Extolled Beauty,' was accompanied by the king himself and would be carried on the shoulders of two groups of priests. The group in front wore falcon masks and the group at the back wore jackal masks, representing the 'Souls of Pe' and the 'Souls of Nekhen' respectively, who were mythical royal ancestors from political centers of Lower and Upper Egypt at the dawn of Egyptian history.

The Temple of Ipet

The smaller, but no less important, Temple of Ipet adjoins Khonsu's temple on the west. This goddess, represented as a standing pregnant hippopotamus, was considered not just the protectress of pregnant women and women in childbirth but also as the mother of Osiris; it was in this latter capacity that she played a significant role in the mysteries of his resurrection. Ipet had a cosmic dimension as well: hers was a constellation depicted as a she-hippopotamus with a crocodile on her back, providing Osiris, that is, the constellation of Orion, with protection from the Great Bear constellation, which Egyptians perceived to represent the god of evil Seth.

In 2006, archaeologists carrying out a survey discovered a stone lintel with an inscription dating the original building of the Temple of Ipet to the reign of Thutmose III. This evidently smaller temple was probably entirely renovated in the Late Period, and later in the Ptolemaic Period it was replaced by a new, but never fully completed, temple. In the entrance to the shrine (the preceding two courtyards in the front part of the temple are today very much damaged) stands a pair of columns. The entrance to the shrine is protected by a bronze bolt in the form of a recumbent lioness, which warns that the lioness will claw to death, eat the heart, and drink the blood of anyone who enters with evil intentions.

Two chapels surrounded the shrine containing Ipet's statue—one on each side—as well as dark crypts for the storage of statues and cult objects that were probably used in the Osirian mysteries that took place in the Temple of Ipet. Archaeologists have found a beautiful statue carved from black-green slate in the temple. The statue depicts the goddess in the form of a standing she-hippopotamus with her forefeet resting on the symbols of protection, the *sa* signs; today it is part of the permanent exhibition in the Egyptian Museum in Cairo. We learn that it was called the 'Seat of Power' from an

Statue of the hippopotamus goddess Ipet-Tweret in black-green slate. Egyptian Museum, Cairo.

inscription on a lintel over the entrance into the south-side chapel. There is a beautiful relief scene, on the interior wall of the lintel, of the young falcon god Horus hiding in the papyrus swamp, protected on one side by a she-hippopotamus and on the other by a lioness, both holding knives. There is a depiction, in the north-side chapel, of the famous scene of Osiris lying on a bier and awaking from his deathly swoon, lifting his left leg and right arm. Osiris's underworld residence was under the shrine. A statue of Osiris is depicted on the wall of one of the crypts; according to the inscription the statue is a bronze, life-size figure, which the accompanying text tells us was brought to life and endowed with the power of "ten *ba* of Amun."

Today French–Egyptian archaeological research is underway in the Temple of Ipet. Probes in the courtyard before the entrance to the temple have shown that during the Middle Kingdom this was the site of administrative and economic brick buildings clearly related to the running of the Temple of Amun in Karnak.

The Temple of Ptah

Closely adjoining the north stretch of the massive mud-brick enclosure wall stands the 'Temple of Ptah South of His Wall in Thebes,' a god worshiped primarily in Memphis. The temple, as we learn from an inscription on a large granite stela found in the temple, was built on the site of an earlier brick building from the reign of Thutmose III. Thutmose III gave the temple a cedar gate with Asian copper hinges and donated precious cult instruments, gold and silver vessels, and precious stones for the production and adornment of cult objects, as well as fine cloth. Later, the temple was subject to a series of alterations and renovations. Its front section, with a series of six gates built one after the other by different kings, is particularly badly damaged. A seventh entrance gives access to the shrine, which has a sixteen-sided column in its antechamber. Apart from the Memphite triad a number of other gods were worshiped in the temple, including the deified Imhotep, here designated the son of Ptah, and Amenhotep son of Hapu. Some parts of the temple date from the Ptolemaic Period.

In the innermost part of the temple are three cult rooms with statues of the triad of Memphis. The middle one belongs to Ptah (a seated red-granite statue has survived here, unfortunately without its head), the left room to his consort Sakhmet, and the third to their son Nefertem. The lion statue of the goddess Sakhmet terrified the Arab workmen on the excavations and they called it 'the monster of Karnak.' Arab workers were afraid of the Temple of Ptah from the very

beginning of the excavations, which were initiated here by Georges Legrain in 1900, and were reluctant to work there. They knew the site as the 'tomb of children,' because of an earlier accident there when a landslide buried seven children whose bodies were never found. After the discovery of the statue of Sakhmet the workers thought it was the monster that had eaten the children.

The temple of Ptah in Amun's temple district in Karnak is a monument unjustly neglected by visitors.

In the Late Period, when the cult of Osiris was on the rise, shrines were built to Osiris west of the Temple of Ptah in the northwestern corner of the Karnak precinct of Amun. Osiris was honored here by his various names and in his different forms, such as Osiris Lord of Life or Osiris Wennefer ('Osiris who became perfect'). The high priests of Amun and Adoratrices of Amun were the main initiators of the building of these shrines.

The Temple Precinct of Mut

Mut's temple precinct in Karnak lies south of Amun's; the two are connected by an avenue of sphinxes roughly 350 meters long and starting from Pylon X. Mut ('mother') was Amun's divine partner and the mother of their son Khonsu. She was worshiped as the god of the sky and represented as a woman. Her character was not unambiguous: on the one hand she was the lady of peace, the mild protectress of motherhood and the family, but she also had her aggressive side, expressed by the lioness form and the name Mut-Sakhmet. Although Sakhmet ('The Powerful One') was the divine partner of Ptah, who with Ptah and Nefertem formed what was known as the Triad of Memphis, the ancient Egyptian mind found no contradiction in the hyphenation. Mut's high position among Egyptian gods is also expressed by her title 'Lady of the Two Lands.'

The history of the Temple of Mut, unfortunately very much damaged in the nineteenth century when the site was exploited as a quarry for local buildings, has yet to be fully clarified. Amenhotep III established the temple here on the site of an older building perhaps dating from the Middle Kingdom. In orientation the new temple continued on the axis of the north–south tract of the Precinct of Amun. Amenhotep III donated numerous statues of Mut-Sakhmet to the new temple, dozens of which are currently scattered in various museums and collections throughout the world. Ramesses II, Ramesses III, and other pharaohs, including the Ptolemaic kings, made alterations or additions to the temple.

The temple façade was formed by the two towers of a pylon, with a gate between them leading into a courtyard lined on three sides by a row of pillars. Beyond this open courtyard, as was the custom in Egyptian temples, there was a hypostyle hall and beyond the hall the shrine surrounded on three sides by smaller chambers. There was a large courtyard with a colonnade running through its center from an entrance gate built by Sethi I to the entrance to the temple. The rear section of the temple was surrounded on three sides by a pool in the form of a half-moon called Isheru. The goddess Mut was therefore also entitled 'The Lady of Isheru.' The precise meaning of the word *isheru* is unknown, but we encounter it in connection with a number of other goddesses as well.

As we learn from inscriptions, the Temple of Mut in Karnak was not just the setting for regular ceremonies in which offerings were brought to the goddess, but was also a place where many festivals relating to other gods and goddesses were held. These included, for

Statue of the lion goddess Sakhmet.

Remains of the temple precinct of Mut in Karnak.

example, the feast of the Two Ladies (Nekhbet and Wadjet, the symbolic protectresses of Upper and Lower Egypt), the Feast of Intoxication in honor of the goddess Hathor, and on the first day of the first month, from sunset to daybreak, the feast of the snake goddess Renenutet, protectress of crops. Some festivals were rather peculiar: for example, on the third day of the first month of the season of harvest, known as the 'day of the strengthening of Mut,' an onion was chewed for the goddess.

A small temple, which is currently seriously damaged—built during the Eighteenth Dynasty and restored under Nakhtnebef I—is situated in the northeastern section of the Precinct of Mut. The temple commemorated the birth of Amun's and Mut's son Khonsu, who was worshiped here as Khonsu-pa-khered ('Khonsu the child'). Ramesses III had a smaller temple built to Mut south of the Isheru pool; it included a pylon entrance adorned by two colossal seated statues. The exterior walls of the temple were decorated with scenes of the king's battles in Syria and Libya. In addition to Mut, Amun and Khonsu were also worshiped in the temple.

Under Nakhtnebef I the temple precinct of Mut, like Amun's neighboring precinct, was enclosed by a massive wall constructed from mud bricks and equipped with a pro-pylon, to which Ptolemy II Philadelphus and Ptolemy VII Neos Philopater later contributed decoration. From the north it abutted the enclosure wall of the precinct of the Temple of Kamutef. An avenue of sphinxes led northward from the front of the propylon to Pylon X of Amun's temple in Karnak. Turning off the avenue toward the west was another avenue of sphinxes that connected the temples of Amun in Karnak and Luxor. Since 2001, an excavation and study of the precinct (Mut Temple Project) has been conducted by a team led by Betsy M. Bryan from Johns Hopkins University in collaboration with the American Research Center in Egypt. The team is cleaning and restoring the temples and the sacred pool, and has discovered buildings used in the practical running of temple operations: workshops and a place where food was prepared.

The Temple Precinct of Montu

The temple precinct of Montu is much smaller than that of Mut; it took up less than half as much ground. It lies north of the precinct of Amun and is not connected to it directly by any avenue of sphinxes or similar ceremonial road. However, the Temple of Montu

Temple precinct of Montu in Karnak.

could be reached from the precinct of Amun through a gate in the north stretch of the enclosure wall. The architectural and operational independence of the two temple precincts was a reflection of the fact that Montu was not originally linked with Amun on the religious level.

Montu was among the more important gods of ancient Egypt; it was he who had originally been lord of the Theban region and its first political center, Armant, where there was an associated cult of the white bull Bekh (Greek: Buchis), the earthly incarnation of the *ba* of Montu. It was under the banner of Amun *and* Montu—a warrior god represented in the form of a falcon with a sun disc on its head—that the local rulers managed to reunify the country at the end of the First Intermediate Period. This was an achievement suitably expressed in the favorite name Mentuhotep ('Montu is satisfied'). Together with the goddess Rattawy and her divine child Harpare, Montu formed a divine triad in theological constructions. In other religious speculations Montu was regarded as one of the forms of Amun.

The precinct of Montu was accessible from the north, where there was a quay on a canal connected with the Nile. The remains of several buildings, some of them not yet thoroughly excavated, are to be found both inside and just outside the precinct. The entrance to the precinct was through a propylon that the local Arabs call Bab al-Abd ('The Slave's Gate'). Beyond it was an avenue of sphinxes with human heads leading to the most important building in the precinct, the Temple of Montu, built in the Eighteenth Dynasty during the reign of Amenhotep II on the ruins of an older temple that may have dated from the Middle Kingdom. Later alterations and additions date primarily from the reign of Ramesses II, the Ethiopian king Taharqa, and the Ptolemaic kings. In contrast to the east–west direction of the main tract of the neighboring Temple of Amun, Montu's temple was oriented parallel to the course of the Nile, that is, toward the northeast. In front of the temple, little of which survives except the foundations and the lowest sections of the wall, there was a large so-called forecourt, with four rows of columns, which was built during Taharqa's reign. Beyond this was another courtyard with a row of columns on all four sides (notably, on the south side the row was doubled) and beyond this a smaller columned hall with only four columns. In the innermost part of the temple was the shrine surrounded by smaller chambers. Montu's precinct, like the others, had a sacred pool, which was situated west of the temple.

Adjacent to Montu's temple on the south is the Temple of Maat, the goddess of truth. Interestingly, during the reign of Ramesses IV, it was here that tomb robbers were interrogated and tried, as we know from surviving papyrus records kept in the British Museum in London and published by the British Egyptologist Thomas Eric Peet (1882–1934). A smaller temple to Amun lay west of Montu's temple. Adjoining its eastern side is the Temple of Harpare (with the same orientation), built by Taharqa and originally surrounded by a grove. The temple to this son of Montu is striking for its narrow, elongated ground plan. Access was through a pylon into a courtyard with just a single row of columns along the two longer sides. Beyond this courtyard was a columned hall, also with just two rows of columns, and beyond this the shrine. In the southwestern part of the temple precinct of Montu, along the southern stretch of its mud-brick enclosure wall, a series of chapels to the wives of Amun was built during the Twenty-fifth and Tweny-sixth dynasties. The massive enclosure wall probably dates from the Thirtieth Dynasty, during the reign of Nakhtnebef I.

Amun's Southern Harim

As the name Ipet reseyet ('Southern Harim') suggests, Amun, or Amun-Re's temple in Luxor, had a very specific significance relating to the *opet* festival and the cult of the divine birth of the king resulting from the union of his mother with Amun-Re. The origins of the temple are still obscure. Two blocks from a stone architrave bearing the name of one of the Thirteenth Dynasty kings, Sebekhotep II, suggest that during the Middle Kingdom a shrine dedicated to Amun probably already stood on the site of today's Temple of Amun in

Dominique Vivant Denon's sketch of the ruins of the temple of Amun in Luxor.

Façade of the Luxor temple with pylon, obelisk, and colossal statues of Ramesses II.

Luxor. During the New Kingdom it had to make way for new, bigger buildings worthy of the greatness of Amun. In the northwestern corner of the courtyard stands a small shrine built by Hatshepsut and Thutmose III, which Ramesses II integrated into his design for the courtyard. In the three chambers of the shrine, in front of which is a portico with four red-granite papyrus columns, rested the sacred barques of the Theban Triad: Amun in the middle and Mut and Khonsu at the sides.

The most extensive reconstruction of the original shrine took place under Amenhotep III. Amenhotep son of Hapu was the supreme director of all building works in the reign of Amenhotep III and an exceptional figure of the period, but the project of the Luxor temple was entrusted to twins, the architects Hor and Suty. The eventual result was a large sandstone temple of elegant proportions. Its northeast–southwest orienation follows the direction of the flow of the Nile, which runs close to the temple. The temple itself was built first, on a slightly elevated site accessible by a ramp; an open columned court was later added in front of the temple, and finally an entrance colonnade.

The entrance colonnade consists of seven pairs of columns, each around sixteen meters tall with open papyrus capitals. The columns, which bear relief decoration and are composed of separate sections, supported the massive blocks of the architrave on which stone ceiling panels originally rested. In the reigns of Tutankhamun and later Haremheb, walls with relief decoration were built on both sides of the colonnade, closing off the colonnade and turning it into a courtyard in its own right. Other alterations and additions to the decoration of this part of the temple were made in the reigns of Sethi I, Merenptah, and Sethi II. The western wall of the courtyard colonnade is decorated with superb scenes of the *opet* festival, including a procession of priests bearing the sacred barques containing the statues of the gods. In these processions we also see soldiers, musicians (drummers, flute players, Nubians with resonating poles, and women with sistra), and men leading the ornamented, fattened sacrificial bulls. The entrance colonnade issues through a massive gate into a columned court built on a slightly rectangular ground plan. Two rows of papyrus columns run on three sides of the court (east, north, and west), but this time they are stemmed in design and with closed papyrus bud capitals. These columns also support the architrave on which the now-lost ceiling blocks once reposed. On festival occasions, the public could come as far as this court, but only priests were permitted farther into the temple.

In 1989 an exceptionally important archaeological discovery was made in the columned court of Amenhotep III in the Luxor temple. The columns on the western side of the court had started to lean, and so the Egyptian Antiquities Organization (predecessor of the Supreme Council for Antiquities) decided to have their bases reinforced. Probes in the paving of the court led to a surprising discovery of statues. This find, not unlike the already noted discovery in Karnak at the beginning of the last century, has entered the history of Egyptian archaeology as the 'Luxor Cachette.' The statues were in different kinds of stone and in a surprisingly good state. They dated from the period roughly from the mid-Eighteenth Dynasty to the Ptolemaic era and represented various kings and gods. They were placed in a separate gallery of the Luxor Museum after being excavated, cleaned, and restored. The 'statue of a statue' of Amenhotep III, made of reddish quartzite, is considered the most beautiful and typologically the most interesting. It represents a statue of the king with one leg placed slightly forward, standing on the drag sleds that are to transport it to its destination, which was undoubtedly the temple in Luxor. The

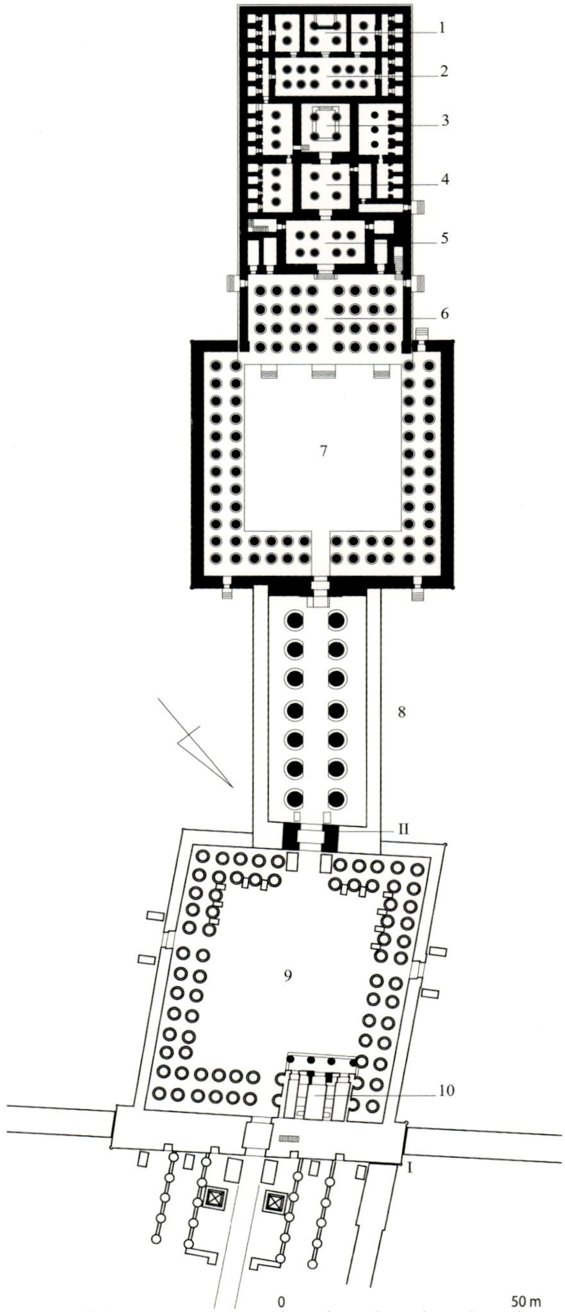

Plan of the temple of Amun in Luxor
1. sanctuary
2. transverse hall
3. hall of the barque
4. second antechamber
5. first antechamber
6. hypostyle hall
7. court of Amenhotep III
8. colonnade of Amenhotep III
9. court of Ramesses II
10. shrine—resting place of the sacred barques

Hypostyle hall of Amenhotep III in the temple of Amun in Luxor.

king statue is dressed in a short tunic and represented with a double crown, that is, a conjoined Upper and Lower Egyptian crown, on his head. Imprints show that the statue was originally adorned with gold leaf on a wide necklet and bracelets. The statues were buried for the same reason those included in the Karnak Cachette were: in the Ptolemaic Period the temple was crammed, and during a clear-out the superfluous statues were simply tidied away without respect to ancestors or gods and buried under the floor of the courtyard.

From the open, sun-drenched courtyard the way led into the temple interior, into a hypostyle hall sunk for most of the day in shadow. The ceiling was supported by thirty- two columns of the same type as in the courtyard, arranged in four rows of eight. The walls of the hall are adorned with relief scenes of Amenhotep III bringing offerings to Amun and his divine partner Amaunet and other gods, as well as depictions of Nile gods offering gifts, and so on. The god Amun, or Amun-Re, is represented in the Luxor temple in two anthopomorphic forms: either as the ruler of the sky with the characteristic tall crown of plumes and body painted blue, or as an

Quartzite 'statue of a statue' of Amenhotep III on a drag sled. Luxor Museum.

ithyphallic creator. Two smaller columned antechambers were beyond the large hypostyle hall, the first with eight columns and the second with four. Chapels to Khonsu (on the west) and Mut (on the east), from which there was access by a staircase to the roof terrace, were situated along the sides of the first antechamber. There are scenes on the walls of the first antechamber that show the king making offerings to Amun, kneeling before the god, and so on. Major alterations were made to the first antechamber in the fourth century AD: the columns were removed and the antechamber was turned into a Christian church with an apse on the southern side. The original relief decoration was masked by stucco bearing wall paintings with Christian motifs. The walls of the second antechamber are decorated with relief scenes, such as one with Amun embracing the king and giving him a symbol of life, the king during the ceremony of 'driving out the four calves,' the king offering a necklace to the god and burning incense for him, and so on.

From the cult point of view, one of the most important places in the temple, which Egyptologists call the 'Birth Hall,' lies east of the second antechamber but is only accessible from the following, intimate part of the temple. Three columns support the hall's ceiling and its western wall is adorned with scenes of theogamy, the divine marriage and resulting birth of Amenhotep III, which infused the temple with its specific meaning. Here we see the parents of Amenhotep III, King Thutmose IV, and Queen Mutemwia in the presence of the gods. Thoth, the god of wisdom, brings Amun, who has taken on the appearance of Thutmose IV, into the queen's private chamber. There, the culminating scene takes place: The goddesses Neith and Selket hold up the sky, on which the queen sits opposite Amun; the two hold hands and Amun declares that the child born from this union will be called Amenhotep. At the same time, Amun is instructing the god Khnum to create the child and his *ka,* by forming them on a potter's wheel. The queen is then led to another chamber where, with the assistance of a goddess, she gives birth to the child, which the goddess then weans and presents to Amun. The scenes end with the presentation of the already adult Amenhotep, whom the gods bless.

The temple's most intimate part, from which the Birth Hall is entered, consists of the barque's shrine and the hall containing the holy of holies at the very southernmost point in the temple. Small columned chapels surround the barque's shrine, the columned antechamber, and the holy of holies. The barque's shrine acquired

>> Amun in the role of god-creator was worshiped in ithyphallic form. Detail of the decoration of the White Chapel in Karnak.

This scene of Amenhotep III's divine birth was badly damaged, probably in the early Christian Period when part of the Luxor temple was converted into a church.

its present form as late as the reign of Alexander the Great; Alexander is represented here offering Amun his high-plumed crown, diadem, eye cosmetic, scented grease, wine, milk, fabrics, and so on. The walls of the following transverse hall with twelve columns arranged in two rows of six are adorned with relief scenes of Amenhotep III bringing Amun various sacrificial gifts. In the holy of holies,

by its southern wall, there originally stood a colossal statue of Amun, which was the main cult statue in the temple. Unfortunately, nothing survives of it but a fragment of the base. Amun is depicted, in the relief scenes decorating this hall, sitting by the sacred *ished* tree and recording the name of Amenhotep on its leaves; the king is seen elsewhere performing the 'opening of the mouth' ceremony.

Extensive changes to the building were made in the reign of Rameses II. In front of the columned court of Amenhotep III a new, even bigger columned court, approximately 57 × 51 meters, was added. Its façade was adorned by a pylon that was twenty-four meters high and sixty-five meters wide with a new entrance. The court, 'The Shrine of Ramesses Meriamun United with Eternity,' has a rhomboidal ground plan. This was necessary to ensure that its long axis carried on without deviation from the Avenue of Sphinxes that connected the temple in Luxor with Amun's temple in Karnak. The sphinxes with human heads, which can be seen today, date from the Thirtieth Dynasty, the reign of Nakhtnebef I, when they replaced older ram-headed sphinxes. Two rows of columns—seventy-four

The procession route from the temple of Amun in Luxor to his temple in Karnak was lined by a long avenue of sphinxes.

papyrus columns with closed capitals—run around all four sides of the court. Ramesses II had colossal statues of himself erected between the columns. Colossi of Ramesses II approximately seven meters tall and carved from red granite (one is in black granite) have survived on the southern side of the court. On the walls of the courtyard there are relief scenes showing captive enemies, Ramesses offering sacrifices to various gods, and also an interesting depiction of the temple pylon with colossal statues, obelisks, and waving banners on poles in front of it. On the exterior side of the western wall of the court there are relief scenes of Ramesses II's military campaign into Syro-Palestine, the attack on the fortress of Dapur, the leading of captives to Amun, and the like. The scenes on the court's southwestern exterior corner also include an interesting detail from an environment very different from that of Egypt: a bear attacking a man in a cedar wood.

Today the attention of a visitor to the columned court of Ramesses II is caught by a very unusual sight: on the east wing of the court, close to the entrance pylon, stands the mosque of Sheikh Abu

The mosque of Abu al-Haggag in the northeastern corner of the columned courtyard of Ramesses II shows the height to which the temple of Amun in Luxor had been buried in rubble and sand at the time when the mosque was built.

al-Haggag, built in the nineteenth century when the court was buried in sand and rubble right up to that level. In fact, the minaret is a great deal older than the mosque; it dates from the eleventh century and was erected to commemorate a victory over the Nubians. Every year on the fourteenth of Shaaban by the Muslim calendar a great festival *(mulid)* is held in Luxor to mark the sheikh's birthday; it involves a barque carried in a procession to the mosque. The feast is a clear echo of the ancient *opet* festival during which the barque of Amun, accompanied by the barques of Mut annd Khonsu, was borne in procession from Karnak to Luxor.

The northern face of the pylon is adorned with relief scenes of Ramesses II's battle with the Hittites at Qadesh: the Egyptian military camp, the king attacking in a war chariot, and so on, including an inscription with a poem glorifying the king's victory. In front of the pylon, which is decorated on its upper edge by a concave cornice, a pair of wooden poles with banners originally stood on each side of the entrance; today all that remains of them are empty niches in the façade. Six colossal statues of Ramesses II, arranged symmetrically on both sides, adorned the entrance. The statue closest to the entrance on each side was seated, with two standing statues beside it. The façade was further adorned by two red-granite obelisks, which the Egyptian regent Muhammad 'Ali gave to France in 1829. Seven years later, in 1836, the obelisk was installed in the Place de la Concorde. Fortunately, the French only managed to take one of them away, the western obelisk. In the 1990s, the French president François Mitterand officially renounced any claim to the second donated obelisk.

The temple gradually declined after the New Kingdom, although building alterations were carried out sporadically, for example, in the Twenty-fifth Dynasty during the reigns of the Ethiopian kings. The last significant Egyptian king, Nakhtnebef I of the Thirtieth Dynasty, had a massive mud-brick enclosure wall built around the temple in Luxor like the wall he had built around the three great temple precincts in Karnak. As we have noted, the barque's shrine in the innermost part of the temple was renovated during the reign of Alexander the Great. In the Roman era, the Temple of Luxor found itself in the middle of a large fortified camp, which became the military and political center of Thebes. The plural of the Arabicized form of the Latin word for camp, *castrum* (singular: *al-qasr*, plural: *al-uqsur*), later gave the place its modern name—Luxor. The enclosure wall of the Roman fortress partly replaced Nakhtnebef's wall, and all that survives of the latter is the northern section in front of the temple entrance. Massive bastions reinforced the wall of the Roman fortress, with gates on all four sides, at roughly twenty-five-meter intervals. In front of the temple, in the northwestern part of Nakht-nebef's courtyard, a Temple of Serapis was built; at the beginning of the Christian period a church was erected in the middle of the court. The centuries that followed brought the Temple of Luxor into oblivion under the ever-deepening drifts of sand.

Abu Simbel

Ramesses the Great

The Nineteenth Dynasty king Ramesses ('Re gave birth to him'), whose family name was Meriamun ('Loved by Amun'), and who took the throne name Wesermaatre Setepenre ('Powerful-is-the-Truth-of-Re Chosen-by-Re')—that is, Ramesses II, later known as 'the Great'—was one of the most powerful and longest-ruling Egyptian kings; he remained on the throne for six and a half decades. In the later tradition he was also one of the most celebrated, although he did not come from the famous royal line of the Thutmoses and Amenhoteps of the preceding Eighteenth Dynasty. Ramesses's line came from Hatweret (Greek: Avaris) in the Eastern Nile Delta; it was there that Ramesses II decided to build his royal city and the new metropolis of Egypt, Per Ramesse ('House of Ramesses'), in the pronunciation of the time 'Piramesse,' the biblical 'City of Ramesses.' His grandfather, the soldier and vizier Paramessu, ascended the throne of the pharaohs after the death of Haremheb—the last king of the Eighteenth Dynasty—and took the name Ramesses. Seth, the god of evil and war, was worshiped in Ramesses I's native region, and so as founder of the new dynasty he honored Seth and regarded him as the 'father of his fathers.' The cult of Seth was widespread in the eastern Delta and had a long tradition that can be documented as far back as the Old Kingdom. It is therefore no surprise that the father of Ramesses II, Sethi I, was the first Egyptian king to adopt the name Seth. Ramesses II had a granite stela raised in Hatweret as one way of glorifying the origin of his dynasty and legitimizing his claim to the throne; the king is depicted in its upper arched niche offering wine in two small vessels to the god Seth. In this depiction the god looks more like the Semitic god Baal with a few Egyptian characteristics; we can conclude that this was the local form of Seth of Hatweret. There is a text beneath the scene (the lower part of the stela is missing) presenting the king's order to raise the stela, information on the king's ancestors, and also a specific date: "Fourth day of the fourth month of the season of inundation in the year 400." The date—which has given the stela its Egyptological name, Stela of Four Hundred Years—as well as the entire text, continue to be the subject of scholarly debate. According to an earlier interpretation, the four hundred years is a reference to the period that had elapsed from the beginning of Hyksos supremacy (the Hyksos were worshipers of Seth), but now the prevailing view is that it refers to the period since the founding of the Temple of Seth in Hatweret. The stela was not actually discovered in Hatweret–Piramesse, but in nearby Tanis, where it had been moved in the Twenty-first Dynasty. Mariette found it in Tanis but then it disappeared and was, luckily, eventually rediscovered by

Torso of fallen colossal seated statue of Ramesses II in the Ramesseum, the king's mortuary temple in Western Thebes. The statue was originally about seventeen and a half meters tall and weighed about a thousand tons.

Pierre Montet in 1932. Today the stela is in the Egyptian Museum in Cairo.

Ramesses II not only inherited the warlike tendencies of his ancestors, but also proved to be a systematic administrator of the country, a resolute politician, and a skillful diplomat. His father Sethi I raised him to be a soldier: he made Ramesses II commander of the Egyptian army when he was only ten years old, and named him co-regent at the age of sixteen. In internal politics Ramesses II concentrated on the economic development of the country and the efficient running of government. His honor for Seth did not prejudice his basic religious orientation to the cult of the three most important Egyptian gods of the time (Re, Amun, and Ptah). He was therefore able to skillfully balance what had previously been the dominant cult of Amun. Nor did he forget his own relationship to godhood: as the third ruler of the New Kingdom, after Hatshepsut and Amenhotep III, Ramesses II had his divine conception depicted in a chapel dedicated to the king's mother in the Ramesseum, his Temple of Millions of Years in western Thebes. He was thorough in his self-deification and identification with the chief gods of the country. In foreign policy his attention and military plans were directed to the east, western Asia in particular.

Heaps of slaughtered enemy cavalry during the conquest of the Asian fortress of Dapur. Detail from the relief decoration of the Ramesseum.

Ramesses II undertook a military campaign, in the fifth year of his reign, which intended to consolidate the Egyptian position in Syro-Palestine, where the interests of Egypt contended with the those of the Hittite Empire. He set out with a large army, but acted very rashly and underestimated the value of intelligence. He prematurely pitched camp west of the enemy fortress of Qadesh (known today as Tell Nabi Mend) on the river Orontes without waiting for all the Egyptian forces—under the standard of the gods Amun, Re, Ptah, and Seth—to arrive. A surprise Hittite attack from the east, across the river, threw the Egyptians into confusion. Defeat and even the capture of the king seemed inevitable, but at the last minute the wheel of fortune turned unexpectedly and the undisciplined Hittites, busy looting the Egyptian camp, were surprised in turn by an elite Egyptian auxiliary formation, which approached the camp quickly from the coast west of the troops. The Hittite army found itself in danger of encirclement and hastily retreated. Ultimately, the battle ended in a draw, but this did not prevent both sides from considering it a victory. In the following years the position of the Hittites in western Asia became more difficult to sustain, and finally, more than fifteen years after the Battle of Qadesh, they started to discreetly negotiate a long-term peace agreement with the Egyptians. The treaty established a commitment of mutual non-agression, provisions for mutual aid in the event of an attack from outside or a domestic revolt, and the handing over of fugitives; it was finally concluded in the twenty-first year of the reign of Ramesses II. It was the first important document of its kind in history. A copy of its text is carved into one of the walls of the Temple of Amun in Karnak. The following is an extract from J.H. Breasted's English translation of the treaty.

The good treaty of peace and of brotherhood, setting peace [between them (?)], forever.
Now, at the beginning, since eternity, the relations of the great ruler of Egypt with the great chief of Kheta were (such) that the god prevented hostilities between them, by treaty. Whereas, in the time of Metella, the great chief of Kheta, my brother, he fought w[ith Ramses II], the great ruler of Egypt, yet afterward, beginning with this day, behold, Khetasar, the great chief of Kheta, is [in] a treaty relation for establishing the relations which Re made, and which Seth made, for the land of Egypt, with the land of Kheta, in order not to permit hostilities to arise between them, forever.

Behold then, Khetasar, the great chief of Kheta, is in treaty relation with Usermare-Setepnere (Ramses II), the great ruler of Egypt, beginning with this day, in order to bring about good peace and good brotherhood between us forever, while he is in brotherhood with me, he is in peace with me; and I am in brotherhood with him, and I am in peace with him, forever...

The children of the children of the great chief of Kheta shall be in brotherhood and peace with the children of the children of Ramses-Meriamun, the great ruler of Egypt, being in our relations of brotherhood and our relations [of peace], that the [land of Egypt] may be with the land of Kheta in peace and brotherhood like ourselves, forever. There shall be no hostilities between them, forever. The great chief of Kheta shall not pass over into the land of Egypt, forever, to take anything therefrom. Ramses-Meriamun, the great ruler of Egypt, shall not pass over into the land of Kheta, [to take anything] therefrom, forever.
(Breasted, *Ancient Records of Egypt* 3, 167–68 §§ 374–76)

The king was also very active in his private life, as is evident from his extensive harem and more than a hundred children. Two of the royal wives and concubines enjoyed exceptional standing as the 'Great Royal Wife': Nefertari and Esetnofret. Nefertari bore the king his first son, Amenherwenemef, whose name Ramesses II later changed to Amenherkhepeshef and whom he designated as his heir; however, this crown prince probably died before the twentieth year of the king's reign, and around the twenty-fifth year so too did Nefertari. Esetnofret then became the king's chief wife. She bore the king several children, among them the celebrated sage Khamwaset, the later successor to the king Merenptah (his thirteenth son), and also the princess Bentanta. After the death of Esetnofret, Ramesses II married Bentanta and had other children. We should point out that the ancient Egyptians did not consider such a relationship incest, but thought it wholly legitimate (in harmony with their myths about the creation of the world and foundation of the kingdom of Egypt) and even a desirable way of maintaining the 'purity' of the royal blood.

One of the many superlatives associated with the name of Ramesses II is that he was also the greatest builder of monuments in the history of Egypt; his grandiose buildings in Memphis, Abydos, Thebes, and many other places are eloquent testimony to this.

Nefertari, the great royal wife of Ramesses II. Detail from the decoration of the queen's tomb in the Valley of Queens.

He was probably also the greatest usurper of other monarchs' monuments: in the case of many earlier monuments, Ramesses simply had the names of their owners and his predecessors removed from the inscriptions and replaced with his own.

The Great and Small Temples in Abu Simbel

Members of the Prussian scientific expedition led by Lepsius saw the façade of the Great Temple in Abu Simbel in the early 1840s when it was still partly buried in sand.

Ramesses II did not neglect the southern reaches of the Egyptian empire, as can be seen from his extensive building program in Nubia. Rock temples (more accurately, semi-rock temples, known in Greek as *hemispeos*) were built on the king's orders in Beit al-Wali, Wadi al-Sebua, Derr, and Gerf Hussein. The best known, however, are the two that stood not far from the Second Nile Cataract on the west bank of the Nile in a place called Meha, which is known today as Abu Simbel. The choice of location was no accident, since the Second Cataract was at the time a kind of southern gate into Egypt, beyond which lay Lower Nubia, already fully colonized by Egyptians. The mere sight of the royal colossi in front of the Great Temple undoubtedly conveyed the greatness of the king, but also the might of Egypt, to people sailing up from the south. An older cult of the god Horus already existed in Abu Simbel, as well as two prominent sandstone hills in the sandy plain, which thus made it a convenient place for

Façade of the Great Temple in Abu Simbel after it was relocated to a new site on the bank of the Aswan Reservoir.

building two temples. The king decided to build the two temples after his accession to the throne. The larger temple was intended as the commemorative Temple of Ramesses II in Nubia, his "Mansion of Millions of Years Hewn in the Rock" (to quote the words of the First King's Cupbearer Ashahebsed, one of the dignitaries involved in the building of the temple), while the smaller temple was intended for the deified royal wife Nefertari and her cult in Nubia. As the local rock inscriptions inform us, the viceroy of Nubia, Iuny, was entrusted with the building works in Abu Simbel, and after him the next Nubian regent, Heqanakht.

The two temples, today known as the Great and Small Temples in Abu Simbel, were the greatest expressions of Ramesses II's efforts to build up Egyptian power in Nubia. They were completed in basic form and consecrated in the twenty-fourth year of the king's reign. Notably, the closing ceremonies may well have taken place in a troubled atmosphere, or at least this is the view of the English archaeologist Kenneth A. Kitchen, an outstanding expert on written records relating to Ramesses II and the late New Kingdom and Third Intermediate Periods. Kitchen bases his conclusions on scenes and texts on a stela that the viceroy Heqanakht had carved into a rock close to the Great Temple. The chief gods of the Great Temple—Amun, Re, and the deified Ramesses II—are represented on the stela as being honored by the king, who is accompanied by his daughter, the princess Meretamun. Beneath this scene is another, in which Heqanakht brings offerings to Queen Nefertari. Kitchen thinks it possible that Nefertari was already seriously ill and could not attend the consecrating ceremonies, thus explaining why Meretamun stood in for her. After the return of the king and his entourage from Nubia, all reports of Nefertari cease.

It is almost incredible to think that the Great Temple in Abu Simbel, the biggest Egyptian rock temple ever constructed, completely disappeared for many centuries, lost under drifts of sand. It was only rediscovered at the beginning of the nineteenth century, in March

The frieze on the upper edge of the façade of the Great Temple in Abu Simbel is adorned by a row of baboons worshipping the rising sun.

Giovanni Battista Belzoni.

1813, when Johann Ludwig Burkhardt (1784–1817), a Swiss traveler and Arabist known among the Arabs as Sheikh Ibrahim, was passing through Abu Simbel. Burkhardt decided to stay for a few days and take a closer look at the place. At the time Abu Simbel (the place was originally called Mekka in Arabic, and acquired its present name, probably a distortion of 'Istanbul,' from Turkish administrators in the nineteenth century), was a sleepy, forgotten corner of the Ottoman Empire, where the conditions were very tough. The local people were exposed not only to the occasional raids of robber Bedouin tribes from the Western Desert, but also to the arbitrary behavior of the Turkish administrators, who themselves occasionally made profits by attacking caravans. As Burkhardt recorded, the people took refuge in the Small Temple, which was the only one known and accessible at the time, when the Bedouin launched raids.

Walking over the rocky hillocks, Burkhardt noticed part of a frieze of baboons sticking a little way out of the sand high on a slope south of the Small Temple. Soon he also managed to uncover part of the head of a colossal statue. He had stumbled on the Great Temple, its façade almost totally buried in a sand dune. Reports of the discovery of the colossal statues spread fast in circles interested in Egyptian antiquities. Three years later, "in a premonition of a great discovery and rich plunder for collectors," the Italian amateur pioneer of Egyptian archaeology and romantic adventurer, Giovanni Battista Belzoni (1778–1823), arrived in Abu Simbel. Small bribes, including a mirror, won him the permission of the local Turkish administrator and he began to remove the sand dune under which he rightly guessed the entrance to the rock temple lay. Unfortunately, he had underestimated the time and money needed for the task. He had to leave Abu Simbel, but returned approximately one year later. Eventually, he managed to find the entrance to the temple and stood in amazement with his partners as they saw before them a hall, its ceiling supported by pillars in the form of colossal statues and its walls covered in inscriptions and scenes in low relief. Yet it was to take many more years and a great deal of labor before the façade of the great temple would emerge in all its beauty and majesty. It was not until 1909 that all the sand was removed from the façade. Once the sand was gone, a thorough investigation and documentation of the statues, inscriptions, and relief scenes was undertaken.

The Great Temple in Abu Simbel was dedicated to the trio of the highest 'state' gods of New Kingdom Egypt—Amun, Re-Harakhty, and Ptah—and to the deified Ramesses II. The majestic façade of the temple, carved into the sandstone rockface, evokes the entrance into a standard Egyptian temple: the carved rock face resembles a pylon with two pairs of colossal seated statues in front of it. Originally, there was a large courtyard surrounded by a mud-brick wall in front of the temple. The entrance to the temple lay between the two pairs of seated colossi representing the deified Ramesses II, each almost twenty-two meters tall. The colossi are set on a slightly raised area accessible from a low staircase leading to the entrance of the temple. Their heads are adorned by the *nemes* headdress and crown: the pair of statues north of the entrance wear the Lower Egyptian crown and the pair south of the entrance wear the combined Upper and Lower Egyptian crown. The head of the second colossus on the south side broke off at some point in the past and fell to the ground, probably during an earthquake, which some scholars believe occurred even before the end of the reign of Ramesses II. The earthquake also caused serious damage inside the temple. As the Egyptian archaeologist Labib Habashi (1906–84) showed, the statues had their own names, which addressed the king with his divine attributes and as the beloved of the gods. For example, the southernmost colossus was called 'Ramesses Ruler of the Two Lands.'

Beside the legs of the colossi stand much smaller statues of members of the king's family: the king's mother Tuya, his chief wife Nefertari, and princesses and princes. On the southern pair of colossi there are numerous pieces of Egyptian, Greek, Carian, and other graffiti preserved from the period when the statues were still partly exposed. Soldiers, Egyptians or foreign mercenaries, who ventured here on expeditions far to the south in the Late and Graeco-Roman

Plan of the Great Temple in Abu Simbel.

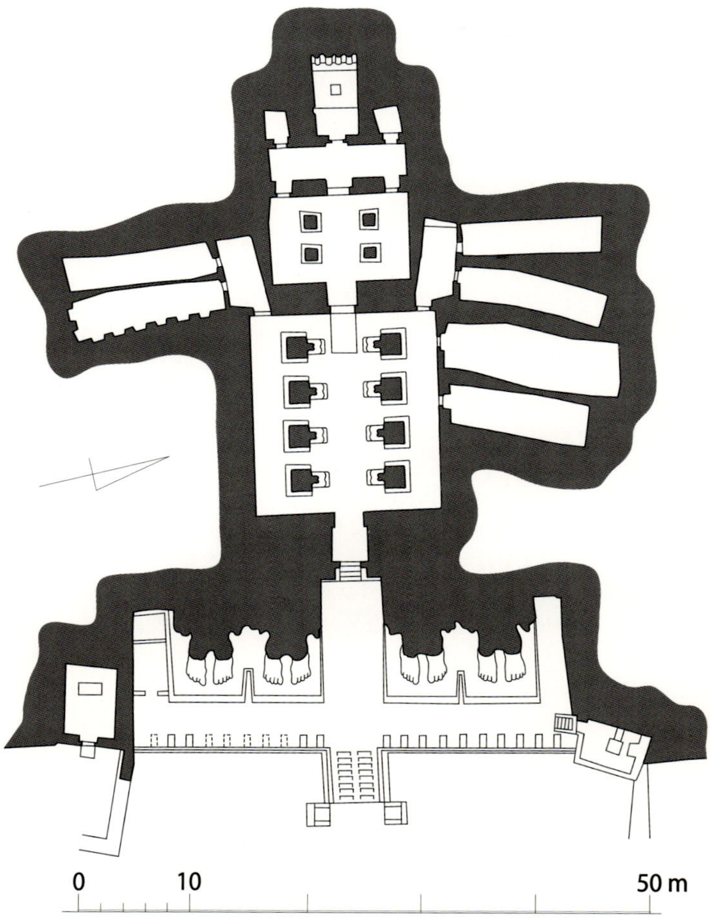

Periods, left these graffiti. It is not without interest that inscriptions were also left on the partially uncovered colossi by British and Egyptian soldiers who passed the same way, nearly two and a half millennia later, to put down an anti-British uprising in Sudan.

Over the entrance into the rock temple, Re-Harakhty is represented in a niche in high relief—as if stepping out of the rock—with a falcon head and solar disc on his head. On the north and south edge of the façade, one on each side of the colossi, are two chapels that are still waiting for thorough Egyptological assessment and publication. The north chapel is believed to be a solar shrine. It is adorned by a few obelisks; an altar in the form of a cabinet containing a scarab, the symbol of the eternally reborn sun; a seated baboon with a sickle moon and full moon on his head, the symbol of the moon and moonlight; and a frieze of baboons with their forepaws raised in a gesture of adoration. The south chapel is considered to be a birth temple.

On the southern edge of the façade is a stela from the thirty-fourth year of Ramesses II's reign, which is known as the 'Hittite Marriage Stela.' The inscription records the king's marriage with the Hittite princess Naptera, daughter of Hattusilis III. This diplomatic union was intended to consolidate peaceful relations between the two great powers. A frieze depicting twenty-two baboons worshiping the sun adorns the upper edge of the façade of the great temple. This was a favorite symbol of the solar cult because the ancient Egyptians, perceptive observers of nature, noticed that at sunrise baboons shriek and stretch their limbs, and considered this an expression of sun worship.

The temple itself consists of a set of halls and chambers carved sixty meters deep into the interior of the rock massif. The halls are arranged, one after the other, along an axis that deliberately has no entirely precise orientation but is roughly east–west. This was because the builders were trying to ensure that twice a year, on February 20 and October 20, the rays of the rising sun would reach as far as the farthest sanctuary and light up the four statues of the gods by the western wall. The first day was perhaps the king's birthday and the second his coronation day. Inside the temple, the king is presented as the 'Lord of the Two Lands' and as the 'Lord of the Ritual.' The presence of his statue among the statues of the gods vividly conveys his co-rulership with them as well as his status as one of them. In overall architectural and artistic conception, the Great and

The great pillared hall of the Great Temple in Abu Simbel is adorned with two rows of pillars featuring Osirian statues of Ramesses II.

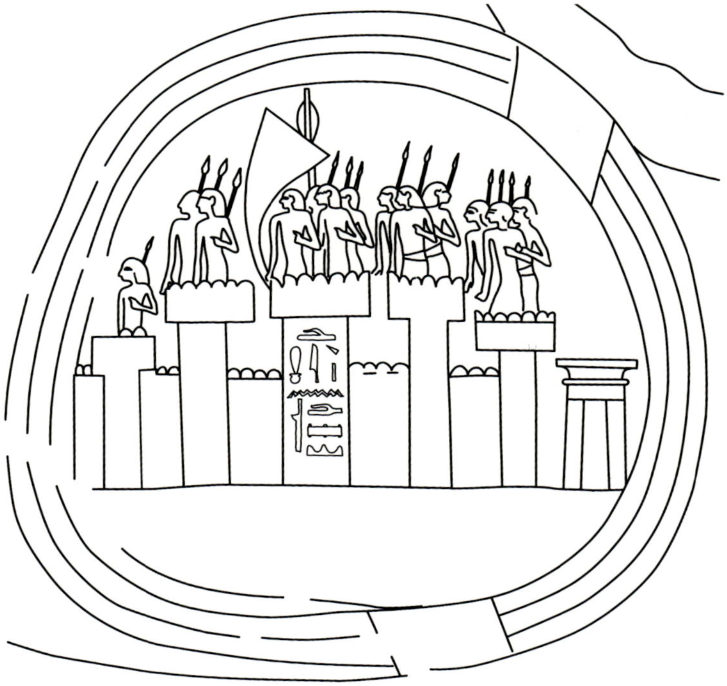

The fortress of Qadesh. Detail of relief decoration from the great pillared hall of the Great Temple in Abu Simbel.

Seated statues of Ptah, Amun-Re, the deified Ramesses II, and Re-Harakhty are situated along the western wall of the sanctuary of the Great Temple in Abu Simbel.

Small Temples in Abu Simbel are a stage for the expression and fulfilment of the king's divine destiny.

Beyond the entrance is the great hall, its ceiling supported by four pairs of pillars arranged symmetrically along the axis of the temple. Standing out from the pillars are Osiris figures of Ramesses II—that is, they take the form of a mummy with an Upper Egyptian crown on his head and hands crossed on the chest, holding the crooked scepter and flagellum. These are not depictions of the king after death, but, as the French archaeologist Christian Leblanc concludes in his studies, symbolic expressions of his powers as renewed by the *sed* festival. The walls of the hall are covered in abundant relief decoration, and in many places the original polychromy has survived. On the south side there are scenes and inscriptions relating to Ramesses II's campaigns in Syria, Libya, and Nubia; there is also a representation of the coronation of the king, including the sacred *ished* tree.

On the north wall there are scenes from the battle by the fortress of Qadesh between the Egyptians and Hittites for supremacy over Syro-Palestine. As we have explained, the battle did not start well for the Egyptians, who were thrown into disarray by a surprise attack and whose king was nearly captured, but the clash ultimately ended indecisively. All the same, not only in Abu Simbel but also in temples in Abydos, Luxor, and the Ramesseum, Ramesses had himself depicted in the battle as a brave general massacring the enemy and then as a victor watching his soldiers counting the severed limbs of their fallen foes.

The façade of the Small Temple in Abu Simbel.

Entrances from the great Pillared Hall lead into long narrow storage chambers, three on the southern and five on the northern side. The ceiling of the following, much smaller antechamber is supported by only four pillars. From the next, so-called transverse hall, we reach the smallest and innermost chamber, which is a chapel with seated statues of the main deities worshiped in the temple—Amun, Re-Harakhty, and Ptah—by the southern wall. In the Great Temple of Abu Simbel the king had a statue in his own likeness added to those of the gods; thus, in some places in the temple decoration we see rather curious scenes featuring Ramesses II bringing offerings to himself. According to Kitchen the deified king identified himself through the other statues with the gods they represented, that is, as the Amun of Ramesses, the Re of Ramesses, and the Ptah of Ramesses. Kitchen also argues that a barque holding a cult statue representing the deified Ramesses II in the form of the god Re originally rested on the base in front of the statues. In his view, the Great Temple in Abu Simbel was dedicated less to Amun than to Re and Ramesses, 'Great God, Lord of Nubia.' As is evident from the relief scenes and inscriptions, some other gods, such as Min, Montu, Thoth, and others, were also venerated in the temple.

The Small Temple in Abu Simbel lies about four hundred meters north of the Great Temple; its building was overseen by Iuny. It was dedicated to the goddess Hathor of Ibshek (the Egyptian name of Faras in northern Sudan) and the deified chief royal wife of Ramesses, Queen Nefertari. Unlike the Great Temple, the Small Temple was not originally protected by a forecourt, which allowed water from the annual inundations to reach right up to its entrance. Like that of the Great Temple, the façade of the Small Temple is carved into a sloping surface resembling a pylon. The façade is decorated by six standing statues, eleven and a half meters tall, representing Ramesses II and Nefertari and arranged so that on each side of the entrance there is a pair of statues of the king and between them one statue of the queen. It is rare in Egyptian art to find statues of a king and queen that

Not only the Great and Small Temples in Abu Simbel, but also stelae in their immediate vicinity, were moved during the rescue operation.

are the same size, and the fact that they are on the same scale here suggests how greatly Ramesses II respected his wife. The statues are set in niches and appear as if they are emerging out of the rock. In the statues south of the entrance the king wears an Upper Egyptian crown, while north of the entrance one king has a double crown, that is, a combined Upper and Lower Egyptian crown and the other the *nemes* head dress and *atef* crown with two plumes and a sun disc. In both cases the queen has a crown with cow horns, plumes, and a sun disc. At the base of the colossi there are much smaller standing statues of the royal children.

The Small Temple is carved about twenty-one meters into the interior of the rock. There is a hall, immediately beyond the entrance, whose ceiling is supported by three pairs of pillars with Hathor capitals, arranged symmetrically along the axis of the temple. The walls of the pillared hall are adorned with scenes and inscriptions in low relief. They include the king slaying the enemies of Egypt in the presence of the queen, Horus and Seth crowning the king, and the king and queen bringing offerings to Hathor, who is depicted as a cow sailing through a papyrus swamp on a boat. From the pillared hall we enter a transverse hall (as in the Great Temple), and then a relatively small chapel where Hathor the cow goddess is depicted on the back wall; Ramesses II appears under her head in this image, thus symbolizing that he has been taken under her protection.

The Rescue of Abu Simbel

In the early 1960s the fate of both rock temples in Abu Simbel hung in the balance. The new revolutionary Egyptian government had decided to build the High Dam at Aswan and a large part of the monuments of Nubia would accordingly disappear beneath its waters. In collaboration with UNESCO, the Egyptian government declared an extensive international archaeological rescue project, focused first and foremost on the relocation of the temple complex at Philae and both temples of Abu Simbel.

The challenge facing archaeologists at Abu Simbel seemed at first an impossible one: to save a temple with more than a dozen rooms, including one large and one smaller pillared hall, carved sixty meters deep into sandstone. Architects presented the Egyptian government with various plans that were immediately rejected by expert committees on technical and financial grounds. For example, one proposal was to have the temples cut out of the cliff in their entirety and then, after the release of the water into the reservoir, supported

View of the interior of the artificial hill into which the Great Temple of Abu Simbel was inserted.

on the surface by concrete pontoons. Another project envisaged the building of a protective dam around the temples, which would be accessible by long elevators, and another plan proposed the building of huge glass houses over both temples. In 1961 the Egyptian government eventually came to favor a plan put forward by an Italian team. This plan involved cutting the temples out of the rock in one piece; constructing a concrete platform beneath them equipped with three hundred strong hydraulic jacks, which would be used to raise the temples thirty centimeters; building another concrete platform beneath them, and so on, in thirty-centimeter intervals, until the desired elevation was achieved. In fact, after further study of the technical problems and especially the expense of the project, the idea was finally abandoned. In 1963 a new project was accepted, this time definitively: the two temples would be cut out in segments and reassembled on an artificially built hillock at another suitable location on the bank of the future reservoir. The realization of the plan was entrusted to a consortium of construction firms from Germany, Sweden, Italy, and France.

The final phase of cutting up and dismantling the two temples into a total of 1,042 blocks—the Great Temple was broken down into 807 blocks and the Small Temple into 235—took place in an atmosphere of great stress and anxiety. As a result of spring rains in the Ethiopian mountains, the annual flood was more intense than usual in 1964 and the water level in the dam reservoir rose higher than had been anticipated. Fortunately, the work was accomplished safely and on time. The blocks were kept in a safe place and restored while work went ahead on building two reinforced concrete houses to form the cores of the artificial hillocks in which the two temples were to be reassembled. With the joint efforts of Egyptian and foreign experts and workers the whole project was successfully completed. On 22 September 1968 the relocated temples were reopened to the public.

The Desert Oracle of Amun

For the nearly four millennia of its existence ancient Egyptian civilization was formed by striking contrasts, not only between the culturally different environments of the south and north of the country (Upper and Lower Egypt), but between the Nile Valley with its abundance of vegetation and water and the unending expanses of parched desert enclosing the valley on each side. The desert—the 'Red Land,' or more precisely, the 'Fiery Land'—terrified and fascinated Egyptians in equal measure. The Western Desert in particular was considered the kingdom of the dead, a fearful world ruled by the god of evil, Seth, a land that it was best to avoid and from which there was no return. This desert world was also a constant source of mundane danger in the form of devastating sandstorms and murderous attacks by savage Bedouin. Yet the ancient Egyptians were descended not only from the first farmers to settle in the Nile Valley, but also from audacious shepherds traveling with their herds in search of scanty green pasture to oases far beyond the horizons of the desert. At the end of the prehistoric age the desert was already crisscrossed by a network of caravan routes linking oases with the Nile Valley and with each other. As time went by the ancient Egyptians came to realize the importance of the oases not just for herding (it is no accident that one of them, Farafra, was called the 'Land of the Cattle'), but also for long-distance trade with the African interior and as a source of valuable raw materials. Military control of the oases was a necessity both because of profitable foreign trade and because the country's frontiers ran through the oases. All of Egypt's conquerors were very well aware of the strategic significance of the oases. The Romans, for example, equipped this southern border of their imperium with systematic fortifications.

The oases of the Western Desert were firmly under the control of the Egyptians as early as the Old Kingdom, in the second half of the third millennium BC. The Egyptians introduced agriculture to the oases and in one of them, Dakhla, they built a fortified administrative center, which was the seat of the administrator. Dakhla's dates, wine, and precious minerals were highly valued in the Nile Valley. The Egyptian colonists, officials, and administrators brought Egyptian culture to the oases and it gradually took firm root in their very distinctive conditions. However much Seth might be ruler of the desert, in the oases he had to yield pride of place to the highest state god, Amun, and the other two deities of the Theban Triad, Mut and Khonsu. In the sixth century BC King Haibre (Greek: Apries) built the famous Temple of Amun in Hebenet ('Town of the plow,' known in Greek as 'Hibis') in the Oasis of Kharga; soon afterward the temple was enlarged by the Persian king Darius I. Darius I founded another temple to Amun not far away, in the fortress of Qasr al-Ghueita ('The Garden Fortress'). Temples to Amun were built in other oases; for example, one was built in Deir al-Hagar on the western edge of Dakhla by the Roman emperors. A golden age of economic prosperity and cultural flowering in the oases was ushered in by Alexander the Great's conquest of Egypt and his diplomatically motivated journey in 331 BC to the Ammonion, the celebrated oracle of Amun in the oasis of Siwa. Veterans from Alexander's army and Greek colonists came to settle in the oases, bringing with them new knowledge, well-planned irrigation systems, and advanced methods of agricultural production. They

founded great vineyards, olive groves, and fruit orchards. In these multicultural conditions the cults of the traditional Egyptian gods, with the Theban Triad in first place, together with new cults such as that of Serapis, found fertile soil.

<< The remains of the temple of Amun on the rock outcrop in Aghurmi rise above the palm groves in the Siwa Oasis.

The Ammonion exceeded all other temples in the Western Desert in importance. The Siwa oasis, originally settled by Berber tribes and previously known as Santaria ('The place of acacias'), lies close to the Libyan frontier and is the farthest oasis from the Nile. It is separated from the Nile Valley by the Qattara Depression, a vast depression full of salt marshes. Siwa had always been a self-enclosed world; the Egyptians were familiar with it but only established control of it in the Late Period. Siwa acquired greater special importance after the founding of the city of Cyrene in Libya in the seventh century BC. Cyrene grew rapidly, and an important trade route from the African interior to Cyrene ran through Siwa. In the sixth century BC, the Twenty-sixth Dynasty king Ahmose II (known as Amasis in Greek) founded the Temple of Amun—which soon after became a famous oracle—in the middle of the oasis on a rock promontory known as Aghurmi that was surrounded by a great sea of palm groves. Thanks to its close ties to long-distance trade with prosperous Cyrene, the Ammonion came to rank with the oracles of Apollo in Delphi and Delos, and those of Zeus in Olympia and Dodona, as one of the most important oracles in the ancient world.

The Persian king Cambyses was resolved to undermine the position of Siwa as a way of striking a major blow against Cyrene. According to Herodotus, Cambyses sent an army from Thebes across the desert with orders to destroy the Ammonion. Many thousands strong, the Persian contingent passed through the oasis of Kharga, known at the time as 'Island of the Blessed,' but somewhere between Dakhla and Siwa in the Great Sand Sea, the Persians were caught and completely wiped out by a severe sandstorm that lasted several days. Many archaeologists and adventurers have tried to find the lost army of Cambyses. In the autumn of 2009, the world press reported that two Italian researchers from the University of Lecce expedition had discovered skeletal remains, weapons, and jewelery near Siwa, which may have belonged to Cambyses' doomed soldiers.

Another conqueror of Egypt, Alexander the Great, was very well aware of the great importance of the Ammonion, but unlike Cambyses he acted very skillfully and diplomatically to win the favor of Amun's priests. After his conquest of Egypt (he crossed its northeastern

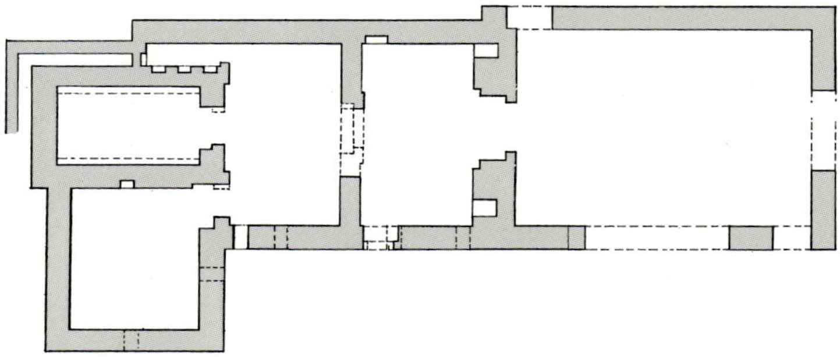

Plan of the temple of Amun in Aghurmi in the Siwa Oasis.

frontier near Pelusium in December 332 BC), he decided to visit Siwa and make obeisance to Amun. He probably made the first leg of the journey by sea to the port of Paraetonium (known today as Marsa Matruh), before reaching Siwa by caravan route on his faithful stallion Bucephalus. When he visited the Ammonion he received favorable prophecies from the god, who declared him to be the son of Amun and thus the legitimate king of Egypt. Returning from Siwa, Alexander took the desert route via the oases of Bahariya and Fayoum to Memphis, where he was crowned king in the Temple of Ptah. This return route was notoriously hazardous; therefore, after safely overcoming the worst section around the southern edge of the Qattara Depression and reaching the oasis of Bahariya, Alexander had a small temple reminiscent of a caravan station—a caravanserai—built in the oasis as an expression of thanks, close to where the Siwa route issues into the oasis.

The Ammonion forms as it were the core of the citadel spreading out on the massive rock promontory of Aghurmi. The palace of the oasis administrator was close to the temple. The temple's plan combines elements typical of both Egyptian and Greek building styles. Its ground plan is a roughly reversed 'L' shape, and it is oriented approximately on a northwest/southeast axis. In the front part of the temple there is an open forecourt, from which an entrance adorned with Doric columns leads into the first antechamber, which has a pair of columns. A second antechamber follows, its ceiling likewise supported by a pair of columns, which gives access to three chambers. The middle chamber is the shrine (with a wooden ceiling) and is adjoined on one side by a hall with one pillar and on the other by a small narrow chamber with side niches. This narrow chamber afforded access to a corridor leading from the shrine and to a well, which provided a water supply for the temple in times of danger.

In the nineteenth century one of the local bosses had the temple of Amun in Umm Ubaida blown up, and so today only a few forlorn remnants of the building survive.

The oracle in the shrine could be manipulated from this corridor. Inscriptions that have survived in the temple mention the Theban Triad (Amun-Re, Mut, and Khonsu) and other gods, such as Herishef and Mahy. The administrator of the oasis held the position of high priest.

The main cult idol of the Ammonion in Siwa was the omphalos, an object of rather uncertain shape, but perhaps oval and convex to judge by a few vague pieces of information from written sources of the period. It has been reported that the omphalos was wrapped in a veil and adorned with emerald. Emerald here may mean the rare 'Libyan glass' (Latin *silica libyca*), which occurs naturally south of Siwa on the southwestern edge of the Great Sand Sea and was used, for example, to make the scarab set in the famous pectoral of Tutankhamun. Like the cult statues of the Egyptian gods, the omphalos also rested on a holy barque, which was placed in an open wooden cabinet and decorated with protective sphinxes.

The temple in Aghurmi was recently thoroughly excavated and researched by a German archaeological team led by Klaus Peter Kuhlmann. This team also undertook very urgent building and reconstruction work to strengthen the stability of the temple and the rock on which it stands. Earthquakes and the occasional torrential rain have damaged the rock, which is now cracked. Despite all the expert efforts the future of this unique monument is somewhat insecure.

The Temple of Amun on Aghurmi was connected by an avenue of ram-headed sphinxes to another temple just a few hundred meters away, which stood on the site known as Umm Ubayda, and was dedicated to Amun-Re and other gods worshiped in Siwa. The temple, probably built during the Thirtieth Dynasty in the very last years of Egyptian independence by King Nakhtnebef, is currently in a very miserable state. At the end of the nineteenth century, even though Egyptian regulations on monument protection were already in existence, one of the local potentates had the temple blown up with gunpowder, and built himself a residence with the shattered limestone masonry. A few walls with remnants of relief decoration are all that remain of the temple. Fortunately, we still have the drawings made by the Prussian expedition led by Baron Heinrich Karl Menu von Minutoli (1772–1846) on a visit to the oasis in 1811. The drawings were published in an interesting work compiled and published in 1824 on the basis of the baron's travel diary.

The cult in both temples ceased sometime in the fifth century after the acceptance of Christianity and the prohibition of Egyptian cults. Christianity never took hold in Siwa, however, and the eventual victor here was Islam, as witnessed by the minaret towering above the rock of Aghurmi.

At first sight it might seem that the Ammonion in Siwa was the westernmost Temple of Amun, and therefore that the spiritual domain of Amun ended in the west at the Egyptian–Libyan border. In fact, from the Late Period his cult gradually spread even among the tribes living still farther to the west and eventually Amun became one of the most important gods of the Berbers. Shrines to Amun from the Roman Period have been found as far away as Djerma on the territory of the Garamants (in present-day Libya) in the heart of the Sahara. If we bear in mind how far the cult reached into Nubia, we can see how huge the spiritual empire of Amun was. It included the greater part of north and east Africa, lasted almost two millennia, and finally succumbed only to Islam.

Second Excursus

The Great Festivals of the King of the Gods

The processions at the *opet* festival included fattened sacrificial bulls. Detail from the decoration of the temple of Amun in Luxor.

Plan of Thebes showing the temples in Luxor and Karnak and the mortuary temples on the West Bank.
1. Hatshepsut
2. Mentuhotep II
3. Ramesses IV
4. Thutmose III
5. Ramesseum
6. Thutmose IV
7. Merenptah
8. Amenhotep III
9. Colossi of Memnon
10. Medinet Habu
11. palace of Ramesses III
12. palace of Amenhotep III
13. Sethi I
14. temple of Luxor
15. temple of Mut in Karnak

The Festival of the Decade

As the very name suggests, the festival was held every ten days (the Egyptian week had ten days). A procession of priests bearing the veiled statue of Amun would set off from Amun's Karnak residence to take the god to the temple complex in Medinet Habu on the west bank of the Nile. The procession would first visit Amun's 'Southern Harim' in Luxor and from Luxor cross in boats to Medinet Habu. There, in a small temple on a mythical sacred site (the mysterious Djeme hillock, surrounded originally by an acacia grove) the god would meet the eight primordial gods and one of his own forms, the primordial serpent Kematef, 'He who has completed his time,' and so renew his creative power. Amun would then return to Karnak to descend into his crypt like the setting sun. During the subsequent rites he would be reborn as the sun god Khepre: at dawn the priests would carry his statue to the roof terrace where the rebirth of the god would culminate in a flood of sunlight. In the Late Period this festival was performed in a temple built in the reign of the Twenty-fifth Dynasty Nubian king Taharqa close to the sacred pool in Karnak.

The Beautiful Feast of the Valley

Besides the *opet* festival, the Beautiful Feast of the Valley was another very important annual Theban festival. It was even older than the *opet* festival, our earliest record of it dating from as early as the beginning of the Middle Kingdom, the reign of Mentuhotep II. It was a festival of the dead, and was celebrated in the second summer month, to which it even gave its name, *paoni* (from *pa en inet*, 'he who belongs to the valley'). The feast would begin at the full moon, when a procession would set out for the western bank of the Nile, visit the tombs and mortuary temples and cult sites of the gods, and end up in the sanctuary of the goddess Hathor, which was situated in the middle of the rock amphitheater in Deir al-Bahri.

From the Nineteenth Dynasty certain changes were made to the Beautiful Feast of the Valley. The gods worshiped in Karnak—Amun, Mut and Khonsu—now took part in the procession. With the appropriate rites, use of incense, recitation of liturgical texts, and so on, the *wab* priests would take the statues of the gods out of their sanctuaries, place them in their sacred barques, and then carry them out in front of the temple on litters borne on their shoulders. Other priests would carry statues of the dead kings whose mortuary temples on the west bank of the Nile the statues of the gods were to visit. Other participants would join them on the way and the whole procession would cross on small boats to the other side of the river and the great temples of kings buried not far away in the rock tombs in the Valley of the Kings. The most important of these temples included (from the north) Hatshepsut's in Deir al-Bahri, Sethi I's in Qurna, Ramesses II's, known as the Ramesseum, Amenhotep III's—its lonely ruins today gazed down on by the colossi of Memnon—and farther to the south the relatively well-preserved Temple of Ramesses III in Medinet Habu.

These temples had a mortuary and at the same time a cult significance and according to the surviving inscriptions were intended to honor and maintain the memory of their royal owners for millions of years. Egyptologists have diverged somewhat in their attempts to express the function or meaning of this type of temple. Some define them as mortuary temples, others as funerary temples or 'temples of millions of years,' or in some cases just as memorial temples. Each temple had its own name; for example, the Temple of Ramesses II, the Ramesseum, was called the 'Temple of Wesermaatre Setepenre

The Ramesseum, the mortuary temple of Ramesses II, in Western Thebes. A view from the rock ridge above the Valley of the Kings.

(called) "United with Thebes" in the Domain of Amun in the West of Thebes.' Some kings built other 'temples of millions of years' in other places; for example, Amenhotep III built one far to the south in Soleb in Nubia between the Third and Fourth Cataracts of the Nile. Sethi I chose Abydos, which was a particularly appropriate place for such a building since it was the site of a kind of national cemetery of Egypt with the tombs of the earliest kings—most notably, the mythical tomb of the god of the dead and ruler of the underworld, Osiris. Ramesses II built himself the most 'temples of millions of years,' including the famous rock temple in Abu Simbel.

In the rock amphitheater of Deir al-Bahri on the west bank of the Nile and opposite Karnak, the sky goddess Hathor was worshiped in the form of a cow emerging from the rocks or from a papyrus swamp. Her sanctuary was one important stop on the Beautiful Feast of the Valley's procession route. A great cemetery, a real city of the dead, spread out in the surrounding rocks, and so the feast was an important opportunity for the public to take part in the procession and visit the tombs of their families here. Each family held a place, close to the entrance of the tomb concerned, to celebrate the mortuary feast; its degree of opulence would depend on family funds. The celebration began with a burnt offering, for this opened the way for the 'blessed spirit' (owner of the tomb) to come out of the tomb into the sunlight, touch the rays of the sun, and draw strength from them. It was also a way of honoring the sun god. The burnt offering most often consisted of poultry or small pieces of meat placed in bowls on burning coals. Butchers were on hand to kill the sacrificial animals and portion out the meat. Other offerings, dishes, and drinks were spread out on mats on the ground and consumed during the mortuary banquet in honor of the owner of the tomb and other worthy ancestors. During the feasts small lanterns were lit, incense was burned, and myrrh was offered. Bouquets and wreathes, initially made mainly of lotuses but later other flowers and even papyrus stems and lettuce, were important adornments and offerings at the Beautiful Feast of the Valley.

At the tombs of important people, a musical element followed the feast: a choir came, men set the beat by clapping, and women sang while shaking sistra and little rattles. At times, a group of female singers known as 'Harim Women of Hathor' performed. The musical performance took place during the feast from the reign of Thutmose IV onward. When all the rituals were accomplished the statues of gods and kings were returned to the Temple of Karnak.

The Mysteries of the *Opet* Festival

The *opet* festival took place between the temples in Karnak and Luxor, beginning on the fifteenth day of the second month of the inundation season. At first it lasted eleven days but the duration of the festival was gradually extended to twenty-seven days. Our earliest record of the festival dates from the reign of Queen Hatshepsut in the Eighteenth Dynasty.

The American Egyptologist Lanny Bell has put forward one of the most interesting and persuasive reconstructions of the course of the *opet* festival. He considered it to have been a mystical and very momentous event for the king and his rule over Egypt. According to Bell, during the successive individual episodes of the *opet* festival, the king's power was symbolically reborn and reinvigorated. In other words, the reigning king was reidentified with the royal *ka*, his right to rule was renewed, and the god Amun, or Amun-Re, recommunicated his power to the king. The *opet* festival also had great significance for Amun-Re himself, for at the end of the year the god

Amun-Re presents Senwosret I with the symbol of life, the *ankh*. Detail from the decoration of the White Chapel in Karnak.

was believed to be exhausted to the point of death. The mysterious events of the feast ensured his rebirth, thus restoring his creative power and the order of the cosmos. The weekly festival of the decade also expressed the idea of the renewal of the powers of the weary god in a shorter cycle. In fact, the ancient Egyptians believed that other gods too, and not just Amun-Re, were so drained by the end of the year that without effective rituals they would be unable to continue to exist and function. This was why, at the New Year, the statues of the gods would be brought out of their storage places in the dark temple crypts and taken up to special shrines on temple roof terraces in order to be reborn and draw new strength in secret rites involving the life-giving rays of the sun.

According to Bell, the *opet* festival would commence in the eastern part of Amun's temple precinct in Karnak, in Akh menu—Thutmose III's cult 'temple of millions of years'—and the place of the king's eternal union with the gods. After the initial rites, a still small group of priests, bearing the royal barque with the statue of the king's *ka* on their shoulders, and led by the king, went from Akh menu to the sanctuary containing the cult statue of Amun. The procession then continued on to Amun's barque. The barque's appearance is known from various depictions: it was made of cedar wood richly adorned with gold. It had its own special place in the temple, a chapel, where it rested on a rectangular stone base. The bow and stern of the barque were decorated with the symbols of Amun: a ram head with a necklace. The cabinet of the god on the deck of the barque was adorned with pictures of protective goddesses and kneeling royal figures. On the bow in front of the cabinet was a sphinx with the king kneeling to it. Also on deck were other symbols of the god and offerings. The junior priests, known as the 'pure ones,' but not the higher priests called 'servants of the god,' carried the barque on their shoulders. They were accompanied by two *sem* priests in leopard skins. The king walked behind the barque.

The processions continued on their route to the space between pylons IV and II, where the two main axes of the Temple of Amun intersected. Here, the procession took the southern route, making a detour to Khonsu's temple where the priests took charge of the god's statue, placed it in his sacred barque, and returned with it to the southern route. This led to the Avenue of Sphinxes on the approach to the Temple of Mut, where after performing the required rites the priests placed the statue of the goddess in her sacred barque. Thus, having collected the statues of the complete Theban Triad and the statue of the king's *ka,* the procession could set out for the temple in Luxor.

After leaving the precinct of Mut the procession could take one of two routes from Karnak to Luxor, and one or the other would be chosen according to circumstances: either the two-and-a-half-kilometer-long Avenue of Sphinxes linking the two temples, or by water along the Nile. Whichever the route, the procession would be accompanied—with singing, drumming, and the sound of other musical instruments—by selected military units in full armor, acrobats, beribboned light carriages bearing members of the royal family, magnates, and dignitaries, and above all by throngs of rejoicing people, who lined either the Avenue of Sphinxes or the bank of the Nile. There would also be offering bearers, including men leading ornamented sacrificial bulls. A Nubian dancer performed a ritual dance during the procession. When the cult statues were transported by water, barges waited for the procession led by the king and priests at the Nile harbor of the Temple of

Karnak. The barques with their statues would be loaded on the barges and the king, priests, and dignitaries would embark. Bargemen pulled the barges by tow ropes. It was considered a great honor to tow the barges with the sacred barques and statues of the gods.

Detail of relief scene with procession at the *opet* festival. Temple of Amun in Luxor.

When the procession took the overland route along the Avenue of Sphinxes, it eventually entered the Temple of Luxor through Amenhotep II's entrance colonnade or, at a later period, through the main gate on Ramesses II's first pylon. When the water route to Luxor was chosen, the procession from the harbor could enter the temple (after completion of the building during the reign of Ramesses II) through the side entrance in the western wall of the columned courtyard. The procession was greeted in the courtyard by throngs of magnates and selected representatives of the public with bouquets and offerings.

The sacred barques were set down for a while in the chapel with three chambers in the northwestern corner of the court (described above). The king and priests continued with the statues of the gods from Ramesses II's columned court, through the colonnade, and to Amenhotep III's columned courtyard, where it was welcomed by other magnates and selected public leaders. Only the king and priests, however, were permitted to go any farther, taking the statues into the hypostyle hall and interior of the temple. Scenes and inscriptions on the walls of the temple's individual inner chambers give us some idea of what happened next.

In the intimate part of the temple, forbidden to the public, the barques with the cult statues would be set down in appointed places. Then, according to Bell, the rite of the renewal of the ruling power of the king, a key episode in the *opet* festival, would be conducted in the 'chamber of the divine king,' which Bell identifies as the smaller hall with eight columns immediately beyond the great hypostyle hall. The king was first ritually purified by the priests with water and then presented to Amun-Re. Then the king knelt with his back to the cult statue of the god, who laid his hands on the king's head (in reality all these acts were carried out through the priests), thus communicating his divine power to him. The priest representing the god would go on to place different royal crowns on the king's head. With this ceremony the king was reborn through the god and once more confirmed in his full royal power. Bell conjectures that the final phase of the ritual took place in the sanctuary (holy of holies) in the innermost part of the temple, where the god Amun was worshiped in his local form of Amenemopet ('Amun in the Harim'). Here the king would present offerings to the god and perform the ceremony of the 'opening of the mouth' on the great cult statue of the god. This involved touching the mouth of the statue with a cult instrument containing an inset blade of meteoric metal, by which the divine power of heaven was reborn in the god.

The god would also make prophecies through the priests during the *opet* festival. It is possible that other rites were performed in the temple as well. There is even speculation that they could have included a rite of a sexual character, performed in the Birth Hall where the 'wife of the god,' as 'hand of the god,' may have played an important part. When the rites were concluded, the king and priests emerged with the statues from the depths of the Luxor temple and into the jubilation of the crowds waiting in the open-columned courtyards. The statues were placed on their movable sacred barques and the procession

returned to Karnak. Feasts, banquets, and offerings to the gods were held not just in Luxor and Karnak but also throughout Egypt in the days following the religious climax of the festival. Indeed, there was a great deal to celebrate: the royal ruling power had been renewed, the power of the gods reborn, and the order of the world reestablished.

<< Even the Luxor Temple guards have to take a rest sometimes.

Plan of Amarna made by the scholars of Napoleon's expedition.

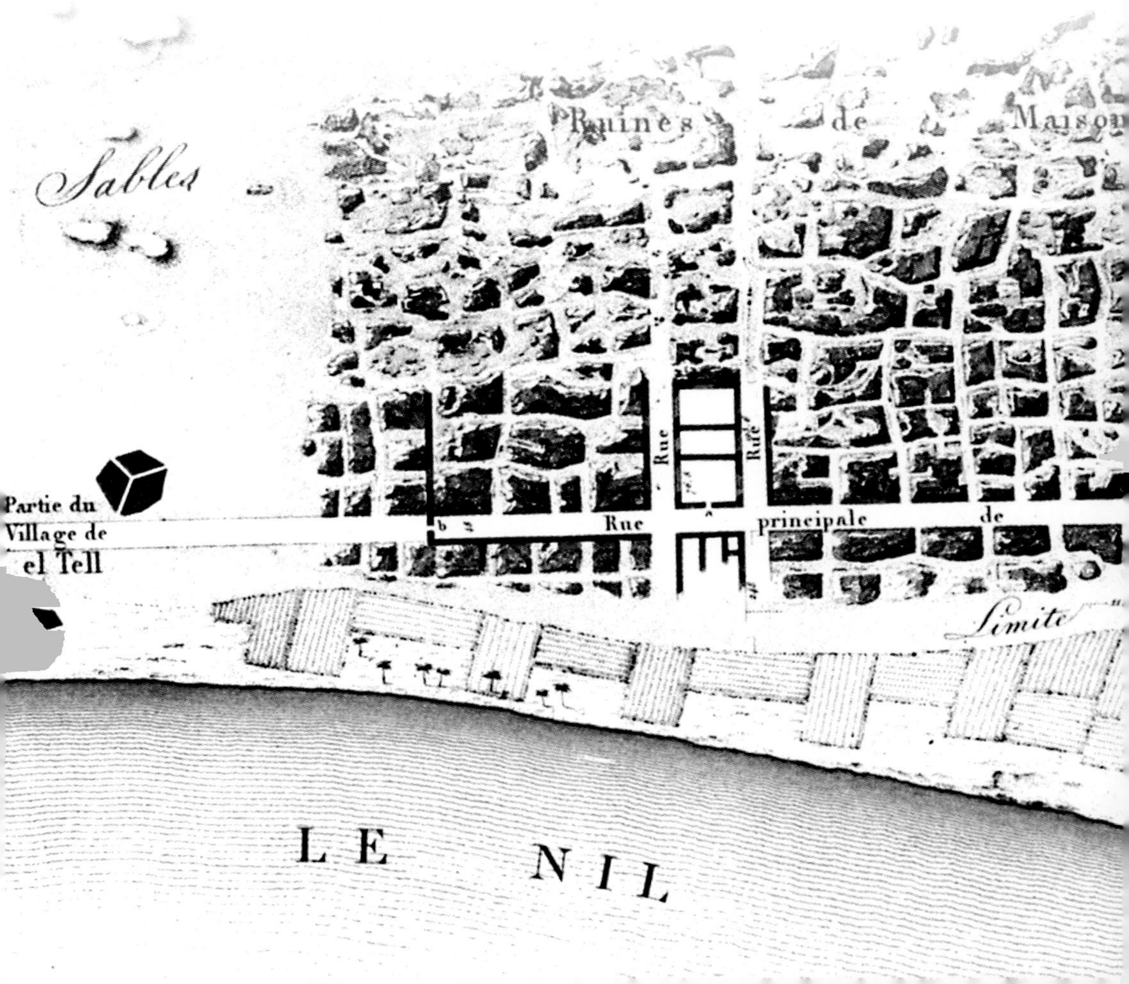

6

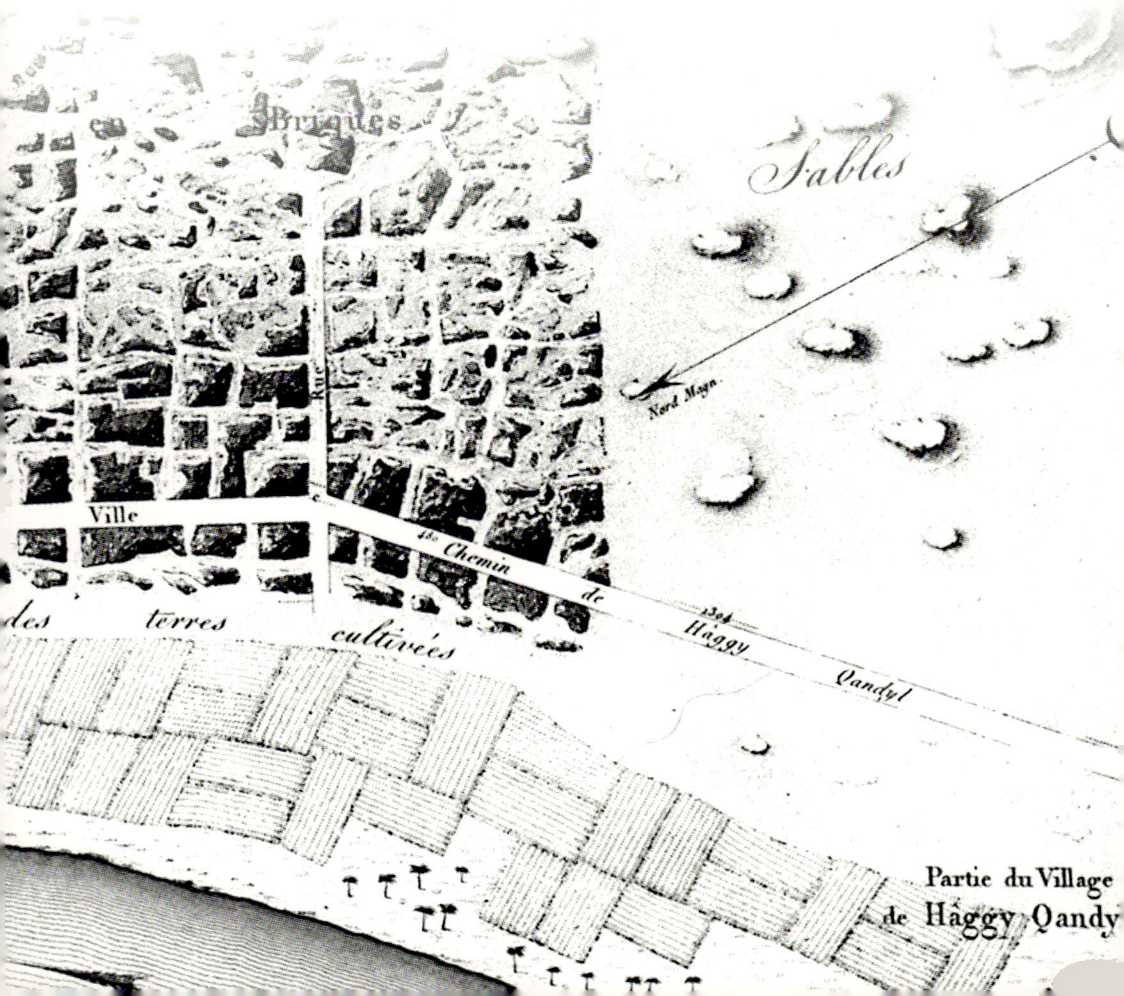
Briques
Sables
Rue
Nord Magn.
Ville
Chemin de Hâggy Qandyl
des terres cultivées
Partie du Village de Hâggy Qandy

Amarna: City of the Heretic

Archaeologists in Amarna

<< Anonymous fragment of relief with a part of the face of a man (Akhenaten?). Amun's temple precinct in Luxor.

Anyone who sets off for Tell al-Amarna with a tourist guidebook in hand may be intrigued to learn that his destination bears this name only as a result of a mix-up between the names of two different places a few kilometers apart: al-Till and Beni Amran. What is more, these are not the only places with modern names on the site of the ruins of the ancient Akhetaten. The others are al-Hagg Qandil, al-Amiriya, and al-Hawata. The names are not of direct interest to tourists, but they are helpful for archaeologists, providing them with orientation in the exploration of the vast parched plain that, thirty-four centuries ago, were the stage on which the drama of Akhenaten's reign reached its climax.

Unlike other sites dominated by grand architectural monuments, Amarna did not initially excite much interest among archaeologists, even though the learned French Jesuit, Abbé Claude Sicard (1677–1726), discovered it at the beginning of the eighteenth century. Napoleon's military expedition to Egypt passed through the locality when pursuing the retreating Mamluks to the south, but it was to be roughly two decades after the French campaign ended that the first archaeological excavations in Amarna were initiated by the English traveler and one of the pioneers of Egyptology, Sir John Gardner Wilkinson (1797–1875). Roughly twenty years after Wilkinson, a German expedition led by Karl Richard Lepsius (1810–1884) arrived in Amarna; the team worked here only briefly but made valuable archaeological documentation. Lepsius was to be followed by a series of other archaeologists, primarily Englishmen and most notably Petrie, who made important discoveries in Amarna. The finds included the beautiful painted floor of one of the halls of the royal palace. Unfortunately, this precious painting was dug up and destroyed by a local fellah, who was infuriated by visitors crossing his field to admire the antiquity. Another Englishman, Norman de Garis Davies (1865–1941), did a great deal of epigraphic work in Amarna, as witnessed by his multivolume treatise on Amarna rock tombs. The virtual English monopoly on excavation of Amarna prior to the First World War was interrupted by a brief but spectacularly successful German expedition led by Borchardt. It was

It is hard to believe that on this plain, which is desolate today, a flourishing city once grew up in a short time, boasting temples, palaces, government and commercial buildings, housing estates, and—last but not least—gardens and large vineyards.

> John Devitt Stringfellow Pendlebury.

Borchardt and his team who discovered the superb sculptures of the Amarna period, including the most famous—the celebrated bust of Queen Nefertiti.

In the late 1920s and early 1930s the key figure in excavations in Amarna was the undoubtedly great and highly eccentric Englishman John Devitt Stringfellow Pendlebury (1904–41). He was not only an outstanding archaeologist but also a man of considerable humor. As a young man, Pendlebury lost one of his eyes; as an adult he wore a prosthetic. The story goes that he sometimes terrified the Egyptian laborers at the excavations by taking out his substitute glass eye. However, the glass eye later played a more serious role in his life. When the Second World War broke out, Pendlebury was in Crete, where he had become the curator of monuments in Knossos for some years after working in Egypt. When the island was occupied by German paratroopers he acted as an important link between the British military command in the eastern Mediterranean and the Cretan partisan leaders. He had an agreement with his friends that if he left the glass eye at an agreed-upon spot it would mean he had gone to the partisans in the mountains. In the end Pendlebury was wounded in an exchange of fire with the Germans and captured. The next day he was summarily shot.

After the Second World War, apart from a brief period of research carried out by Egyptians in the 1960s, it was again primarily British archaeologists, particularly Barry J. Kemp and Geoffrey T. Martin, who carried out further excavations in Amarna.

The Horizon of Aten

The drama that unfolded in Egypt thirty-three centuries ago has no parallel in the history of the kingdom of the pharaohs. It started inconspicuously, several decades before Egyptian internal political conditions erupted in irreconcilable conflict. After long and tough battles Egypt managed to free itself from the overlordship of the Semitic tribes that in the seventeenth century BC, in the period of political decline at the end of the Middle Kingdom, had occupied the northern part of the country.

The Hyksos, as these tribes were known, initially gained the upper hand because they used better weapons than the Egyptians—for example, war chariots drawn by horses and very effective composite bows, which were unfamiliar to the Egyptians. The Hyksos also diplomatically exploited their common strategic interests with the Nubian kingdom ruled from Kerma, halfway between the Third and Fourth Cataracts of the Nile. The fight for independence and reunification culminated at the end of the Seventeenth Dynasty, after roughly a century of Hyksos supremacy. The savagery of the battles is very vividly attested by the maimed body of the Theban ruler Seqenenre Tao, which is full of arrowheads and has a gaping hole in the skull from the blow of a Hyksos war axe. Not even the death of Seqenenre broke Egyptian resistance, however, and his successor Kamose won decisive victories, which Ahmose I crowned by driving the interlopers right out of the country and

destroying the Hyksos fortress of Sharuhen in Palestine. Ahmose I also founded the Eighteenth Dynasty, which ushered in the new era of great political, economic, and cultural upsurge known as the New Kingdom.

It was quite natural that Thebes, from which the struggle against the Hyksos had been organized, should become the new political and religious center of the reunified Egypt, because both the rulers and the country's people believed that they owed their victory to the local god Amun. After the traumatic experience of the battles with the Hyksos the Eighteenth Dynasty kings made a basic change in Egyptian policy: they abandoned the earlier policy of occasional preventive strikes to the north into western Asia and to the south into Nubia in favor of the conquest of extensive territories and the creation of vassal states to form a buffer zone around Egypt in order to protect it from possible threats. Under Thutmose I, who was the grandson of Ahmose I and one of the greatest warriors in Egyptian history, the Egyptians managed to create an empire with frontiers that reached the Euphrates in the north and the Fourth Cataract of the Nile in Nubia in the south. Immense wealth flowed into the country from the wars of conquest that accompanied the building of the Egyptian imperium. The Egyptian kings showered the chief Egyptian gods, Amun most of all, with gifts of booty in gratitude for their victories. Amun's main temple in Karnak experienced a period of unprecedented flowering, the additions of increasingly grand buildings, and full temple coffers. Not surprisingly, the priesthood of Amun also acquired enormous power and gradually came to form a kind of state within a state. Indeed, their position was such that a confrontation between the secular and spiritual powers—that is, between the king and the priests of Amun—was only a question of time and the interplay of circumstances.

<< Fragment of a colossal polychromed limestone statue with a portrait of Queen Hatshepsut. Egyptian Museum, Cairo.

Thutmose II, son of the great warrior Thutmose I, reigned only briefly—a mere three years—and his chief wife Hatshepsut failed to conceive an heir to the throne. He did, however, manage to produce a male heir with a secondary wife, Eset, and the boy was given the name Thutmose III. This was not a particularly uncommon situation in Egyptian dynastic history but the circumstances were such as to make the outcome very unusual indeed. Hatshepsut, like her husband Thutmose II, was the child of Thutmose I. The marriage of siblings was in line with religious ideas (the god Osiris, the mythical first ruler of Egypt, had married his sister Isis) and according to Egyptian royal ideology it guaranteed the 'purity' of the royal blood and so a fully legitimate claim to the throne. The son of Thutmose II and Eset lacked this complete purity of blood. On the other hand, he was the king's only male issue and

>> Striding statue of Thutmose III in black-gray slate, Luxor Museum.

therefore the only possible successor. When an heir had not yet reached maturity, it was usual for the queen mother to rule until her son (even in this case a stepson) came of age. Hatshepsut saw matters differently. Already powerful and highly ambitious, she considered herself the legitimate heir to the throne, and she decided to ally with the priests of Amun to make her claim good. She found crucial support in the very influential high priest of Amun and also the vizier Hapuseneb, and another of the high-ranking priests of Amun—Senenmut—even became her lover and the tutor of her daughter Neferure. With the help of the priests of Amun, Hatshepsut, who was formally co-regent for the minor Thutmose III, had herself proclaimed de facto king of Egypt. A relief scene on the wall of her mortuary temple in Deir al-Bahri shows her divine birth from the will of Amun himself. Hatshepsut's coronation was depicted on the walls of the Red Chapel, which the queen had built for the sacred barque of Amun in his main temple in Karnak. The coronation was an event entirely at variance with the royal ideology associated with the Osirian myth: a woman, with all the insignia of royal power, had ascended the throne of the pharaohs.

Thutmose III grew up in the shadow of his stepmother and the powerful priesthood of Amun and soon realized that if he was to win some independence and build up his own power base he would need to turn to the army. Notably, the army was a rather neglected pillar of royal power during Hatshepsut's reign, in which there were already signs of the weakening of Egyptian influence in the Syro-Palestine area to the advantage of the rising power of the Mitanni Empire. The young king, although at the time he was still only Hatshepsut's co-regent, organized successful military expeditions into western Asia and Nubia that restored and consolidated Egypt's position of power abroad and Thutmose III's position in Egypt. Hatshepsut died after a reign of more than twenty years. Thutmose III, as her successor, eventually ordered the destruction of her monuments, such as her statues, and the erasure of her name and image from all other monuments. It is interesting that he did not give this order immediately after he ascended the throne, but some years later; this is somewhat hard to explain. We might speculate that even after her death Hatshepsut still had influential supporters, who continued to occupy important posts. Thutmose III also took steps to prevent the repetition of a situation in which a woman could ascend the throne. He had more than one son but, most importantly, he did not elevate any of his wives to the position of 'Great Royal Wife,' and in the final years of his nearly forty-year reign he made his son Amenhotep II his co-ruler. Thutmose III did not make any move against the power of

Amun, however. He continued, like his predecessor, to endow the temple with rich gifts from the booty of his military campaigns.

Thutmose III's successors—Amenhotep II, Thutmose IV, and Amenhotep III—did not forget the lesson gleaned from the events of Hatshepsut's accession and her power base. They realistically respected the huge spiritual and material power of the priests of Amun but were aware of the potential risks. Gradually and cautiously, ostensibly just in the interests of internal stability and the balance between the north and south of the country, they started to emphasize the importance of the god Re, whose center was Heliopolis close to Memphis, the ancient Egyptian capital. It was in this way that Thutmose III's successors somewhat diluted the status of the cult of Amun. The policy was made easier by the fact that centuries before, in the period of the Middle Kingdom, the two gods had been merged into the form of Amun-Re, combining and so doubling their individual spiritual power. Trends supporting the solar cult intensified during the reign of Amenhotep III, when one particular external form of the sun god came to the fore: the sun disc known as Aten. A god visible to all and with his life-giving rays embracing all peoples without exception seemed to have good prospects of becoming the universal god not only of Egypt but also of the whole empire.

Amenhotep III displayed immense skill in both domestic and foreign politics during his thirty-eight-year reign. The powerful viziers Ptahmose (who was also high priest of Amun), Ramose, Amenhotep Huwy, and Aper-el (who was also the high priest of Aten), did much to

Detail of the painted pavement from Tell al-Amarna

ensure the stability and prosperity of the land. This was reflected in a whole constellation of important buildings constructed at sites from the southern to the northern borders—or, as confidently declared in royal inscriptions of the time, 'From Karoi [Nubian Kurru] to Naharin [Mitanni],' and decorated with hundreds of statues of the king. Ramesses II was the only later king to be more successful in this respect. On the west bank of the Nile in Thebes Amenhotep III had a vast mortuary temple built for himself and a little farther south, also in western Thebes, a new residence and royal palace called 'House of Rejoicing,' a *harim*, a temple to Amun, and service buildings, including a lake and a great harbor on the Nile. Amenhotep III's relations with the priests of Amun, headed at the time by four 'servants of the god,' were circumspect but generally amicable. The first of the servants of the god, the high priest, was the Ptahmose already mentioned. Good relations between the king and the priesthood of Amun are also evident from the important buildings that Amenhotep III contributed to the glory and greatness of Amun-Re and his temple in Karnak: Pylons III and X (completed by Haremheb), a granite statue by the sacred pool, two obelisks, and so on. It was also on his orders that the royal architects, the twins Suty and Hor, designed and built the most beautiful part of the Temple of Amun in Luxor, the setting for the *opet* festival and the royal cult. Scenes on the wall of the Birth Hall (see above) provide further testimony to the king's more than peaceful coexistence with the priests of Amun. Here, we see Amenhotep III depicted as born from the direct union of the god Amun, who has taken on the form of the king's father Thutmose IV, and the queen Mutemwia.

Amenhotep III's policies abroad were just as successful. The territories conquered by Egypt in the south and their lucrative gold mines in Wadi Allaqi, Wadi Gabgaba, and elsewhere were under the control of the energetic Nubian regent—the 'king's son of Kush'—Merimose. The king took a quite different approach when defending Egyptian interests in the north, in western Asia. There, Egypt controlled three territories—Canaan, Apu, and Amurru—which served as a buffer zone and were ruled by governors. With more distant states, which Egypt did not control, Amenhotep II conducted a successful diplomacy of marital alliance: he married Gilukhepa, daughter of the king of the Mitanni, the daughter of the king of the Arzawa, and two daughters of the king of Babylon. When the Babylonian king requested an Egyptian princess, however, he was curtly rebuffed, but the Egyptian gifts, especially gold, that Amenhotep III sent to these lands was all the more generous in compensation.

Archaeological excavation (directed by Hourig Sourouzian) of the remains of the huge mortuary temple of Amenhotep III in Western Thebes in a place now known as Kom al-Haytan ('Whale Hill'). Groundwater makes the working conditions technically very difficult.

Nor was the power of Amenhotep III in any way affected by the fact that a woman of non-royal blood, Tiye (daughter of a priestess of Min and a royal groom, Yuya, from Akhmin in Upper Egypt), became his chief royal wife. Amenhotep's attitude to his beautiful wife is reflected in a series of what are known as wedding scarabs, which were produced to notify the public of the king's marriage to Tiye. Amenhotep also had a temple built in Tiye's honor far to the south in Nubia, in a place today called Sedeinga, where Tiye was venerated as a goddess along with Hathor. Tiye was even represented as a sphinx, usually the privilege of kings alone. With Tiye, Amenhotep had four daughters (Sitamon, Henuttaneb, Eset, and Nebetah) and two sons. The elder son, Thutmose, was crown prince, but he died prematurely and the position of heir went to his brother Amenhotep. Who knows the direction that Egyptian history might have taken had Prince Thutmose ever been crowned king of the Two Lands? Some people have speculated that Tutankhamun might also have been the son of Tiye and Amenhotep III, but chronological considerations make this unlikely.

The king celebrated his first festival—the *sed* symbolic renewal of his powers as ruler—on the thirtieth anniversary of his coronation, in the context of relatively secure international relations and tranquil domestic conditions. Some scholars conducting detailed research on the reign of Amenhotep III—for example, the Americans Arielle P. Kozloff and Betsy M. Bryan—have noticed that after this jubilee (the king was to celebrate another two, in the thirty-fourth and thirty-seventh years of his reign) certain new elements can be observed in iconography and contemporary texts that suggest a change in the way the king saw himself and his self-presentation. Earlier the king had been represented as the mediator between people and the gods, but now he was fully promoted to the status of god and himself became the sun god: Amenhotep III started to call himself Aten tjehen, 'Dazzling Sun Disc,' or sometimes Aten tjehen tau nebu, 'Dazzling Sun Disc of All Lands.' On seals found in the royal palace in Malqata we even find his new name, Aten tjehen, written with his throne name, Nebmaatre, in the form of a rebus.

Ailing, obese, and far from resembling the beautiful, slightly decadent figure of his statues, Amenhotep III expired soon after his third jubilee. His younger son, Amenhotep IV, who had ruled jointly with him for some years, succeeded him. Amenhotep IV was undoubtedly highly educated if almost certainly indulged by the ostentatious life at the royal court. He too was a supporter of the solar religion in the form that it had acquired in the last years of his father's reign. Some Egyptologists

Nebmaatre tjehen Aten ('Nebmaatre is the dazzling sun disc')—cryptogram of an epithet of Amenhotep III.

>> Akhenaten with Nefertiti making a libation to Aten, who is giving them the *ankh* symbols of life. Detail of decoration of polychromed limestone altar from Amarna. Egyptian Museum, Cairo.

studying his life and personality consider Amenhotep IV to have been a man of exceptional intellect and courage, while others see him as a great mystic and visionary, and yet others brand him a ruthless fanatic. In the first years of his reign he lived in Thebes and there, in the chief seat of the god Amun in Karnak, he launched his ambitious and somewhat provocative construction of temples to Aten.

Akhenaten's buildings in Karnak were a radical departure in architectural, artistic, and ideological conception from what had hitherto been built there to glorify the 'king of the gods,' Amun. They were 'open' temples with very large courtyards full of offering tables bathed in a flood of sunlight. Mysterious mythical events and complex rituals were largely absent from the decoration of these temples, and instead the center of attention was the one god, Aten, who was never represented in anthropomorphic or zoomorphic form, as other gods were, but only in his true form as a sun disc flooding all with his life-giving rays, which always terminate in a hand holding the *ankh* symbol of life. In this flood of solar rays, the married couple, king and queen (in later buildings and objects the royal couple and their children) is accorded the leading place. On the one hand, the thoroughness of the change and the stress on Aten's direct bond to the king and queen represent innovations in the concept of the leading role of the king in the relationship between god and the world of mankind. On the other hand, they can also be interpreted within the existing tradition of Egyptian religious thought as the expression of a new divine triad: Aten as god-creator and the king and queen as the first created divine pair Shu and Tefnut.

The artistic style of the scenes on the walls of the temples of Aten in Karnak was also radically new. The contemporary rock tomb of Ramose, the vizier and governor of Thebes, vividly documents the speed and thoroughness with which the new artistic style was introduced: part of its decoration is still in the spirit of the traditional artistic canon but the rest observes the new style. The new aesthetic involved the representation of people and animals in a far less idealized, far more realistic way than before, and included the expression of emotions. A very peculiar mode of depiction was reserved for the king and his family. The openness with which the royal family was presented, the expression of feeling between the royal husband and wife and between the royal parents and children is a characteristic feature of this new artistic idiom, but above all there is a startling new mannerism in form. The king has an elongated face, a narrow chest, wide hips, and massive calves. The effect is like that of a distorted image of a human figure in a spherical mirror. The queen and the royal daughters are represented in the same way,

Akhenaten. Sculptor's model. Limestone, Tell al-Amarna.

in their case with an emphasis on the elongation of the skull at the back. The very strange appearance of the king has been the subject of a great deal of expert debate and speculation that is certainly likely to continue in future years. Often an explanation has been sought in some endocrine disorder that caused the king real physical deformation of the kind—for example, Fröhlich's syndrome (a metabolic syndrome characterized by obesity, underdevelopment of the genital organs, and other symptoms)—but this is usually accompanied by dementia and impotence, which was certainly not the case for Amenhotep IV. Marfan syndrome (a genetic disorder of connective tissues, slender limbs, scoliosis, and other symptoms) has also been suggested. On the other hand, it is argued that the deformation was a deliberate artistic device, a way of expressing the radical distinction between the king and his family and ordinary mortals. This view is supported by a polychrome limestone figurine found in Amarna, which is currently exhibited in the Egyptian Museum in Cairo. It represents the standing king with a so-called blue crown on his head (the official crown relating to the royal rite) holding a tray of offerings. The young king is depicted realistically here, but while he does not look like an athlete and is rather plump there is nothing to suggest physical deformity arising from some illness.

The temples that Amenhotep IV had built in considerable haste in Karnak were connected with preparations for his *sed* festival. Egyptologists continue to argue over why he should have decided to celebrate

Akhenaten. Polychromed sandstone colossus of the king from one of his buildings in Karnak. Egyptian Museum, Cairo.

the jubilee of his accession so early, in the second or third year of his reign, rather than waiting the traditional thirty years. Some believe that he wanted to follow up the last two jubilees celebrated in quick succession by his father, and so emphasize continuity in their period of joint rule but also set a seal on the changes that had been made in the divine conception of the king at the end of Amenhotep III's reign. He may also have wanted to speed up the process of inauguration of the cult of Aten and the 'new thinking' associated with it. Whatever the case, there seems to have been a rapid escalation of developments soon after, in the fourth year of the reign of Amenhotep IV. We do not know the details, and have no safe way of establishing whether some particular event provoked a confrontation or whether what happened was simply a matter of the king's decision to take strong action to end a long- festering dispute. Inscriptions on the boundary stelae from Amarna suggest that the second version is more likely. A progressively intensifying conflict is evident from the inscriptions: after each year there is a reference to "worse than those things" that the king had heard the preceding year. The king decided to change his name Amenhotep ('Amun is satisfied') to Akhenaten ('Beneficial to Aten') and to leave Thebes. He gave orders for the foundation of a new city and royal residence dedicated only to Aten, Akhetaten ('Horizon of Aten'). It was important that it should be built on a virgin site that "belongs to no god and no goddess." According to Barry Kemp, Akhetaten was intended not as the center for the constantly growing community of adherents of Aten, but as the material expression of the king's personal piety. On the other hand, by founding Akhetaten, Akhenaten delivered another painful blow to the economic might of the domain of Amun; for example, he had several thousand laborers, the many thousands of loaves being offered daily, and much else moved to Akhetaten from the Temple of Amun in Thebes.

The choice fell on a desolate spot on the east bank of the Nile, roughly halfway between the then administrative centers Memphis and Thebes and a few kilometers south of the administrative center of middle Egypt today, Minya. The site was suitable for the founding of a new, potentially expanding city: here the rocky slopes defining the edges of the Nile Valley drew back toward the east and created a natural amphitheater around an area of a few dozen square kilometers. The name of the newly founded city, Akhetaten ('Horizon of Aten'), was very apt, indeed. It is not known whether the natural scenery was the inspiration for the name of the city, but some scholars—such as the British Egyptologist Nicholas Reeves—

believe so because there is a deep ravine in the rock promontory dividing it into two parts and creating the illusion that it is from here that the first rays of the rising sun appear. This would have made it a materialization of the hieroglyphic sign *akhet* ('horizon'), which is formed by a sun disc appearing between two hillocks. This theory is indirectly supported by the fact that it was precisely here,

One of the boundary stelae of Akhetaten is now to be found in the western rock outcrop at Tuna al-Gebel.

deep in the rocky promontory, that Akhenaten had his tomb built, and also by the representation of the rising sun in this tomb. On the other hand, rather than the site itself inspiring the name, the king may simply have looked for and found a place that corresponded to his existing idea.

While the center of Akhetaten lay on the east bank of the Nile, it is clear that Akhenaten envisaged that the city would also spread out on the west bank, for the future boundaries of Akhetaten were defined by huge stelae carved out of the rock walls on the east and west banks of the river. These mark out an area of over two hundred square kilometers for

Plan of Akhetaten
1. North City
2. North Palace
3. desert altars
4. North Tombs
5. North Suburb
6. Central City
7. way to Akhenaten's tomb
8. South Tombs
9. River Palace
10. Maru Aten

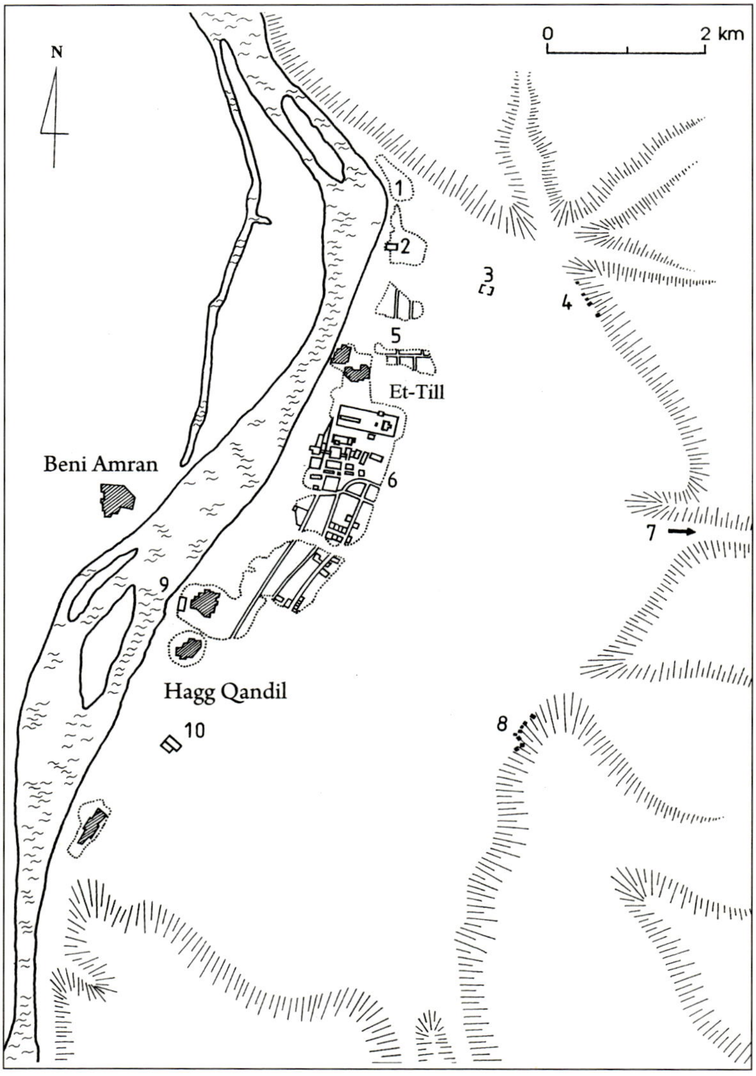

the future city. So far, fifteen such boundary stelae have been discovered, but it is possible that more will be found, for some may be buried in the layers of sand on the rock promontories. Some stelae are dated to the fifth and others to the sixth regnal year of Akhenaten. It would be a mistake to think of them as mere practical boundary markers with a simple text. The stelae are large and are major artistic works of their kind, with considerable historical importance. Akhenaten's royal family making offerings to Aten are depicted on the stelae three-dimensionally and in high relief. The accompanying relatively long text is more than just a glorification of Akhenaten and explanation of the reasons that led the king to found Akhetaten—it is in fact Akhenaten's political program.

The detailed research of the British architect Michael Mallinson has shown that the locations of the stelae on the boundary were not random or merely convenient. Notional lines connect the stelae on the west and the east bank with a single point, the king's tomb in the rock valley east of Akhetaten. The main buildings of the city are composed into the network created by these lines. Thus, unlike the other ancient Egyptian tombs, Akhenaten's tomb was not only the place of the resurrection and eternal life of its owner, but the focal point to which the whole new capital was oriented; it was the place from which, through Akhenaten, the life-giving rays of Aten were supposed to flow toward the city and its inhabitants and, through them, into the whole of Egypt.

The central part of Akhetaten was formed by a group of temples and residential, administrative, and economic buildings constructed according to a pre-established plan and connected by straight roads, usually

Archaeological research at Amarna includes the reconstruction of the ground plan of destroyed buildings.

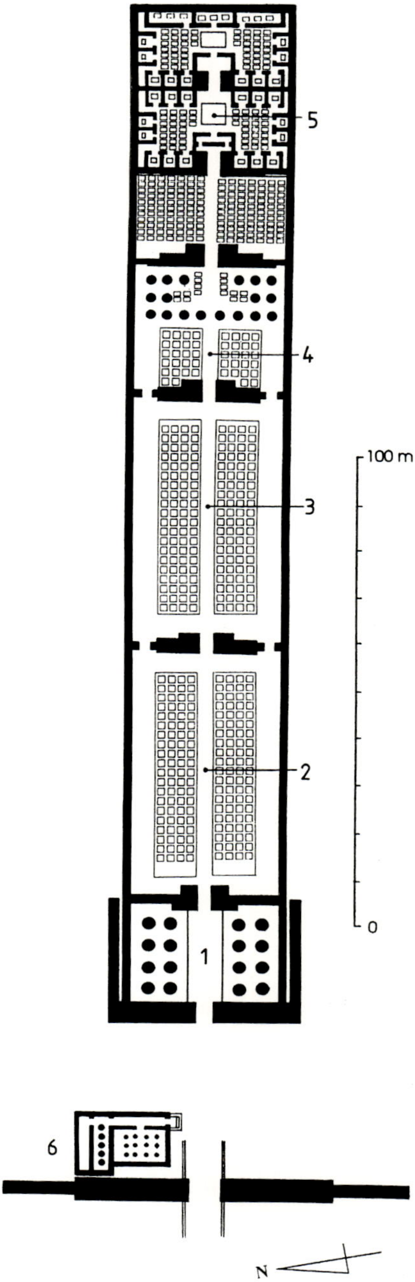

intersecting at right angles. The great majority of the buildings in Akhetaten were built of mud bricks, and their walls then plastered and whitewashed and, in some cases, adorned with paintings. Only some sections of the temples had walls faced with stone and decorated with scenes in low relief. Evidently, it was anticipated that stone sections would progressively replace the brick sections. The whole central precinct was called 'Island of the Aten Distinguished of Jubilees.' The Royal Road ran through it from the north to the south. On the east side of this road lay the Great Aten Temple called 'House of the Aten in Akhetaten,' and about half a kilometer south of it the Small Aten Temple called 'The Sanctuary of Aten in Akhetaten.' Both temples contained many elements of the solar shrines of the 'Re's shadow' type. The Great Aten Temple was a vast east–west oriented complex of buildings 760 meters long and 270 meters broad surrounded by a wall. A picture of it has survived in the Amarna tomb of the chief of the royal *harim* Merire. The complex was formed by two temples lying on the east–west axis of the building, the older in the eastern and the later in the western part. The older temple, known as the 'Mansion of the Benben Stone in the House of the Aten' and originally accessible by an avenue of sphinxes lined with trees, consisted of a courtyard with columned halls, in which stood statues of Akhenaten and Nefertiti, with a large altar in the middle. Beyond the court was an open shrine on a raised area surrounded by roofless chapels exposed to the rays of the sun. Access to the later temple known as 'Aten Is Found' in the front part of the building complex was through a pair of pylons, leading to a courtyard, a columned hall, another large courtyard, and a few more pairs of pylons separated from one another by open courts. A symbol of the *benben* solar cult in the form of a quartzite stela stood on a raised area surrounded by rows of altars in the innermost part of the temple. The open courtyards of the Great Aten Temple were filled with a total of 730 regularly arranged altars, half of them representing Upper Egypt and the other half signifying Lower Egypt. Therefore, each day of the year symbolically fell to one altar from each part of the land. This did not mean, however, that offerings were not placed daily on the others. On the contrary, loaves, cakes, and other offerings were placed on each altar every day.

The Small Temple of Aten also has a rectangular, east–west oriented ground plan, but it differs from the Great Aten Temple in many respects. The face of its enclosure wall was decorated and also reinforced at regular intervals by tower-shaped projections. Inside, the temple was divided by three successive pairs of pylon-like gates into three open courtyards, the middle one being the smallest and the others of roughly equal size. Someone entering the temple through the pair of massive pylons would have been confronted by a raised area with a large altar surrounded on both sides by 110 smaller altars arranged symmetrically in rows. In the third, farthest courtyard stood a temple that in many respects recalled a similar building in the Great Aten Temple. It consisted of two open courts, each with a large altar on a raised area surrounded by smaller altars that were arranged symmetrically in rows. The rear part of the temple was defined on the northern, eastern, and southern sides by two lines of columns. The long axis of the temple was oriented directly into the valley opening out to the rocks to the east, to Akhenaten's tomb, and thus both buildings mystically linked and probably bound the temple to the ruler's life, posthumous life, and cult.

<< The Great Aten Temple, Gem-pa-Aten ('Aten is found'), in Armana.
1. hypostyle hall
2. first court with offering tables
3. second court with offering tables
4. third court with offering tables
5. high altar
6. pylon, with small temple adjacent to it; the pylon was part of the great enclosure wall that surrounded the temple

This fragment of a limestone column shaft is one of the few remains of the Small Temple in Amarna.

Plan of the Small Aten Temple in Amarna

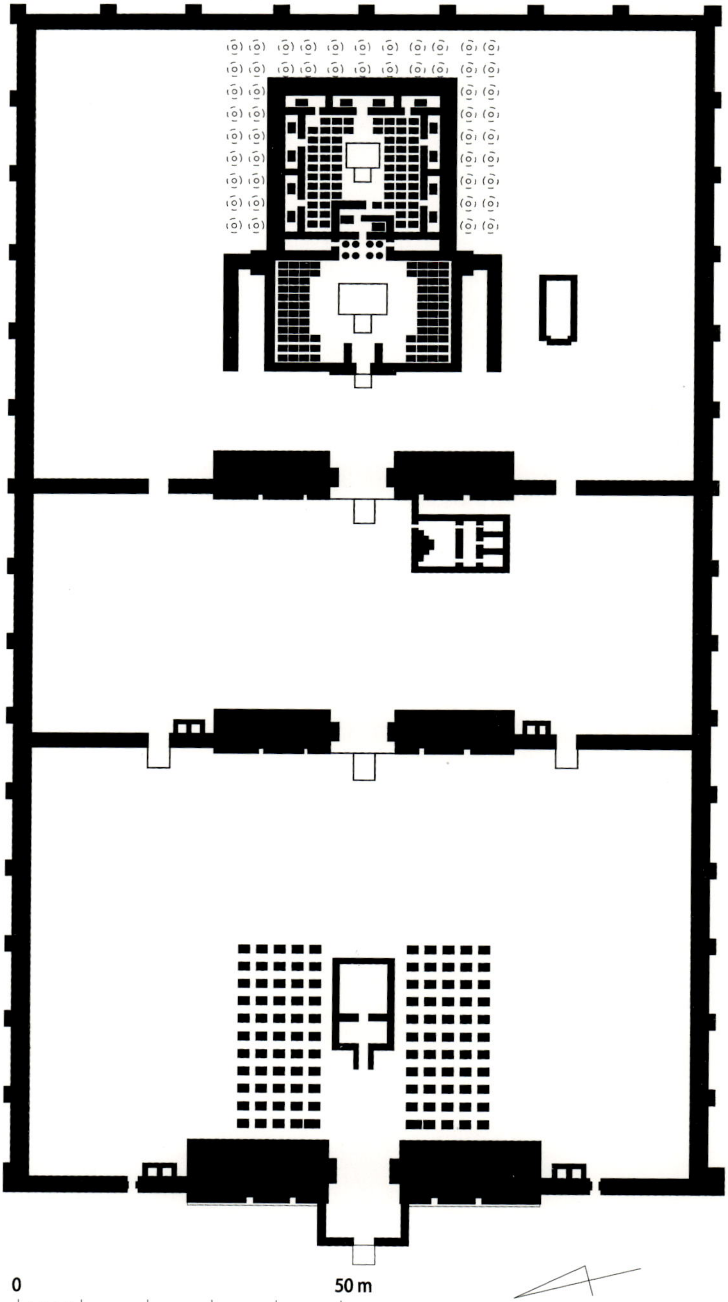

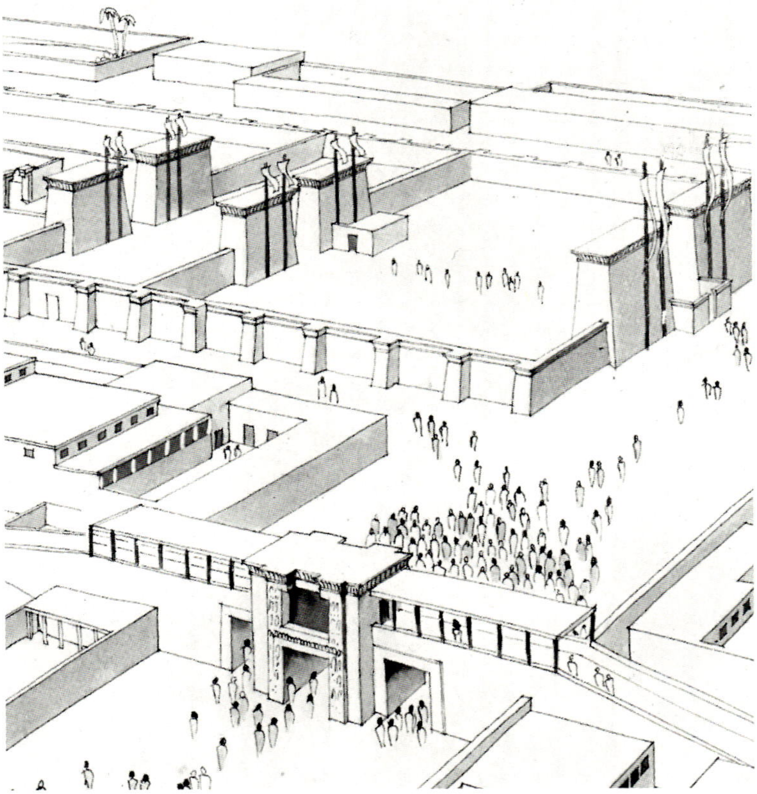

Pendlebury's reconstruction of the central part of Akhetaten with bridge and royal palace. The king would appear in the 'window of appearance' on the bridge to receive homage from the assembled crowds and present rewards and honors.

Between the Great and Small Temples of Aten lay the ruler's residence, the King's House, surrounded by administrative buildings, stores, stables, and other service facilities. Here too was the Office of Records, in the ruins of which a local woman, digging up clay to fertilize her field, discovered the famous Amarna Archive of clay tablets in 1887. These were written in cuneiform in Akkadian, the diplomatic language of the time, and concerned Egypt's diplomatic relations with other more or less important rulers and vassals in Syro-Palestine from roughly the last phase of the reign of Amenhotep III to the years of the reign of Tutankhamun.

The King's House was connected by a bridge above the Royal Road to the Great Palace known as 'The House of Rejoicing in Akhetaten.' Located on the west side of the Royal Road, the Great Palace was a luxurious, richly adorned building with courtyards, hypostyles, and a throne hall, where the king conducted such royal business as receiving envoys from foreign lands. Like the King's House, the Great Palace boasted floors and walls decorated with superb paintings in some of the rooms. The bridge connecting the King's House with the Great Palace had a 'window of appearance,' a kind of balcony from which the king and his closest family and associates would watch the festivals and processions on the Royal Road and from which the king would present, or rather throw, gifts to those he wished to honor for their services.

North of the Central City, several groups of mud-brick buildings lay along the Royal Road. Archaeologists have designated these groups, starting from the north, as the North City, the North Palace, and the North Suburb. The North City comprised administrative and storage buildings. The North Palace, separate from both the North City and the North Suburb, was a building of residential character with rooms decorated by beautiful wall paintings, and with large courts, gardens, and colonnades. Originally it was the residence of Akhenaten's second wife Kiya, and later of his daughter Meretaten. The Northern Suburb was a

The floor of the palace of Maru Aten in Amarna was decorated with superb paintings with nature motifs.

densely built-up area consisting of larger and smaller dwelling houses, farms, and service buildings. It seems to have been the center of the economic life of Akhetaten.

The South Suburb, which was not strikingly dissimilar to the North Suburb, was south of the Central City. The grand residences with gardens belonging to high-ranking officials, priests, and military dignitaries were situated here in addition to a complex of administrative buildings. The famous sculptor Thutmose, the main creator of the unique Amarna art, had his house and studio in the South Suburb. It was in the ruins of his house that in 1912 the German team found the celebrated bust of Akhenaten's chief wife Nefertiti, along with other works of art.

Ay with his wife worshipping Aten. Detail from the decoration of Ay's tomb in Amarna.

The picture of Akhetaten, as archaeologists have managed to reconstruct it so far, includes a number of other buildings, such as the relatively isolated Maru Aten ('Summer house of the Aten') south of the South Suburb. It consists of a whole set of buildings, sacred and secular: pavilions, solar altars, gardens, a pool, and so on. The whole building complex has often been considered to have a deeper, cosmic character symbolizing the role and meaning of the sun. Some archaeologists who study the confused and intricate subject of the Amarna royal family believe that Maru Aten may have originally been built for Nefertiti and then been usurped by Akhenaten's second favorite, Queen Kiya.

East of the Central City are two dwelling quarters for workmen, one containing houses built of stone, and the other surrounded by a wall and comprising small brick houses. Three raised areas where so-called desert altars accessed by mud-brick ramps once stood are located on the plain in the northeastern part of Akhetaten.

Together with the city of Akhetaten a cemetery was founded for the royal family, magnates, and high-ranking officials and priests. The common people and workmen were buried on the empty plain near the rock promontories closing in the city on the east. The grand tombs of the magnates and high officials were carved into the rocks on the northern and southern edges of these promontories. The northern cemetery consists of beautifully decorated rock tombs belonging to the officials closest to the king, that is, the people regarded as the intellectual elite of Akhetaten, such as Panehesy, Huya, and Merire. The relief decoration in the tombs, in some cases only sketched in, has great historical value since it often includes scenes from the life of Akhetaten.

The South Tombs, also carved into the rock, were the burial places of people who had occupied important offices, such as the commander of the local police Mahu or the general Paatonemheb. The most famous of the South tombs belonged to Ay ('God's father'), the gray eminence at the court of Akhenaten, who was later to take part in the restoration of the old order and eventually ascended the throne of the pharaohs. In his tomb in Akhetaten, which is adorned entirely in the Amarna artistic style, the famous solar hymn—'Great Hymn to the Aten'—was recorded on the wall. Fragments of the hymn were preserved in several other tombs of the time, but in Ay's we find it in the most complete form.

It is significant that the new royal cemetery, like the cemetery of the sacred Mnevis bulls that were considered the heralds and earthly embodiments of the *ba* of the sun god, was not founded opposite Akhetaten on the west bank of the Nile, where according to ancient established ideas the kingdom of the dead began, but in the rocks east of the city. In this cemetery, situated in the deep rocky valley of Wadi Abu Hasa al-Bahri, by far the most important but in its way also the most mysterious building is the Royal Tomb. Scholars believe that this tomb was intended to be the first in a projected new royal cemetery that would overshadow the Valley of the Kings in western Thebes. Akhenaten's tomb was supposed to dominate not only the new cemetery but also the entire newly founded city Akhetaten. This is suggested by a relief scene, unfortunately seriously damaged, which has been preserved on the wall of the central room of the tomb. The scene shows the sun disc rising on the horizon and bathing Akhenaten and Nefertiti in its life-giving rays (the *ankh* symbol of life is hung directly in the disc); the royal couple is standing in the middle of the Aten temples in an Akhetaten brimming with life and are paying homage to the dazzling god. As Nicholas Reeves emphasizes, this is why Michael Mallinson is right to consider Akhenaten's tomb to be have been conceived as the life-giving epicenter of the whole of Akhetaten.

The first archaeologist to investigate Akhenaten's tomb, which had long ago been robbed, was the Italian Alessandro Barsanti (1858–1917). Several other archaeologists explored the tomb after Barsanti's initial investigations, including Petrie for the Egypt Exploration Fund. In the

The way to the king's tomb hidden in the rocks east of Akhetaten leads for quite a long way through a ravine.

1970s, the British Egyptologist Geoffrey T. Martin resumed the examination of the tomb and published objects coming from it. The interpretation of the tomb has been a matter of academic controversy for many years. The tomb's plan resembles that of the royal tombs in the Valley of the Kings. It is accessible by a long downward sloping passage with a staircase and its central room is a columned hall, Akhenaten's burial chamber. As is usual in royal tombs of this period, in front of the entrance to the chamber a deep vertical shaft gapes in the floor. The king's red-granite sarcophagus had been smashed and only fragments of it were discovered in the tomb. Likewise, although the king's funerary equipment must have been rich, all that remains are more or less broken remnants: the alabaster cabinet for the canopic jars, the wooden model of a boat, *ushabtis* in limestone, faience, and sandstone, and so on. Nonetheless, one especially important find consisted of fragments of the sarcophagus of Queen Tiye, Akhenaten's mother; she too, then, was originally buried here.

Other burial chambers were carved into the tomb secondarily, and as their surviving remnants of relief decoration show, they were for the princess Meketaton and the king's second wife Kiya. Both probably died prematurely in childbirth. Another addition was a winding passage, which may indicate an intended burial, of Nefertiti, in the tomb. Akhenaten's tomb and the fate of his remains and those of the other main protagonists of the Amarna epoch are shrouded in speculation and mystery, to which the no less mysterious tomb KV55 in the Valley of the Kings in Thebes may provide a key.

Before his final break with the priests of Amun, Akhenaten originally intended his tomb to be in the Valley of the Kings in western Thebes. On the basis of architectural and archaeological findings, but not direct written records, scholars believe that Akhenaten started work on the tomb that is today designated WV25 (archaeologists designate the tombs in the Central Valley of the Kings using the abbreviation of its English name KV and tombs in the Western Valley with the abbreviation WV). Only a few burials from the Third Intermediate Period were found in this tomb, which was discovered at the beginning of the nineteenth century by the Italian adventurer Belzoni.

About ninety years later, in 1907, a rich American named Theodore M. Davis (1837–1915), who was an amateur archaeologist, hired an English Egyptologist named Edward Russell Ayrton (1882–1914) to carry out excavations in the Valley of the Kings. Ayrton and Davis managed to find the entrance to a rock tomb and the remains of a wall that had once closed it up. The tomb was designated KV55. In

the rubble in the passage leading to the burial chamber lay the leaves of a gilded wooden shrine, with decoration indicating that Akhenaten had had it made for his mother, Queen Tiye, but the image of the king and his name had been removed at a later date. In the burial chamber itself other parts of this shrine were found, and a number of other objects that pleasantly surprised the finders but also puzzled and confused them. One was a damaged wooden decorated anthropoid coffin with a nameless mummy. The head was contained in what is known as a Nubian wig and was protected, from behind, by the outstretched wings of a vulture goddess; a golden uraeus remained on the brow. Nor had the long beard attached to the chin been pulled off. The body of the coffin was decorated with the stylized plumage of the protective goddess. Down the middle of the lid ran the vertical band of a gilded inscription from which the royal name in cartouche had been excised. Alabaster canopic jars were found in the smaller side rooms beside the burial chamber, and from these too the original inscriptions had been removed. The finders believed that the canopic jars belonged to Queen Tiye, but today they are considered to belong to Akhenaten's second wife Kiya. Four so-called 'magic bricks' with inscriptions that unambiguously assign them to Neferkheprure Waenre, which means Akhenaten, were also discovered in the chamber. Various other objects of a funerary and religious character were

Only small fragments remain of the original relief decoration of the king's tomb.

unearthed here, including a clay seal with the name of Amenhotep III and Tutankhamun.

The discoveries created a very chaotic picture of the tomb, its owner, and the circumstances of the interment. Unsurprisingly, archaeologists focused primarily on the coffin and mummy. The initial theory that this was the burial of Queen Tiye was soon rejected on the basis of expert anthropological examination: the mummy proved to be male. A century has now gone by since the tomb was discovered and there have been constant Egyptological debates on the problem, but no definitive interpretation of the discoveries in KV55 has yet emerged. In regard to Queen Tiye, archaeologists generally consider (although not without reservations) that she is the 'Elder Lady,' whose mummy had already been found at the end of the nineteenth century in a secondary cache in the tomb of Amenhotep II (designated KV35). In regard to the coffin in KV55, one theory is that it was originally made for Akhenaten's second wife Kiya, but that in the end (as Reeves and Wilkinson, and a number of other Egyptologists, argue) it was altered for Akhenaten himself, and that the male mummy resting in the coffin should in fact be identified as Akhenaten. On the other hand, experts estimate that the mummy was a man who was twenty to twenty-six years old at the time of interment. Another theory (put forward by James P. Allen and others) is that this is the mummy of Smenkhkare, a king who reigned only briefly and whose origin and the circumstances of his rule are also the subject of a great deal of scholarly discussion and dispute. There is only one record of Smenkhkare and Queen Meretaten in Akhetaten; it is contained in the decoration of the tomb of Merire II. Some archaeologists consider Smenkhkare to have been Akhenaten's son and successor, while others believe that Nefertiti adopted the name Smenkhkare with the royal crown around the thirteenth year of Akhenaten's reign as the king's co-regent and later successor. There are other hypotheses that enjoy less scholarly support. The question of the identity of the mummy from tomb KV55 remains unanswered.

The Amarna era ended as suddenly as it had begun, and under very obscure circumstances. After Akhenaten's death, Smenkhkare, whoever he or she was, reigned briefly, perhaps for two years. He or she was succeeded on the throne by Tutankhaten, whose identity seems likely to be another subject of Egyptological controversy for many years to come, since it is not precisely known who his father and mother were. Some Egyptologists believe that his father was Akhenaten, others that it was Amenhotep III. There is an even greater range of views on Tutankhaten's mother. Was she Tiye, wife of Amenhotep III? Or

Akhenaten's second wife, the beautiful Kiya, identified by some Egyptologists with the Mitanni princess Tadukhepa? Or the daughter of Amenhotep III, the princess Sitamon? Nor can we exclude the possibility that his mother was the eldest daughter of Akhenaten and Nefertiti, princess Meretaten. Tutankhaten succeeded to the throne at a very young age—he was not even ten at the time—and was unable to resist

Haremheb kneeling before Amun and offering him two vessels of wine. Luxor Museum.

Tutankhamun's wife Ankhesenamun rubs the king with perfumed grease. Detail from the decoration of Tutankhamun's golden throne. Egyptian Museum, Cairo.

the growing pressure for a return to the old gods. He was far too young to be able to hold the reins of real power. The military commander Haremheb and the 'God's father' Ay acquired enormous influence at Tutankhaten's court. Shortly after the start of Tutankhaten's reign, there began a sharp turning away from the existing political and religious course and a return to earlier conditions. The god Amun, and with him the other gods of the Egyptian pantheon, made a comeback. The victory of Amun was reflected in important events relating directly to the ruler and his closest circle: in the second year of his reign the king changed his name from Tutankhaten ('Living likeness of Aten') to Tutankhamun ('Living likeness of Amun'), left Amarna with his court, and moved to the old royal seat and Egyptian capital city Memphis.

The reign of Tutankhamun did not last long, perhaps only nine years. The cause of his premature death was not murder by a blow to the back of the head, as some Egyptologists believed on the basis of minor damage to his skull (this occurred during mummification). Indeed, in January 2005 the former Minister of Antiquities Zahi Hawass initiated a thorough examination of Tutankhamun's mummy using computer tomography, which was carried out by a medical team of leading Egyptian and foreign experts. This study showed that shortly before his death the young king had suffered a fracture of the femur and a number of other fractures (apart from those that can be blamed on Howard Carter and his team when they were handling Tutankhamun's mummy) that had not had time to heal. It is possible that the young man liked racing a light horse-drawn two-wheeled chariot across the desert, and the pursuit proved fatal to him.

His young widow Ankhesenamun failed in what was a very bold, and in the Egyptian context completely unprecedented, plan. Upon her husband's death she hurriedly asked the Hittite king Suppiluliuma to give her his son as a husband. However, Prince Zanzana was probably murdered on his way to Egypt, and so the daughter of a king of Egypt did not become the wife of a foreigner. We can only speculate whether Haremheb or Ay or both were responsible for the murder. In light of the fact that Ay and then Haremheb—who brought the Amarna era to its end—consecutively occupied Tutankhamun's throne, it would not be surprising to uncover evidence implicating one or both of the men in Prince Zanzana's murder. The destruction of Akhetaten began under Haremheb's rule, as is shown by the fact that the royal pylon in nearby Hermopolis was built of blocks from the demolished buildings. According to Barry Kemp, however, the dismantling of Akhetaten took place in several stages. Indeed, the presence of Haremheb's name on one limestone block from the Great Aten Temple means that he may have still respected Aten at the beginning of his reign. Similarly, on blocks from the Small Temple of Aten we find signs of efforts at erasure that leave the name of Aten and may have been directed only at the royal names. The return to the old order culminated soon after the rule of Haremheb, under the first kings of the Nineteenth Dynasty: during Ramesses II's reign the temples and palaces in Amarna were torn down, and Akhenaten, the king-reformer, was branded the "criminal of Akhetaten."

For long millennia Akhenaten's memory fell into an oblivion from which it was not to be retrieved until the advent of modern archaeology. Even then, it was only the discovery of Tutankhamun's intact rock tomb in the Valley of the Kings that set off the immense wave of still undiminished interest among Egyptologists and the general public in the dramatic events of the Amarna period. In a sense, Akhenaten was ahead of his time. His faith and his attempt to reform Egyptian society, however progressive and audacious for their time, were largely predestined to fail. His language reform brought lasting change and the Amarna artistic style had some continuing influence on the style of the subsequent period, but the main change, the switch to monotheism, could not be sustained. It was too abstract and intellectual a religion, one that could only have an appeal (whether from conviction or cool pragmatism) to the ruler's immediate circle and the governing elite. It was not the expression of a long-term evolution of an idea, but a matter of orders from above, and the mass of the people never ceased to trust in their domestic gods and never abandoned their traditional religious beliefs. Yet, even if it was a premature step and failed in its time, the Amarna era, its protagonists, a religious reform considered to be the first monotheistic doctrine in history, and the superb works of art associated with it, will always be among the most fascinating and inspiring elements in the legacy of ancient Egypt.

Dazzling Aten

Almost a millennium and a half had gone by since the sun god of Heliopolis had started to dominate the Egyptian world of gods and men. In that time, Egypt had undergone great changes: It had experienced an unprecedented rise in the era of the pyramid builders of the Old and Middle Kingdom but also the terrible decline that followed. At the end of the second period of decline, Egypt rebelled against the humiliation of Hyksos supremacy; at the beginning of the New Kingdom the Egyptian kings brought a new confidence and prosperity to a reunified land. The Egyptian rulers from Thebes had fought for the liberation of the country under the banner of their local god Amun; after the final victory Amun enjoyed the favor of all Egypt and a dominant position among the Egyptian gods. The old sun god of Heliopolis was not forgotten, but he changed. The mysterious creator of the gods and the world emerging from the chaos of the primordial waters and journeying through time and the cosmos in the eternal cycle of day and night became more remote from the people and world that he had made. The great creator of the order of the world, the victor over the forces of chaos and evil, and lord of mystic transformations became hidden and lonely. As religious texts of the time show, and as the German Egyptologist and leading expert on Egyptian religion Jan Assmann emphasizes, the solitary sun god was now gazing down on people from afar. This is

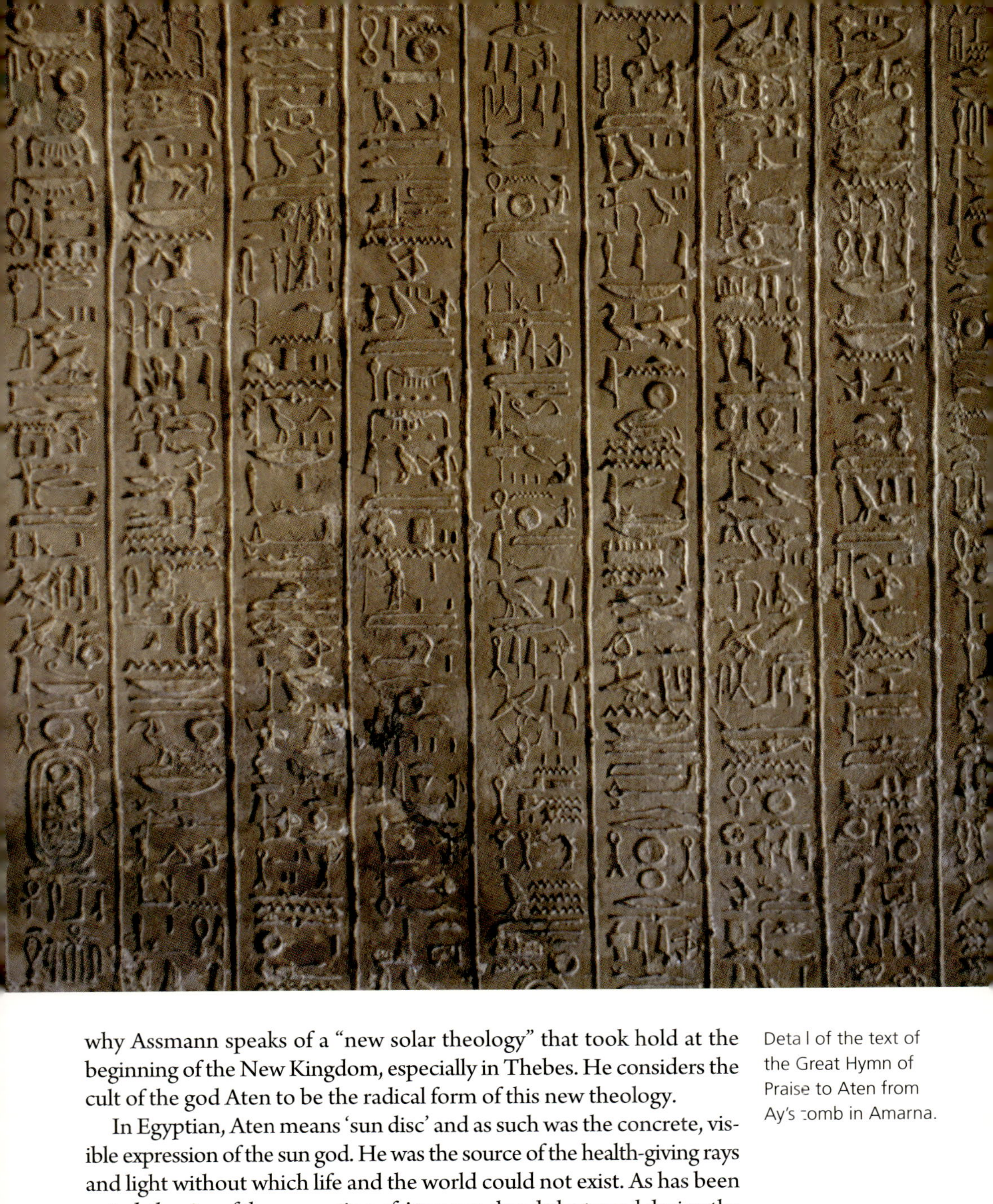

why Assmann speaks of a "new solar theology" that took hold at the beginning of the New Kingdom, especially in Thebes. He considers the cult of the god Aten to be the radical form of this new theology.

In Egyptian, Aten means 'sun disc' and as such was the concrete, visible expression of the sun god. He was the source of the health-giving rays and light without which life and the world could not exist. As has been noted, the rise of the veneration of Aten can already be traced during the reign of Amenhotep III, but the cult immediately acquired far more prominence immediately after the accession of Amenhotep IV, as is evident from the rapid construction of temples to Aten in Karnak. The major rupture with the past came around the fourth year of the reign of

Deta l of the text of the Great Hymn of Praise to Aten from Ay's :omb in Amarna.

Amenhotep IV when the king changed his name to Akhenaten and then left Thebes, founded Akhetaten, and clearly formulated the principles of the religion of Aten. Aten became the only god, and the king his main servant and prophet in the world of men. Aten was a god who created and permeated life and invigorated the world with his radiant light and heat. He required no mysterious rituals and was not associated with any esoteric world beyond the tomb: life after death was believed to resemble life in this world. Aten's greatness and dignity was expressed in the writing of his name in cartouche: the symbol of limitless power. The worship of Aten was simple and consisted of praising and glorifying the god and bringing offerings in the open air. The king did not have priests to represent him and carry out these rites in his absence as had been the case with other gods and kings in previous times; the king conducted the rites himself, accompanied by his family. This did not mean, however, that priests were entirely excluded from the cult of Aten. In the veneration of Aten apart from the king there appears a 'first god's servant of Aten' or Heliopolitan high priest entitled 'the highest of the seers.'

Rather than providing a complicated description of the cult of Aten and its beliefs, we direct readers to another text, entitled "Great Hymn of Praise to Aten," in which the ideas of the new religion are best conveyed. The text is a cogent and passionate confession of faith which is often attributed to Akhenaten himself.

Beautifully you come forth in radiance
On the horizon of heaven,
You, the living sun, giver of life!
You rise on the eastern horizon
And fill every land with your beauty.
You are gracious, mighty, and glittering,
High above every land.
Your rays suffuse the lands, like your creative powers:
As Re you encompass them,
And subdue them for your beloved son.
Although you are so distant, your rays are on earth,
Although you are visible,
Your voyaging is unknowable.

When you withdraw on the western horizon,
The land finds itself in darkness,
In the kingdom of death.

People sleep in their bedchambers with covers over their heads;
One eye cannot see another.
And if all their possessions were stolen from under their heads,
They would not know it.
Every beast of prey comes out of his den,
All vermin sting.
Darkness is like a tomb:
The earth is silent,
For its creator is resting in his horizon.

As soon as you come forth on the horizon at dawn,
Shining as the sun of day,
You drive away the darkness and send your rays
Each day, and the Two Lands can celebrate a festival.
Because of you, all with legs to stand on awake and arise,
Wash their limbs, and put on their raiment,
And with arms raised they worship you, because you have appeared
In radiance. The whole world goes to work.

The farm beasts are content with their feed,
The trees and plants grow.
The birds fly up from their nests
And greet you with their wings.
The wild animals spring up,
And every creature that flies and alights
Lives, when you have risen for them.
The barques people sail upstream and downstream:
All ways are open, for you have come forth in radiance.
The fish in the river
Leap before your face,
For your rays reach even into the sea.

Thanks to you, in women the seed grows
From which you fashion men.
You sustain the son in the womb of his mother
And give him breath,
For your desire is to keep alive all you have made.
And when he descends from the womb
And takes his first breath on his first day,
You open his mouth and take care of him.

When the unhatched chick
Stirs in the eggshell,
You grant him breath to keep him alive.
After the time you have determined for him,
He breaks the egg, and comes out of it,
And straightaway begins to chirp.
And almost as soon as he emerges,
he can already run about.
How manifold are your creations
And hidden from (human) sight!
Sole god, to whom no other is like!

When you were all alone, you created the world according to your will
With people, herds of cattle, and wild beasts,
With all that is on the earth, walking upon it,
With all that is in the air and on the wing.
To all lands—Syria, Nubia,
And the land of Egypt—
You have assigned territory and provided sustenance.
Each one has his necessities and defined span of life.
The peoples differ in language,
As in their natures,
And they have different complexions; thus have you made the foreigners distinct.

You created the Nile in the Kingdom of the West.
And you bring it forth as you wish,
To keep alive mankind whom you have created:
You are their lord, who troubles himself on their behalf.
Lord of all lands,
Who rises for them,
Sun of the day, majestic!
You have given life to all faraway lands.
You have created a Nile in the heavens, so that it should descend to them,
And make waves between the mountains like the sea,
And water their fields by their dwellings.
How excellent are your designs, Lord of Eternity!
You give a celestial Nile to foreign nations
And to the beasts of all mountainous lands that go on their feet.

The Nile comes from the Kingdom of the West into Egypt.
Your rays sustain the meadows:
When you rise, they become green and grow as you desire.
You have created the seasons, in order that all you have made should grow,
Winter, that everything should be cooled,
Summer, that everything should honor you.
You have raised the heavens so that you might come forth in them
And observe all that you made when you were alone.
In the form of the living Sun
You come forth and shine,
Withdrawing and drawing closer.

You create millions of forms of yourself, O Sole One:
Towns and villages, fields, roads, and rivers:
Every eye beholds you
When you are overhead, O Sun of Day!
And even when you depart, and are seen by no eye endowed by you with sight, so that you do not have to gaze on your creatures,
I never cease to remember you, for there is none that knows you
Save your son Nefer-kheperu-Ra Wa-en-Ra.
Only to him do you make known your designs and your power!

The world is in being thanks to you,
For you created it.
When you come forth, life lives. Eyes behold your beauty as you set,
All work ceases when you vanish in the west.
When you come forth again, all blossoms for the king,
Balance has reigned since the moment you created the world.
You established all for your son, who came forth from you,
The King of Upper and Lower Egypt, who lives by the truth,
The Lord of the Two Lands Nefer-kheperu-Ra Wa-en-Ra,
And for the beloved Great Wife of the king,
The Lady of the Two Lands Nefer-nefru-Aten Nefertiti,
Who lives and is young forever.
(translated by A. Bryson from the original Czech translation of the hymn by B. Vachala)

<< This bust of Queen Nefertiti, with the unusual blue crown and uraeus on her head, has become one of the icons of ancient Egypt. Limestone covered with plaster and polychromed. Egyptian Museum, Berlin.

The Beauty Has Come

The polychrome limestone bust of Queen Nefertiti—her full name was Nefernefruaten Nefertiti ('Perfect-is-the-Beauty-of-Aten The-Beauty-Has-Come')—is both a supreme work of art and one of the icons of Egypt. Ironically, it is not exhibited anywhere in Egypt but in the Egyptian Museum in Berlin. The beauty of Nefertiti is timeless and the origin and fate of this exceptional woman continue to be veiled in mystery. In view of her complexion and apparently un-Egyptian appearance, and also the name 'The Beauty Has Come' (Egyptologists concerned with linguistics believe that at the time she lived her name was pronounced Naftet and the name of her husband Akhenaten was pronounced Akhaniati), some Egyptologists were previously inclined to identify her with Tadukhepa, the daughter of the Mitanni king Tushratta, who was married into the Egyptian royal house as an act of royal diplomacy. Other scholars believe that her unusual crown connects her with an eastern Mediterranean region. Today the prevailing view is that Nefertiti was in fact an Egyptian (she had an Egyptian wet nurse), and possibly the daughter of the 'god's father' Ay. Yet obscurities continue to surround Nefertiti's identity. Nor is it clear why she came to have so unusually important a position in her husband's reign—for example, appearing by herself in some rituals previously reserved for the king. Nor are the circumstances in which Nefertiti disappears from the scene, roughly after the twelfth year of Akhenaten's reign, at all clear. On the basis of statues of Nefertiti discovered in Karnak and some epigraphic and iconographic documents today, most Egyptologists concerned with the Amarna era believe that Nefernefruaten Nefertiti probably became Akhenaten's coregent and changed her name to Nefernefruaten Ankhkheprure. The added throne name Ankhkheprure means 'Forms of Re are living.' Some scholars even consider it possible that she changed her name for a third time, to Smenkhkare ('The *ka* of Re is fashioned excellently'). Questions and obscurities surround not just the life of the beautiful Nefertiti, but also, until recently, her superb bust, which remains a bone of contention in Egyptian–German relations. The seeds of discord were sown by none other than one of the most celebrated German archaeologists in Egypt, Ludwig Borchardt.

Borchardt was not only an outstanding archaeologist but also an architect, organizer, and diplomat. His name is associated with the founding of two archaeological institutes in Egypt: the Deutsches Archäologisches Institut in Cairo, and when he later left Germany after the Nazis took power (he was Jewish), he established the

Schweizerisches Institut für Ägyptische Bauforschung und Altertumskunde in Cairo. He was involved in the most important archaeological excavations of his time, such as the sun temple in Abu Ghurab and the pyramids in Abusir. The promising results achieved in Amarna by the British Egypt Exploration Fund, which had started to work there in the last years of the nineteenth century under Petrie's leadership, did not escape his attention. Borchardt was very well aware of the archaeological potential of Amarna; after finishing work in Abusir he persuaded the Deutsche Orient-Gesellschaft (German Oriental Society) to allow a German team to excavate there. The work started in 1911 and continued until the outbreak of the First World War in 1914. Not long after excavations started, they were dramatically justifying the decision to work in Amarna and confirming Borchardt's skill, instinct, and constant archaeological lucky star.

In December 1912, coincidentally at a time when Borchardt was personally present in Amarna, the German expedition found the house of the sculptor Thutmose and in it a whole collection of works of art that are today among the most valuable and beautiful of any known from ancient Egypt. Among these works was the polychrome bust of Queen Nefertiti with the crown that was typical in her representations but otherwise very rarely appears in Egyptian sources. There were various scratches on the surface of the mud-caked bust, both ears were partly broken off, and the left eye was missing, leaving only an empty eye socket. It is only today, after thorough examination of the socket, that we know there was never any eye in it; the bust had served as a sculptor's model and the left eye socket was deliberately left empty.

The dispute between Egypt and Germany over the ownership of Nefertiti's bust is recounted in detail in an article by Rolf Krauss. In January 1913, at the end of the archaeological season, the German finds at Amarna were divided up. Nefertiti's bust was assigned to the German share and was legally exported to Germany with all the requisite official stamps. There it lay for more than ten years in the store of the Egyptian Museum in Berlin, Borchardt having expressly requested that it remain a secret. It was not until 1924 that it appeared in the exhibition, immediately attracting deserved attention from the public, but also provoking a speedy and enraged reaction from the Egyptian authorities. Through the then director of the Antiquities Service, the Frenchman Pierre Lacau (1873–1963), Egypt demanded the immediate return of the bust. Borchardt was even threatened with the prospect of having any future archaeological work in Egypt halted. After a time, passions cooled, archaeological-diplomatic talks were held, and a compromise that satisfied both sides was reached: in exchange for returning the bust of Nefertiti, Germany would obtain a collection of selected antiquities from the collection of the Egyptian Museum in Cairo. In the end, however, the German government (or more precisely the Prussian government, because the management of the Egyptian Museum in Berlin fell within its jurisdiction) withdrew from the agreement. It is related that when Hitler (in another version it is the 'art lover' Göring) came to power, he had the bust of Nefertiti brought to him and was enchanted by it. He gazed at it for some time in deep thought and finally confirmed that it would stay in Germany. He is said to have declared, "What the German nation holds, it will not yield."

Only much later, on the basis of archival documents and the memories of those who took part in the division of finds in 1913, were the circumstances in which the bust was exported to Germany reconstructed with some degree of reliability. Gustave Lefèbvre (1879–1957) represented the Egyptian side, that is, the Antiquities Service. At that time, Lefèbvre—who was not an archaeologist but was an outstanding philologist—occupied the post of chief inspector of antiquities for southern Egypt with its office in Asyut. He was informed in advance about the wonderful German finds in Amarna and so personally attended to the allocation of antiquities in the store of the Germans' excavation house. The division took place by the light of hand-held candles; to the uninitiated it might have looked like some mysterious ritual. The finds were kept packed in chests on the table, but the lids of the chests were open and Lefèbvre was free to take out any object, examine it, and personally decide to whom to allocate it. At the start of the process Lefèbvre and the German expedition had agreed that the plaster models would go to the German side, and the Germans had already placed the bust of Nefertiti among them. In fact, although the bust is covered with a layer of plaster stucco, it is made of limestone. This was not obvious at first sight and at the time of the division the bust had not even been cleaned, let alone restored. Lefèbvre therefore agreed that the Germans should take the bust. He signed the relevant protocol and the chests were sealed and sent to the Egyptian Museum in Cairo, where they were carefully stamped (which counted as customs approval) and dispatched to Berlin without further problems . . . until later.

Archaeological plan of Tanis as it looked at the end of the eighteenth century.

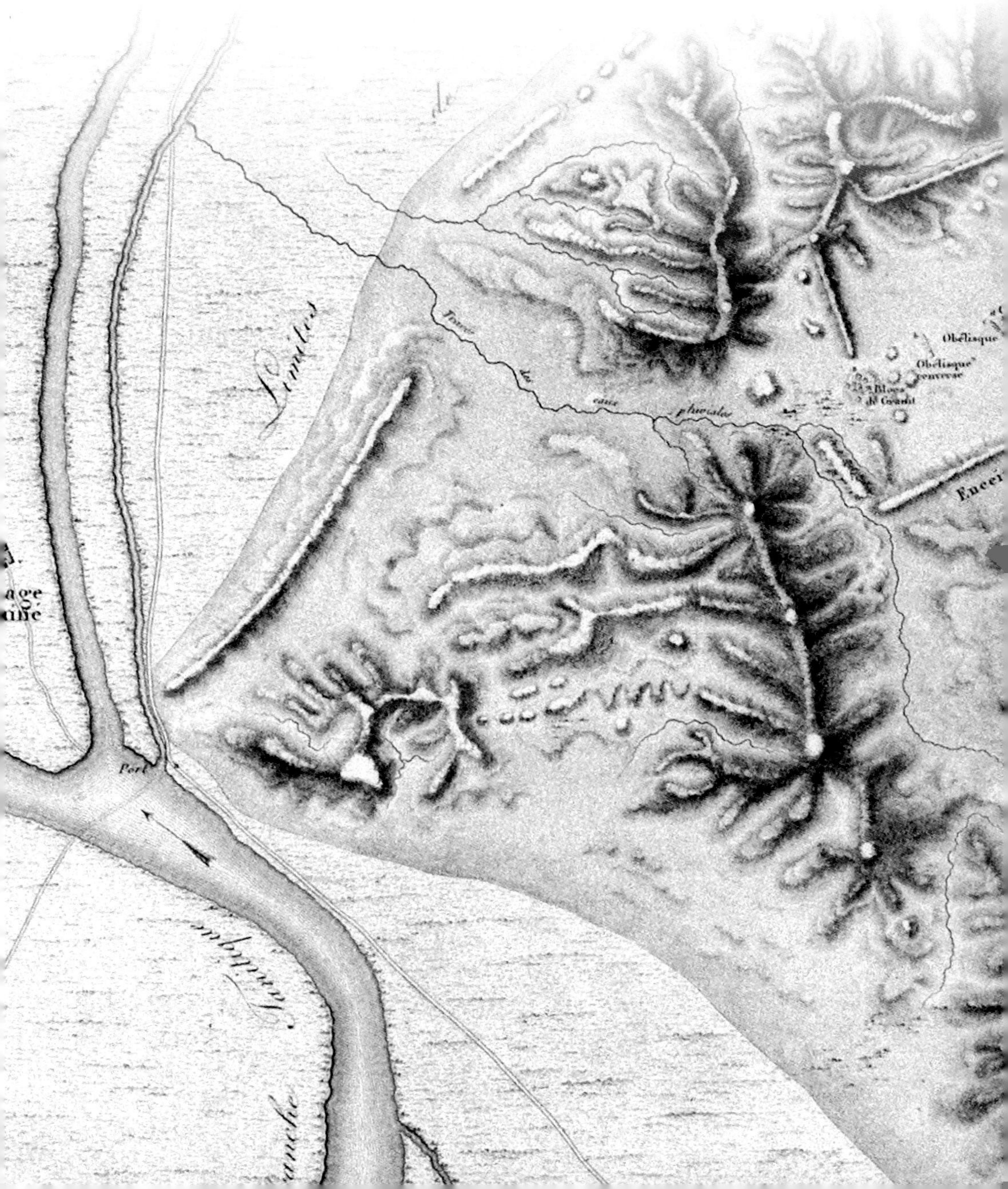

7

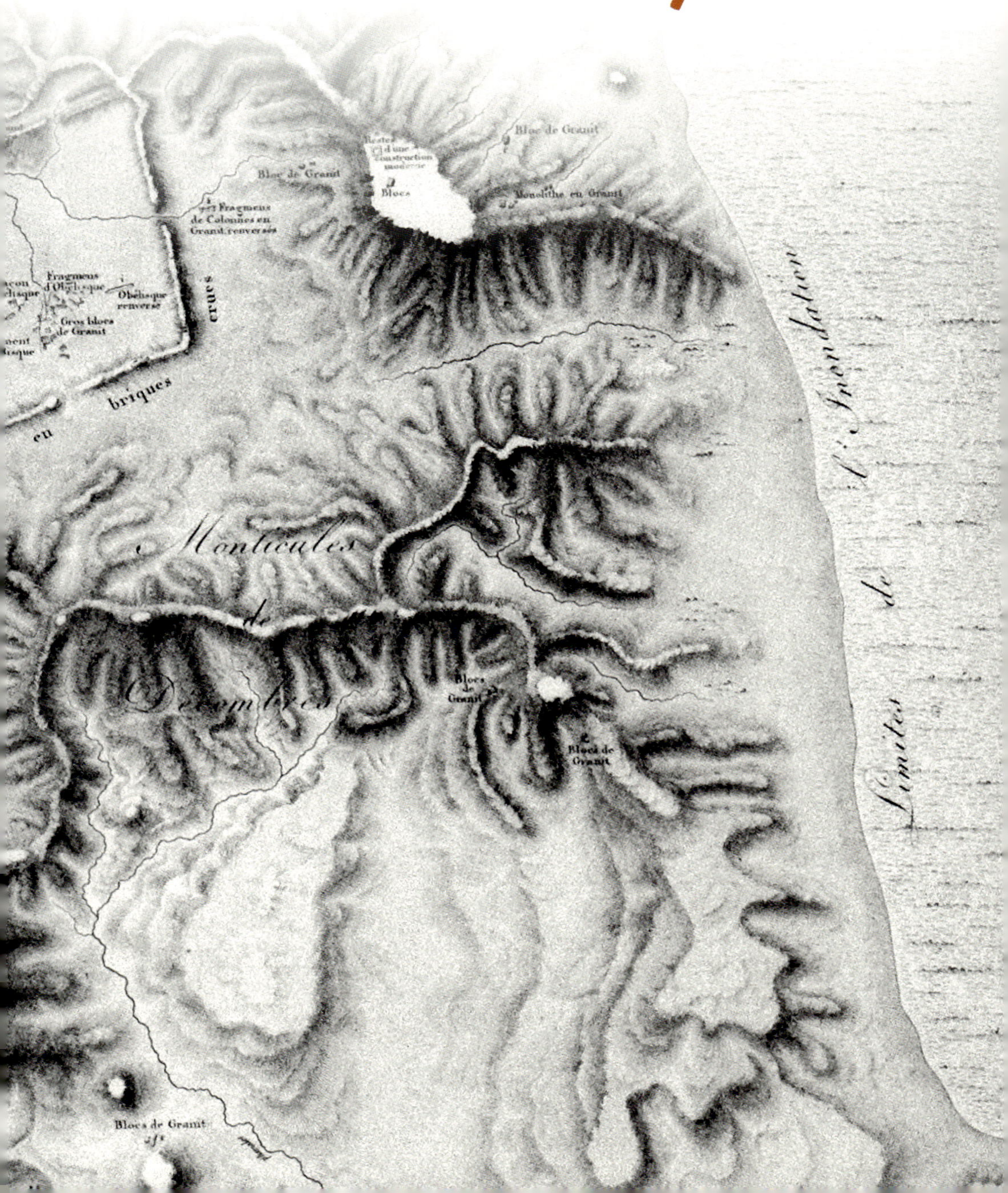
Bloc de Granit
Restes d'une construction moderne
Bloc de Granit
Blocs
Monolithe en Granit
Fragmens de Colonnes en Granit renversés
Fragmens d'Obélisque
Obélisque renversé
Gros blocs de Granit
crues
briques
en
Monticules de Décombres
Blocs de Granit
Blocs de Granit
Limites de l'Inondation
Blocs de Granit

Tanis: The Thebes of the North

<< Broken quartzite colossus of Ramesses II, found by Montet's team in Tanis in the early 1930s.

In 1722, the learned Jesuit Abbé Claude Sicard was the first scholar in the modern era to propose that San in Egypt was the biblical Zoan, mentioned in Psalm 78, verses 12 and 43: "Marvelous things did he in the sight of their fathers, in the land of Egypt, in the field of Zoan. . . . How he had wrought his signs in Egypt, and his wonders in the field of Zoan." Subsequent archaeological research has confirmed this idea. The Egyptian city of Djanet (known in Greek as Tanis, in the Bible as Zoan, and in Coptic as San) lies on the right bank of the Tanis branch of the Nile south of Manzala Lake in the northeastern Nile Delta. The original name and archaeological reality of the place is also reflected in its modern name, San al-Hagar, or 'San of Stone.' Archaeological Tanis consists of the huge low hill of Tell San al-Hagar, roughly one and a half kilometers in diameter, which rises from the sandy and marshy plain and is peppered with huge pieces of stone monuments. Today the mound has been to a large extent excavated and archaeologically investigated.

Originally, Tanis was just a provincial town, the center of the nineteenth Lower Egyptian nome. It owed its rise to its position as the starting point for an important trade route into Palestine and beyond into Syria. At the end of the Twentieth Dynasty the official Wenamun, who was sent from Thebes by the high priest Herihor to procure cedar wood in western Asia for the restoration of Amun's sacred barque, made a stop here. Wenamun's journey, recorded on a Twenty-second Dynasty papyrus, which was found in the Upper Egyptian town al-Hiba and first published by the Russian Egyptologist Vladimir Semionovich Golenischeff (1856–1947), is a famous ancient Egyptian work of literature.

Scholars accompanying Napoleon's military expedition to Egypt made the first modern, if very superficial, plan of this famous archaeological site. Not long afterward, Tanis received a visit from the French sculptor Jean Jacques Rifaud (1786–1845), who was hunting and gathering Egyptian antiquities (it is hard to find a better expression for his 'excavations') for the French consul in Egypt, Bernardino Drovetti (1776–1852). In Tanis, too, he was successful; he obtained four sphinxes, two of which ended up in the Louvre in Paris and the others in the Hermitage in Saint Petersburg. A new, more thorough plan of

Tell San al-Hagar.

the monuments of Tanis was made in the early 1840s by the Prussian scientific expedition led by Lepsius.

The first archaeological research initiated in Tanis in 1860, and as in many other places in Egypt associated with the Frenchman Auguste Mariette, brought remarkable results. On the site of the Temple of Amun Mariette managed to unearth statues of King Senwosret I and Queen Nofret, the so-called Hyksos sphinxes carved in black granite, and many other precious antiquities. Among them were half a dozen stone stelae, of which one—the previously mentioned 'Stela of Four Hundred Years'—was of particularly major historical significance because its text related to the origins of the family of Ramesses II and the cult of the god Seth.

In the years 1883–84 another of the founders of Egyptian archaeology, Flinders Petrie, briefly worked in Tanis for the Egypt Exploration Fund. His conclusions on the founding of the city and its development were in many respects mistaken, which is not surprising given the lack of knowledge at that time and Petrie's limited resources for archaeological research; later it became evident that many antiquities brought from other, and sometimes very distant, sites had been used in the building of Tanis. In Petrie's short period of activity in Tanis, his finds included papyri with hieratic, demotic, and Greek texts. In most cases these were scraps congealed in a homogenous and to a great extent carbonified mass. Despite their very poor condition, parts of some papyri were saved and turned out to date from a very late period. Two in particular proved extraordinarily valuable and their English titles became 'household names' in Egyptology: the Sign Papyrus and the Geographical Papyrus. The first was a kind of primer with a list of hieroglyphic signs and their explanations. It is a pity that only part of what is a unique find among Egyptian papyri should have survived in fragments, for if we had the complete text it would tell us much of interest about Egyptian hieroglyphs, their development, and how they were taught. The fragments of the Geographical Papyrus contain not only the names

Sphinx of Amenemhet III (the so-called Hyksos sphinx) in gray-black granite. Egyptian Museum, Cairo.

of places and calendar of festivals celebrated in them, but also information on local cults, cemeteries, and the like. There is no need to stress what a tremendous resource for knowledge of Egypt in the Roman Period this papyrus would have been if only it had been preserved intact.

After Petrie's departure there was no significant archaeological work undertaken in Tanis for decades. It was not until 1929 that a French expedition led by Pierre Montet (1885–1966) arrived in Tanis to conduct research; further research on this extremely important archaeological locality has remained in French hands since. Initially, the working conditions were very tough and primitive: no bathroom or shower, no darkroom for processing photographs, and the Nubian cook had to prepare food in the open air or, at best, in a tent. As time went by the situation improved, however, and French archaeological work has continued in Tanis to this day. Indeed, current excavations and research in Tanis are being led by Philippe Brissaud.

Tanis's rise in status from a provincial center to country's capital city at the beginning of the Twenty-first Dynasty was sudden and Egyptologists continue to debate the causes that led to this shift. This is because a mere fifteen kilometers southwest of Tanis, close to present-day Khatana and Qantir, lay Piramesse, the royal city and seat of Ramesses II. Piramesse was built on the location of an earlier Hyksos center, Hatweret, and in terms of its position played an important role in Ramesses II's campaigns of conquest in Palestine and Syria. Why did

Pierre Montet.

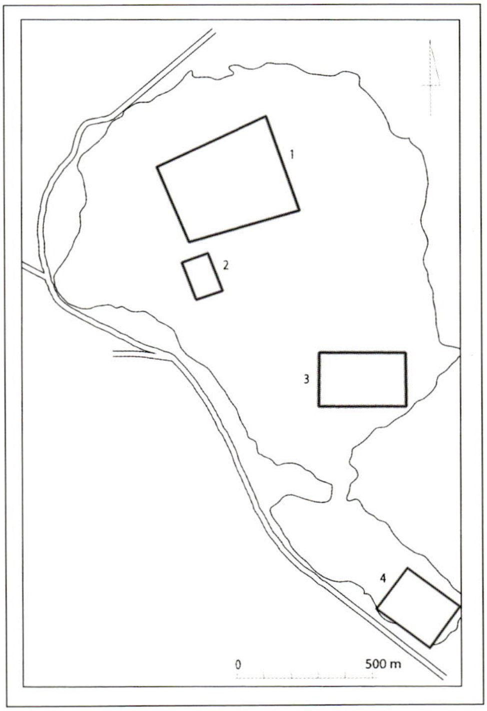

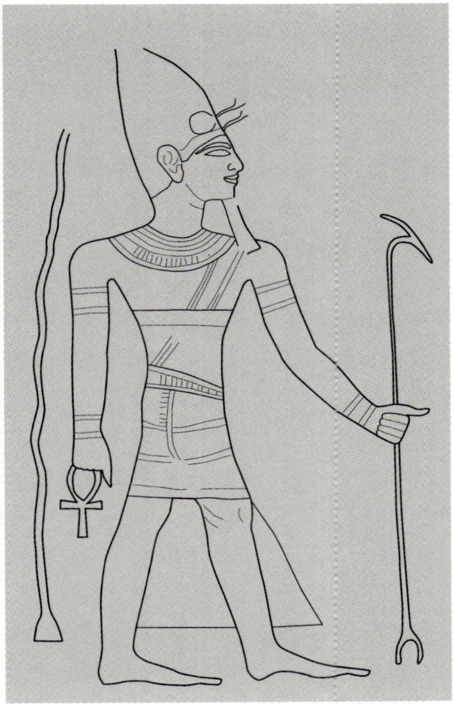

Piramesse fall into oblivion and Tanis rise? The most probable explanation is the one put forward on the basis of archaeo-hydrological research of the Nile Delta by the Austrian Egyptologist Manfred Bietak, who has also been involved in archaeological projects and finds in Avaris. According to Bietak, at the end of the Twentieth Dynasty the Pelusiac branch of the Nile silted up, increasing the importance of the Tanis branch, where the water flow became correspondingly stronger.

(left): Schematic orientation plan indicating the position of the main monuments in Tanis.
1. Amun's temple district
2. temple of Mut and Khonsu
3. temple of Horus of Mesen
4. temple of Amun of Opet

(right): Seth of Ramesse Meriamun. Detail of a scene from the Four-Hundred-Year Stela.

Modern archaeological research projects have only recently allowed scholars to resolve the long controversy over precisely where Piramesse stood. The famous German Egyptologist Heinrich Brugsch (1827–94) published a theory in 1872 in which he identified Tanis with either Avaris, Piramesse, or Sile, the latter of which was the metropolis of the fourteenth Upper Egyptian nome. Other Egyptologists disagreed but, due to the large quantity of monuments in San al-Hagar bearing the name of Ramesses II, many authorities (including Pierre Montet) continued for years to believe that Tanis was the celebrated city of Ramesses. Subsequent archaeological excavations have demonstrated quite clearly, however, that the oldest architectural monuments in Tanis are associated with the much later Twenty-first Dynasty king Pasbakhaenniut I (ca. 1048–999 BC).

The great building program initiated in Tanis by Pasbakhaenniut I was ideologically based on the cult of the Theban Triad: Amun, Mut, and Khonsu. Because there were no quarries with suitable stone close to Tanis, materials from older buildings—particularly in nearby Piramesse, but also Heliopolis, Memphis, and elsewhere—were used. Therefore, in Tanis we find stone blocks bearing the names of the pharaohs of the Old Kingdom—Khufu, Niussere, Teti, and Pepi I—with column capitals from the same time, and royal statues from the Middle Kingdom. It is ironic that the buildings erected in Tanis using usurped monuments eventually met the same fate. When Tanis was no longer the political center, the city became a convenient quarry supporting construction efforts elsewhere; today Tanis consists only of ruins from which it is hard to identify even the original ground plan of the buildings. Furthermore, the limestone sections of the ruins were often used by the local people to burn lime.

The Great Amun Temple founded by Pasbakhaenniut I and built up by subsequent kings of the Twenty-first and Twenty-second Dynasties must have been a grand structure comparable to Amun's temples in Karnak or Luxor once it was completed. It was almost a quarter of a kilometer long, spread out on an area of around thirteen hectares, and was surrounded by a massive mud-brick wall on an irregular but partly rhomboid ground plan, which was strikingly skewed toward the south. The temple was oriented in a roughly east–west direction and the main entrance was accessed through a granite gate built by Sheshonq III in the western stretch of the enclosure wall. Visitors would then pass between two colossi of Ramesses II, one carved out of sandstone and the other out of black granite, and beyond them another two colossi in red granite. On the basis of surviving remnants of masonry and especially architectural and decorative elements (obelisks, columns, statues, sphinxes, stelae, and so on) the front part of the temple is believed to have consisted of three successive monumental gates—pylons—with a courtyard adorned with columns behind each of them. Obelisks (twenty-six have been found in Tanis and, with one exception, they all bear the name of Ramesses II) and colossal statues stood in each case in front of the pylon towers, along the sides of the entrance. In the courtyard between the second and third pylons—where there was originally the greatest concentration of sphinxes, statues, and obelisks—there once stood two huge, very majestic, and even terrifying-looking black-granite sphinxes of King Amenemhet III with great manes, sometimes mistakenly called Hyksos

sphinxes, one on each side of the main route. Today, these sphinxes are exhibited in the west wing of the Egyptian Museum in Cairo.

The Temple of Amun stood beyond the third pylon, which was built out of granite by the Twenty-second Dynasty king Osorkon III. The Twenty-second Dynasty kings Pasbakhaenniut I and Siamon were primarily responsible for the construction of the Temple of Amun, which today is unfortunately so damaged that it is impossible to reconstruct even its basic ground plan. It is thought that like other Egyptian temples it contained a hypostyle, with columns usurped from earlier buildings. Beyond the columned hall there would have been an intimate part of the temple with a shrine most likely made of granite. However, there is not enough evidence to allow us to reconstruct its basic design. Closely abutting the eastern wall of the temple is a massive mud-brick wall dating from the time of Pasbakhaenniut I. There were three gates in the wall, on the eastern, northern, and western sides.

This red-granite palm column came originally from one of the royal buildings from the Old Kingdom in the neighborhood of Memphis.

Fallen colossus of Ramesses II.

> Plan of Amun's temple district in Tanis.

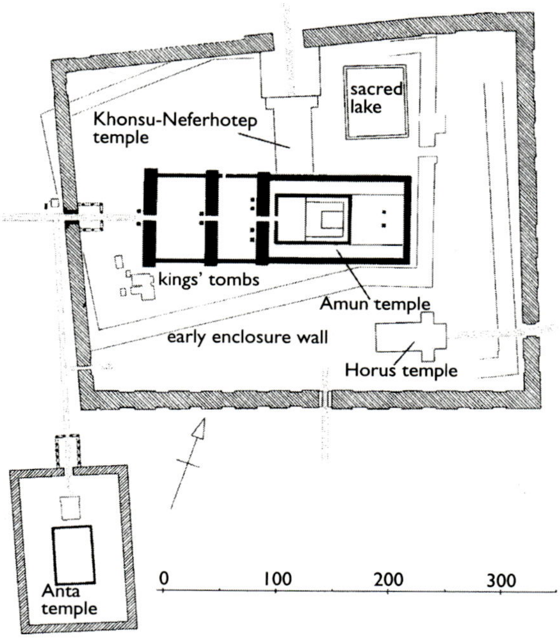

So little remains of the formerly grand temple of Amun in Tanis that we cannot even reconstruct its basic layout.

As we have already noted, the enclosure wall has a very irregular ground plan, with its central and western parts skewed strikingly toward the south. This meant that there was space in the northern section of the enclosed temple precinct for another temple, dedicated to Khonsu, that was built at right angles to the Temple of Amun in the Thirtieth Dynasty, under Nakhtnebef I. It was probably in the Ptolemaic Period that a small sacred pool was added in the northwestern corner of the precinct, with a rim constructed from recycled limestone blocks taken from two important buildings of Sheshonq V: the temple dedicated to Khonsu in Waset Neferhotep and a temple of the royal jubilee type, whose original location has not been identified.

Soon after the completion of the Temple of Khonsu, during Nakhtnebef II's reign, a new massive enclosure wall made of mud bricks was constructed, thus enlarging the temple district to approximately 430 × 370 meters. The wall was sixteen meters thick at its base and was built in the same ingenious way as similar walls from the same period around the Karnak temple precincts, that is, with regularly undulating layers of bricks.

East of the Temple of Amun and between the two enclosure walls stood a small temple, which was built using granite columns with palm

<< Torso of quartzite statue of Ramesses II.

capitals, which had already been usurped twice (by Ramesses II and Osorkon II) and that originally came from one of the Old Kingdom buildings in the Memphis area. The small temple is no longer extant. In the Ptolemaic Period a temple dedicated to Horus of Mesen was built in the northeastern section of the newly enlarged precinct. The cult of the god Horus was very popular at the time. One reason the temple was built in this particular location is because Mesen, probably situated where Sile is today, lay not far from Tanis and was the place, according to legend, that Horus had harpooned his enemy Seth, who at the time of the attack was in the form of a hippopotamus. The entrance to the Temple of Horus was directly opposite the eastern gate in the new large enclosure wall. Another three gates gave access to the temple district from the other three points of the compass. By the main, western granite gate, which was common to both enclosure walls and lay on the main axis of the Temple of Amun, there originally stood a granite colossus of Ramesses II. To judge by the size of the fragments it is thought to have weighed around a thousand tons and been more than twenty meters tall.

Outside the walled temple precinct and close to its southwestern corner lay the Temple of the goddess Anat ('Mistress of heaven'), which had its own enclosure wall. The laborers working on the French excavations had to remove thirty thousand cubic meters of sand and rubble to uncover the temple. Anat, originally venerated in Palestine and Syria, was the partner of the god Baal, who is regarded as the Semitic counterpart to the Egyptian Seth. Her cult, which was probably brought to Tanis from Piramesse where she was called 'Anat of Ramesses, Mistress of Heaven,' had already been adopted in northeastern Egypt under Hyksos rule. The cult of Anat proliferated significantly during the Nineteenth Dynasty when the goddess acquired features of the Egyptian Mut and became a royal protectress. Apart from Anat—represented as a woman with a tall hairstyle—the Theban Triad, Wadjet, and the gods of the Osiris circle were all worshiped in the temple. The buildings in the large temple precinct in Tanis were not all sacred in character: Secular buildings such as a brickworks, a bronze foundry, and stores have also been discovered here.

During and especially following the Second Intermediate Period the cults of Asian gods began to penetrate into Egypt. During the New Kingdom these cults became widespread not only among foreigners but in the Egyptian government elite. Their adoption owed much to the Egyptian wars of conquest in western Asia and the establishment of vassal states subordinated by Egyptian rulers. Unsurprisingly, it was the most warlike of the Asian gods that found favor with the Egyptian pharaohs. For example, Ramesses II gave himself the title 'Son of Anat,' and Sethi I named his team of horses 'Anat is satisfied.' The best-known Asian gods worshiped in Egypt were Baal, Reshep, Horan, Anat, Astarte, and Qadesh.

Baal ('Lord'), the Canaanite lord of heaven and king of the gods, but also the god of storms and fertility, was according to one version the son of the god El, who made him king of both gods and men. In Ugarit he was considered the son of the corn god Dagan. In Egypt, Baal was associated with Seth and represented with a crown on his head, in a short skirt, with a dagger at his waist and with the *was* scepter in his hand. Baal's important Egyptian cult center was his shrine in Peru nefer, a suburb of Memphis containing the shipyard of Thutmose III and a military port. Baal was often accorded the attribute 'of great strength.' Sethi I called himself 'stout-hearted as Baal,' 'of great terror over foreign lands like Baal,' and the like. Also documented are votive stelae offered up to Baal by ordinary people.

In the Egyptian cult of Reshep, a Canaanite god, it is mainly two aspects that come to the fore: war and fertility; his name is connected with the terms 'fire' and 'lightning.' In Egypt, he was sometimes associated with Min and at other times with Montu. He is usually represented in a robe reaching below the knee, with one leg forward, and his right arm raised and gripping a sickle sword or a thresher, lance, and shield. He often has the attribute 'lord of strength,' but we also encounter him as a healer god.

(left): Reshep.

(right): Anat.

Qadesh.

Horan, or Hauron, was a Syro-Palestinian god who may have originated from Hauron in east Jordan. He was probably a chthonic god, that is, connected with the underworld. Hauron was a protector against wild animals. There is evidence of his cult in Egypt from the reign of Amenhotep II by the Great Sphinx in Giza, regarded in the New Kingdom as the representation of the Egyptian god Haremakhet (Greek: Harmachis). The similarity of the names of the two gods led to their merger. Hauron also had a shrine in Piramesse; one of the titles that Ramesses II awarded himself was 'Favorite of Hauron.'

The Canaanite warrior goddess of fertility Anat ('Mistress of the Sky and Mistress of the Gods') standing at the side of Baal, does not appear in Egyptian sources until the Ramesside Period. She is usually depicted in tight-fitting transparent garb. On a stela from western Thebes she sits on a throne with the *atef* crown on her head, holding a shield and lance in one hand and waving a mace above her head with the other. She was venerated particularly in Piramesse and Tanis, where she was called the mother of Ramesses II.

Astarte was a very ancient Semitic goddess of fertility, who had the features of a healer as well as those of a warrior. She is usually represented with a horned crown on her head. The Greeks identified her with Aphrodite. In New Kingdom Egypt Astarte merged with the Semitic warrior goddess Ishtar, who was represented riding on a horse while holding either a lance or a shield and bow and arrows.

The New Kingdom also saw the spread in Egypt of the cult of Qadesh, the Syro–Palestinian goddess of fertility and love. She was depicted naked, standing on a lion, and holding a bunch of lilies and snakes in her hand. Qadesh's cult was centered in Memphis, where she was considered a daughter of Ptah and sometimes compared with Ptah's partner Sakhmet. The closeness in character of all these Asian goddesses is evident from the inscription on a stela from Thebes, where the goddess is represented in the typical form of Qadesh and named as Qadesh-Anat-Astarte.

The Treasures of Tanis

In their first ten archaeological seasons the French archaeologists led by Montet formed a basic archaeological conception of Tanis, at least an outline, but their eleventh season, in 1939, was to change the picture radically. It was then that the team made the epochal discovery of the tombs of the Twenty-first and Twenty-second Dynasty kings. The breakthrough was made in the area around the southwestern corner of the great Temple of Amun, on a site where Montet's team had worked several years before. While excavating smaller brick buildings here the laborers had come upon limestone panels, which the archaeologists initially thought were mere remnants of the paving of some earlier dismantled building. In their disappointment they had even ruefully nicknamed the panels the 'dance floor.'

Thorough examination of the place was to show, however, that this was not the flooring of a building of temple or palace type but the ceiling of a tomb, even though there may perhaps have been an aboveground section above it. One panel of the 'flooring' stone was missing, and as later became apparent, this was because it had been pried out by thieves in antiquity, who accessed the tomb and robbed the interior by removing the panel. After a while the laborers started to pick up fragments of *ushabtis* bearing the name of King Sheshonq, son of Bastet, from the rubble as they cleared a way for Montet to descend into the underground section along the same route taken by the ancient thieves. Montet found himself in a chamber with walls covered in relief scenes

The entrance to one of the royal tombs in Tanis.

and inscriptions resembling the decoration of the royal tombs in the Valley of the Kings in Thebes. The chamber turned out to be an antechamber from which a smaller passage led into a burial chamber with a sarcophagus, and thence to yet another burial chamber in red granite with a sarcophagus sticking out from a mixture of sand and mud. Montet and his colleagues were on the threshold of a discovery of immense value.

The French archaeologists soon realized that they were in the middle of a group of tombs, each having more than one chamber. These tombs were relatively small structures accessed by shafts and constructed from limestone ashlars with granite used in some places, especially for the burial chambers, either to face the walls or to block the entrances. Pieces of obelisk had often been used for the latter purpose. The walls of some of the chambers were adorned with religious scenes

Plan of the royal tombs in the Amun temple district in Tanis.

>> Gold mask of Psusennes (Pasbakhaenniut) I. Egyptian Museum, Cairo.

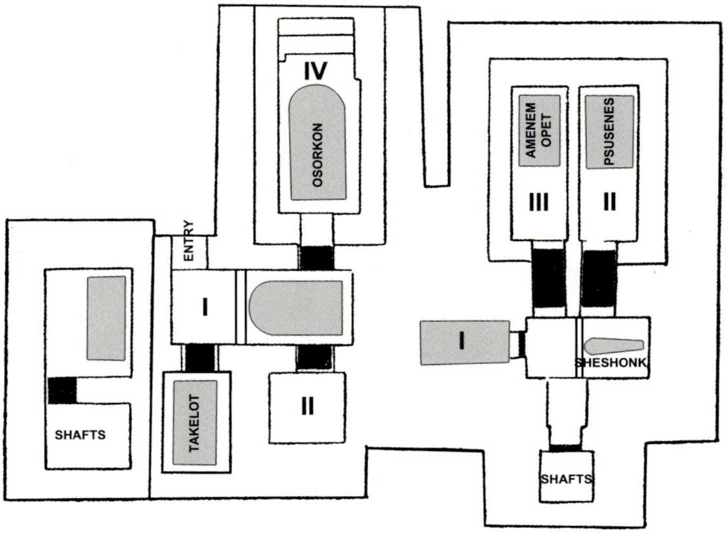

and inscriptions in polychrome low relief, while on the ceilings were stars and in some cases observed astronomical phenomena.

Despite becoming extraordinarily excited at the sight of the sealed sarcophagi in the first moments of the discovery, Pierre Montet remained cool-headed and did nothing to breach regulations. He immediately halted the excavation, secured the site, and called a police patrol. He then went to Cairo to notify the Antiquities Service authorities. He returned to the excavation site several days later accompanied by the young Egyptian king Faruq (1920–61) and canon Étienne Drioton, who was the director of the Antiquities Service at that time. The research commenced in the presence of the dignitaries with the opening of the silver sarcophagus of Sheshonq II. When the lid was raised they saw the superb golden mask resting on the face of the king's mummy. The mask and other pieces of precious jewelry were then removed from the sarcophagus. Those pieces included, among other items, a heavy gold necklace with four rows of golden beads, and a large gold pectoral in the form of the façade of a shrine decorated with colored enamels, in the middle of which was a large inset heart scarab with the text of chapter 30 B of the *Book of the Dead,* beseeching the heart not to bear witness against the deceased at the last judgment. The mummy of Sheshonq also received appropriate attention when it was later examined by the famous British anthropologist Douglas Erith Derry (1874–1961), a professor at the medical faculty of Cairo University.

The excavation and removal of the royal burials and their precious funerary equipment continued for weeks. It should be noted that not every burial found in these tombs was royal; some were of high-ranking dignitaries. Thus far a total of seven tombs have been found in Tanis; these have been designated, following the practice of Montet's time, using Roman numerals, which today the French team prefix with the French abbreviation for the royal necropolis in Tanis—NRT.

The largest number of precious finds was made in NRT III, the family tomb of Pasbakhaenniut I (known in Greek as Psusennes). It was originally intended for the king and his wife Mutnedjemet but was soon enlarged to include a second burial chamber, also made of granite, in which the king's son Ankhefenmut and the high royal official and military commander Wendjebaunedjedet were buried. Other kings were buried here subsequently; the French Egyptologist Jean Yoyotte (1927–2009) argued for their identification as Siamon and Sheshonq II. The walls of the antechamber to the tomb are decorated by inscriptions and scenes with religious themes, in places damaged, relating to the king's fate in the next world, such as Pasbakhaenniut I offering incense to Osiris, a ritual *nemset* libation vessel, and so on. Both the burial chambers are also decorated. For example, on the west wall of the first burial chamber we find the scene of the ceremony of the 'opening of the mouth' showing the standing mummiform king and the set of instruments and vessels used in the ritual; on the south wall there are hymns glorifying the Theban Triad of Amun, Mut, and Khonsu.

In the burial chamber of Pasbakhaenniut I yet another great surprise, in fact a puzzle, was in store for the French archaeologists. The king's mummy reposed in a superb red-granite sarcophagus, its lid adorned with a three-dimensional representation of the king's figure in mummiform, already merging with the ruler of the underworld, holding the flagellum and crooked scepter in his hands, which were crossed over his chest. The king's head is enclosed from the back and protected by the outstretched hands of the goddess Nut. When the French archaeologists carefully examined the inscriptions on the lid, along the sides of the king's figure, they could not believe their eyes: the name of the Nineteenth Dynasty king Merenptah, son and successor to Ramesses II, was written into the cartouche. Initially they concluded that the tomb was originally intended for Merenptah, but the prevailing view among Egyptologists today is that the sarcophagus of Merenptah had been usurped, and was most likely a gift to Pasbakhaenniut I from the priests of Amun in Thebes. Merenptah's tomb in the Valley of the Kings in Thebes would not in fact have suffered much by the gift, for Merenptah had

Broken obelisk of Ramesses II looming above the ruins of Tanis.

been interred in four sarcophagi, one inside another. The one used for the burial of Pasbakhaenniut was the third in order. It is also possible that the lid of Merenptah's sarcophagus was conveyed to Tanis after his tomb was robbed, when sometime at the beginning of the Twenty-first Dynasty the king's mummy had already been taken and, together with a few other mummies, placed in a cache in tomb KV35 belonging to Amenhotep II. Usurpation of the sarcophagus is a logical explanation, but the question concerning Merenptah's name in an inscription on a lintel in Pasbakhaenniut's burial chamber in Tanis remains unanswered.

Tomb NRT I is the burial place of Osorkon II, and his son Harnakht, high priest of Amun, is buried in its later extension. The precise interpretation of the archaeological situation in the tomb is rather ticklish. According to Brissaud, the tomb was reopened after the original burials and a large red-granite sarcophagus was placed inside, which—before it was looted—contained the burial of Hedjkheperre Takelot, as indicated by the cartouche recorded on the lid in red. Others argue that this burial was of Takelot I, father of Osorkon II. Yoyotte has pointed out that some of the jewelry bearing the king's name may have belonged to family members, not the king himself, and so using these names to date the burials can be misleading. The decoration of the tomb is very interesting: there is an installation depicting the resurrected Osiris on a throne on the primordial mound emerging from the primordial waters on the southern wall of the antechamber; on the western wall there are scenes from *Book of the Day* and *Book of the Night* and the voyage across the heavenly ocean. The decans—constellations of stars in the night sky—are represented on the ceilings. There were a total of thirty-six decans in Egyptian astronomy; they were used to tell the time at night. The walls of the burial chambers are also decorated, and here we find scenes from the solar cycle, *Amduat* ('What Is in the Nether World'), the metamorphosis of Osiris into Re with a ram head and solar disc on his head, and other subjects.

Archaeologists found the burial of Takelot II in one of NRT I's burial chambers. King Sheshonq III had tomb NRT V built with older limestone blocks from private tombs constructed during the Twenty-first Dynasty. The looted tomb contained fragments of the canopic jars of Sheshonq I, who was probably interred here alongside Sheshonq III. Only the burial chamber was decorated with themes relating to the *Book of Night* and the *Book of the Dead*.

Georges Goyon, one of the archaeologists involved in the great discovery in Tanis, later recalled how the French team—when the tomb containing the burial of Sheshonq II was opened—could not quite suppress their hope that they might discover sources (for example, cylinder seals, hieroglyphic texts, or tablets with cuneiform script) referring to the biblical Shishak, his military expedition to Palestine, and the sack of Jerusalem as described in the Old Testament (Kings 1:14): "and he took away the treasures of the house of the Lord, and the treasures of the king's house; he even took away all; and he took away all the shields of gold which Solomon had made." Alas, in this respect, the dreams and hopes of the French archaeologists in Tanis were not to be fulfilled.

It is impossible to enumerate in this chapter all the precious objects of funeral equipment that accompanied the burials of the individual kings. The sarcophagi themselves are remarkable, although these have only been found in some chambers and not all of them contain a burial or bear inscriptions that would help us identify their owners. They were made of various materials: red granite, reddish quartzite, and limestone. In some stone sarcophagi there had been inner coffins of wood, long ago rotted away, so that all that remained on the mummies were certain ornamental elements in more durable materials; for example, the eyes and eyebrows. Two silver coffins were found in Pasbakhaenniut I's tomb, one belonging to Sheshonq II and the other to Pasbakhaenniut. The heads of the coffins differ: Sheshonq's was a falcon head and Pasbakhaenniut's human. Importantly, silver was very rare in ancient Egypt and Egyptians considered the metal to be the bones of the gods (gold was likewise deemed the flesh of the gods).

There was a staggering amount of gold and jewelry in the funerary equipment. For example, Pasbakhaenniut II's entire mummy was covered in gold; the gold mask along with the *nemes* headdress and broad necklace forms one single piece reaching down to the lower edge of the chest (as with the famous mask of Tutankhamun). There was also a beautiful gold mask on Sheshonq II's head, whose mummy was wrapped in fine cloth adorned with gold leaves. Selected texts from the *Book of the Dead* were written on the back of this shroud. In fact, the most beautiful objects come from Pasbakhaenniut I's and Sheshonq II's tombs: massive gold and lapis lazuli necklaces; gold pectorals adorned with colored enameled inlays; pendants, bracelets, and rings; belts and even gold funeral sandals. The funerary equipment included canopic jars, faience, and bronze figurines of *ushabti*, scepters, weapons, cult vessels in gold and silver, and much else. Some objects from the funerary equipment of the kings buried in Tanis were gifts from the Theban high priests of the god Amun. The Egyptian Museum in Cairo currently has a room—right next to the room where treasures from the tomb of Tutankhamun are on display—devoted to the exhibition of part of this treasure, including some royal coffins.

It is entirely appropriate that the cache of finds from the royal tombs in Tanis should occupy a place of honor in the Cairo Museum; after all, it represents the second-largest royal treasure trove—or more precisely, set of treasure troves—after that of Tutankhamun. Yet despite the involvement of King Faruq and the exceptional historical and artistic value of the antiquities found, the discovery of the royal tombs in Tanis did not arouse the kind of international interest and admiration that it deserved. The Second World War had begun and, as is all too true, when guns speak, the muses fall silent.

Plan of the cemetery in Abydos made by the Prussian expedition led by Lepsius.

8

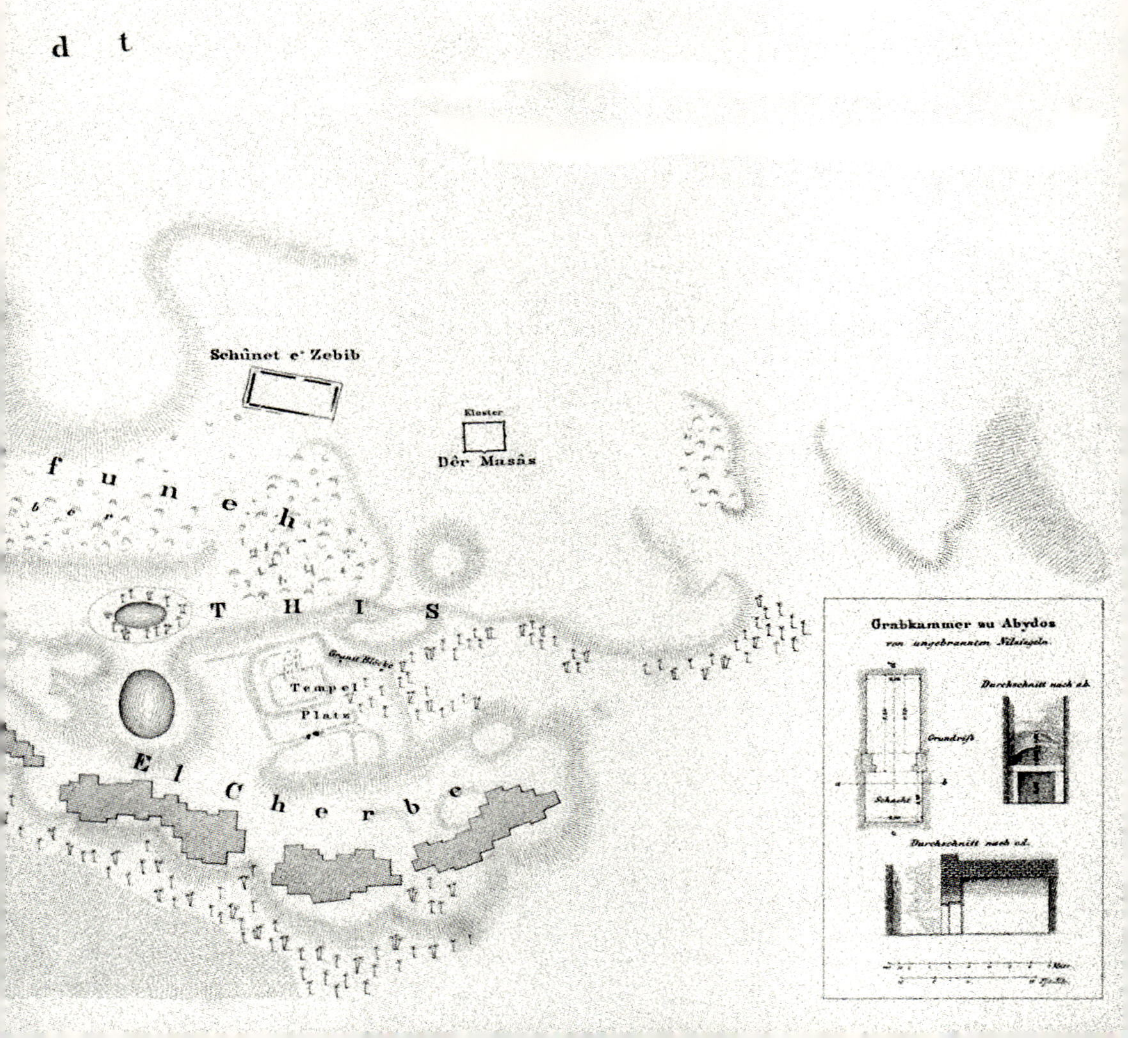
d t
Schûnet e' Zebib
Kloster
Dêr Masâs
f u n e h
T H I S
Tempel
Platz
El Cherbe
Grabkammer zu Abydos
von ungebrannten Nilziegeln
Durchschnitt nach ab.
Grundriß
Schacht
Durchschnitt nach cd.

Abydos: The Sacred Land

The Temple and Tomb of Osiris

Another of Egypt's most important archaeological sites is Abydos, the Greek name for the very important ancient Egyptian town of Abdju, which lies close to the modern village of Araba al-Madfuna. Its origins go back a very long way, into the Early Dynastic Period, when a place called Tjeny (known in Greek as Thinis or This), evidently close to Abydos although not archaeologically identified and known only from written sources, became the center of power in an emergent, newly unified Egypt. It is probable that the area's rise to prominence had much to do with the cultural interaction of the local population with people who were moving from the Western Desert as a result of climate change; as a long wet period with occasional rains was coming to an end, the inhabitants of the eastern part of the Sahara experienced ecological stress that compelled them to migrate, via the oases, toward the more substantial source of water in the region—the Nile.

<< The size of the blocks and the building method of the Osireion are reminiscent of the royal architecture of the Old Kingdom.

Abydos became the capital of the eighth Upper Egyptian nome during the Old Kingdom and also became the administrative seat of Upper Egypt from the Fifth Dynasty onward; this important government office intended to shore up the then shaky authority of central state power in the southern part of the country. Abydos was to confirm its strategically important position in the following First Intermediate Period when Egypt was in political and economic disarray and an armed struggle ensued between two regional power centers: Nennisut (in Greek Herakleopolos Magna) in Lower Egypt and Waset (in Greek Thebes) in Upper Egypt. The decisive battle is reported to have occurred close to Abydos, and involved the partial destruction of the local cemetery. With pacification and the restoration of a strong centralized state at the beginning of the Middle Kingdom, Abydos once again became an important center of the cult of the god Osiris, whose tomb was believed to lie here in a place today known Umm al-Ga‘ab ('Mother of Pots'—because of the quantity of shards of small offering goblets on low feet that are found here).

The tombs of the kings of the First and Second Dynasty at Umm al-Ga‘ab were built close to a cemetery, which had already been established

Wadi Kebir, a deep ravine in the rock reef on the western edge of the cemetery in Abydos, opens the way into the Western Desert, the ancient Egyptian kingdom of the dead.

by the end of the Prehistoric Age, in the late Naqada Period, and the cemetery of the Dynasty 0 rulers which was continuous with it. Archaeologists use the letters B and U to designate these older cemeteries. It was not by chance that the kings chose this remote place, quite a long way from the edge of the fertile Nile Valley. A rocky massif rises west of the site; it is cut through by a deep gaping ravine known as Wadi Kebir ('Great Valley'), running westward. The kings believed that their spirits would take this route to the nether world, the kingdom of the dead that lay in the endless expanses of the desert to the west.

During the First Dynasty, for a time, it seems that the brutal custom for dead kings to be accompanied to the other world by their retinues, whose members would be killed and buried in small graves closely surrounding the tomb of the ruler, continued. There are 325 such secondary burials around the tomb of King Djer. Another 269 have been found by Djer's great enclosure near Kom al-Sultan, which means that almost six hundred people were sent to the other world with the king. David O'Connor, an American Egyptologist, has no doubt that they were ritually sacrificed because the roofs of their simple graves were laid at the same time, indicating that the burials were more or less simultaneous.

The tombs at Umm al-Ga'ab were not as monumental as the later pyramids, but they were impressively large for their time and embodied several basic religious beliefs that were to shape the history of ancient Egypt. The tombs of the kings of Dynasty 0 were soon far outshone in size and splendor. The tomb of the last king of the Second Dynasty, Khasekhemwy, for example, was roughly seventy meters long with as many as fifty rooms in its underground section. The superstructure of the tomb was a sand tumulus approximately thirty-four meters long and four meters high, faced with stone masonry, and symbolizing the primordial mound that emerged from the chaos of the primordial waters at the beginning of the world. It was the place where life was born by the will of the creator god. This concept—expressed architecturally—shows that the tomb was becoming a place symbolizing the mystery of rebirth and eternal life. The dozens of rooms in its interior were filled with gifts intended to secure the king's life in the other world forever.

Although this was a site of immense archaeological significance, excavation of the cemetery at Umm al-Ga'ab got off to a poor start at the very end of the nineteenth century. Émile Clément Amélineau (1850–1915), a French archaeologist, conducted the first excavations

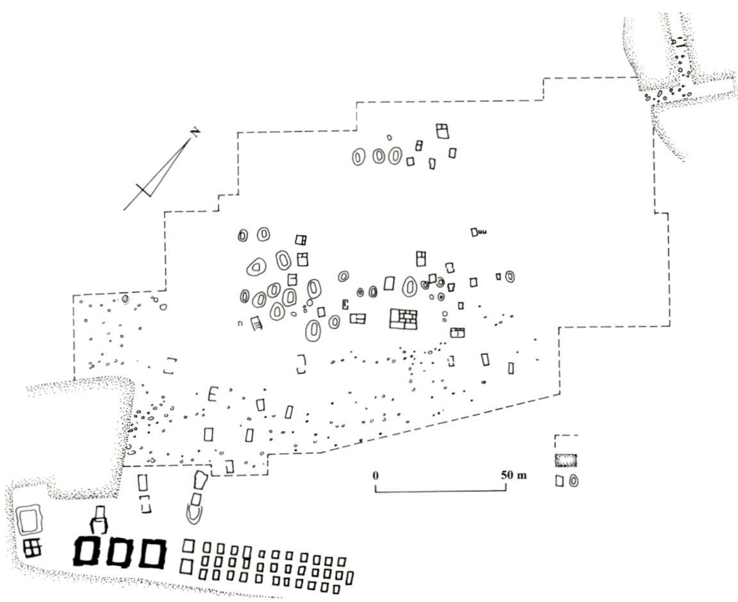

Plan of cemeteries U and B at Umm al-Ga'ab in Abydos. The earliest Egyptian predynastic rulers (U, above) and the early dynastic kings (B, below) are buried here.

Umm al-Ga'ab. In the foreground are the so-called secondary graves surrounding one of the royal tombs.

quite irresponsibly. For example, he allowed wooden parts of the tomb structures to be used as fuel. Soon afterward, Petrie, an English archaeologist, did his best to repair the situation. In recent years, German archaeologists have been carrying out thorough research and have brought to light new, valuable, and often surprising evidence about early Egyptian history.

In fact, the tombs at Umm al-Ga'ab are not the only funerary monuments built in the Abydos area for the Zero and First Dynasty kings. Other structures—great mud-brick enclosures located about half a kilometer farther north on the edge of the Nile Valley—were also associated with the tombs. These enclosures probably served as places for the practice of funeral rites; smaller temporary structures inside the enclosures were torn down when the rites were over. The site for the burial-ritual enclosures was not chosen randomly, for it is close to Khentamentyu's shrine. Khentamentyu was originally the dog or jackal god and the ruler of the cemetery in Abydos, who by the early Old Kingdom had been merged with Osiris. Today this place is known as Kom al-Sultan ('The Sultan's Hill'). An American archaeological team led by O'Connor in the 1990s discovered in one enclosure fourteen

Shunet al-Zebib (the 'raisin storehouse'), the great brick enclosure in Abydos in which rituals accompanying the burial of the Second Dynasty king Khasekhemwy were carried out.

wooden funeral boats around fifteen meters long, which had been ritually buried and walled in with mud bricks.

Like many important Egyptian archaeological sites, the Temple of Osiris-Khentamentyu and the adjoining town on Kom al-Sultan did not undergo thorough archaeological research until the beginning of the twentieth century. Petrie worked in the temple as early as 1901–1903. More than seventy years later another Englishman, Barry Kemp, carried out systematic research there, followed in the 1970s by an American Egyptologist named William Kelly Simpson, and by O'Connor in the 1990s. Petrie started to excavate Kom al-Sultan at a time when the hill was still approximately twelve meters tall. He unearthed the remains of mud-brick buildings, dating from various periods, that were enclosed by a mud-brick wall that was constructed during the Early Dynastic Period.

The older parts of the Temple of Osiris-Khentamentyu had been dismantled and replaced by others, and this made interpretation of the buildings at Kom al-Sultan a complicated problem. Kemp was convinced that the mud-brick buildings excavated by Petrie belonged to the oldest part of the local god Khentamentyu's original cult center and had later been covered by stone buildings that were erected by various kings during the New Kingdom (Amenhotep I, Thutmose III, Ramesses II, and others) and the Late Period (Ahmose II and others). O'Connor takes a quite different view, inspired by Simpson's study of a group of brick buildings from the Middle Kingdom on the southwestern edge of Kom al-Sultan. Simpson showed convincingly

The ruins of the temple of Osiris on Kom al-Sultan, the oldest shrine in Abydos, lie at the northeastern edge of the cemetery.

that these buildings were in fact what are known as *ka* tombs, that is, symbolic tombs constructed of mud brick. They were usually small simple structures with one room and an arched ceiling surrounded by a low enclosure wall with one entrance. Inset in the front wall or inside the chapel there would be a stone stela with a representation of the deceased venerating Osiris and an accompanying text. A pair of trees would be planted inside the enclosure by the entrance to the tomb. According to O'Connor, then, the brick buildings that Kemp believed made up the original Temple of Khentamentyu were probably *ka* chapels dedicated to the kings of the Old Kingdom, their friends, and high-ranking officials. The main Osiris temple that once stood in the oldest part of Abydos has not yet been found. It is probably situated somewhat close by, in the vicinity of the Temple of Nakhtnebef I in the southern part of Kom al-Sultan.

O'Connor discovered the remains of a town in the northwestern section of the enclosed area, which is currently being excavated by Matthew Adams. He also discovered the remains of a temple to Osiris in the southwestern section of the same enclosed area. Petrie dated the most recent

The remains of non-royal cenotaphs of the Middle Kingdom at Abydos.

parts of the structure to the Thirtieth Dynasty, during which the earlier temple from the New Kingdom was replaced, on Nakhtnebef I's orders, by a new temple. We do not know exactly when the earliest parts were built, but they date at least as far back as the Early Dynastic Period. The temple was originally dedicated to Khentamentyu but in the late Old Kingdom his cult merged with that of Osiris; people, therefore, started to venerate Osiris-Khentamentyu in the temple at Kom al-Sultan.

Petrie found a number of historically valuable antiquities of offerings in the ruins here; the quality of those offerings bear testimony to the great age and religious significance of the temple. A fragment of a faience vessel bearing the name of King Aha suggests that the origins of the temple can be traced as far back as of the First Dynasty, at the turn of the fourth millennium BC. One find from the Fourth Dynasty was an ivory figurine of Khufu; it is the only surviving reliably identified portrait of the famous owner of the Great Pyramid. An anecdote associated with the find tells us a lot about archaeological excavations carried out in Egypt in the past, and today too. Originally, the workmen found the headless torso of this seated statuette of the king, which was only a few centimeters tall. When Petrie was cleaning the artifact, he noticed a cartouche with the name Khufu on one side of the throne. He immediately realized the exceptional significance of the find, for no portrait of Khufu was known at that time, and at once offered a particularly generous reward if the workmen could discover the missing head. It was eventually found after several days of painstaking sifting of the sand in

This seated ivory statuette discovered in Abydos is the only definitely identified representation of King Khufu. The enthroned king wears the Lower Egyptian crown and holds a flagellum in his right hand against his breast. The king is identified by the inscription containing Khufu's Horus name, Medjedu, on the right front side of the throne.

the dump. Today, the statuette is one of the most precious exhibits at the Egyptian Museum in Cairo.

Apart from the statuette of Khufu, Petrie managed to find votive monuments to other kings, such as a limestone statue of Djedkare (now in the Egyptian Museum in Cairo) from the Fifth Dynasty. He also unearthed limestone blocks of masonry bearing the names of the

Plan of the ruins of the temple of Osiris in Abydos and monuments in its immediate vicinity, made by scholars on Napoleon's expedition to Egypt.

Sixth Dynasty kings Merenre and Pepi I. By having their statues placed in the temple, the kings were paying tribute to the god and also uniting the cult of the god with their own. Stelae bearing inscriptions of King Neferirkare from the Fifth Dynasty and Teti from the Sixth Dynasty are also historically valuable. A stela of the influential governor of Upper Egypt, the vizier Djau, also dates from the Sixth Dynasty. Djau had two sisters with the same name, Ankhesenmerire, who successively married King Merire (Pepi I). These political marriages were strategies used by the king to maintain control over Upper Egypt.

During the Middle Kingdom, commoners as well as those of royal blood started building small mud-brick cenotaphs in Kom al-Sultan in the hope of being close to the god Osiris after they died, trusting in his resurrection and eternal life. As time went by, other beliefs and practices came to be associated with the temple, including one practice concerning the fertility aspect of Osiris—as is shown by a small limestone

The symbol of Abydos: a wig on a stand decorated with plumes, the sun disc, and a uraeus, with the symbols of life, the *ankh*, and of duration, the *djed*, hanging from it. The symbol is accompanied by the canine god Wepwawet.

tablet with a representation of a man and woman having sexual intercourse; the Nineteenth Dynasty tablet was discovered during the current American excavation of the temple mound in Kom al-Sultan. This was an isolated discovery at Kom al-Sultan, but in terms of discoveries made in all of Egypt it is not exceptional. For instance, ithyphallic and other votive fertility statuettes have been found in various places: temples, cemeteries, and dwelling complexes. These objects were supposed to secure fertility and prosperity in this world and the next for their owners or donors. Incidentally, classical authors such as Herodotus and Plutarch wrote about processions in honor of Osiris in which people carried the symbol of the male sexual organ; the phallus was believed to guarantee a good harvest and prosperity.

The American team led by David O'Connor (comprising participants from the University of Pennsylvania, Yale University, and New York University's Institute of Fine Arts) has been working at

Kom al-Sultan since 2002. The conditions are very challenging, both because the site has been devastated by *sabakhin* (fellahin tomb robbers, who come to the mud-brick ruins to dig clay from the disintegrated bricks to fertilize their fields), and because the remains lie partially under the adjacent village Beni Mansur. If we could only turn back the clock to the time of Napoleon's expedition to Egypt! Although the plan of the remains made by the scholars on that expedition was very superficial, it nonetheless shows how extensive the ruins at Kom al-Sultan were two centuries ago.

Two important routes for religious processions started from the Temple of Osiris. The first led southwest to Umm al-Ga'ab. Notably, from the topographical-archaeological point of view, a line connecting Kom al-Sultan and Umm al-Ga'ab continues directly into the mouth of the Wadi Kebir, mentioned above, through which—it was believed at that time—the dead departed for the other world. The second route led southeast from the temple at Kom al-Sultan along the edge of the Nile Valley to mortuary (or memorial) temples.

The procession road to Umm al-Ga'ab was the first of the two to be established. From the beginning of the Middle Kingdom at the latest, more than a thousand years after the founding of the cemetery of the earliest Egyptian kings, pious pilgrims were coming from all over the land to take the road from Kom al-Sultan to Umm al-Ga'ab and the Osiris mysteries, while a symbolic 'voyage to Abydos' became an inseparable part of funeral rituals and the decoration program of ancient Egyptian tombs. The development of the pilgrimage was based on the belief that

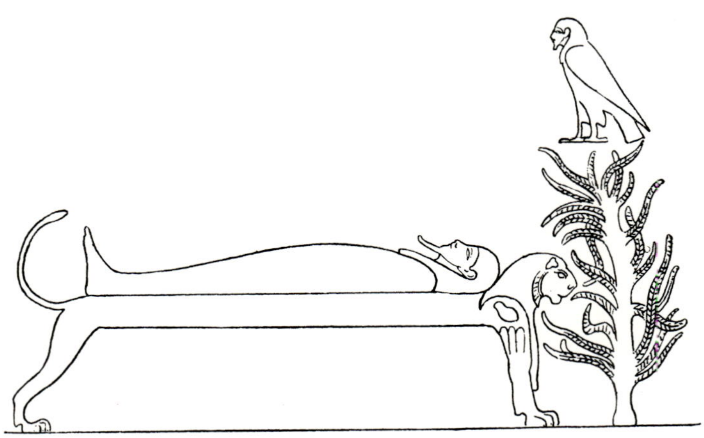

The bier of Osiris. Above it, Osiris's soul, or *ba*, nests in the form of a bird with a human head, on a tree in the sacred Menta grove. Drawing of a detail from the decoration of the Isis temple in Philae.

one of the royal tombs here, that of Djer, was the place where the body (according to later tradition just the head) of Osiris had been buried.

Amélineau found a unique sculpture made of black basalt—the sacred couch of Osiris—in Djer's tomb. The sculpture represents the dead god Osiris lying on a bier in the shape of a stylized pair of lions. Osiris takes the form of a mummy. The crown of Upper Egypt

This standard with the canine god Wepwawet, 'Opener of Roads,' was carried at the head of military expeditions and religious processions.

is on his head, and in his hands, which are crossed on his chest, he holds the insignia of royal power: the *heqa* (crooked scepter) and the *nekhakha* (flagellum). The outstretched wings of falcon gods protected his head and legs. In mystic sexual union with the dead god, his wife Isis perches on Osiris's mummy in the form of a kite with outstretched wings. Through this union the god king, although treacherously murdered by his brother Seth, begets a son and heir, his avenger Horus. Dating from the late Middle Kingdom, this unique sculpture is now part of the permanent exhibition in the Egyptian Museum in Cairo. It is a pity that even though the sculpture is displayed in the central part of the entrance lobby, most of the tourists who flood into the museum each day from every part of the world pass it by with scarcely a second glance.

The course of the Osiris festivities is recorded in a number of written records dating from different periods—for example, in inscriptions on the walls of Hathor's temple in Dendera from the Ptolemaic and Roman Periods.

Much of our information on the festival procession in Abydos comes from inscriptions on stelae found in the local cemeteries. The procession began at Kom al-Sultan in the Osiris temple. A standard of the protective canine deity Wepwawet ('Opener of the ways') was carried at its head. A barque containing a statue of Osiris and other holy reliquaries accompanied the standard from the temple onward. In front of the temple the believers and pilgrims would line up to form a procession of mourners behind Wepwapet and priests carrying the reliquaries, and then set off on the route through the shallow desert valley to the tomb of Osiris in Umm al-Ga'ab. In ancient Egyptian texts this episode is designated 'setting out for Peqer.'

The sacred district of Peqer had the tomb of Osiris at its center, and although we do not know precisely where it began, it was not far from the temple. Particularly in the Late Period, pilgrims brought with them offering goblets of burnt clay, and many also carried sycomore branches. The procession route was lined with stone stelae bearing inscriptions, which were set up by people who hoped by this gesture to take part in the Osiris mysteries forever. As time went by, important people had their tombs built along the way, and also sacrificial or mummified animals (birds of prey, ibises, cats, snakes, shrews, and even scarab beetles) were buried here to honor the gods venerated in Abydos. Burials of donkeys (embodying Osiris's enemy Seth), lions (symbolizing royal power), and dogs (perhaps royal hunting dogs) have also been found close to the oldest tombs at Umm al-Ga'ab. Boundary stelae with inscriptions clearly marked out the 'sacred land,' on which no one but the priests conducting the rituals could set foot. Violaters were subject to severe punishments, including being burned alive.

The final act of the festivities took place by Osiris's tomb at Umm al-Ga'ab; only priests and a few chosen others were allowed to take part in the secret rites. Unfortunately, no written records providing information about the details of these rites have survived. However, in the course of continuing archaeological excavations at Umm al-Ga'ab, a few antiquities that offer at least some clues about the rituals at Osiris's tomb have been discovered. These finds include fragments of a stone altar and just a few shattered remains of what was evidently a now entirely obliterated large stone memorial. Once again we can only lament Amélineau's irresponsibility in carrying out the first excavations; it looks very likely that many similar fragments were casually thrown onto dump heaps, making it quite impossible for us to reconstruct the precise location and circumstances of their discovery. One of the items that met this fate is an unidentifiable alabaster object with relief decoration, which may have belonged to the stone memorial. We have already noted that pilgrims would leave small offering vessels at

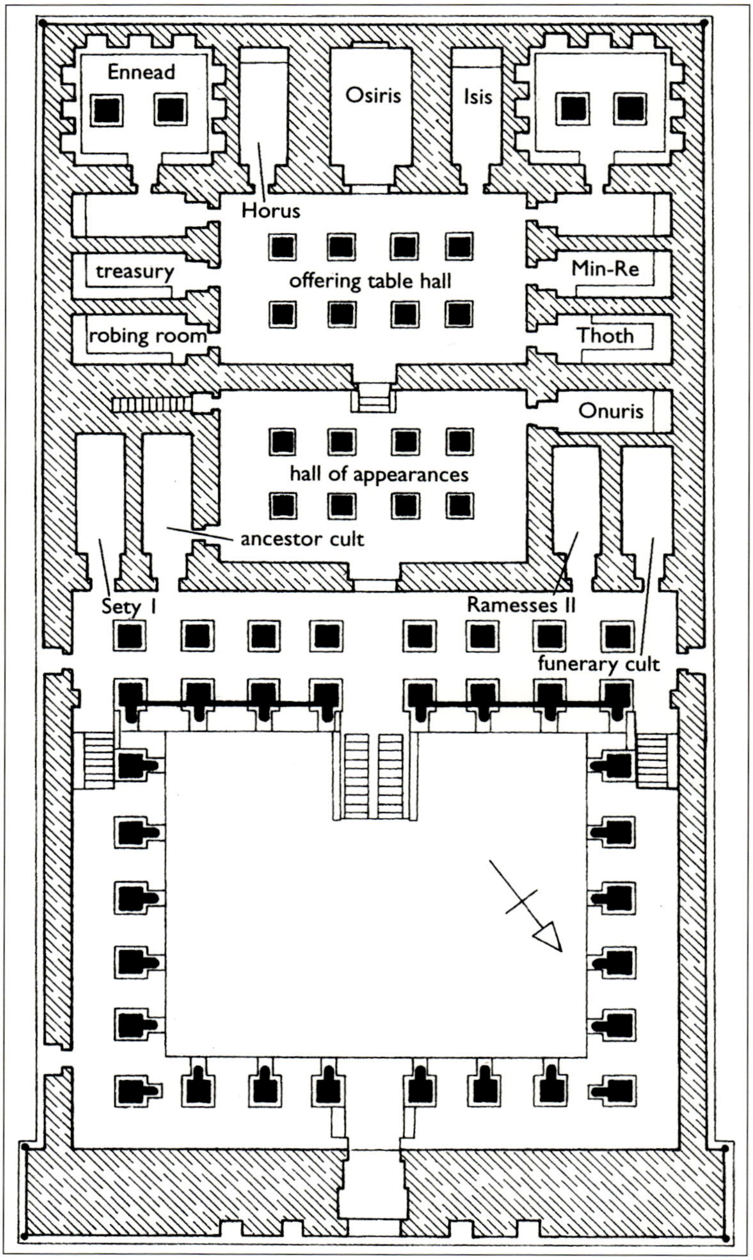

Plan of the Temple (House of Millions of Years) of Ramesses II at Abydos

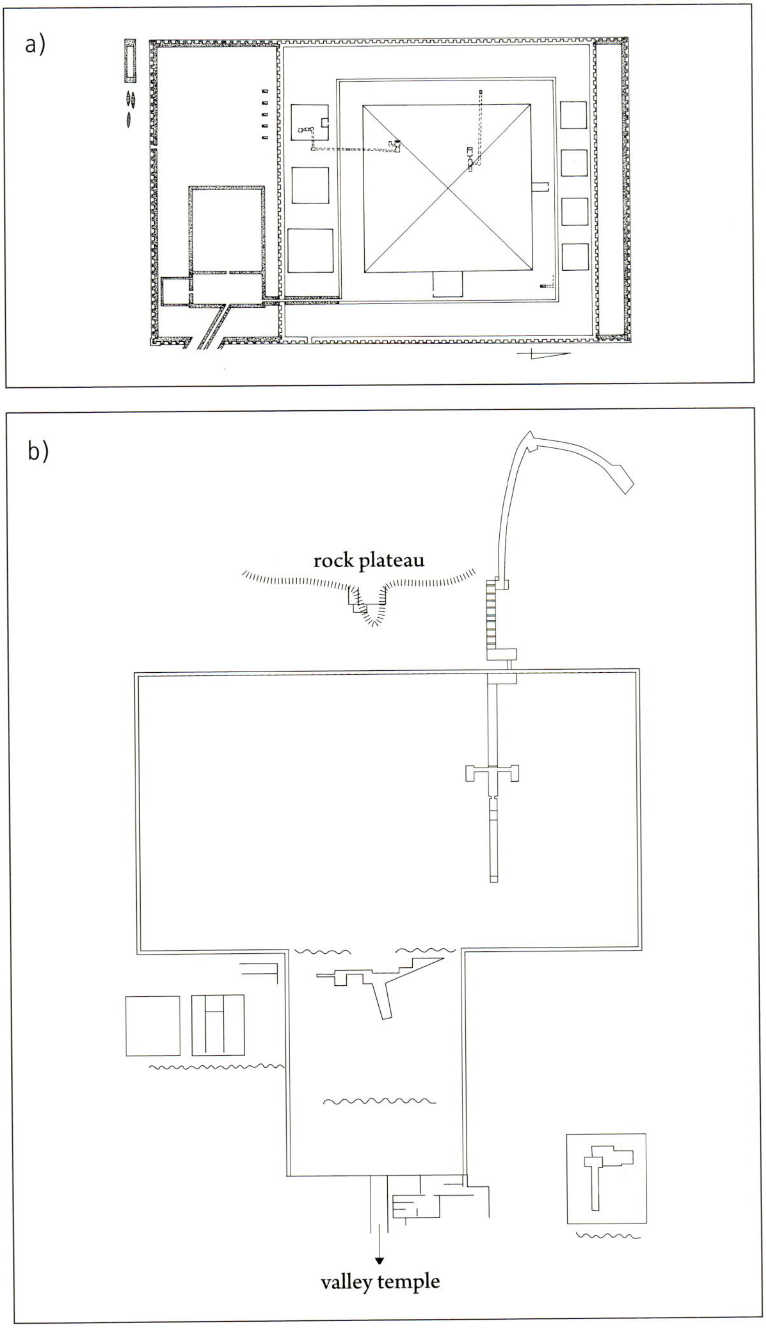

Plan of the pyramid of Senwosret III in Dahshur (top) and the king's tomb (or cenotaph) in Abydos (bottom).

Osiris's tomb and should add here that the deposits found here by Amélineau, which were nearly five meters deep, testify to their enormous quantity and the intensity of the cult. In addition to the vessels, branches of sycomore were placed at the tomb and statuettes of Osiris were buried in the ground. Numerous finds of traces of incense show that censing was part of the ceremonies. The rites probably culminated in the symbolic resurrection of Osiris.

The processions to Peqer and the cult of Osiris continued long after Egypt lost its independence and fell under Greek and subsequently Roman dominance. They ceased only when Christianity gained the upper hand as the state religion, and put an end to them sometime in the mid-sixth century. Their demise is expressed in various Coptic artifacts and symbols found in Umm al-Ga'ab, and in the Coptic inscriptions left on the walls of the nearby Memnonion and Osireion by Coptic monks from the local monasteries.

Royal Mortuary Memorials

The other procession route, which was established after the route to Peqar, headed south from Kom al-Sultan and connected the Osiris temple with the mortuary temples (sometimes also known as memorial temples). Before we turn our attention to these temples, however, we should mention the very unusual building that lies even farther to the south. It is almost half a millennium older than the mortuary temples and was built by the Twelfth Dynasty king Senwosret III. Often known as the cenotaph (symbolic tomb) of Senwosret III, this unique building was the subject of rather superficial and sloppy excavations carried out at the beginning of the twentieth century by a Canadian archaeologist named Charles Trick Currelly (1876–1957). The monument attracted renewed archaeological attention in the 1990s, this time from an American Egyptologist named Joseph Wegner. Wegner has suggested that the cenotaph in Abydos, known as 'Enduring are the (cult) places of Khakaure, justified in Abydos,' might in fact have been more than just a symbolic tomb, partly because no trace of the king's actual burial has been found in the burial chamber Senwosret III's pyramid in Dahshur.

The cenotaph of Senwosret III is a huge building complex with a very unusual plan. There is a temple that once had a limestone chapel and two quartzite seated statues of the king in front of it situated on the edge of the Nile Valley. A road about one kilometer long connected this temple with a large building on a ground plan resembling the letter T, which stood at the foot of the rock massif and has an underground structure consisting of four parts. The first is a long, limestone-faced hall with two side chambers; the second is a long passage leading to a pair of shafts approximately six meters deep. Beyond the shafts is a downward-sloping passage that issues into a chamber faced in red granite and containing a sarcophagus; the latter was discovered to be empty. There was yet another long crooked passage beyond the chamber, which led to a room faced in quartzite.

It is extremely difficult to interpret this building. On the basis of its arrangement and decoration, which emphasizes the union of Senwosret III with the god Osiris, it has been regarded as some peculiar form of symbolic mortuary chapel. Wegner, however, has put forward the theory that Senwosret III was actually buried in this large and complicated funerary complex in Abydos, not in Dahshur. Wegner's theory is backed up by the discovery of fragments of a case that once held canopic

The mortuary temple of Ramesses II in Abydos has superb polychrome relief decoration.

Mortuary temple of Sethi I in Abydos.

jars in the burial chamber in Abydos; notably, no trace of a canopic jar case has been found in the king's pyramid in Dahshur. Fragments of alabaster bowls decorated with duck motifs were also found in the burial chamber in Abydos, and during the Twelfth Dynasty such bowls were typical parts of royal funerary equipment. Wegner's theory, which is bold and has not yet been confirmed, is further supported by the fact that a town had grown up around the complex of Senwosret as early as the Middle Kingdom, thus suggesting the importance and intensity of the king's cult in this location.

Kings in subsequent periods, especially the New Kingdom, also built memorials in Abydos. At the beginning of the Eighteenth Dynasty, King Ahmose I built himself a pyramid and another memorial in the form of a small pyramid for Queen Tetisheri, his mother, and Nefertari, his sister and queen, in the southern part of the cemetery. An American archaeologist named Stephen Harvey is currently conducting research on Ahmose's pyramid and the temple situated to the east of it. Some other royal buildings present in Abydos during this period are known only from written records; however, a number of others have been discovered and excavated. Those discovered include the fairly small Temple of Thutmose III, discovered in 1996 by the American expedition made up of scholars from the University of Pennsylvania, Yale University, and New York University's Institute of Fine Arts. This temple is located southwest of the Osiris temple at Kom al-Sultan. The façade consists of a massive gateway—a pylon. The gateway leads into the the temple's courtyard, within which stood two sacred trees; two large Osirian statues (that is, mummiform and wearing the Upper Egyptian crown) of Thutmose III stood before the entrance to the temple's interior. The chapel of Ramesses I, which has been only partially excavated, stands between the temples of Sethi I and Ramesses II on the edge of the Nile Valley.

The memorial of Ramesses II known as the 'Temple of Ramesses Meriamun in the Sacred Land,' which lies next to the chapel of Ramesses I, has been excavated and researched much more thoroughly. The temple, which was uncovered by Mariette, resembles the mortuary temples of the same period in Thebes. The entrance is located on the northeast—the temple's orientation respects the course of the Nile—through a second pylon, since the first pylon and first courtyard have been entirely destroyed. A large open court with Osirian pillars on all four sides stands beyond the second pylon; farther on there are two halls, each adorned with eight pillars, surrounded by chapels to various gods. In the innermost part of the temple there is a trio of chapels, the middle one dedicated to Osiris and known as the 'alabaster' chapel because it is made of very fine limestone. There once stood a red-granite group statue in this chapel that depicted Ramesses II standing between Osiris and Horus; the remaining two statues, one on either side, have not been precisely identified. There are small square halls with ceilings supported by a pair of pillars in the southeastern and southwestern corners of the temple. Originally, statues stood in the nine niches cut into in the walls of each of the two halls. In one of the niches the king is depicted bringing offerings to Osiris; a *djed* pillar stands behind the god and protects him with outstretched wings. Although the temple was still in good condition at the time of Napoleon's campaign, today it is seriously damaged, missing the upper parts of the walls and the roof. Nonetheless, very high quality polychrome relief decoration, relatively well preserved in places, has survived to this day. There are scenes from the battle of Qadesh on the exterior walls of the temple.

The biggest temple in Abydos, and one of the most important in all Egypt, is the huge and unique building complex of Sethi I, which the writers of antiquity called the Memnonium. The complex, which presents significant problems of interpretation for Egyptologists, consists mainly of a mortuary temple built during the Nineteenth Dynasty mostly by Sethi I, but completed by Ramesses II, and called 'The House of Millions of Years of Menmaatre Rejoicing in the Heart of Abydos.'

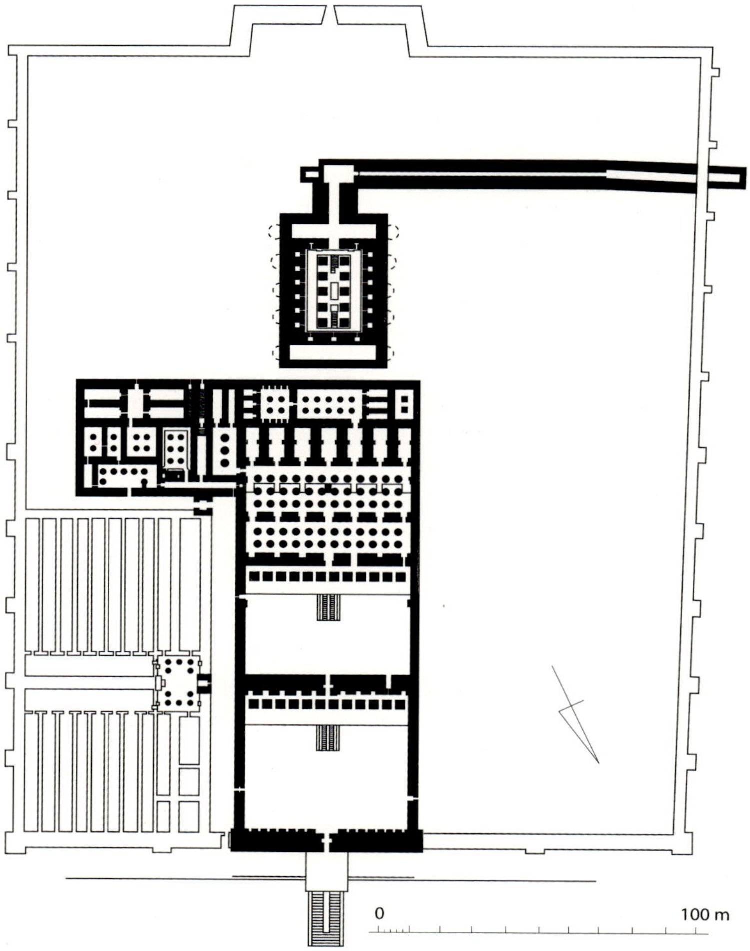

Plan of the mortuary temple of Sethi I in Abydos.

The complex also included the Osireion, the symbolic tomb of the god Osiris, as well as enormous temple storerooms, which were long chambers adjoining the temple from the south with vaulted roofs constructed of mud bricks. The whole complex was surrounded by a massive mud-brick wall pierced in its western stretch by a monumental gate in the shape of a pylon. Its founder endowed the temple with revenues from the gold mines in present-day Wadi Abadi.

The Temple of Sethi I is made of fine limestone and has an unusual L-shaped ground plan. The main tract (the longer side of the L) has an entrance on the northeast through a big pylon, leading into the first open courtyard, which is considerably damaged. The walls of the courtyard bear remnants of relief decoration, including scenes from Ramesses II's battle with the Hittites at Qadesh. Originally, there were also two wells here that were used for the ritual purification of the priests.

A stairway ramp on the main axis of the temple provided access to a raised terrace with a pillared hall. There were three entrances at the

Fallen Asian warrior. Detail from scene of Ramesses II's battle with the Hittites represented in the first court of the temple of Sethi I in Abydos.

back of the hall that led to what is known as the second courtyard. Its walls are also decorated with relief scenes, which show Ramesses II bringing offerings to various gods and slaughtering the enemies of Egypt before the face of the god Amun.

There is another staircase ramp from the second courtyard to another raised terrace on which the interior covered part of the temple is located. The façade is formed by a pillared portico, from which seven gates provided access to the first hypostyle hall. The hall is fifty-two meters wide and eleven meters deep, with twelve pairs of papyrus sandstone columns with bud capitals. Between the columns, which

Pillared portico of the temple of Sethi I in Abydos.

are decorated with relief scenes depicting the king and the gods, the way continues through another seven gates into the second hypostyle hall, which has thirty-six columns of the same type found in the first hypostyle hall (apart from the third row consisting of columns without capitals). On the western wall there are superb polychrome scenes—for example, one showing Sethi I kneeling before Amun-Re and Re-Harakhty and accepting the symbols of the millions of years of rule, the *sed* festivals, duration, power, and life from both of these gods. On the same wall there is a wonderful depiction of Sethi I kneeling by the *ished* tree as Re-Harakhty writes the king's name on its leaves in the presence of Ptah, who is presenting the king with the symbol of the *sed* festival.

There are entrances from the second hypostyle hall into seven chapels, which are dedicated to the main Egyptian gods; originally, sacred barques rested in front of these chapels. The middle chapel belongs to Amun, at that time the most important god of Egypt. South of Amun's chapel are the chapels of Re-Harakhty, Ptah, and the deified Sethi I; the chapels of Osiris, Isis, and Horus are situated to the north of Amun's chapel. In the chapels, which originally had doors, there are relief scenes depicting the ruler bringing offerings to the gods, and the king receiving the symbols of life and duration and the insignia of the royal office from the gods. In liturgical practice these scenes were complemented by ceremonies reflecting the complex course of the Osirian transformation of the king, which the priests would perform inside the chapels while reciting the sacred texts from papyrus scrolls by the light of little oil lamps. None of the rear walls of the chapels are equipped with false doors, but there is further access from the chapel of Osiris into the first hall of Osiris, which has ten columns without capitals. The second hall of Osiris has four columns and is situated to the left of the first hall; in contrast, there are three deep niches located to the right of the first hall. These niches are the chapels of Osiris, Isis, and Horus; there is a small, entirely inaccessible secret chamber with two pillars situated behind the chapels. This area formed the most intimate part of the temple, and was forbidden to all but selected priests, for it was where the Osiris mysteries were conducted.

It is no coincidence that the mysterious tomb of the god Osiris, the Osireion, was located westward on the main temple axis precisely beyond the exterior walls of these halls and shadowy chapels—the setting for the peculiar cult of Osiris connected with the mystical transformation and resurrection of King Sethi I. Nor is it unimportant that the temple axis, extrapolated farther, was oriented toward what was known as the South Hill about 150 meters south of the cemetery at Umm al-Ga'ab, which seems to have had special, though not yet explained, cult significance.

The secondary tract (the short side L-shaped plan) adjoined the chapels from the southeast, and contained the 'Gallery of the Ancestors' with the Abydos King List. There are depictions of Sethi I and his son Ramesses II (still as a youth with a sidelock) on the western wall of this rather narrow hall, in which they are honoring their royal predecessors whose names are recorded here, starting with the legendary unifier of the land and founder of the First Dynasty, Meni, and ending with Ramesses II, who completed this part of the temple after the death of his father. Some kings were deliberately omitted from the list, for example, the Hyksos rulers, the religious reformer Akhenaten, and his immediate successors.

According to the American Egyptologist Alison Roberts, it was here in the 'Gallery of Ancestors' that the temple rituals would commence. The procession of priests would visit the seven chapels and then reach the small chapel of Osiris. The rituals, which may have been inspired

The Osireion submerged in groundwater.

by the text of the so-called Ritual of Amenhotep I (also called the 'Ritual of the Ancestors'), were intended to honor the dead kings, emphasize the continuity of rule and its cosmic dimension, and culminate in the transformation of Sethi I into Osiris. The secondary tract also contained the chapel of Ptah-Sokar and Nefertem, the 'Hall of the Barques,' where the cult barques used in temple ceremonies (to carry statues of the gods) were kept, and the unfinished 'Hall of the Butchers' (the temple slaughterhouse), which in the Roman Period was to become the oracle of the god Bes. Beyond it, in the far northeastern corner of the temple, there was a small chamber well supplied by groundwater. It was from the secondary tract, by way of a passage with a staircase ramp, that there was access to the west of the whole building, that is, to the Osireion.

The Mysterious Osireion

Osiris's cenotaph, the symbolic tomb known in Greek as the Osireion, is a very peculiar and even puzzling building. It is an integral part of the Temple of Sethi I and in a certain sense enhances the latter's religious significance. Discovered at the beginning of the twentieth century by Margaret A. Murray (1863–1963), a British Egyptologist, it was excavated and studied for the British Egypt Exploration Society shortly before and after the First World War by a Swiss Egyptologist named Henri Édouard Naville (1844–1926), and then a Dutch Egyptologist named Henri Frankfort (1897–1954).

The Osireion is very unusual in architecture, in building materials (red granite and silificated sandstone, in striking contrast to the adjacent temple), and in treatment of the materials. Built at the level of the water table, it has a rectangular ground plan and its main axis is identical with that of the main tract of the Temple of Sethi I. The main hall of the building is in the middle, and is largely taken up by a rectangular granite platform. Five red-granite pillars, which originally held up the ceiling of the entire hall, stand along each of the longer sides of this platform. There are two hollows in the middle of the surface, one rectangular and one square, for a sarcophagus and a chest for canopic jars respectively; notably, no such objects were found here. Given that Sethi I was buried in his tomb in the Valley of the Kings, and that Émile Brugsch, a German Egyptologist, discovered Sethi I's mummy (together with fifty other mummies of kings, queens, and magnates in 1881 in a cache in Deir al-Bahri near the Valley of the Kings where they had been hidden from tomb robbers at the turn of the Twentieth/Twenty-

Coptic graffito discovered in the temple of Sethi I in Abydos.

had mixed up the tombs of Khufu and Osiris, especially since according to another legend the latter was close to the Sphinx in Giza, in Osiris's underworld dwelling Ra setau ('Mouth of the underground galleries'). Today, the main hall of the Osireion is submerged because of the permanent rise in the water table following the construction of the Aswan dams.

Originally, a hill of sand planted with trees had been constructed above the cenotaph in order to evoke both the tomb of Osiris and the mound emerging from the primordial waters. It is clear from surviving archaeological artifacts and written records that the Osireion was among the epicenters of the cult of Osiris and was still the object of veneration long after most of the Temple of Sethi had been submerged in sand by nature and neglect, not by man. The Osireion even remained a cult place until the sixth century AD, when Christianity had definitively triumphed in Egypt. At that point Moses was venerated here, as is evident from the surviving visitors' graffiti left by monks from the nearby Deir al-Sitt Damiana monastery and the hermitages they built for themselves in some of the cemetery's tombs.

Although the Osireion is an integral part of the temple complex of Sethi I, and the king's name and the names of his successors Ramesses II and Merenptah appear in inscriptions in it, its dating has provoked controversy among Egyptologists. The prevailing view is that the Osireion dates from the reign of Sethi I and essentially mimics the royal tombs of that time, but in view of its archaic form some have suggested that the basic part of the building, which in its appearance and materials used strongly resembles Old Kingdom monuments (for example, the valley Temple of Khafre in Giza), might be much older and might date precisely from that early period.

The Temple of Sethi I is associated with a rather bizarre episode from the recent past, and an account of this famous Egyptian monument would be incomplete without a mention of it. The heroine of this story was an Englishwoman named Dorothea Eady (1904–81), who had been interested in ancient Egypt from childhood. She believed in reincarnation and came to the conclusion that she had lived in ancient Egypt and been a priestess in the Temple of Sethi I in Abydos. She moved there, and in 1950 built a very humble dwelling place for herself beside the temple, living in it with her cats and a few books until her death. She used to visit the temple several times a day and make offerings to the gods. The villagers started to call her Umm Seti ('Mother of Sethi') and treated her with respect mingled with a certain apprehension. In fact, anyone who thought that this small, wiry woman of rather neglected appearance and shabby dress was mentally backward or impaired would have been quite mistaken. Those who visited her and got to talk with her thought quite the opposite. Although timid, she was very well read, and absorbed in her long-vanished world of ancient gods, among them King Sethi I. (See the accounts of Cott, Eady, el-Zeini, and www.mysteriouspeople.com/Omm_Sety.htm.)

The Ruler of the Kingdom of the Dead

The origin of the god Wsir (known in Greek as Osiris), and the etymology of his name, have been the subjects of scholarly debate for a long time. Most often he has been traced back to the central Nile Delta and in particular the ninth Lower Egyptian nome known as Andjet ('region of pastures'). The emblem of the region was Andjety ('He who belongs to Andjet'): a striding male figure with two plumes on his head, a crook, and a flagellum. This was probably a deified nomad leader and original local god. At all events, as time went by, the name Andjety became one of the names of the god Osiris, and the capital of the region Djed(et) became a center of the cult of Osiris. Osiris's *ba*, the animal believed to be the earthly embodiment of his spiritual power, was the ram (the Egyptian word for ram was *ba*), which was originally worshiped under the name of Ba neb Djed ('Ram, Lord of Djed'). In Djed the tomb of Osiris was believed to lie in the local sacred grove called Nebeh by the Egyptians. The Greek name for the town of Busiris was derived from the shortening and mutilation of the original Egyptian name Per Wsir (neb-Djed) or 'House of Osiris (Lord of Djed).' On the other hand, an earlier scholarly view was that Osiris had originated outside the borders of Egypt, in the Near East, and was perhaps linked with the gods Assur or Marduk. There is a wide range of theories of the interpretation of Osiris's name, but none are completely persuasive.

Osiris is usually represented as a standing, or enthroned mummiform male figure wearing the *atef* crown (a high crown adorned on each side by an ostrich feather). He holds a crooked scepter and flagellum in his fists, which protrude on his breast from a tight-fitting white robe. His face and hands are sometimes black, sometimes green. In the ancient Egyptian symbolism of colors, white was the color of mourning and Osiris was the god of the dead, the ruler of the other world, the kingdom of the dead. Green symbolized freshness, prosperity, and rebirth, and black the fertile soil of the Nile Valley. Thus Osiris was also the god of vegetation and fertility, and his story reflected the life-giving powers of nature and the agricultural cycle from sowing to harvest, and the expectation of new crops.

The cult of Osiris is very ancient and goes right back to the dawn of the history of ancient Egypt. Osiris already occupied an important position in the earliest Egyptian religious doctrine associated with the solar cult and Heliopolis, that is, he was one of the gods of the Heliopolitan Ennead. Together with his sister and wife Eset (known in Greek as Isis), he was the child of the gods Geb and Nut. Indirect proof of the great antiquity of the cult of Osiris is provided by remnants of relief decoration from a shrine built by King Djoser in Heliopolis at the beginning of the Third Dynasty. Next to Geb is a fragment of a representation of the god Seth, one of the protagonists of the Osiris myth. We also encounter Osiris in the Pyramid Texts, the oldest set of religious texts, first historically documented in Wenis's pyramid in Saqqara from the end of the Fifth Dynasty but thought to be much older. A fragment of a scene in low relief on a piece of limestone block from Djedkare's pyramid complex in Saqqara from the second half of the Fifth Dynasty is generally regarded as the oldest known representation of Osiris. This is not unchallenged, but some archaeological finds (which we shall discuss later) even suggest the existence of the cult of Osiris back in the Early Dynastic Period.

<< Osiris, ruler of the underworld. The goddesses Isis and Nebthet stand behind the enthroned god. Detail from decoration in the Huneferef Papyrus. Nineteenth Dynasty. British Museum in London.

In any case, there is no doubt that during the first half of the fifth century the cult of Osiris came to the fore and in a relatively short time became so widespread in Egyptian society that it began to overshadow the hitherto dominant solar cult. In subsequent centuries, and throughout Egyptian history right up to the Late Roman Period, the cult of Osiris continued to flourish and was an integral part of the piety of both rich and poor. A major reason for its appeal was the deep connection between Osiris and vegetation, the Nile inundation, good harvests, and the cycle of nature. At harvest time the god Osiris symbolically died, only to be reborn with the sowing of new seed, and so the first reaping of the corn was an occasion for both lamentation and joy.

The earliest version of the legend of Osiris is briefer and differs in detail from later versions, the most famous of which appears in Plutarch's account, *De Iside et Osiride* ('On Isis and Osiris') (see Third Excursus). The cult of Osiris was based on the myth of a noble, beneficent ruler, which was simultaneously a great drama of betrayal, lust for power, and fratricide, as well as one of love overcoming all obstacles and eventual deserved retribution. Here the eternal struggle between good and evil is entwined with a state-generating myth of the founding of the kingdom of Egypt. According to Plutarch's account, Osiris was the first ruler of Egypt, who brought culture to the people, reformed their brutish mores, taught them to plow the fields and harvest the corn, laid the foundations of learning, and taught them to honor the gods. Osiris's envious brother Seth hated him; he treacherously murdered Osiris by a cunning ruse, cut up his body, and scattered the pieces throughout Egypt. Osiris's sister and wife Isis so loved her husband that she searched out the pieces of his body, put them together again, had intercourse with the dead Osiris through her divine powers, and so conceived a son, Horus. Horus grew up to avenge his father, defeating the embodiment of evil, Seth, in single combat. He then delivered the bound Seth to Isis, but the goddess untied him and released him, and so evil continued to exist alongside good. In a dispute between Horus and Seth over power and the rule of Egypt, the gods finally decided in favor of Horus. Osiris and Horus were ceremonially presented with the "wreath of justification" as an emblem of victory over their enemies. From the New Kingdom onward the wreath became the mortuary cult symbol of passing the test of final judgment. The dead man or woman who had spoken the truth at the final judgment and been vindicated was known as *maa kheru* ('true of voice' or 'justified'), which became the word for 'deceased.' A question that sometimes arises in Egyptological discussions is whether the Osiris myth might actually reflect a prehistoric ritual in which the old chieftain was removed by violence to clear the way for his young successor in order to guarantee better prospects for the tribe's survival.

According to myth, Osiris's envious, violent, and power-hungry brother and arch enemy, Seth (identified by the Greeks with Typhon), soon came to be seen as the embodiment of evil and danger in various forms. He was the god of war, anger, thunder and storms, and the perilous desert that closed in on the Nile Valley on both sides. It is therefore no wonder that we encounter his cult in the oases and that his animal forms included not only the hippopotamus and crocodile but also the donkey, the basic means of transport on routes through the desert. Seth's color was red, but in the temples in the oases, which were usually dedicated to the Theban Triad of Amun, Mut, and Khonsu, his body was colored blue. Seth was most often represented as a mythical beast resembling a seated dog with a raised tail that was split at the end, and a head like that of an anteater or aardvark; sometimes he was portrayed as a man with such a head. Seth's principal cult center in Upper Egypt was Nubt (known in Greek as Ombos), close to Thebes, and in Lower Egypt it was Hatweret (known in Greek as Avaris), the seat of the Hyksos conquerors of Egypt in the Second Intermediate Period. From Avaris the cult came to the new royal seat of Piramesse that Ramesses II founded close by. Seth's partner was the goddess Nebthet (in Greek, Nephthys).

The places where the pieces of Osiris's body fell came to be known as *iat wabet* ('pure place,' known in Greek as *abaton*). There were more than a dozen of these and they became centers for the veneration of relics of Osiris. For example, his spine was supposed to have fallen in Busiris in the north, and his legs in the southernmost, first Upper Egyptian nome, where the local *abaton* on the islet of Biggeh near Philae was to become the most important cult center of the relics of Osiris in the Ptolemaic and Roman Periods.

The Osiris myth was adopted into the foundations of the state dogma and royal ideology of ancient Egypt. According to this ideology, Egypt was created at the beginning of the world by the gods, who gave the land laws and made it an island of order, albeit always surrounded by the forces of chaos and evil. Maat, daughter of the sun god Re,

When Osiris's body was cut up and scattered by Seth, his legs landed as far away as the island of Biggeh by the First Nile Cataract, where water—the source of the Nile—sprang from them. Detail from the decoration of the Isis temple on Philae.

embodied this order and her name meant not only order, but also truth, right, and justice. The guarantor of the divine order of Egypt was the pharaoh, who was considered to be a god living on earth, and the mediator between men and gods. His duty was not just to prevent the internal and external forces of evil from overcoming and destroying the work of the gods, but also to ensure the prosperity of Egypt and its people. He did this during his lifetime, but also after his death, when he would join the rest of the gods yet continue to rule the 'people of his time' beneficently for all eternity. The legitimacy of royal rule and the continuity of the monarchy were expressed in terms of the Osiris myth by the identification of the king with the embodiment of the god Horus. When a king died, it was said that 'Horus has departed for the heavens,' so becoming Osiris, while his son, Horus's new earthly embodiment, acceded to the throne. This idea corresponded perfectly to the ancient Egyptian conception of time, which was largely cyclical. With the succession of a new king, the old myth was always enacted anew: the gods recreated Egypt, and the new terrestrial expression of the god Horus was crowned. Any situation in which the succession was not secured in this way and someone other than the son of the reigning monarch became king was always potentially, and sometimes all too actually, a moment of crisis in Egyptian history.

The potency of the myth of Osiris, a god who symbolizes the fertility of the land itself as well as rule over it, enabled his cult to put down deep and also very extensive roots in all classes of Egyptian society. In the spirit of the ancient Egyptian tendency to syncretism, which permitted gods to acquire new aspects and qualities by merger and hybridization in order to gain additional and mightier powers, Osiris started to absorb features of other gods of a similar kind. Very early, perhaps even by the end of the Old Kingdom, he was merging with Sokar, who was likewise a god of the dead and the ruler of the Memphite necropolis, originally venerated in the form of a falcon. Like that of Osiris, Sokar's cult had originally incorporated certain ritualized agricultural activities like the digging of the earth, for example, or the driving of herds to the fields and the carrying of onions. Later on, Osiris also merged with Ptah, the main god of Memphis, thus developing the form of Ptah-Sokar-Osiris, who was the powerful protector god of the dead from the New Kingdom onward: this threefold god's characteristic wooden polychrome mummiform figurine standing on a low base, which sometimes contained a papyrus scroll with a text from the *Book of the Dead*, became a common article of funerary equipment. Osiris was already merged in a similar fashion with the local god of the dead, Khentamentyu, as Osiris-Khentamentyu, in Abydos in the Old Kingdom. From the Middle Kingdom onward pilgrims from all over Egypt came to the Osiris festivities at Abydos, which overshadowed the god's original cult center in Lower Egyptian Djed because of the belief that the tomb of the god lay in the middle of the cemetery of the earliest rulers at Umm al-Ga'ab.

Where Osiris was supposed to reside in the religious sense is less clear from surviving textual records. Sometimes such sources speak of a kingdom of the dead lying in the west in the endless depths of the desert. Sometimes they refer to the 'mysterious chambers of the dwelling of Osiris' in the underworld called the Duat, through which the dead had to pass on their journey to final judgment. Often the dwelling of Osiris is identified with Ra setau ('The mouth of the underground passages'), which was originally the seat of Sokar. In texts from the New Kingdom this was frequently localized to the area of the cemetery in Giza, in some cases including a wider territory from Giza through Zawiyat al-Aryan and Abusir as far as Saqqara. The Temple of Osiris the 'Lord of Ra setau' is supposed to have stood close to Giza.

As time went by, the myth of Osiris acquired a further, cosmic dimension. The constellation of Orion came to be regarded as the spirit of Osiris and the star Sirius as the heavenly expression of Osiris's partner Isis. This interpretation had an impact on ancient Egyptian funerary customs: the mummification and preparation of the deceased for burial had to be carried out during seventy days, for this was the period of the temporary disappearance of Sirius from the visible sky.

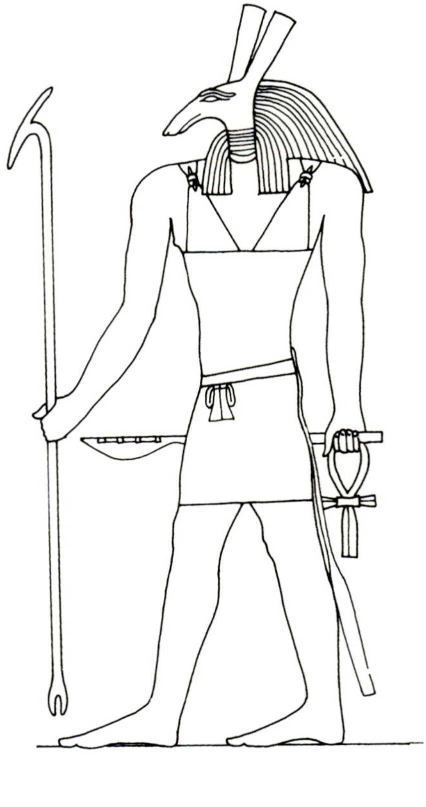

Seth, who killed his brother Osiris.

As has already been noted, the death and glorious resurrection of Osiris was connected not only with ideas of the afterlife but also with the veneration of nature: the fertility and powers of the soil quickened by the inundation of the Nile leading to the resurrection of the god, and the expectation of a new harvest in a constant cycle of death and rebirth. The intermingling of the funerary and fertility aspects of the cult of Osiris found expression in what was known as the bed of Osiris, sometimes also called 'corn (germinating) Osiris.' In preparation for funerary rites a form would be made in the shape of the silhouette of Osiris's body and then filled with fertile soil that would be sown with corn. This form with its germinating corn would be placed against the coffin in the dark underworld of the burial chamber, magically reinforcing the hope of the deceased in resurrection and eternal life. The origins of the cult of Osiris in the form of corn are very ancient, and are believed by some scholars to go right back to the Early Dynastic Period. One beautiful example of the custom is the Osiris form with young seedlings found in the tomb of Tutankhamun, which is currently on display in the Egyptian Museum in Cairo. The corn Osiris was not just a part of funerary customs, however, but played a key role in the Osiris festivities and mysteries.

Popular festivities accompanying the veneration of Osiris culminated in Khoiak, the fourth month of inundation (see Third Excursus). Various written sources, particularly inscriptions in the Temple of Hathor at Dendera, give us an idea of the course of the festival. The Osiris festivities were celebrated annually in all the places where the limbs of the god fell down and all the nomes of Osiris, which meant all the places with a cult of Osiris and the dead, and therefore all large cemeteries throughout the land. The 'mysteries' (Herodotus already used this term for the Osiris festivals) lasted from fourteen days to a month and consisted of a series of precisely defined cult rites carried out on a fixed schedule. Their conclusion was signaled by the ceremony of the 'raising of the *djed* pillar'—Osiris's symbolic resurrection and triumph over the evil personified by his enemy.

The *djed* pillar was a characteristic symbol of Osiris, but also a fetish. In religious symbolism the *djed* pillar, which as a hieroglyphic sign means 'to endure,' and 'to be firm,' was identified as the spine of Osiris. Helck came to the conclusion that originally it had been a stylized sheaf symbolizing crops and the cult of fertility, but this theory has often been challenged. A faience frieze from Djoser's pyramid complex suggests that it might have been a construction element from buildings made of reeds and matting. Other scholars believe that the

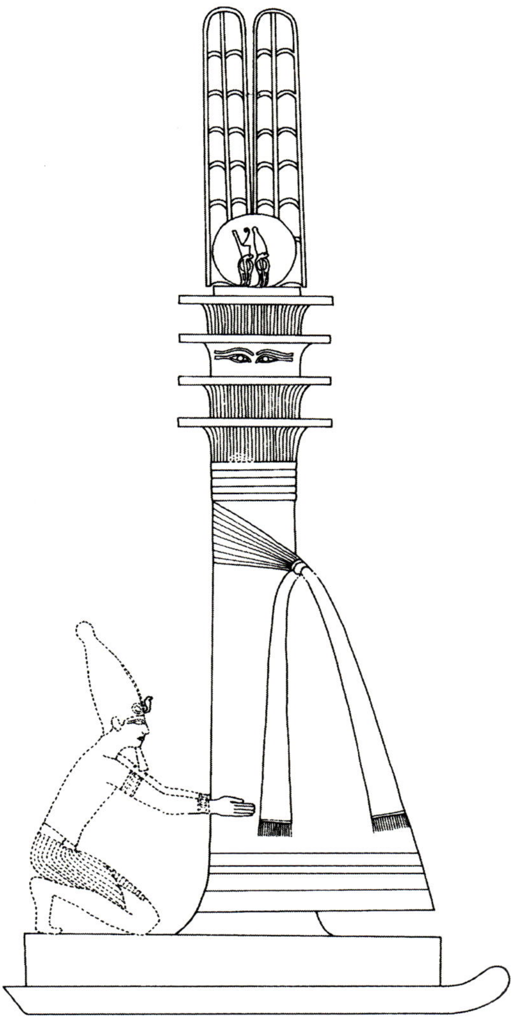

Sethi I raises and worships the *djed* pillar. Detail from the decoration of the mortuary temple of Sethi I in Abydos.

djed was originally a fetish in Memphis and a part of the local cult of the god of the dead, Sokar, and the god-creator, Ptah, with whom Osiris later merged into Ptah-Sokar-Osiris.

The Osiris myth was expressed and conveyed to the public in the form of festivities, feasts, dramatic rituals, and cult plays, sometimes called mysteries. Written sources that survive in only fragmentary form provide us with some notion of the content of these cult plays, which cannot be simplistically compared to modern theater. In these fragments the text is usually divided into scenes, sometimes accompanied by illustrations, and the dialogue is differentiated from the rest of the text. The plays involved reenactment of the myth and were performed by priests taking the roles of gods under the direction of the lector-priest.

The mysteries were not just illustrative but were held to have real spiritual effects, offering salvation to participants. Some parts of the mysteries took place in public and were accessible to ordinary pilgrims to Abydos, for example, but the latter were not allowed to go beyond the designated boundary of Peqer and get close to the supposed tomb of Osiris at Umm al-Ga'ab. Unfortunately there are no surviving detailed accounts of the non-public part of the mysteries, which was performed directly at the tomb of Osiris and involved only priests and a few elect persons. Some limited idea of their course in the Roman Period can be obtained from a relatively late, and not directly Egyptian, source: the eleventh book of *Metamorphoses* by the second-century Roman author Lucius Apuleius. Apuleius's narrative suggests that a man wishing to be initiated into the mysteries had first to confess his sins, ritually cleanse himself, and go through a period of fasting. After this, a priest could initiate him into the mystery preserved in papyrus scrolls in the part of the temple accessible only to priests. In the night the adept had to undergo a symbolic death, descend into the underworld, honor the gods, and pass through the four elements of earth, air, fire, and water. At midnight he was awakened by a bright light, a symbolic resurrection, and was then able to worship the gods in immediate proximity to them. In the morning he awoke as an initiate. Some elements of this initiation ritual strikingly recall the journey of the sun god through the underworld as described in Egyptian religious texts.

As we learn, for example, from inscriptions in the large temples from the Ptolemaic Period, hourly watches or vigils by priests later became part of the cult of Osiris. In the part of the temple known as the *wabet*, priests would take turns holding vigils (each hour being under the protection of different gods) by the symbolic bed where the corpse of Osiris lay, mourning and guarding him. During the vigils they would read out selected religious texts, make offerings to Osiris, and throw little balls to the four points of the compass with recitation of magic rhymes, among other things. These balls were called *benenet* and were identified with the protective goddesses Wadjet, Sekhemtet, Ubastet, and Sakhmet; they were believed to ward off any approaching evil that might threaten Osiris.

In the Ptolemaic and especially the Roman Period, the cult of Osiris as a god of the dead and fertility, and the associated Osiris mysteries, spread far beyond the borders of Egypt. Roman soldiers who spent part of their service in Egypt and were then ordered away to other parts of the empire played a particularly important role in disseminating the cult. Evidence of the worship of Osiris has been found as far away as Gaul or Pannonia, for example, although its main center outside Egypt was Rome. We find veneration of the mummy of Osiris in Pompeii, as witnessed by paintings in the local temple of Isis. Apart from Osiris, Isis became an especially revered and popular goddess outside Egypt. She was considered the protectress of mothers (the so-called Isis *lactans* represented with the child Horus in her lap) but also the giver of victory (Isis-Nike *victrix invicta*) and a goddess who could ensure good fortune. The center of her cult in Rome was a shrine on the Field of Mars.

Elements of the Osiris myth and the mysteries have played a part in the more esoteric traditions of European thought during the Renaissance and later in the rites of the Freemasons, who sometimes identified Osiris with Hiram, the legendary builder of Solomon's temple in Jerusalem. Some argue that it is thanks to the Freemasons that ancient Egyptian symbols related to the Osiris cult can be found on the American one-dollar bill.

Serapisdienst in Rom.

Romanticizing nineteenth-century reconstruction of rites in the Roman Serapeum.

Third Excursus

Osirian Mythology

Osiris, ruler of the kingdom of the dead. Behind his throne the owner of the tomb kneels and pays the god homage. Detail from decoration of the tomb of Pashedu in Deir al-Medina. Nineteenth Dynasty.

Of Osiris and Isis

The myth of Osiris (Usir), treacherously slain by his brother Seth, resurrected by the devotion and power of his wife Isis, and avenged by his son Horus, is one of the most famous of ancient Egyptian myths. It can also be considered the most important historically since it became the foundation of the ideology of the ancient Egyptian state. Although from a comparatively late period, the most complete form in which it has been preserved is in a Latin version of the previously cited work by the Greek historian and philosopher Plutarch.

Here we present excerpts from an English translation of Theodor Hopfner's German translation of the myth.

De Iside et Osiride

12. It is related that Rhea had intercourse with Cronus secretly, and that when this was observed by Helios he placed a curse upon her, that she should be unable to give birth to a child in any year or month. But Hermes [too] loved the goddess and consorted with her. Later, he was playing draughts with the moon goddess [Selene] and won from her the seventieth part of each day, and he combined these parts into five days and added them to the 360 days [of the year], and [so] the Egyptians even now call these days the 'super-added' days and celebrate them as the birthdays of the gods.

Thus on the first of these days was Osiris born, and at the moment of his birth a voice was heard announcing that the Lord of All had come into the light of the world; some, however, say that a certain Pamyles, while drawing water in Thebes, heard a voice from the temple of Zeus telling him to proclaim the birth of a great king, the beneficent Osiris; and for this he brought up Osiris, who was entrusted to him by Cronus. This gave rise to the celebration of the festival of Pamylia, which is similar to the processions with phallus. On the second day Arueris was born, whom many call the elder Horus, and on the third day Typhon,* but not at the due time from the proper place, for he is said to have leapt out, tearing and wounding the groin [of his mother]. On the fourth day Isis was born in all moistness, and on the fifth day Nephthys, who is called Teleute and Aphrodite, and by some also Nike [Victory]. Osiris and Arueris were fathered by Helios, Isis by Hermes and Typhon, and Nephthys by Cronus. For this reason the kings regarded the third of the added days as unlucky and on this day did no business nor took any care of their bodies until night came. Typhon married Nephthys, but Isis and Osiris had made love already before their births in their mother's body in darkness. Some claim that it was in this way that Arueris was conceived.

* Typhon is the Greek interpretation of the Egyptian Seth.

13. It is related that as King of the Egyptians Osiris first delivered the Egyptians from their wretched and rude manner of life by showing them how to grow crops in the fields, by giving them laws, and by teaching them to honor the gods. Later he journeyed all over the earth, teaching mankind to abandon savagery without as far as possible using force of arms, for he won over the majority by charming them with persuasive words and enlightening them at the same time with every kind of song and music. Therefore he seemed to the Greeks to be identical with Dionysus.

They say that in his absence Typhon made no attempt to stir up trouble, because Isis was very vigilant and used her power to counter any hint of rebellion. But on his [Osiris's] return Typhon set a trap for him, with seventy-two conspirators and the assistance of a queen from Ethiopia whom the Egyptians call Aso. Typhon secretly measured Osiris's body and made

Osiris wearing the *atef* crown (the Upper Egyptian crown adorned by plumes on both sides) and holding the insignia of royal rule: the crooked sceptre and flagellum. Osiris's spirit, or *ba*, stands on a pedestal behind him, in the form of a bird with a human head; above it, the scorpion goddess raises her protective hand. Detail of decoration from the temple of Isis on Philae.

the trunk that contained the invisible chest, and used it as a pillar to support his roof.

It is said that Isis was apprised of all this from the divine breath of Rumor, and came to Byblos, where she sat down dejected by a spring, wept, and would speak with nobody, except that she was friendly and kind to the queen's maidservants, and braided their hair and breathed an enchanting scent into their skin. When the queen saw her maidservants, she yearned for this stranger whose hair and skin were imbued with ambrosia. She therefore had Isis brought to her, became friends with her, and made her the wet nurse of her little boy. That king is supposed to have been called Malcander. And according to some people the queen was Astarte, while according to others she was Saosis or Nemanus, whom the Greeks would probably term Athenais.

16. Isis now nursed the boy by giving him not her breast but her finger to suck, and in the night she burned away the mortal parts of his body. She herself turned into a swallow and flew around the pillar lamenting, until the queen who was watching shrieked when she saw her child in the flames, thus depriving him of immortality. Now the goddess, who revealed who she was, asked for the pillar supporting the roof. She took it out from under the roof with considerable ease, and cut the trunk of the *ereike* away from the chest. She wrapped the wood in linen, poured scented unguent on it, and gave it to the royal couple. Today the people of Byblos still venerate the wood, which is kept in the Temple of Isis. But then she threw herself on the coffin and lamented so piercingly that the king's younger son died on the spot. She took the older son with her, placed the coffin on a boat, and departed. When towards dawn the river Phaedrus whipped up a sharp wind, she was enraged and caused its stream to dry up.

17. As soon as she was alone, she opened the coffin, laid her face upon the face of the corpse, and wept. At that moment the little boy came up behind her silently, seeing it, and when the goddess noticed his presence she turned and gave him a terrible look in her anger; the boy was not strong enough to endure the fright, and died. Others claim that this was not how he died, but that in the manner already described [when he had been wanting to pluck an onion] he fell into the sea. He has nonetheless enjoyed honor on account of the goddess, for they say that he is the Maneros of whom the Egyptians sing at their banquets. But some claim that he was called Palaistinus or Pelusius, and that the city [Pelusium] founded by the goddess was named after him, and that the Maneros of the song was the inventor of music. Against that, many insist that Maneros is not the name of a person at all, but a saying fit only for drinkers and feasters, which is "May it bring you joy!," and that this is always what Egyptians mean by the word 'maneros' when they use the exclamation. Likewise, the picture of a corpse in a case that is shown and carried about is not a reminder of the fate of Osiris, as many believe, but is a way that people remind each other, as they imbibe their wine, that what exists in the present should be used and enjoyed, because soon everyone will be the same [as the picture of the corpse]; this is reported as the reason why they introduced this dismal addition to the banquet.

18. Isis [then] journeyed to see her son Horus, who was being brought up in Buto, and left the coffin away from the beaten track, but Typhon chanced on it while hunting by moonlight. Recognizing the body, he tore it into fourteen pieces and scattered them. Isis learned of this, however, and sailing through the swamps in a papyrus boat she found the pieces and put them together again. This is why crocodiles do not harm those who sail in

In ancient Egypt the king was considered the embodiment of both Horus and Seth. The idea is vividly expressed by this red-granite statue of Ramesses III, where the two gods are placing the crown of Upper Egypt on his head. Egyptian Museum, Cairo.

papyrus boats, for the creatures either feared the goddess or sensed a sacred pool in her presence. It is likewise why so many supposed tombs of Osiris are mentioned in Egypt, for wherever Isis found a limb, she held a burial. Others deny this, and say that rather than giving the body itself she made and gave effigies of the body to different cities so that the body would be honored by more, and so that if Typhon managed to defeat Horus and searched for the real tomb, he would despair of ever finding it when so many were pointed out to him.

The only part of Osiris's body that Isis did not find was his male member, for this had been thrown straightaway into the water and had been devoured by the lepidotus, the sea-bream, and the pike, which [for that reason] the Egyptians are most careful to avoid eating. But Isis made a replica of the male member and consecrated the phallus, which the Egyptians still honor with a festival today.

19. It is related that Osiris then came from the underworld to Horus. He armed him and trained him for the battle, and asked him what he considered the most beautiful of all things. When Horus answered that it was "to avenge one's father and mother whom evil has befallen," Osiris asked him which animal he thought the most useful for those going into battle. "A horse," Horus replied. Osiris was puzzled and inquired why he had said a horse, not a lion. Horus is said to have answered that a lion was needful for one who needed help, but a horse was useful for cutting off the enemy in his flight and utterly destroying him. When he heard this answer Osiris was pleased, thinking that Horus was now sufficiently prepared. It is further related that when many had changed their allegiance to Horus, Typhon's concubine Thueris also came over to his side, and that the men around Horus cut in pieces a serpent that had pursued her; this is why today the people still throw down a rope and slice it in pieces.

The battle [then] lasted several days, and Horus emerged the victor. Typhon was delivered bound and captive to Isis, but she did not kill him. Instead she untied him and let him go free. Horus was outraged, and laid hands upon his mother and tore the crown from her head. But Hermes placed a helmet with cow's horns upon her brow instead. Typhon later accused Horus of being illegitimate [and so unqualified to rule], but with the help of Hermes he was declared the rightful heir. Typhon was then defeated in another two battles. In the meantime Isis, having lain with Osiris even after his death, brought forth Harpocrates, whose birth was premature and who was weak in the lower limbs.

20. These are roughly the main legends, leaving aside repulsive episodes such as the dismemberment of Horus and the beheading of Isis. . . . [But that most of the narratives need to be understood just in symbolic-allegorical terms is shown by opinion on the Tomb of Osiris.] For even though the body is supposed to rest in many places, the Egyptians claim there is only one small town that owns the one body; rich and high-ranking Egyptians are eager to have their own tombs in Abydos alongside the body of Osiris. Furthermore, Apis in Memphis where his body [likewise] lies is considered the image of his spirit; some also translate the name of the city as "Harbor of the Good," whereas others translate it as "Osiris's tomb." Finally, however, the island of Philae in the region of Aswan is supposed to be inaccessible and closed to all, and is a place where even birds do not alight or fish draw near; but at a certain time priests go there to make a funerary offering and adorn [Osiris's] tomb, which lies in the shade of the plant Meditha, which in height exceeds all olive trees.

21. For that matter, Eudoxus claims that although there are many tombs [of Osiris] in Egypt, the body in fact lies only in Busiris, because this town is the birthplace of Osiris. In the case of Taposisir no special argument would be required, for the very name means "Tomb of Osiris." I pass over the cutting of wood, the rending of cloth, and the making of libations, however, because much of this is related to the teaching on the mysteries. Nonetheless, the priests say that the bodies not only of these but of the other gods, being neither engendered nor transient, rest in their care after death and are venerated, and that these gods' spirits shine in the sky as stars. The spirit of Isis is called the Dog Star by the Greeks and Sopdet by the Egyptians, Orion is the spirit of Horus, and the Great Bear is the spirit of Typhon.

Khoiak: The Month of the Mysteries of Osiris

Inscriptions in the Temple of Hathor in Dendera are among the best surviving sources of information about the Osiris mysteries of the month of Khoiak. Using these inscriptions, which have survived in abundance and in a relatively good state, the French Egyptologist Émile Chassinat (1868–1948) reconstructed the course of the rituals that took place in the temple during the Osiris mysteries in the month of Khoiak, and compiled a list of temple instruments and cult objects used in them. The rituals included, for example, a vigil by the tomb of Osiris, the mourning of the god, the rather bizarre 'throwing of four little balls' already mentioned above, and so on.

The calendar of the mysteries, always starting very early in the morning, was as follows, as described by Chassinat:

Clay mold for the 'corn Osiris.' Late Period. Roemer-Pelizeus Museum, Hildesheim.

12th day	Beginning of the mysteries, at the fourth hour preparation of barley and sand, and creation of a statuette of Khentamentyu by pressing this into a mold [in the shape of Osiris's body—author's note].
14th day	At the third hour the preparation of a mold for the statuette of Sokar; the figurine is then laid in a silver vessel lined with sycomore sprigs.
15th day	Preparation and adornment of a coffin for the statuette of Sokar; the god is then marked with the name Osiris-Khentamentyu.
16th day	At the third hour the *fekti* priest takes the silver vessel containing the statuette, takes out the statuette and lays it on the lap of the (statue) of the Great Mother of Gods Nut; then the statuette is placed on a couch in a covered pavilion; the god sets out with an escort (priest with the mask of Anubis) to process around the temple.
19th day	Sokar's figurine is taken out of the mold, placed on a gold base, exposed to the sun and at intervals covered with ointments, and sprinkled with water.
20th day	At the eighth hour the weaving of fabric starts, ending at the same hour on the following day.
21st day	Khentamentyu's statuette is taken from its coffin; the two parts of which the statuette is composed are censed with incense and then bound together again with four strings, and allowed to dry in the sun until the fifth hour; Sokar's mold is sprinkled four times with water infused with myrrh.
22nd day	Procession in boats to the sacred lake at the eighth hour; this involves thirty-four little papyrus boats, one cubit and three palms long, bearing statuettes of the gods including Thoth, Anubis, Isis, Nebthet, and Horus. At the end of the procession the statuettes are wrapped in the four fabrics of the South and North House and taken to the tomb; offerings are placed.
23rd day	The statuette of Sokar is placed on a red-granite pedestal; it is allowed to dry in the sun for two hours; then it is placed on a rush mat, ritually cleansed, and fourteen amulets are placed on its swathing bands; various funerary rituals are carried out.
24th day	The statuette of Sokar is taken out of the swathing bands, funerary rituals are conducted with it, and it is then placed on sycomore twigs and rests in the [chapel?] of Khery-djedet until the thirtieth day, when it is to be buried in the sacred cemetery.
25th day	Burial of the three figurines—Sokar, Khentamentyu, and the piece of the god [a symbolic piece of Osiris's body—author's note]—molded the previous year; the burial takes place at the third hour in the cemetery; raising of the *djed* pillar in Busiris.

Into your land
To this your sacred place.
Horus hallowed it for you [?],
Isis mourns you,
. . . enemies . . .

4. Glorification in the Abaton
You will be introduced into the House of Osiris.
You rejoice to the heavens.
You speak to Re.
Amun has hallowed you.
Thoth has honored your name.
Shine from the ocean, you Shining One.

C. The Decree. . . and Thoth blessed them with this written decree:
Abaton [is] the superb golden land
of Osiris and his sister Isis.
From the beginning it has been ordained for
Osiris . . . in Thebes.

Milk must never run out
in this place, on which lies the sacred grove Menta
and the shrine in which Osiris is buried.
Around this holy place 365 offering tables will be set up to him
and palm branches laid on them.
Libations on them will never cease
And in its surroundings water must never run out.

Each day a service to the god will be performed
by the great priest who has the monthly service.
Libation to Isis, Lady of Philae, will be conducted every day.

There must be no drumming on a small drum there
nor playing on the harp or flute.

Nobody may come here,
nobody low may set foot here.

Nobody who is here may speak out loud
during the sacred time of the days,

which Isis, Lady of Philae spends here on her throne,
in order that she may conduct a libation on every tenth day.

Isis, Lady of Philae, is conveyed to Abaton
at festivals in the barque called . . .

Re signed this document.
Shu, son of Re, signed this document,
Geb, son of Shu, signed this document
and Thoth himself signed it.

From another decree we learn that Isis, together with her son Harendotes (that is, statues of these gods), would always visit Abaton on the twelfth day of the third month of the season of harvest, and that it was forbidden to catch fish or birds on Abaton.

Philae: The Pearl of Egypt

"This (temple) came into existence when nothing yet existed and the land lay in darkness." (inscription in the temple on Philae)

"Every part of Egypt is interesting and strange, but only one place deserves the attribute Beautiful, the island of Philae," wrote Robert Curzon (1810–73), who visited Philae in 1834, in his *Visits to the Monasteries of the Levant.* It is hard to disagree. With its grand monuments mirrored in the waters of the Nile, the island of Philae, by the southern edge of the First Nile Cataract not far from Aswan, is one of the most enchanting places in Egypt; it was justly christened the 'Pearl of Egypt' by the French traveler Pierre Loti (1850–1923). According to one theory the island's Greek name is derived from the Egyptian Pa lek, in Coptic Pilak ('Island of the End,' that is, the island at the southern end of the First Nile Cataract), but some experts are skeptical, and consider the origins of the name to be unclear, possibly Nubian. In the Late, Ptolemaic, and Roman Periods a huge complex of sacred buildings was progressively created on the island. Dominated by the temple of the goddess Isis, the complex owes its splendor not only to the Egyptian and Ptolemaic kings but also to Nubian Meroitic rulers. It should be emphasized that the set of buildings on Philae was created with great feeling for the natural setting. Today it still impresses the visitor with its balance and the sense of timelessness eloquently conveyed by the English traveler and admirer of Egypt and its antiquities, Amelia Edwards, whom we have already encountered several times in this book.

≪ One of the last Egyptian hieroglyphic inscriptions. Temple of Isis on Philae.

> *Seen from the level of a small boat, the island, with its palms, its colonnades, its pylons, seems to rise out of the river like a mirage. Piled rocks frame it in on either side, and purple mountains close up the distance. As the boat glides nearer between glistening boulders, those sculptured towers rise higher and ever higher against the sky. They show no sign of ruin or of age. All looks solid, stately, perfect. One forgets for the moment that anything is changed. If a sound of antique chanting were to be borne along the quiet air—if a procession of white-robed priests bearing aloft the veiled ark of the God, were to come sweeping round between the palms and the pylons—we should not think it strange.* (p. 207)

Amelia Edwards thought Philae the embodiment of the harmony of perfect charm and refined beauty, but the times and events that the monuments on Philae have witnessed were not always so harmonious.

The temple complex on the island of Philae lay on the geographical and political boundary of the two worlds represented by the First Cataract—the southern frontier of Egypt. South of the cataract lay Nubia and the way to the African interior. There is no need to stress the sensitivity of this frontier: the First Nile Cataract was the gateway for Egyptian incursions into Nubia, but whenever Egyptian power was internally compromised, it would become a gateway for predatory forces to enter into Egypt. This is why from the Early Dynastic Period the Egyptians strove to bring Nubia and its natural wealth under their control, but also why ambitious rivals from the south sought to do the same with any parts of Egypt accessible to them. In the eighth century BC the Nubian ruler Kashta managed to gain control not only of the First Cataract but also of the whole first (then southernmost) Egyptian nome; his successors finally won the whole of Egypt. From that time onward, the First Nile Cataract was to pass from hand to hand as a series of foreign conquerors succeeded each other in Egypt. Alexander the Great, after subduing Egypt,

<< Philae, the 'Pearl of Egypt,' after its move to the artificial islet of Agilkia; view from the west.

<< The temple complex on Philae as recorded in the 1840s by an artist on the Prussian expedition to Egypt led by Karl R. Lepsius.

The First Nile Cataract forms the natural geographical southern border of Egypt.

Roman temple in Maharraka in Lower Nubia on the southern boundary of the Dodekaschoinos.

exchanged diplomatic civilities with the Nubian *kandake* (the title of the Nubian Meroitic queens and queen mothers who sometimes occupied supreme political and military positions), but his successor Ptolemy I Soter was soon to send a military expedition to Lower Nubia in an attempt to gain control of this territory and its gold mines. In addition to gold, the king and his successors had their eye on yet another African resource: elephants, an important element of the ordnance of the Ptolemaic army. It was probably during Ptolemy I Soter's reign that the Temple of Isis was founded on Philae.

Control of the First Cataract and Lower Egypt was hard to maintain, however, and so eventually the Ptolemaic kings of Egypt and the Nubian rulers started to look for non-confrontational ways of achieving a balance of interests in some areas that would help to preserve peace in Lower Nubia. Ptolemy IV Philopator and the Nubian king Ergamenes II eventually agreed that the Dodekaschoinos (a territory of twelve schoini; 1 schoinos = 6,349 kilometers) between the First Cataract in the north and Hiera Sykaminos in the south would become part of the southernmost Egyptian nome and a royal and priestly territory (donated to the priests of Isis on Philae). In practice it was more of a buffer zone because unrest and resistance in the Theban area permanently destabalized the Ptolemaic kings' rule over southern Egypt.

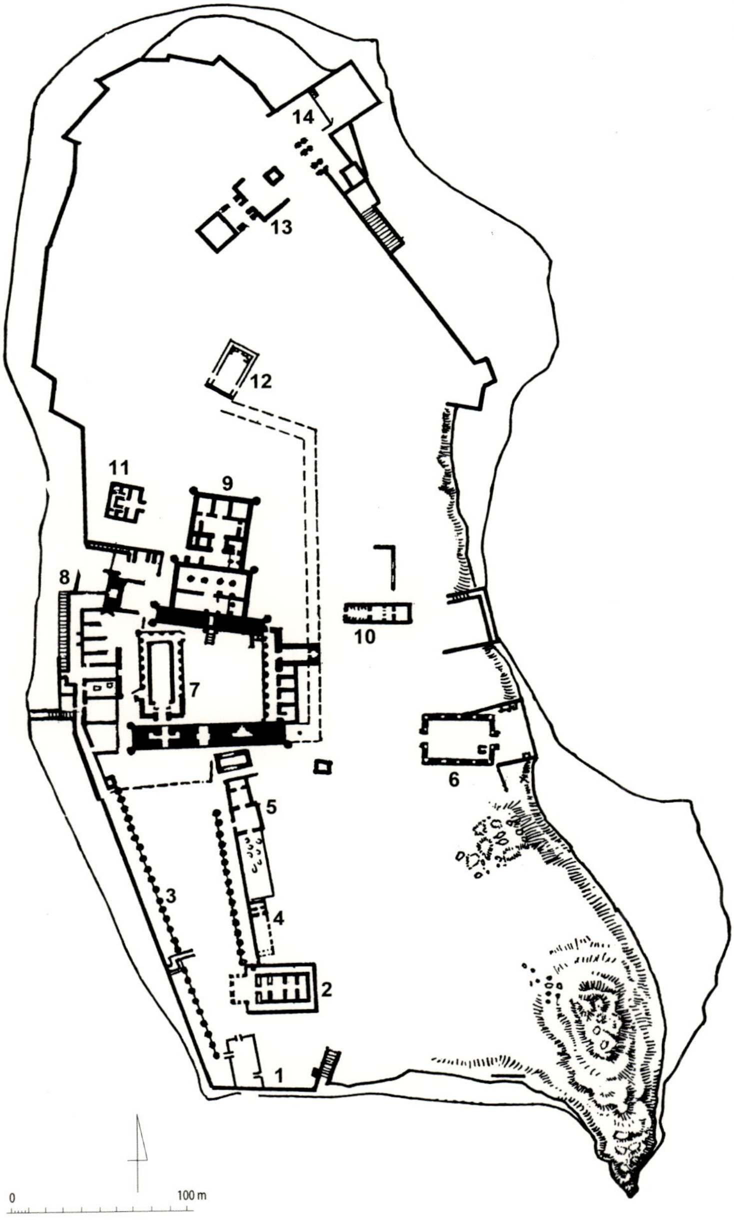

Plan of Philae (after Brunner-Traut and Hell)
1. hall of Nakhtnebef I
2. temple of Arensnufis
3. western colonnade
4. chapel of Mandulis
5. temple of Imhotep
6. Trajan's kiosk
7. *mammisi*
8. Hadrian's Gate
9. temple of Isis
10. temple of Hathor
11. temple of Harendotes
12. church
13. temple of Augustus
14. gate of Diocletian

Western colonnade in the court in front of the First Pylon of the temple of Isis on Philae.

Ptolemy VI Philometor extended the Egyptian-controlled territory to the south as far as Qasr Ibrim. This resulted in the establishment of a larger administrative region known as Triakontaschoinos (thirty schoini), but it was not to last long.

One of the areas of mutual tolerance related to temples and religious cults in the ever-expanding sacred district on Philae, to which Nubians also had access. The Egyptian side not only tolerated the Nubian gods but also gradually incorporated them into the originally Egyptian religious system. For example, in addition to Khnum, Lord of the First Cataract, the Nubian god Iryhemesnefer (in Greek Arensnufis), the 'Good Companion,' came to be worshiped here, while the Nubian god Merul (in Greek Mandulis) was identified with Horus and became part of a triad with Osiris and Isis as Horus-Mandulis.

The influence of the last Ptolemaic kings in Lower Nubia was already very weak, while Nubian Meroitic influence was on the rise. When the Romans conquered Egypt they therefore made considerable efforts to consolidate their control over Lower Nubia and, despite Meroitic resistance, temporarily managed to do so in the area of the Triakontaschoinos. In the reign of Augustus, however, the Romans realistically abandoned any illusions about their chances of conquering the kingdom of Meroe and concentrated on fortifying their positions in the Dodekaschoinos; a settlement was reached and the 'Pax Augusta' came into force. As far as the temple district on Philae was concerned, the Roman emperors kept to the policy of the Ptolemies, continuing to build in the district and permitting Nubians to visit it. Under Hadrian, large-scale fortification projects were undertaken on the southern frontier of the empire and new buildings were constructed on Philae with the aim of consolidating cult ties between Philae and the nearby islet of Biggeh—the Abaton, the place of the tomb of Osiris.

Yet ultimately there was no way of halting the gradual decline of Roman influence in Lower Nubia. Under Diocletian the Romans withdrew militarily from the Dodekaschoinos and building work on Philae essentially ceased. A new religion, Christianity, was spreading, and this created a particularly complicated situation on the sensitive southern frontiers of the empire because the Nubian tribes known as the Nobads and Blemmyes were very attached to the cult of Isis, Mistress of Philae, and the Osiris rituals. The Decree

Isis and Harendotes. Detail of decoration of the east tower of the First Pylon of the temple of Isis on Philae.

of Theodosius in 391, prohibiting pagan cults in Egypt, overshadowed the final phase of the existence of the original Egyptian cults at Philae. It ended with the Decree of Justinian in 535 by which the Temple of Isis on Philae was closed definitively, and the era that allowed Nubians access to the cult statue of Isis in the interests of peace came to an end.

<< First Pylon of the temple of Isis on Philae, viewed from the west.

The Temple of the Lady of Philae

The main temple on Philae was dedicated to the goddess Isis, but other Egyptian and Nubian gods, and not only those in Osiris's circle, had shrines there too. Hathor was worshiped here, as was the deified Imhotep, and the gods of the First Cataract of the Nile Khnum and Satet. Mandulis and Arensnufis, who enjoyed great honor especially among the Nubian Blemmye tribespeople, were also worshiped on Philae. In inscriptions on a number of blocks from the Nineteenth and Twenty-fifth Dynasties, discovered when the temple complex on Philae was being dismantled as part of the UNESCO rescue operation, we find the name of the god Amun, but the origin of the blocks is unclear; rather than being remains of some older, smaller shrine to Amun on Philae, this is probably recycled building material brought from elsewhere.

Parts of some of the buildings on Philae, especially on the edges of the island, have succumbed to the ravages of time or, more precisely, the fierce waters of the Nile inundations. Egyptologists such as the Frenchman Georges Aaron Bénédite (1857–1926), the Austrian Hermann Junker (1877–1962), the German Erich Winter, and others devoted great research efforts to the monuments here, but a great deal still remains to be done. The international archaeological rescue project sponsored by UNESCO, which involved moving the whole temple complex to a safe place, provided a unique opportunity for thorough measurement and documentation of the antiquities on Philae. An important study by Elena Vassilika, "Ptolemaic Philae," is a welcome harbinger of future thorough and detailed research and scientific publications on the Philae monuments.

The entrance to the temple complex is located on the south bank, where we find a small open kiosk built by the Thirtieth Dynasty king Nakhtnebef I and dedicated to 'Mother Isis, Mistress of Philae' and Hathor, a temple to the Nubian god Arensnufis, known as the Eastern Temple, an unfinished colonnade (adjoined by the chapel of Mandulis), and the Western Colonnade from the

Temple of Isis and Trajan's kiosk on Philae as seen by members of Napoleon's expedition

Late Ptolemaic and Roman Periods. The Western Colonnade, from which a staircase leads down to a Nilometer, consists of columns more than five meters tall with capitals carved in a variety of floral motifs; there are scenes on the columns and walls of the passage (colonnade) of the emperors Augustus and Tiberius making offerings to the gods.

The entrance to the Temple of Isis is located in the south by the first pylon, which is approximately eighteen meters high. Work on the temple was started during the reign of Nakhtnebef I and completed by the Ptolemaic kings. On the front of the eastern half of the pylon is a mythical scene in which Ptolemy XII Neos Dionysos, accompanied by Isis, Horus, and Hathor, is slaying the enemies of Egypt. An inscription carved in the pylon in the "seventh year of the Republic" is a reminder that the soldiers of Napoleon's expedition got as far as Philae. In the western part of the courtyard between the first and second pylons lies the *mammisi*, the 'birth house' built by the Ptolemaic kings and Roman emperors in honor of the goddess Isis and her son Horus. On its walls there are scenes of the birth and childhood of Osiris, Isis nursing Horus, and so on. A row of columns with capitals bearing floral motifs, and including a stylized sistrum, runs around the whole temple. The second pylon is only twelve meters high. On this pylon, too, we see Ptolemy XII Neos Dionysus making offerings to the gods.

In the northwestern part of the courtyard between the first and second pylons there is an inscription forbidding priests and bearers to bring donkeys, dogs, goats, or the uncircumcised into the temple, or to consume specific plants relating to the cult of Osiris, such as lettuce and certain medicinal herbs, in the temple. The Byzantine military commander Besarion's inscription in the nearby Nubian temple in Kalabsha, which prohibits letting pigs inside the temple, gives the impression that animals sometimes wandered freely in close proximity to the temple, and sometimes even inside it.

There is a small forecourt beyond the second pylon in front of the columned vestibule of the entrance into the interior of the Temple of Isis. The walls of all the interiors are thickly covered with religious scenes and inscriptions in low relief. The courtyard was once roofed with a baldaquin to protect it from the sun; in the Christian period it was converted into a Coptic church. In the

Trajan's kiosk on Philae, viewed from the east.

innermost part of the temple there is a shrine with a base for the sacred barque, which once held a statue of the goddess Isis. A staircase in one of the rooms in the western part of the temple leads to a roof terrace; the chambers of Osiris are accessible from the terrace. The walls of these chambers are likewise covered with abundant relief decoration relating to the Osiris myth: the dead Osiris lying on the bier with the grieving Isis and Nebthet kneel-

View of the island of Biggeh from the east, from the temple of Isis on Philae.

ing beside it, demons carrying away Osiris's mummy, and other scenes. In the precinct of the Temple of Isis, which was originally surrounded by an enclosure wall, there is also a small temple dedicated to Isis's son Harendotes (the Greek version of the Egyptian name Harnedjitef, 'Horus, avenger of his father').

On the eastern side of the second pylon lies a rather small and very badly damaged temple to Hathor, which was built by Ptolemy VI Philometor and enlarged by the emperor Augustus. The columns in the vestibule are adorned with merry scenes of the dancing god Bes, whose cult was particularly popular in the Roman period, monkeys playing a lyre, musicians, and so forth. A superb small open temple kiosk built by the emperor Trajan is situated south of the Temple of Hathor. The unfinished kiosk's ceiling is

10

Edfu: The Throne of Horus

<< Detail of the row of columns in the courtyard of the temple in Edfu.

The town of Edfu, situated about halfway along the road between Luxor and Aswan, was an important Upper Egyptian religious center and the focus of the worship of the falcon god Horus of Behdet. The original Egyptian name of the town was Djeba, in the later Coptic pronunciation Etbo, from which the modern form Edfu is derived. Identifying Horus with Apollo, the Greeks called the town Apollonopolis Megale. Edfu lies on the west bank of the Nile, and in the past a secondary branch of the Nile used to run west of it (today the Qandafiya Canal partially follows the course of this older branch), giving the town greater defensive potential. Edfu also had the advantage of a position on the crossroads of crucial routes: the desert route westward to the Kharga oasis started at Edfu, while eastward, from the other side of the Nile, ran the route to the gold mines in Barramiya (in Greek Kanais) and to the southernmost Ptolemaic and later Roman Red Sea port of Berenike.

Throughout the centuries, the ruins of the ancient town have been devastated by the *sabakhin*—fellahs digging out decayed mud-brick structures to fertilize their fields. Archaeological excavations of the town were carried out in the inter-war period by a Franco-Polish expedition headed by Maurice Alliot (1903–60) and Kazimierz Michałowski (1901–81), and finds dating from the Predynastic Period right through to the Roman Period have demonstrated its great age and continuity of development. Old Kingdom tombs have been found here, too, for example. One of them, the tomb of Isesi from the Fifth Dynasty, was evidently a much-visited place during the Middle Kingdom and the Second Intermediate Period, as indicated by the votive and commemorative objects left in its vicinity. Isesi seems to have become a local saint. In the Second Intermediate Period the town cemetery was shifted about four kilometers west, to the very edge of the desert. In the Late Period a new cemetery was founded near Nag al-Hassaya about twelve kilometers south of Edfu.

Over the centuries several temples were built in Edfu; some of them were demolished or rebuilt during antiquity. The temple district was surrounded by a massive mud-brick enclosure but only a

The façade of the temple of Horus in Edfu is dominated by the towers of the pylon. In the foreground are remains of the *mammisi*.

>The temple in Edfu at the end of the eighteenth century.

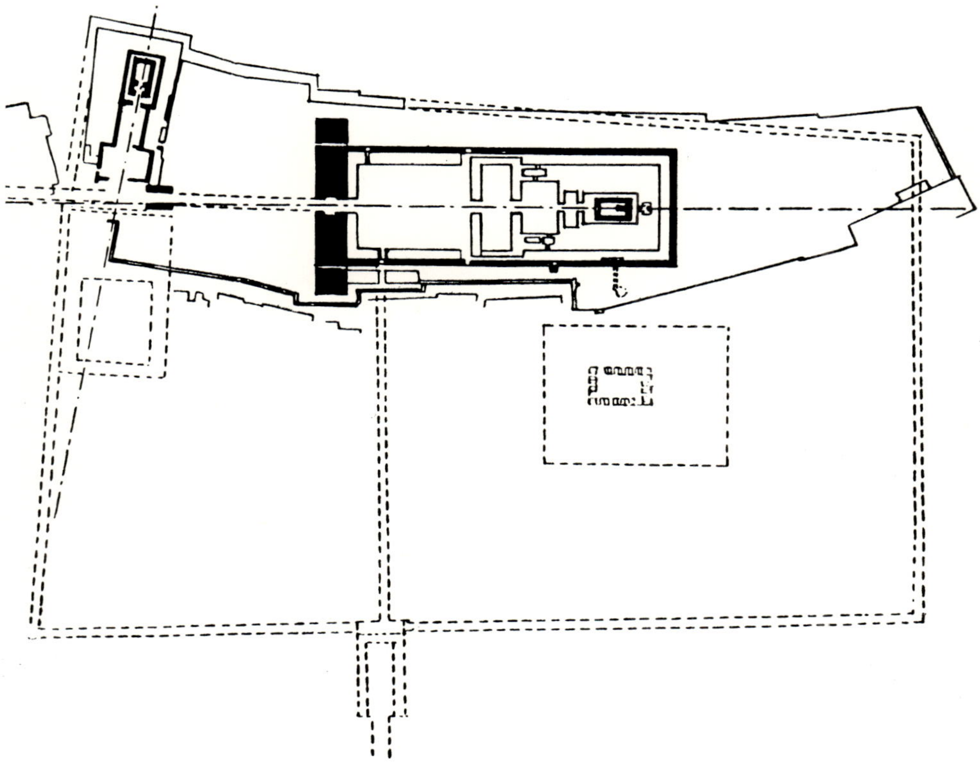

Overall plan of the temple district in Edfu.

small part of the southwestern corner of the wall survives. The dominant building in the town was always a temple dedicated to the falcon god Horus, or more precisely Horus and his solar form Harakhty. In its final form, in which we know it today, this temple is quite exceptional because it is the best preserved temple not only from ancient Egypt, but also in all of antiquity. The original decoration, including an immense quantity of religious scenes and inscriptions, has survived, as well as the building itself, which has been invaluable for our understanding not only of the functions of the temple and individual rooms, but also of the complex world of the ancient Egyptians' religious beliefs at a time when their civilization, under the Ptolemaic kings, was already past its zenith.

When Mariette started archaeological excavations in the temple district in 1860, a small village of sixty-four huts stood on the temple roof terrace. After Mariette, a series of archaeologists, above all the Marquis Maxence de Rochemontieux (1849–91), Chassinat

(1868), and Alliot, contributed to the documentation and interpretation of the inscriptions and scenes densely covering the walls of the temple courtyards, halls, and passageways. Even so, only a tenth of the inscriptions had been translated by the mid-1970s. Research on this epigraphic treasure trove made a great leap forward in 1986, when the German Research Society (Deutsche Forschungsgemeinschaft) initiated a long-term project for the translation of all the inscriptions in the Temple of Edfu under the direction of the leading German expert on Ptolemaic texts, Dieter Kurth. French Egyptologists have also continued their tradition of interest in the temple, as is evident from the research carried out by Sylvie Cauville, for example. The published works of Kurth and Cauville are the main sources for the following account of the temple in Edfu.

The well-preserved scenes on the walls of the temple provide direct information on the founding, building, and dedication of the temple as well as basic technical data. King Ptolemy III initiated construction of the building in the tenth year of his reign on 23 August 237 BC. The temple was built from the rear to the front and work continued for twenty-five years. A rebellion then broke out, leading to two decades of loss of Ptolemaic control of the south of the country (where two kings of merely regional significance, Herwennefer and Ankhwennefer, ruled successively). Work on the temple was restarted in 176 BC under Ptolemy VI and was eventually completed on 3 December 57 BC, while Ptolemy XII was lingering in Rome and his daughter Berenike IV was ruling Egypt. Construction and decoration of the temple therefore took a total of 180 years.

Originally, a mud-brick enclosure wall surrounded the complex. There was also a sacred pool and sacred grove nearby, where the falcon god nested. According to Kurth, the architecture of the temple and the scenes and inscriptions on its walls are very closely integrated and express the conception of the temple as microcosm of the world. This is why the ceiling of the hall is covered with stars and in some places with astronomical phenomena and inscriptions, while the temple floor is conceived as the earth, with floral decorations on the lower edge of the walls and the lower edge of the shafts of the columns. The temple was also a materialization of ancient Egyptian beliefs about the falcon god Horus. It was believed that after rising on the eastern horizon each day, the sun god Horus flew down to the temple and nested there. He would descend from the sky and alight on the highest part of the temple, which was the roof terrace of the tower of the pylon that formed the monumental entrance;

this is why Horus appears alternately in the form of a falcon and a phoenix in the decoration of the pylon. As a perfect image of the world the temple was a place of order and harmony, embodied by Maat, the goddess of truth. For this reason, scenes of offerings brought specifically to this goddess appear by the main entrance. The idea of the temple as a special sanctuary dedicated to the gods, which must be protected from the threats of external evil and chaos, is emphasized by the massive enclosure wall and the even more massive entrance pylon, as well as the depiction of protective deities and scenes of the slaughter of enemies on the outer side. The idea is even elaborated in the details: spouts in the shape of lions drain off and 'disarm' rainwater during rare downpours, because rain and storms were regarded as expressions of chaos and the work of the god of evil, Horus's ancient enemy Seth, while Horus himself took the form of a lion at times.

The falcon god Horus would manifest himself on the monumental gate of the temple in Edfu between the two towers of the pylon.

According to Kurth, three dimensions mingle between the architectural elements and the decoration of the temple. These are the real, the theological, and the integrative. For example, the dimension of the real is represented by the raw materials and minerals that would be brought into the temple and processed in three small rooms called the 'Golden House,' where artists created statues which priests brought to life using the 'opening of the mouth' ritual. One of the rooms was also a 'laboratory' and on its walls we find lists of various substances and recipes for unguents, incense, and so on.

In the ruins of the temple of Horus in Edfu.

The dimension of theology is conveyed by the very names of the temple and its component parts, such as 'Seat of the Two Gods [that is, Horus and Re],' 'Island of the Raging [against the enemies of gods],' or 'House of the Leg' (referring to the Osiris myth).

The architecture of this late temple respects principles established over preceding millennia, primarily the approach through open and larger exteriors to ever more enclosed and smaller interiors as a way of increasing spiritual concentration until the focal point is reached: the small closed sanctuary enveloped in shadow. The decoration of the temple was also governed by established rules on the location of scenes and accompanying inscriptions in the different parts of the temple, their arrangement in rows, and their succession. For example, themes of the daily cycle of the sun, its rising and setting, are very prominent on the entrance pylon. Its eastern tower was conceived as the mountain on the horizon from which the sun emerged, and the western tower as the mountain behind which it set; directly above the entrance there is a large winged sun, at the zenith. In scenes devoted to specific religious

The first courtyard of the temple of Horus in Edfu.

themes, the gods and their epithets and addresses, the king and his epithets and addresses, and religious symbols, all have their assigned places, and the ancient Egyptian color symbolism is appropriately deployed.

The Horus temple in Edfu is a little over 137 meters long, and its main axis is oriented roughly in the northeast direction. It was entered from the southwest. Its monumental entrance between the two towers of the pylon, which is more than seventy-six meters wide and more than thirty meters tall, has an immensity that projects a sense of stability and protection from the restlessness of the outside world. The decorative scheme of all the walls of both towers of the pylon enhances and supports this impression. Scenes in high relief, which show King Ptolemy XIII killing the enemies of Egypt before Horus and Hathor, bringing the symbols of rule (the diadem and uraeus) to Horus as offerings, bringing Horus and other gods the symbol of the goddess Maat, and so on, are prominent on the front wall. Tall wooden poles with waving banners—two stood at the foot of each of the pylon towers—emphasized the temple's majesty. The entrance, where a fourteen-meter-tall cedarwood gate was once set, was further embellished by a pair of obelisks on each side.

The open court immediately beyond the pylon was called 'The Palace of Nut—the place where Seftekh [the primal serpent Apophis], enemy of Harakhty, was defeated,' because the sky—the goddess Nut—arched above it as symbolic roof. The walls of the

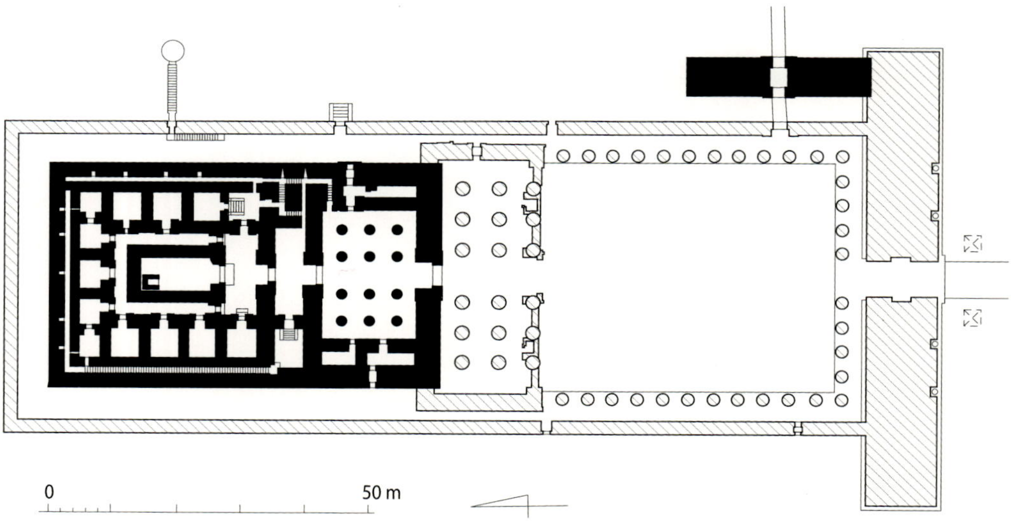

Plan of the temple of Horus in Edfu.

courtyard, like the line of thirty-two columns with composite capitals that runs along the eastern, southern, and western sides of the courtyard, are covered with various religious scenes and inscriptions. For example, on the western wall of the courtyard we find depictions of Horus's divine partner, Hathor of Dendera, visiting Edfu, the king following the sacred barques of both gods, priests and musicians accompanying the festive procession, and so on. The courtyard's eastern wall includes scenes of the king in the presence of the divine triad of Horus, Hathor, and their son Ihy followed by personifications of the nomes of Upper Egypt. The way to the sanctuary, the holy of holies, led from the court along the axis of the temple. There were entrances in the northwestern and southeastern corners of the court that led to a circular passage, which ran between the enclosure wall of the temple and its entire intimate, western end. A staircase from the eastern section of the passage led to a well.

Colossal granite statues of the falcon, Horus of Edfu, stood on each side of the entrance from the courtyard to the first columned hall; the statue on the western side has survived intact but only a fragment of the other remains. The walls of the hall and its eighteen columns, symmetrically arranged in three rows, are covered with scenes and inscriptions that feature Ptolemy VI, Ptolemy VIII Euergetes II, and Ptolemy X, in whose reigns the hall was built and decorated. Two small but important chambers are inset between the front interior wall and columns of the first row: the one on the eastern side is 'the Chamber of the Book,' and the one on the west 'the Morning Chamber.'

The decoration of the Chamber of the Book (that is, the library) is dominated by the god of writing and knowledge, Thoth, and the scenes and inscriptions make it clear that cases of papyrus scrolls bearing religious, astronomical, medical, magical, and other texts, including lists of their titles, were kept here, as well as writings relating to the performance of the daily temple ritual and ceremonies during temple festivals. The Morning Chamber was the space in which the king—or the priest deputizing for the king at ceremonies—carried out his symbolic purification rituals before meeting with the god. On the western and eastern side of the second columned hall there are entrances to a circular passage. In the eastern entrance to the circular passage there are some fascinating astronomical scenes, including the solar and lunar barque with the fourteen gods of the waning moon, pictures of the decans, planets, constellations, and the fourteen gods ascending up a lunar staircase to Thoth, who was the god of the moon as well as of writing and knowledge.

The second columned hall is smaller than the first, but also has an abundance of relief scenes and inscriptions. Its ceiling is supported by twelve pillars. On the western side of the hall there is an entrance to the chamber that archaeologists call the 'laboratory.' Its walls are covered with inscriptions and scenes relating to preparation of various aromatic unguents and incense and the offering of these substances to Horus, Hathor, Osiris, Isis, Min, and other gods. On the opposite, eastern side of the hall there is an entrance to the 'treasury,' a chamber where precious cult objects were kept. The relief scenes on the walls of this chamber show figures representing the regions that were sources of gold and precious stones; the eastern figures are being led to Horus and Hathor by the god Sopdu, and the western figures by the god Ha.

On a boat, Horus holds the bound Seth, in the form of a hippopotamus, captive on a rope and spears him with a harpoon. Detail from the decoration of the Horus temple in Edfu.

and ritual practices of Egyptian religion had endured through the centuries, even if with certain modifications.

In the temple at Edfu religious ideas reflected the local theological doctrine focused on the god Horus of Behdet (Behdet was the name of the seat of Horus here, and was therefore the theological name of Edfu)—'great god, lord of the heaven, foremost one of all the sanctuaries of the south and north.' In the temple texts we encounter him in his ten forms expressed by corresponding names, and wearing seven different crowns. In addition to Horus we meet more than sixty other deities, which in itself testifies to the extent to which the local theological doctrines were intertwined with religious teachings from other temples in Egypt, above all Heliopolis, Memphis, Abydos, and Thebes. The specific religious significance of the Horus temple in Edfu, on the other hand, is highlighted by the scenes relating to the great festival of Behdet, when the goddess Hathor would come from Dendera to visit Horus, the myth of Horus, and the choice and enthronement of the living divine falcon of Edfu.

The Horus temple in Edfu was not just the dwelling of gods, but had a political and dynastic rather than purely religious significance. The ceremonies performed in the temple were supposed to renew and consolidate the power of the king, guarantee the legitimacy of the ruling dynasty, emphasize the ties between the kingdoms in heaven and on earth, and strengthen the order of the world.

The Birth Temple

The good fortune of the splendidly preserved Horus temple was not shared by another Ptolemaic temple about fifty meters to the southwest. This is the much more damaged 'birth temple' or 'birth house,' *mammisi,* built under Ptolemy VIII Euergetes II and modified under Ptolemy XII Neos Dionysus. It is much smaller than the great Horus temple and is oriented east–west with an entrance from the east. Its façade is not a monumental pylon; one enters the temple by climbing up a short flight of steps into a wide courtyard, followed by another courtyard, this one lined with columns connected by low partitions. The core of the western part of the temple is the sanctuary, which is entered from the columned courtyard via two antechambers. The sanctuary is surrounded on all four sides by a line of columns connected by low walls adorned with religious scenes and inscriptions. The basic meaning of the temple as the place of the birth of Horus's and Hathor's son Hor-sema-tawy, 'Horus Unifier of the Two Lands' (known in Greek as Harsometes, and in Latin as Harsomtus), and his identification with the king, is reflected in the

Drawing of idealized reconstruction of the *mammisi* ('birth temple') in Edfu by the artists on Napoleon's expedition.

The *mammisi* ('birth temple') in Edfu. In the background are the still-impressive remains of the massive brick enclosure wall.

decorative scheme of the shrine. This is dominated by scenes of divine creation and birth, showing the god Khmun modeling the figure of the child Harsomtus and Ptolemy VIII Euergetes II on a potter's wheel, then the goddess Hathor suckling Harsomtus, and then Hathor presenting Harsomtus to the divine triad of Edfu, Ptolemy VIII making offerings to the gods, and so on. The scenes have suffered a lot of damage, and the figures in particular were systematically chiseled off in more recent periods.

The Festivals of the Falcon God

The whole temple district in Edfu was the setting for everyday rituals but also major festivals of more than local and sometimes more than regional significance. Apart from the festivals common to all ancient Egyptian temples at the time, for example the festival of the New Year (see First Excursus), there were some festivals particularly associated with Edfu.

The Triumph of Horus

The festival of 'The Triumph of Horus,' which took place in the season of budding a month after the resurrection of Osiris, was very famous and important. British Egyptologist Herbert Walter Fairman (1907–82) concluded on the basis of the surviving written sources that the text of 'The Triumph of Horus,' probably compiled at the end of the New Kingdom, was conceived as a drama and that the festival took the form of a theatrical performance. The first act introduced the main protagonists of the Osiris myth, above all Horus in his dual form as Horus of Behdet and Horus of Mesen, representing Upper Egypt and Lower Egypt respectively. Then followed the ritual of the 'Ten Harpoons,' when both Horuses would spear a small model of a hippopotamus, the form taken by Horus's arch enemy Seth. As reconstructed by Fairman, the next act involved a celebration climaxing in the coronation of Horus as king of Upper and Lower Egypt and the presentation of the royal insignia, the scepter and flagellum. In the final act, Horus was presented in a triumphal attitude on top of the defeated hippopotamus, Seth, while Isis relates how the hippopotamus is cut into pieces. Finally, Horus together with the king would spear the model hippopotamus once again, a lector-priest would recite the formula on the destruction of Seth, and another priest would cut up a cake in the form of a hippopotamus. The performance, in which a chorus would repeat certain lines in refrain, would end with the assurance that the enemies of the king and gods had been defeated. After the defeat of these enemies, Horus took on the form of a winged sun providing protection for Egypt and its people.

The Festival of Behdet

The festival of Behdet was one of the five great Edfu festivals that are described in considerable detail by inscriptions and scenes on the walls of the temple. It has sometimes been presented as a 'conjugal reunion of the gods' (Horus and Hathor), but it was more an opportunity for the chief gods from Edfu and other places to visit the tomb of the primordial gods in the Behdet necropolis in order to be rejuvenated by offerings and rituals and achieve regeneration in all their aspects.

Once a year, at the new moon in the month of Epep, the goddess Hathor would visit Edfu from Dendera. Her statue, conveyed in a case on her sacred barque, would be placed on board a large riverboat, which would be accompanied by many other boats and

The façade of the temple
of Hathor in Dendera.

11

Dendera: The Heliopolis of Hathor

<< Fragments of the relief decoration of Hathor's temple district in Dendera.

The main seat of Hathor, one of the most important goddesses of ancient Egypt, was her temple in Dendera, the metropolis of the sixth Upper Egyptian nome. The town lay on the west bank of the Nile and its remains, including the important Hathor temple, are to be found a few kilometers south of Qena, the administrative and economic center of the modern region. Originally the principle god of the nome was a crocodile represented with what appears to be an ostrich plume on its head. This was no coincidence; crocodiles were common in the region and the people who lived here feared them but were also famous for their skill in hunting them. The importance of the region is evident from the fact that it is mentioned in the earliest Egyptian written records: for example, in a biographical inscription from the tomb of Metjen in Saqqara from the end of the Third Dynasty, or as one of the personified nomes in the valley Temple of Snofru in Dahshur. Even earlier than the first mentions of the sixth Upper Egyptian nome are references to Iunet '(Upper Egyptian) Heliopolis,' with the full name Ta-Iunet-ta-netjeret, or 'The Heliopolis of the Goddess.' This is the theological title of the seat of Hathor here, which dates back to the Early Dynastic period and appears later in the Pyramid Texts. The Greek form of the shortened version of this title, Ta-netjeret, known in Greek as Tentyris, was the basis of the Coptic name Tentore and its current form Dendera. The Egyptians liked to style Hathor 'the Golden One,' and the Greeks identified her with Aphrodite.

From written records it is clear that the Hathor temple in Dendera was already in existence at the beginning of the Fourth Dynasty in the reign of Khufu. Pepi I later endowed it with a statue, and many subsequent rulers through the whole history of ancient Egypt enlarged, embellished, or reconstructed it. The temple that is the dominant feature of Dendera today dates from the Ptolemaic and Roman Periods and was devoted primarily to the goddess Hathor, although Horus too was worshiped there. There are other important monuments close to it: two *mammisi,* a temple of Isis, a Coptic church, and so on. The sacred district was surrounded by a massive mud-brick enclosure wall, most of which has survived. In the vicinity of the temple complex

Vues et Temples de Tentyris.

View of the ruins of the Hathor temple in Dendera at the end of the eighteenth century.

there is a cemetery, the earliest tombs dating from the Early Dynastic Period. The precise extent and location of the oldest town remains, however, are still the subject of academic discussion.

One picture in the *Description de l'Égypte* shows that the grand ruins of Dendera, particularly the Temple of Hathor and massive enclosure wall of the temple district, did not escape the notice of the scholars and draftsmen of the French expeditionary corps who came this way at the turn of the nineteenth century. Excavations in Dendera were started by the French consul in Egypt Jean François Mimaut (1774–1837), but the Temple of Hathor was to be fully cleared of sand and rubble only later, in 1859, by August Mariette. Archaeological projects at the cemetery at the end of the nineteenth century are associated with British archaeologist Flinders Petrie and in the years of the First World War with the American archaeologist Clarence Fisher (1876–1941). Excavation and study of the Temple of Hathor and other architectural monuments in the temple district in Dendera have remained largely the preserve of French Egyptologists, particularly Emile Chassinat and François Daumas. The French Egyptologist Sylvie Cauville has produced a very erudite archaeological and religio-historical description of the temple.

Northern gate of the Hathor temple precinct in Dendera.

<Northern gate and façade of the temple of Hathor in Dendera at the end of the eighteenth century.

The Dwelling of the Golden Goddess

The Temple of Hathor in Dendera is a superlative work of ancient architecture. Today even the less impressionable visitor is awestruck by the exterior and once inside the temple has the sense that a long-vanished world is rematerializing before his eyes. The temple is built of sandstone and, like the Temple of Horus in Edfu and that of Isis on Philae, has survived in a relatively good state of preservation. Hathor's temple stands roughly in the middle of the sacred district, which covers an area of approximately 300 × 300 meters defined by an enclosure wall built in the Roman Period (possibly under the emperor Nero). The main monumental gate, a propylon, is in the western stretch of this wall. A dromos—that is, a ceremonial road connecting the temple with a quay at the end of a canal leading from the Nile, which takes a bend here and flows almost from east to west—leads to the gate. At the quay there once stood a small open temple, a kiosk. A second, smaller gate was set in the eastern stretch of the enclosure wall. In the Roman period a well was sunk in front of the main entrance to provide water for visitors to cleanse themselves before entering the temple.

>> Drawing of the façade of the temple of Hathor in Dendera.

As the written records and surviving building show, the temple, which is oriented roughly north–south, underwent a long and complex development involving the progressive replacement of older sections with later ones. The innermost part of the temple as it is now, the naos, dates from the Ptolemaic Period. In the Roman Period the emperor Tiberius built a large pronaos, which is also sometimes termed an external hypostyle, and Nero had an enclosure wall built around the temple in addition to the wall around the whole sacred district, thus creating an extensive open forecourt in front of the pronaos. The temple is eighty-six meters long (the naos takes up sixty meters of that total space) and thirty-six meters (the naos) or forty-three meters wide (the pronaos). The naos reached a height of twelve and a half meters, while the pronaos is five meters taller. Abundant relief decoration, scenes, and inscriptions cover not only the walls of the individual interiors but also the exterior walls of the temple. On the southern wall, for example, there is a large head of the goddess Hathor in high relief as well as a procession of gods.

>> Plan of the temple of Hathor in Dendera.

The façade of the pronaos, which unlike the naos is oriented east–west, is adorned on each side of the entrance by three columns with Hathor capitals. These are four-sided capitals with the head of a goddess with cow ears and above it a sistrum, Hathor's characteristic symbol, on each side. There are low cross-pieces between the façade columns bearing relief decoration dominated by the main gods honored in the temple: Hathor, Horus, Harsomtus, and Isis. Roman emperors (Tiberius, Claudius, Caligula, and others, depending on the period when the scenes were created) are depicted here bringing gifts to the gods; for example, a sistrum to Hathor, scented grease to Horus, a lotus to Hersomtus, and the *maat* symbol of order to Isis. The ceiling of the pronaos, which has two side entrances as well as the main entrance on the axis of the temple, is supported by eighteen columns bearing relief scenes arranged according to strictly established religious and iconographic principles. There is also abundant relief decoration on all the walls of the pronaos and the ceiling. For example, on the northern side we find the emperor Augustus honoring the gods of the Hermopolitan Ogdoad, or bringing Hathor and Horus the gift of an obelisk, while another scene shows the emperor

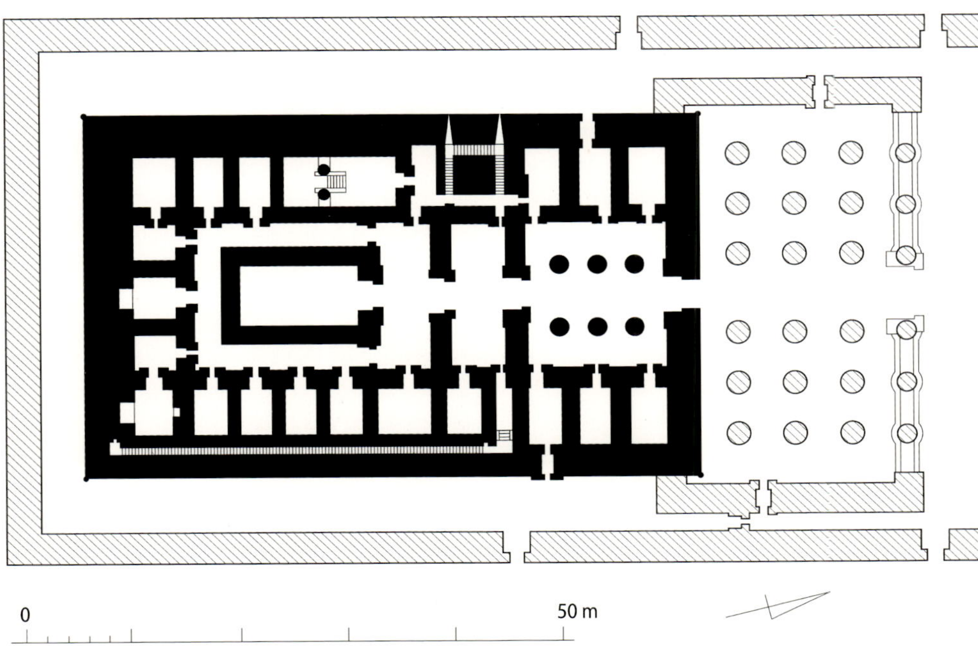

Caligula bringing offerings to Thoth and other gods. The astronomical scenes on the ceiling of the pronaos are very valuable, presenting a kind of summary of Egyptian knowledge of astronomy: here we find the constellations, the decans (thirty-six groups of stars, each visible in the sky for ten days), the planets (Mars, Venus, Mercury, Saturn, and Jupiter) and of course the sun and moon. The Egyptians conceived of the sky as an ocean across which the sun sailed for twelve hours in his day barque and for twelve hours in his night barque but they also imagined it as the overarching figure of a woman, the goddess Nut, or represented it as a cow scattered with stars.

The passage that led deeper into the temple went through the center of the pronaos, and respects the Egyptian temple principle by which the floor is raised and the ceiling lowered in each interior in the direction of the sanctuary. Immediately beyond the pronaos is a smaller internal hypostyle hall with six columns arranged in two rows along the axis of the temple. As in other temples, this is called the 'hall of appearance,' for here the goddess, that is, her statue, would make an appearance on festival occasions. On both sides of this hall, on the east and the west, there are entrances to three smaller chambers. The decoration of the walls of the hypostyle hall includes scenes of the ceremonies of the founding of the temple: the king leaving the palace accompanied by standards with symbols of the gods; the king carrying out the digging of the foundations of the temple; the king offering founding bricks to the goddess Hathor, ritually purifying the temple, and finally presenting it to the goddess. The columns are also decorated, for example, with scenes of the king offering wine to Hathor, planting a willow in the presence of the gods, and so on. It is interesting that the cartouches in the inscriptions accompanying the scenes have been left empty, merely prepared for the recording of the king's name.

In the first chamber on the eastern side of the hypostyle hall the king is depicted offering perfumed unguents to Hathor, and in another scene sacrificing incense to Isis; there are also representations of the gods of the Nile and fields. The inscriptions include recipes for the preparation of scented unguents and perfumes used at temple ceremonies and during mummification. The room served for storage and preparation of these products; today archaeologists refer to it as the 'laboratory.' The inscriptions on the walls of the neighboring chamber are historically very valuable, for they include a complete list of the festivals of Hathor celebrated in the temple in the course of a year.

The capitals of Hathor columns in the pronaos of the temple in Dendera are adorned on all four sides by the face of the goddess and a sistrum.

On the walls of the chamber on the western side of the hypostyle hall, opposite the 'laboratory,' the king is depicted bringing Hathor a basket of precious stones, while in other scenes in the room he offers her a pectoral and a richly adorned necklace; here too the gods of the Nile and fields appear. The scenes of the offering of precious stones and jewelry have a meaning more specific than merely suggesting luxury and largesse: Hathor was patron of the desert areas containing precious stones and of the people who mined them. The room is known as the 'treasury'; it served as a storage room for jewelry and the precious minerals and stones used to make it.

The columned 'hall of appearance' is separated from the sanctuary in the innermost part of the temple by another two halls. The first of these is called the 'hall of the offerings'; here, priests presented various sacrificial gifts to the goddess: food, drink, flowers, perfumes, and so on. The function of the hall is emphasized by the scenes on the walls: the king making a libation to Hathor and offering her wine, or bringing Isis (with whom Hathor was often merged) the gift of a bouquet. Other gods—Harsieset ('Horus, son of Isis'), Horus, Harsomtus, and Osiris—are also partaking of the offered gifts. The inscriptions on the walls include the duties of the priest performing service in the hall. On the eastern and western sides of the room there is access to a staircase leading to the roof terrace, where the very important New Year and Osiris ceremonies were conducted. The priests would ascend to the terrace by the western staircase and descend by the eastern staircase.

Another hall, from the functional point of view an antechamber, was known as the 'Hall of the Nine.' It immediately preceded the sanctuary and was the place where the gods assembled in order to be close to Hathor, to protect her, and to share in the offerings made to her. Its walls are decorated with pictures of the king and the gods Thoth, Re-Harakhty, Shu, Montu, and others. In other scenes, the king is offering the *maat* symbol of the order of the world to Isis, four cases for cult statues to Harsieset, four calves to Osiris, and so on. On the eastern side of the antechamber is an entrance to the 'chamber of materials,' which was used to store the various woven materials used to adorn the statues of the gods at ceremonies and festivals. Recorded on the walls of the chamber are the names of the fabrics, their protective gods, bearers of materials, and so forth.

On the west side of the hall there is an entrance to the cult space known as the *wabet* ('pure place'). This consisted of a small courtyard separated by two columns with Hathor capitals and a low wall from a chapel entered via a short flight of steps. There are scenes on the walls of the courtyard showing the goddess Renenutet (known in Greek as Termuthis), the protectress of the fields and crops, offering food, gold, and silver to Hathor and Re-Harakhty and turquoise and lapis lazuli to Isis. The chapel's decoration includes depictions of the king and queen, the four *ka* of the god Re, and a female musician and male harp player; there is also a scene in which the king is offering the day solar barque *mandjet* to Isis, an oryx antelope to Hathor, and also spearing a turtle, the symbol of evil, with a lance in the presence of Harsomtus. The *wabet* played a very important part in the New Year festival, when the priests would gather together the statues of the gods worshiped in the temple and all kinds of offering gifts in this small courtyard. After the initial offering rites in honor of Hathor the priests would process with the statues (Hathor's statue in front) up the stairs to the roof terrace. The procession is depicted on the walls of the staircase. The king would lead the procession holding in his hand the symbol of Dendera, in front of a priest holding a golden tablet engraved with the texts to be recited during the ceremony. In addition to the priests with statues of the gods there would be symbols of the Hermopolitan primordial gods—frogs and snakes—in the procession.

Leading off one of the landings on the staircase was the entrance into a small room called 'House of Gold.' The scenes on the walls highlight its function: the final phase of the statues' creation took place here, their adornment and, most importantly, the rituals performed to bring them to life. The ancient Egyptians attributed great importance to statues and thus devoted an extraordinary amount of care to their production. After performing the 'opening of the mouth' ritual, the statue of a god, a king, and even a common person would become the seat of magical forces. This idea was expressed in the

The 'Hathor capital' of a column.

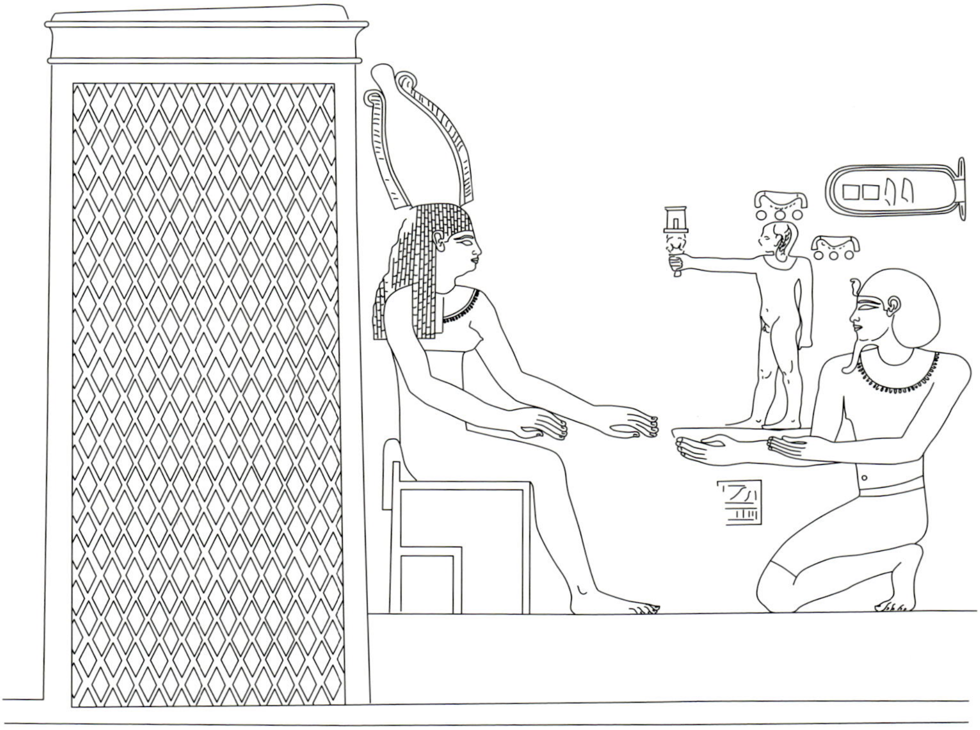

Pepi I offering a golden statue of Ihy to Hathor. Detail from the decoration of the temple of Hathor in Dendera.

Egyptian figure of speech used for the creation of statues, that is, the statue was 'born.' The mystery of the birth of a statue is depicted on the chamber wall: the king touches the finished statue with special instruments in the presence of the god Sokar and thus brings the statue to life. Sokar is present because he was not just a god of the dead, but deputized for the god of artists and craftsmen, Ptah, with whom over time he merged.

The sanctuary, where the daily ritual took place, outwardly resembles a miniature version of the whole temple. It originally contained a stone case holding the statue of the goddess and two sacred barques were placed in front of the case. Pictures and inscriptions on the interior walls of the shrine show that the eastern barque belonged to Hathor and Horus and the western one to Isis and Harsomtus. There is a hymn glorifying Hathor recorded in the shrine's entrance and inscriptions on the interior walls invoking the goddess in her various names and forms, as well as the other goddesses with whom she merged (Bastet, Sakhmet, and Sothis).

The shrine is surrounded on three sides by a passage that provides access to eleven chapels. Seven of those chapels are dedicated to Hathor; the remaining four are dedicated to Isis, Sokar-Osiris, Harsomtus, Horus of Edfu, and to the divine symbols of Hathor—the sistrum and *menat* necklace. The walls of the chapels are covered in scenes and accompanying inscriptions, which together summarize the religious doctrine of the temple. The most important of the chapels to Hathor is the one that lies on the axis of the temple behind the sanctuary and contained sacred statues of Hathor. On the chapel wall Hathor is represented wearing a double, conjoined Upper and Lower Egyptian crown and sitting on a throne in front of her chapel. The Sixth Dynasty king Pepi I, accompanied by the goddesses of Upper and Lower Egypt, Nekhbet and Wadjet, kneels before the goddess. The king is presenting the goddess with a statue of Ihy, the god of music and son of Hathor and Horus of Edfu. As we learn from the text, the one-cubit-high (52.5 centimeters) statuette was made of gold. This scene is considered to be evidence of the antiquity of Hathor's cult in Dendera, because two millennia separated the existing temple from the time when Pepi I donated the golden statue to the chapel of Hathor as it was then. Another interesting feature of the chapel is the depiction of two mobile cases (these probably originally stood directly under the picture) containing cult statues of the goddess in the form of a falcon: one with a human head and cow horns topped by a sun disc and the other with a falcon head and conjoined Upper and Lower Egyptian crown.

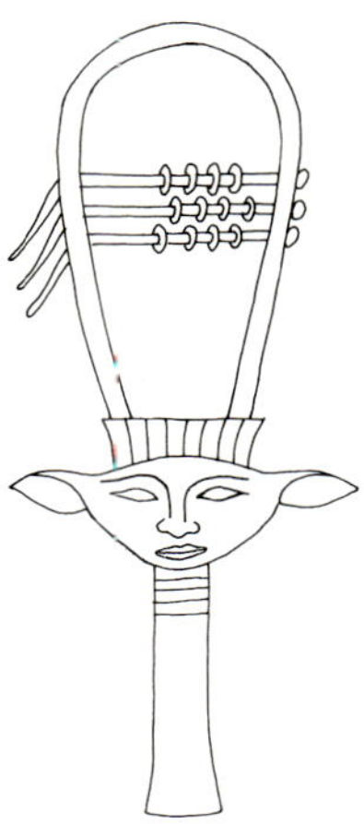

The sistrum, the musical instrument and symbol of the goddess Hathor.

In Hathor's temple in Dendera one very important element, from a religious point of view, are the crypts. These are chambers set into the masonry of the exterior walls at three levels differing by approximately three meters: under, on, and above the level of the temple floor. These are accessible by passageways, roughly half a meter wide, which lead to the crypts from various places in the temple. The length of some crypts is impressive, as much as around thirty meters. Eleven crypts have relief decoration with religious but sometimes also important historical themes. For example, the chapel immediately behind the *wabet* provides access to a crypt, where we find representations of the chief gods of Dendera and Edfu and inscriptions containing detailed information on the town, its names, and gods and their shrines. This crypt may have served as a temple archive. Another crypt is accessible from one of the chapels in the southwestern corner of the temple. The sacred symbols of the goddess Hathor, sistra, are depicted on the wall. The scene includes information about their dimensions (as much

The skylight letting in the first rays of the morning sun intensified the Osiris mystery in a chapel on the roof of Hathor's temple in Dendera.

Apart from the kiosk, on the roof terrace above the columned 'hall of appearance' there were also two trios of chapels, on the eastern and western sides of the temple. These chapels were associated with the Osiris mysteries. The eastern trio was known as the 'House of the Life of the Models,' which referred to statues. These were models of the so-called corn Osiris, and were made and animated here in secret ceremonies. Similar models of Sokar were also made here. Inscriptions and scenes on the walls of the first of the three chapels provide us with a detailed picture of the successive phases of the rites, which were performed here during the month of Khoiak. An important role in these rites was accorded to the goddess Shentayet, who was represented in the form of a recumbent cow with a sun disc on her head and the *bat* symbol (in the shape of a female face with cow ears and horns) hung around her neck. The model of Osiris rested on a couch known as 'the garden of Khontamentyu [that is, Osiris] in the House of Shentayet'; the goddess Shentayet herself was known as 'She who each year makes the garden green in her time.'

The ceiling of the second chapel in the eastern trio was originally adorned with the famous 'zodiac of Dendera,' but the original was taken to France in 1823 and is today in the Louvre. Unfortunately, this happened with the consent of Egypt's viceroy Muhammad 'Ali at a time when the French and British in particular could do almost anything they liked in Egypt. In 1920, the French installed a copy of the zodiac at the original site, but it is not very good. The constellation of the Great Bear is depicted at the center of the zodiac, other constellations suround it, and the thirty-six decans are depicted along the edge.

The third chapel in the eastern trio is also adorned with religious scenes and inscriptions in low relief. Here we see the body of Osiris in a sarcophagus, with the kneeling Isis and Nebthet weeping beside it; the falcon god Harendotes is already standing on the lid of the coffin. In the decoration's concluding section we see the victory of Osiris in his main cult centers, Abydos in Upper Egypt and Busiris in Lower Egypt. The culminating religious drama is intensified by the skylight, with depictions of Osiris on all its four sides, which allows the life-giving rays of the sun into the chapel where they fall first on Osiris lying on the bier.

The western trio of chapels on the sun terrace of the temple in Dendera was called the 'House of Isis Shentayet.' As is evident from the religious scenes and inscriptions covering their walls, these chapels were also the setting for Osiris mysteries. In the first of the western chapels a scene of Osiris lying on the bier and waking from his deathly

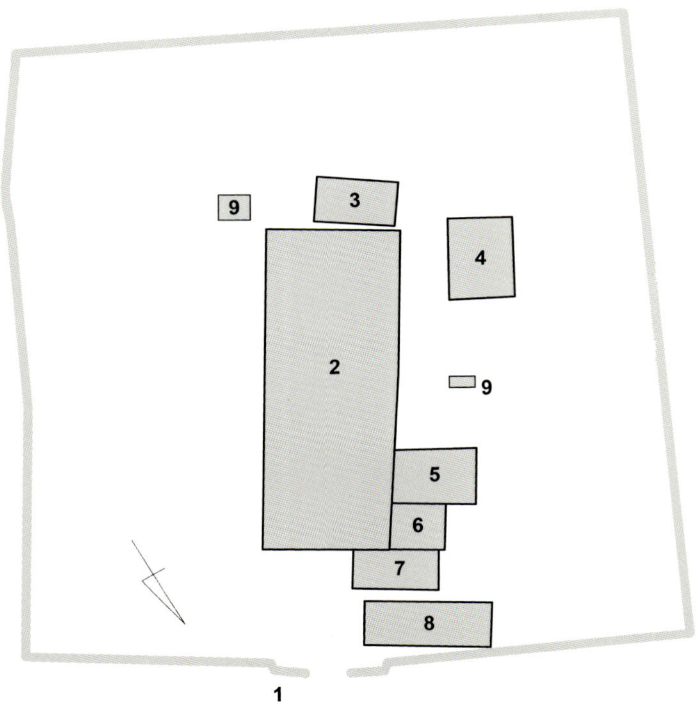

Schematic orientation plan of monuments in the temple precinct of Hathor in Dendera.
1. propylon and mud-brick enclosure wall
2. temple of Hathor
3. temple of Isis
4. sacred lake
5. sanatorium
6. *mammisi* of Nakhtnebef I
7. Coptic basilica
8. *mammisi* of Trajan
9. well

swoon occupies a prominent place. He is lifting his right forearm and his divine wife Isis is perching in the form of a hawk on his erect sexual organ. This is the mystical union that will create Osiris's son Horus ('avenger of his father'). Anubis is standing by the bier and raising his hands above them in a protective gesture. The second of the chapels was the place where Osiris models from the preceding year were kept. The scenes and inscriptions from the *Book of the Dead* on its walls commemorate the eventual victory over Osiris's enemy Seth in his different forms, from a donkey to a hippopotamus; here he is killed in the form of a red bull (red is Seth's symbolic color).

The texts and scenes on the walls of the chapels dedicated to the Osiris mysteries and on the walls of the other interiors make Hathor's temple in Dendera an extraordinarily rich source of knowledge about the religious thought of Egyptians in Ptolemaic and Roman times. Here we encounter myths, litanies, hymns, and the various priestly functions, but also historical and geographical information, astronomical texts, and much else. Altogether, these texts are direct and indirect testimony to the great religious, political, and economic power and social prestige that the temple in Dendera (but likewise the temples in Edfu and elsewhere in Egypt) possessed at the time. Last but not least, at a time when the country was under foreign rule, the texts reflect the efforts of the Egyptian priests to return to the roots of Egyptian identity and learning, to maintain continuity with domestic religious traditions, to demonstrate their greatness and spiritual depth, to give them new impulses, and thus to bolster the people's self-confidence and pride in their country.

Today the Hathor temple in Dendera, with other Ptolemaic and Roman temples in Egypt, is very important not only for the quantity of evidence that it provides on Egyptian religion and the political and economic conditions in the country at the time, but also because the texts preserved here offer so much information about the Egyptian language and Egyptian hieroglyphic script of the period. At the time of these inscriptions, in the nearly three millennia since the foundation of the ancient Egyptian state, both the language and the script had changed greatly. For example, the number of hieroglyphic signs, which was around seven hundred in texts written in classical Egyptian, had grown to several thousand. What is more, many signs had retained the same form as in the past but changed entirely in meaning. As a result, study of the religious beliefs themselves with their complex interrelations is not the only challenge for Egyptologists in the field; the understanding of the extensive sets of religious texts from the

Ptolemaic and Roman Periods presents immense difficulties, complicated even further by instances of cryptographic writing.

Temples of Divine Birth

The Temple of Hathor is by no means the only important monument in the temple district of Dendera. In the area surrounded by the massive enclosure wall there are also two *mammisi*, a temple to Isis, a Christian church, a sacred pool, and a few other buildings. The older of the two birth temples is the *mammisi* of Nakhtnebef I from the Thirtieth Dynasty. It is a relatively small building, oriented east–west in contrast to the Hathor temple, and located by the northwestern corner of the enclosure wall. The eastern part of the *mammisi* was originally a court, while the western part consisted of a sandstone shrine with two mud-brick chapels, later also faced with sandstone along the sides. The temple was architecturally altered in the Ptolemaic Period. The walls of the sanctuary carry relief decoration thematically centered on the birth of the divine child. This is a theme that, with some differences in the divine and mortal cast and treatment, was depicted on the walls of the 'birth hall' in the Temple of Luxor (where it was related to Amenhotep

View from the roof of Hathor's temple over the remains of the *mammisi* of Nakhtnebef I and Trajan, with the early Christian basilica wedged between them.

III). In Nakhtnebef's *mammisi* in Dendera the creator is likewise the god Amun, accompanied during the mystical act by gods from his circle, but in this case it is with Hathor, Lady of Dendera, that he wishes to beget a child. Here Hathor sits beside him on a couch protected by Neith while he gives her the *ankh*, the symbol of life, to inhale. In another scene Khnum is modeling the divine child Harsomtus on a potter's wheel while the frog goddess Heqet kneels in front of the wheel and holds out the *ankh* for the child to inhale. Next, Thoth, the god of knowledge, proclaims the birth of the divine child, who is weaned with the milk of divine cows and placed on the Egyptian throne.

In the Ptolemaic and Roman Periods the temples of the divine birth acquired considerable significance for the whole country. In Dendera, the mystery of the divine birth was celebrated on the eleventh day of the month of Pakhon, but in other parts of Egypt the timing may have been different. The mysteries that took place in the *mammisi* were in many respects like a mixture of Greek dramas and medieval Christian mystery plays. Their purpose, wholly in the Egyptian tradition, was the annual commemoration of the birth of the young god with which the actual ruler was identified. In this way, the ruler's divine origin was emphasized, the connection between the land and the gods was confirmed, and the order of the world renewed.

The other birth temple in Dendera is the *mammisi* of Trajan, and lies a little to the north of Nakhtnebef's close to the propylon that forms the main entrance into the temple district. While it also has an east–west orientation, it is bigger than Nakhtnebef's and in many respects resembles the *mamissi* of Augustus in Edfu. The temple was later quite seriously damaged when a Christian church was build next to it. Running around its perimeter is a line of columns with composite capitals and abacus bearing a picture of Bes, a very popular god in the Roman Period. As is usual in *mammisi*, between the columns of the peristyle there are low crosspieces with religious scenes and inscriptions in relief. The upper edge of these crosspieces is adorned by a frieze in the form of a row of uraei, while the upper edge of the temple terminates in a concave cornice. The interior part of the temple consists of a forecourt (today destroyed) and a hypostyle hall, leading successively into a 'hall of offerings,' an antechamber, and the sanctuary with two long narrow chambers on either side of it. Here, too, there are scenes of the birth of the divine child, which with a few divergences resemble the scenes in Nakhtnebef's *mammisi*. In addition to Khnum modeling the divine child on a potter's wheel, we find the god Ptah engaged in similar activity,

carving the divine child out of stone. Cult instruments were stored in the chambers on each side of the sanctuary. A staircase in the north-eastern part of the temple gave access to the roof terrace. Its walls are adorned with figures of offering bearers.

Trajan's *mammisi* in Dendera.

Close to the southern stretch of the enclosure wall of Hathor's temple lies the Temple of Isis. The Greek inscription on its wall dates

Detail of a fragment with a representation of the god Bes in high relief. Dendera, sandstone. Roman Period.

from AD 1, the reign of the emperor Augustus, but in the temple there are cartouches of earlier kings—not just Nakhtnebef I, who founded the temple, but also several Ptolemaic kings who made alterations and additions and contributed to its decoration. The temple is north–south in orientation and consists of an antechamber and a shrine, which has one chamber on either side. There is rich relief decoration on the exterior of the temple and in its interiors; for example, Augustus is depicted in the antechamber honoring Isis, Osiris, Ihy, and other gods. The decoration in the shrine and in the chambers on each side is seriously damaged. A court with a central path along its axis between pairs of columns, leading into a hall with four columns, was added from the east. At the beginning of the Christian era, both the court and the columned hall suffered extensive deliberate destruction, probably an attempt to make sure that the still-popular cult of Isis would not be carried on.

Not far from the southwestern corner of the enclosure wall of Hathor's temple is a sacred pool, today full of sand and overgrown with palms. It is roughly 31 × 25 meters in size. There are flights of steps down to the pool on all four sides. Just as in the other Egyptian

View of the Isis temple from the roof terrace of the temple of Hathor in Dendera.

The sacred pool in Hathor's temple district in Dendera, overgrown with palms.

temples, the pool was not only a source of water for the purification of priests and ritual tasks but also symbolized the primordial waters. It had an important role on certain festivals, such as the Osiris mysteries or the Festival of the Beautiful Union. Close to the pool lay a small chapel for Hathor's barque dating from the reign of Ptolemy VIII Euergetes II; on the first day of every month Hathor's statue would be taken in this sacred barque to sail on the sacred pool for the biggest local festival in Dendera: Hathor's Voyage.

One very interesting profane building here was a 'sanatorium,' which lay close to Nakhtnebef's *mammisi*. It was made of fired bricks and had a pool with curative water for baths at its center. Water was channeled here from the sacred pool and flowed in from the pedestal of a statue of Osiris. There were small chambers around the pool, where patients could rest after their baths. People came here for treatment of various disorders and injuries, seeking the help of the Egyptian gods such as Imhotep (the deified builder of the Step Pyramid in Saqqara, whom the Greeks identified with Asclepius), Hathor, and Isis. It is believed that what was known as therapeutic sleep was also practiced here.

a human face and cow horns and ears. In the case of the Narmer Palette this is not in fact Hathor but another, similarly ancient cow goddess called Bat, who was to merge with Hathor at the beginning of the Middle Kingdom.

Hathor was the goddess not just of fertility and maternity, as her various attributes suggest, but also of love and the song and dance associated with love. Her symbol was the sistrum, a kind of rattle much used in temple rituals, with a head that was sometimes in the form of Hathor herself. The goddess was also associated with various jewels and precious stones. She was the patroness of miners and prospectors and the mountainous desert areas where deposits of precious stones were to be found; this is the source of her title 'Lady of the Turquoise.' By extension she came to be regarded as the ruler of foreign lands such as Sinai, Byblos, or Punt. Hathor's face (she and the god Bes are the only gods characteristically represented *en face* in Egyptian art) appears as a decorative element in Egyptian art and architecture, for example, on column capitals. Hathor played an important part in the life of Egyptians from birth to the afterlife. She assisted at births as a fate (that is, a godmother or goddess midwife) in the form of the 'seven Hathors,' which were seven forms of the goddess supposed to protect the child and predict his fortune. After death the individual would meet Hathor in the form of a sycomore, for example, offering shade where he could rest on his journey to final judgment and refresh himself with fruit and drink water from a spring at its roots. Hathor was worshiped as the 'Lady of the Sycomore' in many places, including Memphis.

Hathor was venerated in Thebes as Mehet Weret ('Great Flood'), represented in the form of a cow stepping out of her local rock shrine, or sometimes emerging from a papyrus swamp symbolizing the primordial waters.

Hathor plays a significant role in various myths, such as the "Contendings of Horus and Seth." In another myth she appears as the 'eye of Re': The god Re, burning sun disc and ruler of gods and men, was weary of his creative activities and growing old, and so decided to send down his 'eye' to punish those who were conspiring to overthrow him. Hathor changed into the frenzied lioness Sakhmet, 'the Mighty,' and started to hunt and kill all that lived. Out of control, her raging threatened to destroy everything. Therefore, on Re's order, the high priest in Heliopolis made a red-colored drink resembling blood and went off to seek the goddess, who had meanwhile fled far to the south. In the end the goddess, also known as the 'Mistress of

Intoxication' and sometimes as 'the Estranged,' was tricked and tranquilized and mankind was thus saved.

As has already been suggested, Hathor was worshiped in many places not only in Egypt, such as Memphis and Thebes, but also in the Sinai and Nubia. Her shrine in Dendera was nonetheless the most famous. The temples were the centers of Hathor's local cult, but also the setting for Hathor festivals that were nationwide and had a state character. We are relatively well informed about Hathor's chief festivals from inscriptions in the temple in Dendera and especially the temple in Edfu, the cult center of her divine partner Horus (see chapter 10). However, there is insufficient evidence about the smaller local festivals.

Hathor's Festivals

The great festivities of the goddess Hathor in her principal temple in Dendera started at the New Year, the first day of the month of Thoth. Well before daybreak the priests would carry Hathor's statue, the seat of her *ba*, to the *wabet*. Here, offerings were assembled in the small open courtyard and the statue of the goddess would be dressed and adorned with the jewels and insignia symbolizing her power. Shortly before dawn a procession of priests bearing the statue of the god went up the staircase to the roof terrace. In the kiosk on the terrace, with the requisite liturgical prayers and songs, the priests performed the 'union with the sun disc' ceremony, in which the spirit of the goddess would draw new strength from the first rays of the sun, revive, and so be enabled to fulfill her task in the world of men and the world of the gods with full vigor for another year.

'The Brought Back [goddess]' festival was also quite famous; it was celebrated starting on the nineteenth day of the month of Tobi and culminated in the coronation of Hathor on the fourth day of the following month, Mekhir. The festival commemorated the myth of the Eye of Re: the transformation of the goddess into a raging lion, her flight south, her eventual calming, and her return to Egypt, restoring peace and prosperity. The festivities took place throughout Egypt; they involved the voyage of the statue of the goddess on the Nile, commemoration of the life-giving flood that heralded a good harvest, singing, dancing, and offerings to the goddess. On the twelfth day of the month of Thoth another festival connected to the Eye of Re myth took place in Hathor's temple in Dendera. This was the 'Feast of Intoxication,' when the high priest would dance and sing in front of the statue of Hathor and bring her the *menu* vessel as an offering.

According to inscriptions preserved in the temple at Dendera, the 'Festival of the Beautiful Union' was already being celebrated at the dawn of Egyptian history. It took place in the month of Epep, when Hathor, after all the necessary rites were performed, would set out in her barque to visit her divine partner Horus in Edfu, about seventy kilometers to the south of Dendera. A suite of other boats accompanied her on this voyage, people on the banks helped to tow the barque, and crowds came to greet her on her journey, and would join Hathor's procession in other small boats. The grand festival lasted two weeks.

Hathor's temple in Dendera was not only the setting for celebrations of Hathor. Many other festivals linked to other gods were held there. We have already given a detailed account of the great Osiris festivities celebrated in the month of Khoiak. On the fifth day of the month of Paopi there were festivities in honor of the god Nun, Hathor's primordial father, when offerings including white bread and a special pastry known as *shenes* were brought. We do not know the precise meanings of some of the festivities, which involved the raising of a willow and a procession through the House of Harsomtus. The festival of the Night of the Child in the Barque, the birth of the

Harsomtus: Horus, Unifier of the Two Lands.

goddess Isis, was held on the penultimate day of the year, the fourth epagomenal day. The mystery of the Divine Birth was also celebrated here. It is curious that the inscriptions in Dendera do not mention celebration of any great festivals in the month of Athyr, which was actually named after Hathor and dedicated to her. This has not yet been satisfactorily explained.

Fourth Excursus

The Lady of the Turquoise

Sinai landscape close to Serabit al-Khadim.

Wadi Maghara, a rock valley in the Sinai Peninsula where the ancient Egyptians were already mining copper ore during the Old Kingdom.

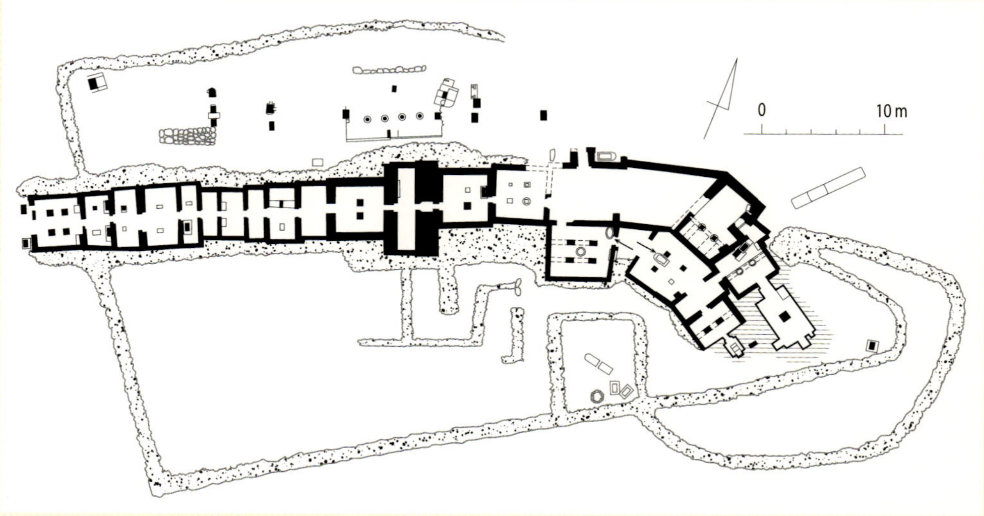

Plan of the Hathor temple in Serabit al-Khadim.

≫Fragment of a pillar in the ruins of the Hathor temple in Serabit al-Khadim.

deposits of turquoise in the mountains in the southern part of the peninsula, around Wadi Maghara and Serabit al-Khadim. This blue to greenish mineral, which symbolized eternal life and resurrection, was extracted by tunneling into the interior of the cliffs—a process which also gave Wadi Maghara its name, 'Valley of the Caves.' The turquoise deposits here were being exploited as early as the Old Kingdom. The turquoise was used above all in the creation of jewelry. In these locations the Egyptians also found other ores containing copper, malachite, and azurite. The Egyptians sent military expeditions to obtain these precious minerals from the Sinai

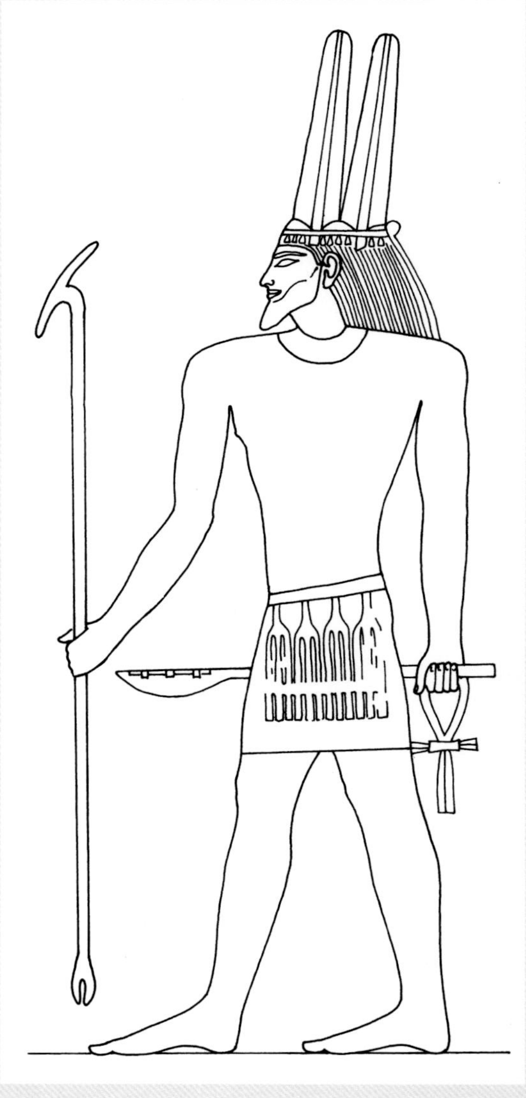
The god Sopdu, lord of the East. Drawing of a detail from the decoration of Sahure's mortuary temple in Abusir.

mountains because, in that place, they were at constant risk of raids by hostile Bedouin. The risk of clashes was reduced by the fact that the Egyptian expeditions traveled to Wadi Maghara and Serabit al-Khadim by water rather than by land. The starting point of the expeditions was a fort and harbor close to what is today the village of Abu Zeneima on the shore of the Gulf of Suez. The mined material was brought through the valley of Wadi Matalla to this harbor for transport back to Egypt.

Stelae were carved in the rock walls close to the mines as a way of trying to avert the perils that threatened the miners. The rock stelae include information about the expedition and its date as well as representations of the king massacring the hostile Bedouin with a stone mace. The images had commemorative as well as magical apotropaic significance. The earliest stela raised here was carved on the instructions of the Third Dynasty king Djoser, while later stelae were erected by kings Snofru, Khufu, Sahure, Pepi I, and many others.

The Mountain Temple of Hathor

The goddess Hathor, venerated here as the 'Lady of the Turquoise,' was considered the ruler of the Sinai turquoise and copper-ore mining areas and the patroness of the miners. On the mountain plateau of Serabit al-Khadim, almost nine hundred meters above sea level, the miners built a temple to her and then progressively enlarged it. The building has a very unusual ground plan that was partially dictated by the uneven mountain terrain but is more reminiscent of a Canaanite rather than an Egyptian type of temple. It has a roughly east–west orientation and its oldest part is a rock chapel from the Middle Kingdom. Another artificial cave, also from the Middle Kingdom, adjoins it from the north and includes a pillared portico and resembles a rock tomb of the period. According to Petrie, who excavated the temple in Serabit al-Khadim at the beginning of the twentieth century, Sopdu, 'The Pointed One' or 'Lord of the East,' was worshiped in the first chapel and Hathor in the second. Each chapel is fronted by a hall; Sopdu's chapel has four pillars and Hathor's has two columns.

Successive additions were made to the temple from the New Kingdom onward, and these shifted the whole orientation of the temple farther to the southwest. First an open court was added, with the original entrance to the temple on its north side, and also two rooms, one of which has four pillars and dates from the time of Hatshepsut and Thutmose III. Petrie believed that both rooms served for ritual purification. During the reigns of the rulers already mentioned and other kings of the New Kingdom, further halls were added on the southwest, and even a pylon, with two stelae raised in front of it. The last hall with four pillars was built under Sethi I and included a new entrance in its western wall. By this time the temple was around one hundred meters in length.

Numerous stelae attest that apart from Hathor and her divine partner Sopdu, other gods were worshiped in the temple: Thoth, Ptah, and surprisingly also the deified Fourth Dynasty king Snefru. Possibly one contributory factor to the cult of Snofru and his positive reputation in later times was his 'positive'-sounding name, which has as its root the word *nefer* ('good, perfect'). The miners, expeditions, and individual travelers passing through this place brought offerings to Hathor and other gods and asked for their favor and protection when working or traveling in the wild and dangerous terrain. There is some evidence that Canaanite cults may also have been practiced in the Hathor temple in Serabit al-Khadim.

The temple has been very seriously damaged, not just by vandals but also—in the mid-nineteenth century—by a British colonial mining project intended to extract turquoise once again. Israeli archaeologists carried out research here during the Israeli occupation of the Sinai following the Six Day

Drawing of a stela with a proto-Sinaitic text.

War in 1967. They were also looking for evidence of the Biblical exodus of the Jews from Egypt, but in vain. Numerous archaeological finds were later returned to Egypt as part of the Camp David Accords. Currently the Egyptian government is seeking to have Serabit al-Khadim registered on the UNESCO world cultural heritage list.

Proto-Sinaitic Inscriptions

Shorter texts written in a peculiar script have been found on the rocks and also on a number of objects in the vicinity of the turquoise mines of Wadi Maghara and Serabit al-Khadim. These have been given the name 'Proto-Sinaitic inscriptions.' Some experts consider them to be Hyksos, and others think they are merely meaningless scribbling, so they continue to present an interesting philological puzzle. They are written using roughly three dozen signs, some quite obviously derived from Egyptian hieroglyphs and heavily stylized. Researchers concerned with this script have concluded that it is an alphabetical script derived from hieroglyphics, which records a Semitic language on the principle of acrophony. As yet only a few words have been deciphered. Some scholars date the Proto-Sinaitic inscriptions to the Twelfth Dynasty, others ascribe them to the Eighteenth Dynasty. The prevailing view is that the authors of the Proto-Sinaitic inscriptions were probably Canaanites who may have taken part in the Egyptian expeditions as guides, or worked alongside Egyptians mining turquoise in the Sinai.

Alexander's City by Egypt

≪ Detail of a frieze discovered by the Polish–Egyptian archaeological expedition at Kom al-Dikka in Alexandria and dating from the Roman Period.

Where should this account of ancient Egyptian temples, cults, and mysteries end if not in Alexandria? In Egypt, but not wholly of Egypt, Alexandria was the meeting place of the civilizations of ancient Egypt, the Near East, Greece, and later Rome—all of them sources of a religious, intellectual, and cultural heritage on which the world still draws.

Historians have inevitably wondered why Alexander the Great founded his city on what seems an inconvenient site for a great metropolis: a narrow strip of land confined between the limestone cliffs of the Mediterranean coast and the extensive marshes around Lake Maryut (known in Greek as Mareotis). Plutarch reports that Alexander decided on this location for the new capital of his world empire because of a dream, but it was more likely that he was thinking very wakefully of the island of Pharos, which lies close to the shore here and could provide ships with safe anchorage. Alexander, the educated pupil of Aristotle, most likely knew of Pharos from the *Odyssey,* in which it figures as the island where the immortal Proteus slept and where Menelaus was shipwrecked. Alexander the general was certainly interested not just in the island of Pharos with its value for control of the eastern Mediterranean, but in control of Egypt and the trade routes into the African interior; east of Pharos, by the town of Canopus on the edge of Abuqir Bay, lay the mouth of the western branch of the Nile, which offered fast and easy access to the historical capital city of Egypt, Memphis.

Alexandria was founded shortly after Alexander's conquest of Egypt in 332 BC (the famous general crossed the border at Pelusium in December 331 BC), but it is not clear whether the founding of the city took place before or after Alexander's celebrated visit to the oracle of Amun in the Siwa Oasis.

At the time there was a small village called Ra qedu ('The Wall'), already known to the Greeks as Rhakotis, on the coast opposite Pharos. It was later incorporated as the Egyptian quarter in the planning of the new city, which Alexander entrusted to the architect Deinokrates of Rhodes. Alexandria was planned as a Greek fortified city with streets intersecting at right angles and two main streets: the Canopic Way and the Soma Way. The Canopic Way ran from east to west between the

Portrait of Alexander the Great with Amun's horns on a silver coin.

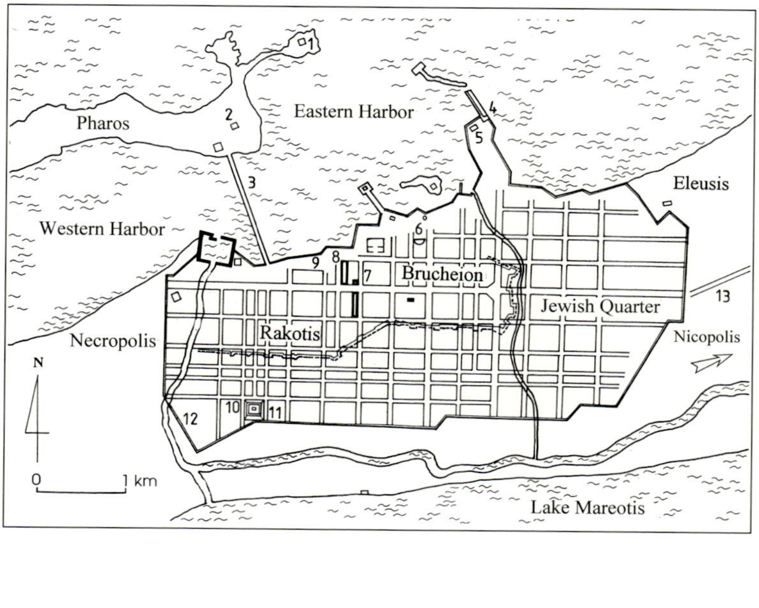

Plan of Ptolemaic Alexandria (based on the plan originally drawn by G. Botti in 1898 and republished in Tkaczkowska, *Topography*, fig. 10a) showing harbors, main neighborhoods, and monuments.

1. lighthouse
2. temple of Isis
3. Heptastadion
4. temple of Artemis
5. royal palace
6. theater
7. mausoleum
8. Museion
9. library
10. Serapeion
11. Pompey's Column
12. Kom al-Shuqafa
13. hippodrome

Kom al-Dikka.

Gate of the Sun and the Gate of the Moon, while the Soma, named after the district Soma (or 'body,' although according to another version the true title was Sema, or 'sepulchre'), ran from the Maryut lake in the south to the sea in the north. The city had two harbors, Megas Limen ('The Great Harbor') west of Pharos, and Eunostos ('The Harbor of Happy Return') east of Pharos. The city eventually consisted of Rhakotis, the Greek quarters of Neapolis, and the Brukheion, with Eleusis and Nikopolis in the east and Nekropolis to the west. The agora, the center of civic life, lay south of the royal Basilea district, by what today is Kom al-Dikka. We owe a detailed description of Alexandria and its main districts and buildings to the geographer and historian Strabo, who visited Egypt in the reign of Augustus in the years 25–24 BC. According to Strabo, the city was thirty stadia long (1 stadion = about 180 meters).

The Basilea district with its royal palaces and gardens, its own harbor, and many other buildings was by the sea in the center of the city. The Soma, the royal cemetery containing the grand tombs of the first

Ptolemaic kings, was probably situated in the Basilea. Alexander the Great did not live to see the fulfilment of his dream of a city bearing his name on the boundaries of Europe, Asia, and Africa, but was possibly buried in Basilea in a glass coffin. He had no time to return after the foundations were laid; he died in 323 BC in Babylon, on his return journey from campaigns in Persia and India. The cortege bearing his body back to Greece on a carriage, in a provisional but predominantly golden coffin, was seized in Syria by Ptolemy, one of Alexander's generals entrusted with the government of Egypt, who conveyed the corpse to Memphis and had it buried there. Ptolemy was very well aware of the important role that would be played by Alexander's tomb in the new order in the eastern Mediterranean. It is not known where in Memphis Alexander's tomb was located, although there is speculation that it might have been in the Memphite cemetery in Saqqara close to the Serapeum. Nor is it clear how long Alexander was buried in Memphis. There are some indications that it might have been just a few years, but others suggest as long as thirty-six years. Nonetheless, his body was then taken to Alexandria; despite the efforts of generations of archaeologists no one has yet managed to find Alexander's final resting place.

After the death of Alexander the Great's half-brother Philip Arrhidaeus and his posthumous son by Roxanna, Alexander IV, his former generals divided up his empire among themselves. Ptolemy, son of Lagus, became king of Egypt in 306 BC as Ptolemy I Soter, founding the dynasty that ruled the country until it fell under Roman control in 30 BC. The first Ptolemaic kings consolidated Egypt politically and did much to improve economic conditions. As many documents of the period attest, they made a series of important administrative and economic reforms concerning administration of the regions, allocation of land to clerouchs (military veterans), tax collection, improvement and extension of the networks of irrigation canals, the establishment of a schedule of work in the fields, and purchase of crops for fixed prices. One particularly important set of documents in this context is the papyri of Zenon, the private archive of the administrator of a large estate who lived during the reign of Ptolemy II Philadelphus. The renewed prosperity of the country was what made it possible for Alexandria to be built up into a great and flourishing city, although unfortunately this was, to a great extent, at the expense of older monuments: the sphinxes, obelisks, statues, and whole buildings from Heliopolis, Tanis, and elsewhere that were usurped or, even worse, exploited as building material.

Nothing testifies more vividly to the wealth of Alexandria and the new rulers of Egypt (and their aspirations to rule the world) than the

Reconstruction of the lighthouse on Pharos by H. Thiersch.

ostentatious dynastic festivals, or Ptolemaia, described in sources from the reign of Ptolemy II onward. These took place under the aegis of the favorite gods of the Ptolemies—Dionysus, Serapis, and Isis—and involved heavily subsidized and unconstrained hedonism including banquets lasting several days, rivers of wine, and the slaughter of two thousand bulls. The royal court and foreign envoys took part in processions of tens of thousands of people through the center of the city, with infantry and cavalry troops, musicians, dancers, priestesses with snakes in their hair,

Qaytbay's fortresss was built from the ruins of the collapsed lighthouse.

exotic animals, and men leading nearly two and a half thousand dogs. Merrymakers dressed as satyrs and sileni would carry a huge silver krater full of wine and a wine press, and others a long golden phallus—a symbol of fertility and prosperity. Bearers of statues of Alexander the Great and Ptolemy I Soter I brought up the rear of the procession.

Alexander's dream of Alexandria becoming the capital of the ancient world, an aspiration not relinquished by the Ptolemies, was not as unrealistic as it might seem at first sight. Fertile Egypt, with its abundant wealth, was initially a very promising hinterland for these plans. The building of a lighthouse on the island of Pharos, under the direction of Sostratus of Cnidus, started immediately in the reign of Ptolemy I Soter I. Completed during the reign of Ptolemy II Philadelphus, it was of key importance for sea transport along the Egyptian coast. Ptolemy II with his wife Arsinoë II ceremonially opened the lighthouse in 283 BC. The island was connected with the mainland by an artificial isthmus seven stadia long and therefore known as the Heptastadion. In its time the lighthouse, largely constructed out of stone taken from earlier buildings in different places in Egypt, was justly considered one of the seven wonders of the ancient world. It was approximately one hundred meters high and consisted of four parts. The first section was square in ground plan, the next octagonal, and the uppermost, with the fireplace and mirrors, was circular. The lighthouse was topped with a gigantic bronze statue of Poseidon, ruler of the sea. In the early Middle Ages the lighthouse was seriously damaged by earthquakes and eventually collapsed altogether during a major earthquake in 1376. On the site of the lighthouse, and reusing its ruins, the sultan Ashraf Qaytbay built a fort in the mid-fifteenth century.

The Metropolis of Learning

In the spirit of Alexander's vision and the plans of the Ptolemies, Alexandria was meant to be not merely the capital city of the known world but the center of all knowledge and learning. The intention was to bring all accessible and movable important monuments, works of art, and learned texts together in Alexandria, and the key element in the plan was the creation of an institution known as the Museion, so called because all the muses would have their seats there. The building, which according to Strabo was part of the royal palace, was the work of the architect Demetrius of Phaleron and funded by the state. A priest (probably a priest of Serapis) appointed by the king oversaw the institution, which had a promenade, conference hall, and a common refectory for the schol-

View of the roof of the new Library of Alexandria.

ars. The process of bringing works of art from Greece, Egypt, and foreign countries began once the building was completed. Written works were concentrated in the library, which was probably an annex to the Museion, and these included Greek and Egyptian papyri, the treatises of the Chaldean scholars, Indian, Armenian, Hebrew, Persian, and many other manuscripts. The office of librarian was socially very prestigious from the outset and occupied by leading scholars of the period, such as the publisher Zenodontus of Ephesus and the philosopher and poet Eratosthenes of Cyrene. The arrangement of the library owed a great deal to Callimachus of Cyrene. His "tables of persons outstanding in every field of knowledge, together with a list of their writings" formed the basic annotated 102-volume catalogue of the library, which at the time may have boasted as many as half a million texts. Its destruction by an accidental fire in 48 BC, which broke out during Caesar's short so-called Alexandrine War, was a tragic and irretrievable loss to the cultural heritage left to us by antiquity. Today a new Library of Alexandria has been built under the patronage of UNESCO and was opened in 2002, in an effort to symbolically revive and continue the tradition of the ancient library.

The first Ptolemaic kings did not want to acquire works of art and scholarship merely for reasons of prestige; they wanted to understand the wisdom of foreign nations and integrate it into the cultural environment of the society that they were creating in Alexandria. For example, the Ptolemaic kings and the learned men in their courts were interested in the Hebrew texts not only for religious and philosophical reasons but for security reasons as well, because from the beginning of the sixth century BC colonies of Jewish settlers had been living in various places in Egypt and Jewish soldiers served in the Egyptian army. Up to the beginning of the second century BC Palestine was part of the Ptolemaic monarchy, and Jews were permitted to settle in Alexandria from the city's very foundation. Their community here had notable features of autonomy.

At the suggestion of Demetrius of Phaleron, Ptolemy I Soter I gave the order for translation of the Hebrew scriptures into Greek, a project connected with reforms of the legal system at the time and their consequences for the Jewish community in Egypt. Seventy Jewish scholars were chosen, the symbolic seventy elders of the community (originally there were supposed to have been seventy-two, six for each of the twelve tribes of Israel), all with an excellent knowledge of Greek, to translate the Torah in seclusion on the island of Pharos. Incidentally, this is the reason for the title of the translation, the Septuagint, derived from the Latin for 'seventy.' The translation of the Torah (whose five books then came to be known in Greek as the Pentateuch) had far-reaching importance, since apart from its significance for the Jewish community in Alexandria and Jews in Egypt it later played a major role in the spread of Christianity. The meeting of Judaic and Hellenic thought in Alexandria is epitomized at the turn of the common era by Philo of Alexandria (circa 25 BC–AD 45), a Jewish thinker strongly influenced by Greek philosophy, particularly Platonism and Stoicism. Philo studied the Old Testament using

Marble bust of Serapis with a corn-measuring vessel on his head. Greco-Roman Museum in Alexandria.

allegorical interpretation. His work was later a source of inspiration for emergent Christianity, and he was an influence on Origen, Saint Augustine, and others.

design and the nature of later alterations are subjects of academic speculation and controversy. Rather paradoxically, however, archaeologists have found gold, silver, bronze, and glass founding tablets with hieroglyphic and Greek text relating to the founding of the temple.

According to some contemporaneous sources, for example Rufinus of Aquileia, a staircase with a hundred steps led up to the temple, which

Entrance to the underground cemetery at Kom al-Shuqafa.

was square in ground plan. In the middle was a colossal polychrome seated statue of Serapis made of wood and metal (bronze, gold), inlaid with precious stones (for example, the eyes), with Cerberus at his feet. On his head he wore the *kalathos* adorned with ears of corn and olive branches. A small window in the eastern wall of the temple was set in a position that allowed the first rays of sunlight at dawn to bathe the face of the statue. According to surviving archaeological evidence and written sources, work on building the Serapeum started during the reign of

Ptolemy I Soter I or Ptolemy II Philadelphus. Archaeological research has confirmed that under Ptolemy III Euergetes the temple was surrounded on three sides by a peristyle enclosing the whole hill. The approach to the temple was from the northern, open side of the peristyle. Only the building's foundation trenches have survived. West of the Serapis temple stood a temple to Isis, and yet another temple, to Harpocrates, was built here under Ptolemy IV Philopator. A Nilometer connected by an underground canal with a secondary branch of the Nile was part of the temple complex. Incidentally, supplying Alexandria with drinking water was a serious problem, and was solved by canals bringing Nile water, which was then retained in hundreds of huge cisterns, some several stories high.

The cult of Serapis gradually spread throughout Egypt, probably aided by his reputation as a healer god. Shrines to him were built all over the country, particularly in larger towns and important religious centers such as Hermopolis, Thebes, and Krokodilopolis in the Fayoum Oasis. It is worth noting that the spread of the Serapis cult in Egypt owed a great deal to the efforts of the Egyptian priest Manetho. He came from Sebennytus in the Nile Delta and achieved fame by writing a history of Egypt, the *Aigyptiaca hypomnemata* (Egyptian Antiquities), at the wish of Ptolemy I Soter I. This work, in which Manetho divided the history and rulers of Egypt into thirty dynasties, has not survived in its entirety; only small extracts and citations in the writings of later authors remain. Serapis and his divine partner Isis became major cosmopolitan gods of the empire in the Roman Period. Shrines to them were built in the eastern Mediterranean and southern Europe, and some were also places of initiation ceremonies. The festival of Serapis was very popular, involving offerings of wine, honey bread, and other delicacies; in Egypt it was still being celebrated at the beginning of the fourth century AD.

The relative religious freedom of the predominantly Hellenist but multicultural society of Alexandria is evident from the building of a whole series of other temples dedicated not only to Greek (Hermaion, Hephaesteion, Nemeseion, Paneion) and Egyptian gods, but also to foreign gods (that is, the Mithreion). There were also temples dedicated to rulers, for example the Arsinoeion dedicated to Queen Arsinoë II.

In the final years of Ptolemaic rule and at the beginning of the Roman era the importance of the Serapeum declined somewhat, since it was overshadowed by the new center of the imperial cult in the eastern part of the city, the Caesareum, on which work started in the reign of Cleopatra VII. The Temple of Serapis was later destroyed in AD 392 by a frenzied crowd of Christians at the instigation of the patriarch Theophilus,

Pompey's Column, which was re-erected on Kom al-Shuqafa, originally stood in the temple of Serapis in Alexandria.

who justified the destruction by appealing to the edict of the emperor Theodosius, issued the previous year and forbidding pagan cults. Today the site of the temple is commemorated by what is known as Pompey's Column, which is twenty-nine meters tall (including the base), and made of Aswan granite; it was originally topped by a statue. Scholars once believed that the pillar was raised by Theodosius in AD 391 as a sign of victory over paganism, but today the academic consensus is that it was set up in honor of Diocletian in AD 292.

The Greeks had great respect for ancient Egyptian culture and in many respects greatly admired it, without fully understanding many of its peculiarities. Not only the Greek historian Herodotus, but many other learned men in the classical world (Pythagoras, Eratosthenes, Euclid, Strabo, and Plutarch, to mention only a few) were attracted to Egypt. The great antiquity of Egypt suggested to Greeks that it was the cradle of knowledge, while the peculiarities of a culture veiled in mysteries encouraged them to believe that it could only be penetrated by the elect and initiated. Therefore, many learned Greek men traveled to Egypt to get to know the culture first hand, to learn wisdom from the priests in Egyptian temples, and so (it was hoped) to learn the meaning of life and the world. For the Greeks, Thoth, the Egyptian god of wisdom and knowledge—in their interpretation, Hermes Trismegistus—seemed to be the embodiment of the Egyptian cultural and spiritual inheritance. It is therefore no wonder that in the Roman Period it was the authority and indeed alleged authorship of Thoth that guaranteed the venerability, mystery, and holiness of Egyptian religious writings.

The Cultural Legacy of Alexandria

The multicultural milieu of Alexandria, so favorable for the mutual enrichment of all the ethnic groups and artistic and religious movements that thrived there, retained its character for a long time after the Roman conquest of Egypt in 30 BC. Christianity—a new religion at that time—found a place beside the other spiritual currents of the unique city in the first centuries after Christ's death. Early Christianity in Egypt is associated with the evangelist Mark, who according to the fourth-century historian Eusebius arrived there early in the reign of the emperor Claudius, around the year AD 41. (Christian tradition also holds that the Holy Family had found refuge in Egypt when fleeing from Herod's soldiers). The new religion attracted ever more adherents in Egypt despite persecution. Indeed, it found relatively the best conditions for development in places where few would have expected it to flourish, that is, in the oases and towns on the edge of the desert. One reason must have been that state power was relatively weak on the very boundaries of the imperium and so persecution was less thorough and effective. These peculiar conditions also encouraged the emergence and growth of monasticism, the specific Christian institution to which Egypt made a unique contribution.

Not only the desert fathers, however, but also the learned men of Alexandria were formative influences on Christianity. Among the philosophers who were interested in the new religious movement and brought it from Athens to Alexandria, the most prominent was Titus Flavius Clemens, known as Clement of Alexandria, who lived in the second half of the second century and the beginning of the third century. Clement came to the conclusion that Christianity and Greek philosophy, above all

Platonism and Stoicism, were not mutually exclusive but complementary, and that Greek philosophy was even in its way a preparation for the acceptance of Christianity. He became the head of the Didascalion, the famous catechetical school of Alexandria, which tried to demonstrate the compatibility of philosophy and theology and contributed significantly to the birth of the universal Church. In his thought and works, among which we should mention at least the *Stromateis* (Miscellanies) and the *Paidagogos* (Teacher), Clement of Alexandria took an eclectic line and sought in 'symbolic style' to combine elements of Greek philosophy, the Old Testament, and incipient Christianity. Like some of the Gnostics he believed that religious knowledge was the foundation of Christian perfection, understood as enlightenment, and that conversely ignorance was a sin.

The life of another man of learning, Origen called Adamantios ('the Iron') (185–254), who was Clement's pupil and successor at the head of the Didaskalion, tells us much about his times and the major changes affecting Alexandria and Egypt during that period. Like Clement, Origen had been educated in Greek philosophical thought before developing an enthusiasm for Christianity. He was fascinated by the relationship between the world and God, questions of the origin and end of the world, and the freedom of rational beings. He identified Christ with the Logos and believed in the pre-existence of souls and the multiplicity of worlds. He had a strong tendency to asceticism and his work and spirituality became a great source of inspiration for many later thinkers. However, as a result of disputes with the Christian community's leaders he was banished from Alexandria and stripped of his clerical status in 232. He eventually settled in Caesarea in Palestine. Origen produced an extensive body of work. Apart from his treatises on dogma, the most outstanding is the *Hexapla* (Sixfold). As the Greek title suggests, here Origen lined up the Hebrew text of the Bible and its five different Greek translations, including the Septuagint, in six columns and made critical comparisons among them. Some previously unknown writings by Origen were only discovered at the beginning of the 1940s in a limestone quarry in Tura near Cairo; monks from the nearby monastery, who considered the texts heretical, had discarded them fifteen centuries before.

By Origen's time the cosmopolitanism and tolerance of Alexandria were increasingly becoming things of the past. One great era in the history of the ancient land on the Nile was drawing to a close. Today we can only look back with admiration and a certain nostalgia at the cultural flowering, the 'Indian summer,' achieved in Egypt under the Ptolemies and the first centuries of Roman rule. The grand and well-preserved

Detail of decoration from the catacombs at Kom al-Shuqafa, in which Egyptian and Greek funerary beliefs are combined.

temples in Dendera, Edfu, and elsewhere, as well as many other material and written monuments, offer eloquent testimony to this achievement. Indeed, almost every day there is news of more remarkable archaeological finds in Alexandria and its coastal waters, and in such remote places as the oases in the Western Desert or obscure settlements where no one would expect to discover antiquities of major international significance. One example of this kind is Bahnasa in Middle Egypt (known in Greek as Oxyrhynchos), a little-known provincial town on the edge of the desert on the west bank of the Bahr Yusuf Canal. This was the starting point of a caravan route to the Bahriya Oasis in very ancient times, but the first

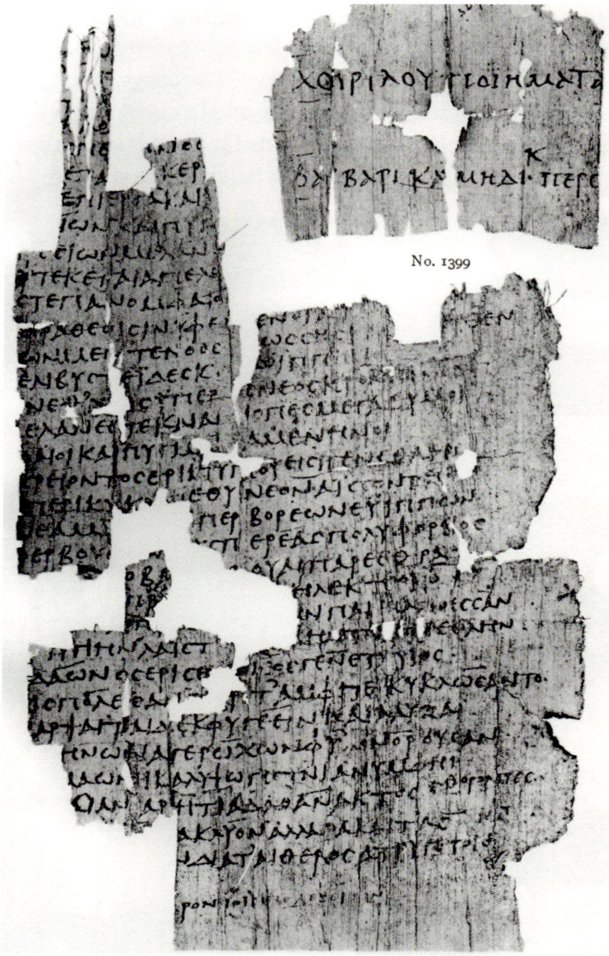

Papyrus from Oxyrhynchus.

of papyrus written in Greek containing sayings attributed to Jesus that had not been recorded in the gospels and dated from a time around the year 200. Grenfell and Hunt immediately published these noncanonical Jesus traditions, called Logia, under the title "Sayings of Our Lord," and these became an important source for New Testament research.

Dozens of chests containing the papyri were transported from Bahnasa to the British Museum, where they have been conserved, studied, and progressively published in what is today a multivolume series entitled The Oxyrhynchus Papyri. No less important, but written in Coptic, are the fourth-century papyri containing religious, gnostic texts that local fellahs found at Nag Hammadi (in Greek Khenoboskion) in Upper Egypt. Sayings of Jesus known from the Oxyrhynchus papyri appear in scrolls, too. Excavations in Egyptian oases and villages have brought us not only religious writings and administrative and legal records, but also many important works written in Greek from a period earlier than the papyri at Oxyrhynchus. These have included excerpts from Homer's *Iliad*, Aristotle's *Athenian Constitution*, and works by Plato, Aeschylus, Sophocles, Thucydides, and Sappho. Probably the oldest Greek work yet found in Egypt is *Persai* (The Persians), by Timotheus of Miletus from the fourth century BC, discovered in the pyramid cemetery in Abusir not far from Cairo.

It is generally thought that far more Greek literary works were preserved in Egypt than in Europe, but of course even in Egypt, what has actually survived (or what we have so far managed to find) is a mere fraction of what were the ordinary contents of the libraries of educated people in Ptolemaic, Roman, and Byzantine Egypt. The cultural level achieved by Egyptian multicultural society over the roughly six centuries from Alexander the Great's conquest of the country to Theodosius's adoption of Christianity as the state's religion was amazing. It is almost incredible that the millennia-old spiritual heritage of the relatively closed Egyptian society, highly distinctive, with a somewhat superior and distrustful attitude to surrounding nations, should ultimately have fused so profoundly with Greek culture and the intellectual currents of other eastern Mediterranean countries. This happened not only in Alexandria, which was a city both Egyptian and at the same time very un-Egyptian and significantly known as Alexandria ad Aegyptum ('Alexandria by Egypt'), but also in distant provincial towns and communities and even oases lost in the desert. When you pass through such places today, it is difficult to believe that a prosperous and sophisticated society once flowered here, a society that was part of the cultural elite of the ancient world, and where people took pleasure in reading Aristotle, Bacchylides, Sophocles, or the love poetry of Sappho. When Alexander the Great founded the capital of his empire by the island of Pharos he intended it to become the cultural as well as the political and economic center of the world. This dream was not to be fulfilled, but Alexandria—and Egypt by extension—has given more to Europe, the Orient, and the world than we can even imagine.

Final Excursus

A Brief Outline of the Overall Architectural History of the Ancient Egyptian Temple

View of the Great Hypostyle Hall in Karnak, from the south.

From its almost four millennia of continuous development from the Predynastic Period to the closure of the last ancient Egyptian temple (the Temple of Isis on the island of Philae by the First Nile Cataract), ancient Egypt might seem to the reader or tourist to have left behind so many temples, some in a surprisingly good state of preservation, that tracing their general architectural development ought to be quite a straightforward matter. Surely it should be quite easy to define overall stages in Egyptian sacred architecture, and create a classification of different types. In fact, it is very difficult indeed. From what we know at present, it is clear that there was no standard type of temple in ancient Egypt. We can therefore talk only of certain general features and general trends that came more or less to characterize their layout and design. Moreover, any attempt to reconstruct the development of temple architecture encounters serious problems of archaeological evidence. First and foremost, this evidence is often very scanty or absent, especially for the earlier periods of Egyptian history. Second, the Egyptian Temple of the god, unlike the royal mortuary temples, was never a finished, one-off work of architecture; each successive king would continue building activities in the temples of gods—demolishing, reconstructing, enlarging, embellishing—to show he could achieve "what had not been accomplished since the times of his forefathers."

Another set of problems arises when we try to classify temples into different types. For example, one possible typological distinction is between temples built of stone or brick on the one hand and rock temples—that is, temples carved wholly (speos) or half (hemispeos) from living rock—on the other hand. Another is between the temples of gods and the mortuary temples of kings. Yet then we find that the so-called 'temples of millions of years' fit on neither side of these distinctions. The British archaeologist Barry Kemp has put forward a classificatory framework for Egyptian temples that avoids these pitfalls by concentrating more on general form and style. His starting point is the premise that up to the late Middle Kingdom the Egyptian state had no great interest in provincial temples, and so he calls the latter 'pre-formal,' as opposed to the royal tomb complexes, which he calls 'early formal.' 'Pre-formal' temples are small, simple structures made of plant materials and mud bricks and reflecting local tradition. According to Kemp, the New Kingdom saw the emergence of the 'classical' type of large stone temple, which he terms the 'mature formal' style. Architectural development then ended in the Ptolemaic and Roman Periods with what he calls the 'late formal' temple. Kemp's classificatory scheme has been criticized by the American archaeologist David O'Connor, and it is obvious that it has numerous inadequacies when applied to many questions of the development of ancient Egyptian temples, but nonetheless Egyptologists use it as a working terminology.

The Predynastic Period

We are unable to establish just how far back into the past the roots of Egyptian temple development reach. As already mentioned, one major obstacle in this context is the lack of sufficient relevant archaeological evidence for the earlier periods. Even where it may be assumed to exist, it is often inaccessible as a result of natural conditions in the Nile Valley and Delta—that is, the earliest architectural monuments are buried beneath many layers of mud deposits. Frustratingly, in cases where it is technically possible to excavate them (as is evident, for example, from German archaeological research in the important Predynastic and Early Dynastic site of Tell al-Fara'in, or ancient Buto), this is almost prohibitively expensive. The groundwater level can be artificially lowered by sets of powerful pumps, and so archaeologists can gain a temporary, limited chance of getting down to the cultural layers at the bottom, that is, the earliest layers. Even where this is feasible, however, there is no need to emphasize that most buildings made of plant materials (and it was these that were used for the earliest shrines) have long ago completely disintegrated in these conditions.

The Neolithic calendar from Nabta in the Egyptian Western Desert has been moved to the garden of the Nubian Museum in Aswan.

The Cave of Swimmers in Wadi Sura in al-Gilf al-Kebir.

Fortunately the Nile Valley and Delta are not the only areas where we can hope to improve our scanty knowledge of the earliest Egyptian temples and cult places. Remarkable finds are being made in areas where nobody would have expected them, in very remote desert localities. A good example is the Nabta Playa ('playa' is an archaeological term for a dried-up lake) about a hundred kilometers west of Abu Simbel, which has been discovered and excavated by an American team headed by Fred Wendorf. Here, there are remains of a Neolithic dwelling complex and cemetery as well as two structures loosely assembled from stones. One of the latter consists of two long rows of monoliths, and is hard to interpret. The second is circular, with two pairs of larger monoliths placed opposite each other inside the circle. Detailed study has shown that a line running between these two pairs, or 'gates,' corresponds to the course of the sun at the summer solstice about six thousand years ago. The solstice was a key event in the life of the semi-nomadic shepherds who lived there at the time, because it heralded the arrival of the wet season, when there would occasionally be rain. The circle at Nabta is sometimes enthusiastically described as a "desert Stonehenge" and is believed to have been both a cult place and a calendar. It is likely that the inhabitants of Nabta and people from the wider surrounding area met here for various festivities and rituals marking important events.

In the cemetery at Nabta archaeologists have discovered large monoliths, sometimes weighing several tons, which must have been dragged from quarries about thirty kilometers away. Some of the monoliths have a roughly pyramid shape. A number of researchers believe that the origins not only of a fondness for megalithism, but also of the animal cults that were to become so characteristic a feature of ancient Egyptian religion and religious buildings, are to be found here in the desert, in the environment of the hunters, shepherds, and the first semi-settled farmers of the playa culture in the eighth to fourth millennia BC. In the desert areas of Egypt there are other sites where rituals (about which, unfortunately, we still know little in terms of what they involved or meant) were already conducted in the prehistoric age. One such site may be the Cave of Swimmers in the rugged and inaccessible al-Gilf al-Kebir range at the southern edge of the Great Sand Sea on the Egyptian–Libyan border.

The Early Dynastic Period and the Old Kingdom

Evidence of temples begins to mount up in the Nile Valley at the end of the prehistoric age, in the Late Naqada and Early Dynastic Eras. This is mainly a matter of writings and representations, but includes the first archaeological evidence for buildings of a sacred character. The earliest were simple buildings made of the plant materials so abundant in the Nile Valley—wood, rushes, and matting—but during the Early Dynastic Period the first buildings made of mud bricks start to appear. It is remarkable how typologically diverse such buildings were even at this early stage, as we can illustrate from the following selected examples.

In the first row from the top of an ivory tablet of King Hor Aha, which was discovered in Abydos by the English archaeologist Petrie, there is a representation of a shrine of the goddess Neith, venerated in the town of Sais in the Western Delta. It appears to be a structure made of wooden stakes with rush matting stretched between them. The front section of the

Drawn reconstruction of the shrine of the goddess Neith, worshipped in Sais, based on a depiction on the ivory tablet of Horus Aha from Hierakonpolis.

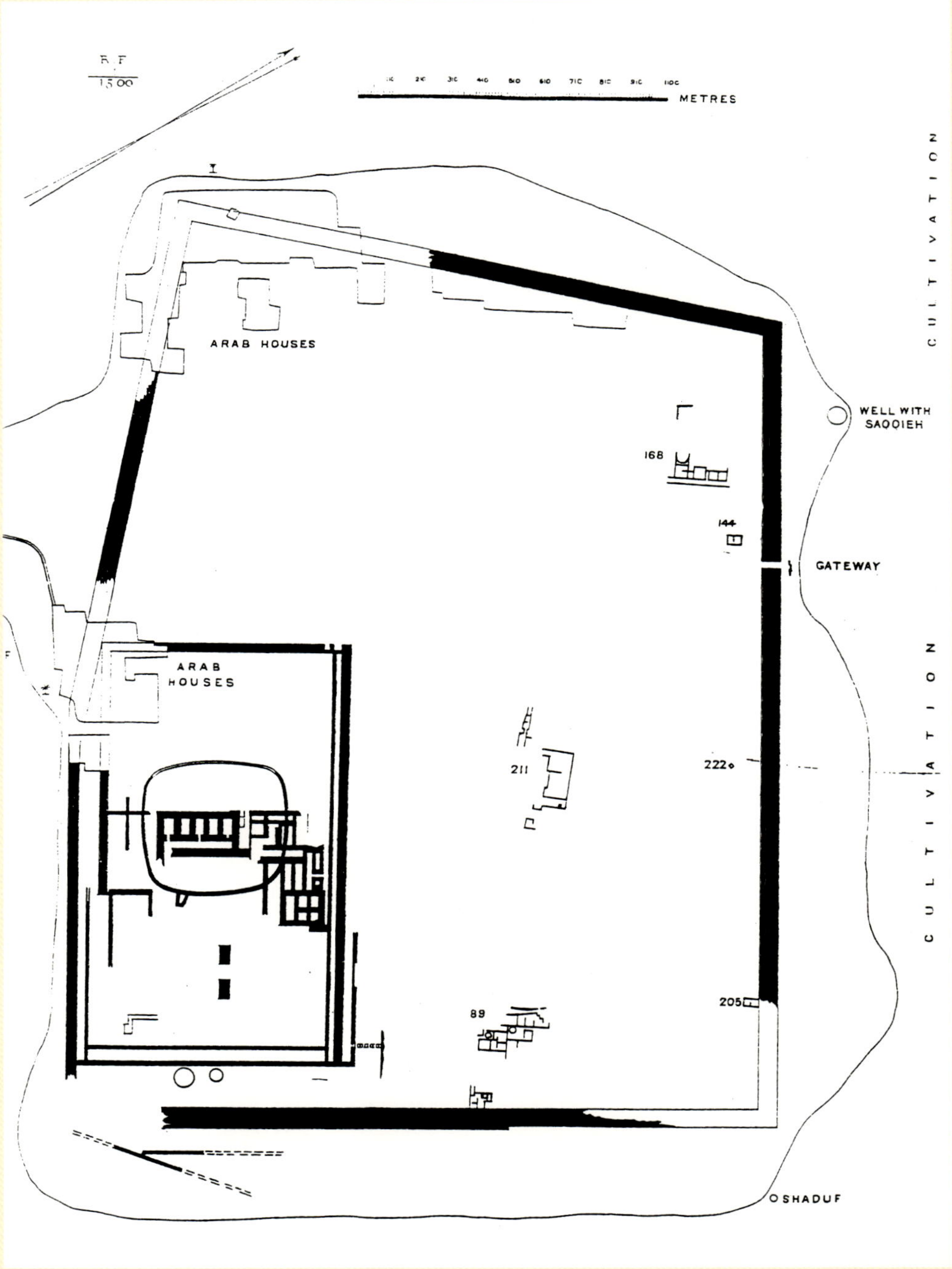
R.F.
1500
METRES
CULTIVATION
ARAB HOUSES
WELL WITH SAQQIEH
168
144
GATEWAY
ARAB HOUSES
211
222
CULTIVATION
205
89
SHADUF

building is an enclosed courtyard, its façade adorned with a pair of poles with banners. In the middle of the courtyard is a standard with the characteristic symbol of the goddess: a shield with two crossed arrows on it. The rear section consists of a simple building with arched roof: a sanctuary with a cult statue.

≪Plan of the Horus temple district in Hierakonpolis.

At the end of the 1890s the English archaeologists James Edward Quibell (1867–1935) and Frederick William Green (1869–1949) discovered a large, roughly circular mound faced with pieces of sandstone in the Upper Egyptian locality of Kom al-Ahmar, in Egyptian Nekhen (known in Greek as Hierakonpolis), which was the place of the cult of the falcon god Horus called Nekheny ('of Nekhen') and the political center of predynastic Egypt. On the mound, which probably symbolizes the mythical primordial mound, the archaeologists found the remains of a building that may be reconstructed as having been a simple, roughly north–south oriented temple made of mud bricks on a rectangular ground plan. It had an entrance from the south and consisted of a courtyard and sanctuary with three rooms. It is thought that in sanctuaries of this type the middle room was an offering chamber (offerings were placed on an altar here), while there were cult statues in each of the side chambers. This building may date from the Middle Kingdom but could be older. The English archaeologists discovered a set of cult objects in the ruins, including the famous slate palette of the First Dynasty king Narmer.

An American team working in Hierakonpolis for more than two decades made another important find. South of a circular mound the team found the remains of a building dating from the Predynastic Period, and which is now considered to be the earliest archaeological evidence of an Egyptian temple. The word 'remains' is perhaps something of an exaggeration, since what survives of the building is mainly just imprints in the ground, which show that it was built of wooden stakes and rush matting. The open façade of this temple, evidently devoted to the worship of the local falcon god, was adorned with four wooden poles. In front of the temple there was an oval court enclosed by a rush fence.

The Shrine of Min.

Petrie had made another significant discovery during archaeological excavations in the years 1893–94 in Upper Egyptian Koptos, center of the cult of the fertility god Min (originally perhaps a god worshiped by the nomad Medjau in the Eastern Desert). On the site of the main Min temple, among many other valuable artifacts, Petrie found fragments of three colossal ithyphallic limestone statues. Typologically these are very old statues that are now dated to the late Naqada period or the reign of the First Dynasty king Narmer. According to the American Egyptologist Bruce Williams, the name of Min was carved into one of the statues secondarily (that is, at a later date than the statue was made). The statues were originally almost four meters high. It is believed that they originally stood in a temple, which, given their size, must have been quite large. The Temple of Min was originally constructed of rushes and to judge by later representations had a circular ground plan and arched roof. A post with the symbol of Min stood by the temple.

Not every Early Dynastic shrine was built of wooden posts, matting, and rushes. By this time some were already built of mud bricks, while others were constructed in more unconventional ways. One example is what is so far the oldest shrine known to us; it is on the island of Elephantine by the First Nile Cataract. This was a shrine to the lady of the island, the goddess Satet. Her cult place was hollow, roughly 4 × 3.5 meters and 3.5 meters tall between huge granite blocks. The origins of the shrine go back to the end of the prehistoric era, the period of Naqada culture, and so before the unification of Egypt. The cave shrine was gradually enlarged and at the beginning of the Middle Kingdom was replaced by a new temple to Satet.

Cave shrine on Elephantine dedicated to Satet, the goddess of the First Nile Cataract and partner of Khnum, lord of the cataract.

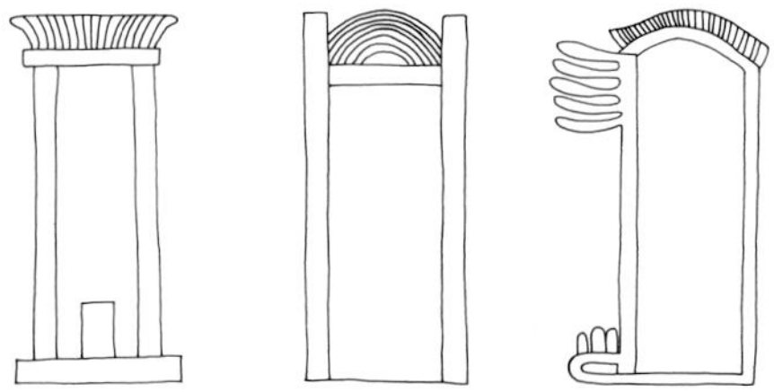

Stylized form of the earliest types of ancient Egyptian shrine (from the left, *seh-netjer*, *per-nu*, and *per-wer*).

In the Early Dynastic Period two main types of shrine building gradually crystallized: the Upper Egyptian type, known as *per wer*, and the Lower Egyptian type, *per nu*. The shrine of the falcon god Horus in Hierakonpolis mentioned above probably represented the *per wer* ('great house') type, while the shrine of the vulture goddess Nekhbet, the protector goddess of Upper Egypt worshiped in nearby Kab, may well have been similar. A *per wer* was a structure made of wooden stakes and matting and seen from the side may have resembled the silhouette of an elephant or rhinoceros. Later, this type of building became identified with the land (whole region), acquiring the name *iteret Shema* ('the shrine of Upper Egypt'). It was a coronation shrine in the royal town, where the White Crown of Upper Egypt was placed on the king's head. The stylized façade of a *per wer*, rendered in fine white limestone, was used in the decoration of the courtyard of the *sed* festival in the pyramid complex of Djoser.

The *per nu*, later the land and coronation shrine of *iteret Mehet* ('the shrine of Lower Egypt'), seems to have had its original prototype in the shrine of the cobra Wadyet, the protector goddess of Lower Egypt worshiped in Buto. This shrine was also made of wooden stakes and matting. It is thought that the earliest rulers of Lower Egypt were buried in tombs resembling in shape this shrine in Buto, in a sacred grove on the bank of a winding canal. We can find a stylized form of this shrine in the decoration of the *sed* festival court by the Step Pyramid. As early as the Old Kingdom, the royal type of sarcophagus also acquired the stylized form of *per nu*.

At the beginning of the Third Dynasty, king Netjerikhet, later called Djoser, managed to consolidate the country after a period of political instability in Egypt at the end of the Early Dynastic Period and to establish a powerful, well organized, and effectively governed state. The prosperity of the state as well as the king's exclusive position within it was expressed in Djoser's tomb complex: a set of stone temples, chapels, stores, colonnades, and courts, all dominated by the king's tomb in the shape of a step pyramid and all enclosed by a huge ditch and stone wall. The complex is partly functional, partly symbolic in character, and is conceived as the

The Step Pyramid of King Netjerikhet, later called Djoser, which is the earliest known example of monumental stone architecture in the world. In the foreground is what is known as the courtyard of the *sed* festival with stylized models of the chapels of Upper and Lower Egypt.

king's residence in the other world. It is probable that the architects were inspired by the ruler's earthly residence. From the point of view of architectural history, the complex is a unique example of the combination of Early Dynastic archetypes taken over from the buildings in light plant materials and the new building material—limestone. Stone, for example limestone or red granite, had been used before and has been identified in Early Dynastic royal buildings made of mud bricks, but it was in Djoser's complex in Saqqara that it was first used on a large scale. It is here that we encounter the oldest stone columns in shapes copying plant models such as papyrus, lilies, sedge, or just bundles of reeds. Here, for the first time, we find typical Egyptian building elements emerging through a literal copying in stone of certain details from the archaic structures made of plant materials. The torus (originally the fastening of the external corners of the matting walls using string or a strap, but then figuratively in stone as a rounded band with a zigzag line), or the concave cornice (originally the outward-curving and slightly shaken-out upper edge of the rushes or matting stretched on a frame of wooden posts) are two examples of such elements. In architectural history the combination of the concave cornice with a torus is known as the 'Egyptian gorge' and appears in ancient Egyptian architecture throughout its several millennia of continuous development.

Djoser's complex was also the material embodiment of the fundamental idea of the ancient Egyptian state: The king was the mediator between gods and men and at the same time the chief guarantor of the order of the

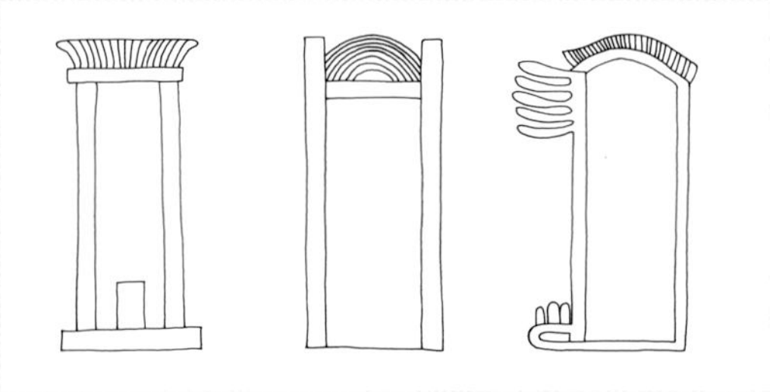

Stylized form of the earliest types of ancient Egyptian shrine (from the left, *seh-netjer*, *per-nu*, and *per-wer*).

In the Early Dynastic Period two main types of shrine building gradually crystallized: the Upper Egyptian type, known as *per wer*, and the Lower Egyptian type, *per nu*. The shrine of the falcon god Horus in Hierakonpolis mentioned above probably represented the *per wer* ('great house') type, while the shrine of the vulture goddess Nekhbet, the protector goddess of Upper Egypt worshiped in nearby Kab, may well have been similar. A *per wer* was a structure made of wooden stakes and matting and seen from the side may have resembled the silhouette of an elephant or rhinoceros. Later, this type of building became identified with the land (whole region), acquiring the name *iteret Shema* ('the shrine of Upper Egypt'). It was a coronation shrine in the royal town, where the White Crown of Upper Egypt was placed on the king's head. The stylized façade of a *per wer*, rendered in fine white limestone, was used in the decoration of the courtyard of the *sed* festival in the pyramid complex of Djoser.

The *per nu*, later the land and coronation shrine of *iteret Mehet* ('the shrine of Lower Egypt'), seems to have had its original prototype in the shrine of the cobra Wadyet, the protector goddess of Lower Egypt worshiped in Buto. This shrine was also made of wooden stakes and matting. It is thought that the earliest rulers of Lower Egypt were buried in tombs resembling in shape this shrine in Buto, in a sacred grove on the bank of a winding canal. We can find a stylized form of this shrine in the decoration of the *sed* festival court by the Step Pyramid. As early as the Old Kingdom, the royal type of sarcophagus also acquired the stylized form of *per nu*.

At the beginning of the Third Dynasty, king Netjerikhet, later called Djoser, managed to consolidate the country after a period of political instability in Egypt at the end of the Early Dynastic Period and to establish a powerful, well organized, and effectively governed state. The prosperity of the state as well as the king's exclusive position within it was expressed in Djoser's tomb complex: a set of stone temples, chapels, stores, colonnades, and courts, all dominated by the king's tomb in the shape of a step pyramid and all enclosed by a huge ditch and stone wall. The complex is partly functional, partly symbolic in character, and is conceived as the

The Step Pyramid of King Netjerikhet, later called Djoser, which is the earliest known example of monumental stone architecture in the world. In the foreground is what is known as the courtyard of the *sed* festival with stylized models of the chapels of Upper and Lower Egypt.

king's residence in the other world. It is probable that the architects were inspired by the ruler's earthly residence. From the point of view of architectural history, the complex is a unique example of the combination of Early Dynastic archetypes taken over from the buildings in light plant materials and the new building material—limestone. Stone, for example limestone or red granite, had been used before and has been identified in Early Dynastic royal buildings made of mud bricks, but it was in Djoser's complex in Saqqara that it was first used on a large scale. It is here that we encounter the oldest stone columns in shapes copying plant models such as papyrus, lilies, sedge, or just bundles of reeds. Here, for the first time, we find typical Egyptian building elements emerging through a literal copying in stone of certain details from the archaic structures made of plant materials. The torus (originally the fastening of the external corners of the matting walls using string or a strap, but then figuratively in stone as a rounded band with a zigzag line), or the concave cornice (originally the outward-curving and slightly shaken-out upper edge of the rushes or matting stretched on a frame of wooden posts) are two examples of such elements. In architectural history the combination of the concave cornice with a torus is known as the 'Egyptian gorge' and appears in ancient Egyptian architecture throughout its several millennia of continuous development.

Djoser's complex was also the material embodiment of the fundamental idea of the ancient Egyptian state: The king was the mediator between gods and men and at the same time the chief guarantor of the order of the

Passage, with entrance columns, into the precinct of the Step Pyramid, Djoser's residence in the next world.

world and prosperity of the people during their lives and after death. The building of his eternal, indestructible tomb was the principal task of the whole country during his lifetime, because to preserve the king even after death in mummified form guaranteed the eternal prosperity of the "people of his time" as well. The king's exceptional position in the Old Kingdom was also reflected in the fact that the temples of the cults of gods were far more modest buildings than the divine temples of the royal cult. The former were usually constructed from mud bricks, while the latter were large, complex stone structures with rich polychrome relief decoration. The difference in economic position was also very great: the temples of the royal cult, also known as mortuary temples, were richly endowed with revenues from numerous estates allocated or newly established for the purpose, whereas the temples of the gods had far more modest incomes. Furthermore, the royal mortuary temples were not freely accessible to the public and employed a relatively large number of priests and secular staff.

Yet even in the Early Dynastic Period there were already signs that the advancing cult of the sun god was starting to undermine the unambiguously supreme position of the king, despite the fact that on the theological level the king's destiny in life and after death was so closely linked to the sun god. A temple of the sun god already existed in Heliopolis and from the beginning of the Old Kingdom, at the latest, had become the most important religious center of the country. We can only speculate on its appearance at this time, since although Heliopolis is one of the most

Remains of the Ptolemaic–Roman temple of Montu in Medamud.

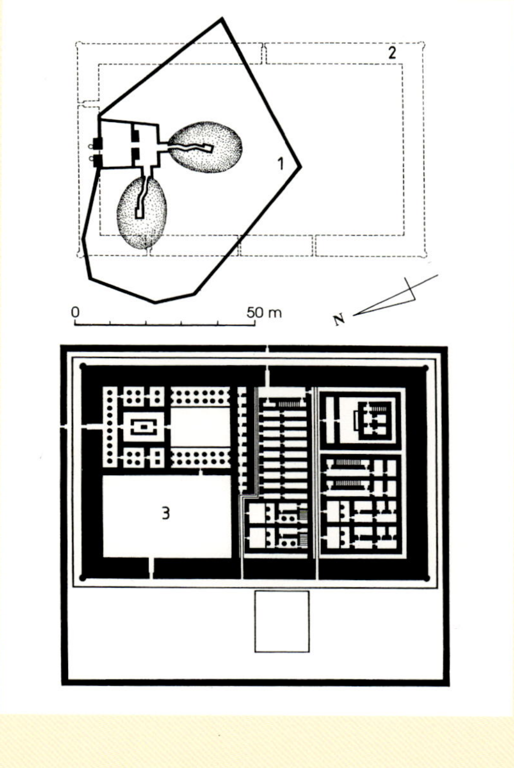

>Plan of the temple of Montu in Medamud.
1. original Old Kingdom temple
2. enclosure wall of Middle Kingdom temple
3. Middle Kingdom temple with enclosure wall and sacred pool.

important archaeological localities of Egypt and the entire ancient world, it has not been systematically excavated and its monuments and history have not been thoroughly researched. On the basis of written sources it is thought that the cult fetish the *benben* stone, which some believe to have been a conical or pyramidal boulder possibly of meteoric origin, was kept in the temple in Heliopolis. This fetish then found stylized symbolic form in obelisks. At present, our earliest material evidence of a sacred building in Heliopolis consists of fragments of a limestone case from the early Third Dynasty, perhaps originally located in the sun temple complex, with remnants of relief scenes and inscriptions mentioning the gods of the Heliopolitan Ennead (see chapter 2).

From the time of the unification of Egypt and the founding of the capital city Memphis at the beginning of the First Dynasty the Memphite Temple of Ptah must also have been very important. In this case too we have no idea of its earliest form. Ptah's epithet 'Ptah Who Is South of His Wall,' which already appears in texts from the Old Kingdom, means that logically it must have been south of the capital, which at this time was the fortress of 'White Wall.' Some recent archaeological finds during British explorations in Memphis suggest that the oldest part of the Temple of Ptah might lie under the hillock of Kom al-Fakhri, today covered by the village of Mit Rahina (see chapter 3).

The remains of a remarkable mysterious mythical cult site resembling an Old Kingdom temple were discovered in the 1930s by the French archaeologists Clément Robichon (1906–99) and Alexandre Varille (1909–51) in Medamud in Upper Egypt. The temple, probably devoted to the worship of Osiris, consisted of two courtyards each entered through a pylon. From the second courtyard there was access by two irregular passages to the sanctuaries buried under artificially created oval hillocks. Numerous remains of charcoal found at the same site suggest that the hillocks originally lay in a sacred grove. Originally, the whole temple precinct was enclosed by an irregular whitewashed wall of polygonal ground plan; Senwosret III later built a large new temple on its ruins.

In the eastern Delta at the locality Tell Ibrahim Awad, which was already a small provincial town by the beginning of the Early Dynastic Period, a Dutch archaeological team found a small temple that is regarded as an example of the 'pre-formal' type. It was a simple building on a right-angled ground plan made of mud bricks and oriented roughly north–south. In the middle of the temple the statue of a god had stood in a case on a low pedestal. It is not known which particular god it was. Two deposits of cult objects were discovered under the case. It is notable that this 'pre-formal' temple existed with minor alterations for another twelve centuries.

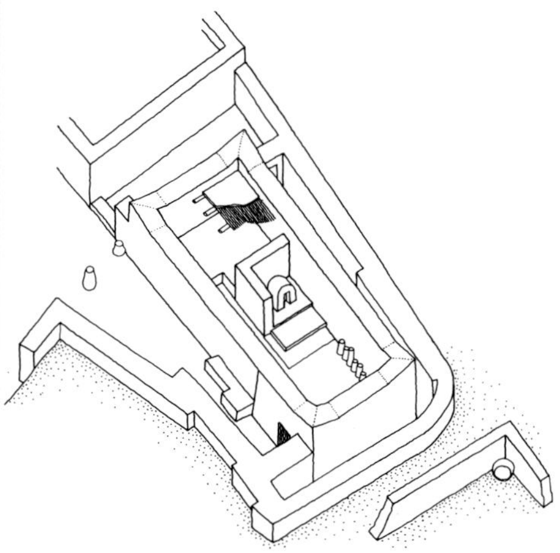

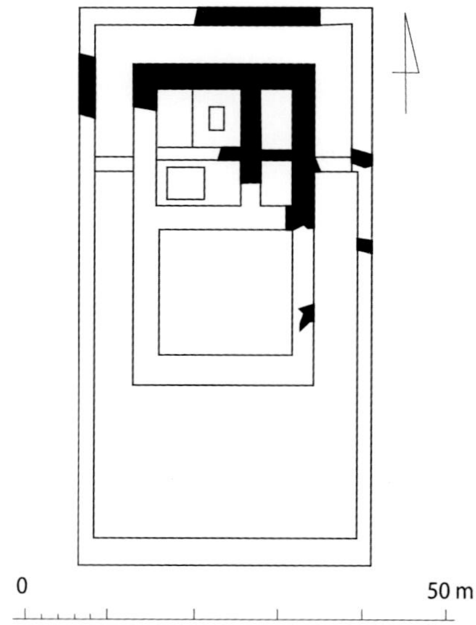

Reconstruction of an Old Kingdom temple of Tell Ibrahim Awad.

>>Unfortunately, a few sad ruins are all that is left of the *ka* house of Pepi I by the temple of Bastet in Bubastis.

The end of the Old Kingdom saw the appearance of a type of temple called a '*ka*-house.' These chapels were built by both kings and private individuals. It is thought that cult statues of the *ka* of those to whom the chapels belonged were placed inside. In this way, the owners of the chapels wanted to pay homage to the god and also secure permanent participation in his cult. The remains of the almost entirely destroyed *ka*-houses of the Sixth Dynasty kings Pepi I and Teti are to be found in Tell Basta, for example; as far as private persons are concerned, the *ka* house of the administrator of the southernmost Egyptian nome, Heqaib, on Elephantine Island is particularly well known. Numerous *ka*-houses have been found in Abydos (see pp. 350–51).

In this brief selection of Old Kingdom temples we should not forget two kinds of temples that were characteristic of the period but are also surrounded by many obscurities. The solar temples built during the Fifth Dynasty in the Memphis necropolis represent the first type (they have been discussed in more detail in chapter 2). The never satisfactorily explained Temple of the Sphinx in Giza is considered to be a peculiar type of solar temple. The second type of temple, about which we can only speculate at present, is that of the *meret* sanctuaries. None have yet been found and they are known only from written records of the period. It is thought that Hathor and her son Ihy, and also the god Re, with whom the dead king was perhaps identified, were worshiped in these sanctuaries. They may well have

been closely connected with the royal mortuary cult and it is possible these were the places where the mystery of the 'sacred marriage' (known in Greek as *hieros gamos*) was conducted—a rite that was supposed to ensure the fertility of people, cattle, and the fields, and thus the entire country's prosperity.

However patchy the archaeological evidence, it is clear that a number of basic features and elements characteristic of ancient Egyptian temple

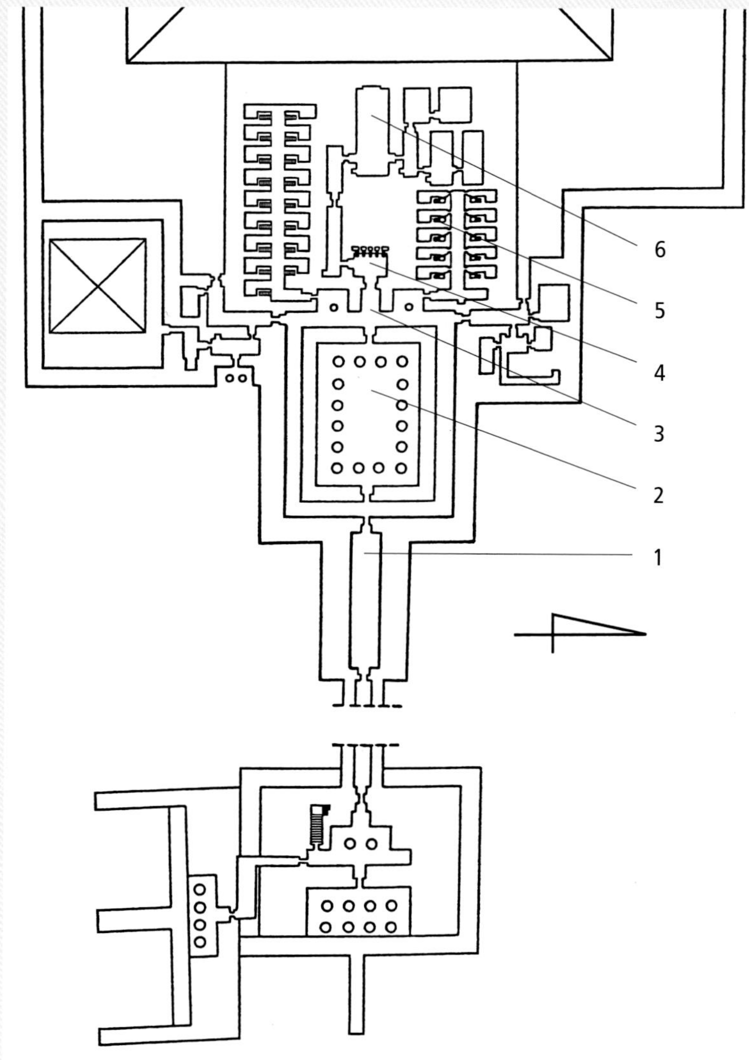

Plan of the mortuary temple of Sahure in Abusir.
1. entrance hall
2. columned court
3. transverse passage
4. chapel with five niches
5. storerooms
6. offering hall

architecture stabilized during the Old Kingdom. Temples were now generally buildings on a rectangular ground plan oriented to the points of the compass and protected from the outside world by a massive enclosure wall, its outer side sloped slightly inward from the base in the interest of greater stability. Inside the wall, the temple was divided into right-angled, symmetrically arranged sections. In the front part of the building there would be an

The rather mysterious temple in Qasr al-Sagha on the western edge of the Fayoum Oasis. We do not know to whom it was dedicated.

open courtyard accessible to the public, and in the rear section the shadowy cult sanctuary with the statue of the god, permitted only to the priests.

As far as the royal mortuary temples are concerned, it is thought that their architecture made use of elements copied from the royal palaces; for example, the Temple of Raneferef contains the oldest known great hypostyle hall, which may have been inspired by the throne hall of the ruler's earthly palace. Various architectonic elements like pillars, simple and stemmed columns inspired by floral models (papyrus, lotus, and palm), and statues became usual features of mortuary temples in this period. The types of column have a deeper religious meaning relating to ideas of rebirth, eternal life, peace, and fertility. The statues were mainly of the king in his various ruling and mythical roles, but we also find statues of kneeling bound enemies with Asian, Nubian, and Libyan features, embodying the mythic external evil that threatened Egypt and its god-given order.

The First Intermediate Period and the Middle Kingdom

The political and economic decline of the Old Kingdom ended in a period of upheaval and chaos. Egypt fell apart and armed conflicts, unrest, and hunger resulted. Although conditions were eventually stabilized and consolidated, the events of this First Intermediate Period had serious social consequences. As several literary works of the period show, what had previously been fundamental values, including faith in the divine authority of the king, were seriously shaken. The royal tombs were looted. What is more, belief in the gods, the divine order of the world, and even life after death was undermined. It was not until the end of the Eleventh Dynasty that the Upper Egyptian rulers based in Thebes managed to reunite Egypt, impose order, renew the authority of the king, and centralize the power of the state, ushering in what we know as the Middle Kingdom. The circumstances of the unification of the country, as well as the memories of the preceding period of anarchy and decline, had a major effect on future development. One of the new features of the state was a change in the status of the king and the gods. At the risk of oversimplification, it can be said that while the authority of the king was restored, it was no longer comparable to royal power and prestige at the height of the Old Kingdom (which had in fact already been weakening toward the end of that period). By contrast, the importance of the gods increased, especially Amun, the local god of the Theban nome from which the line of rulers who reunited Egypt came. Osiris dominated ideas about the afterlife.

One important expression of the renewed power and prosperity of the ancient Egyptian state was the initiation of extensive temple building. The architecture of these temples drew on the tradition of the Old Kingdom as created, above all, by the builders and artists in the milieu of the former political center, Memphis, but other elements characteristic of Southern Egypt make an appearance, such as façades adorned with a row of pillars. The pattern that emerged was one of symmetrical arrangement of spaces along the main axis of the temple; in the rear part there would be a building with three chambers and in the front an open court, all of this surrounded by an enclosure wall. There could be fewer chambers than three, or more; for example, the temple in Qasr al-Sagha in the Fayoum Oasis has seven chambers. Another development was the appearance of a vestibule, sometimes with columns or pillars, in front of the chambers. The front wall of the enclosure wall of the temple acquired the form of a pylon—a massive structure with two towers and between them an entrance gate on the main axis of the temple.

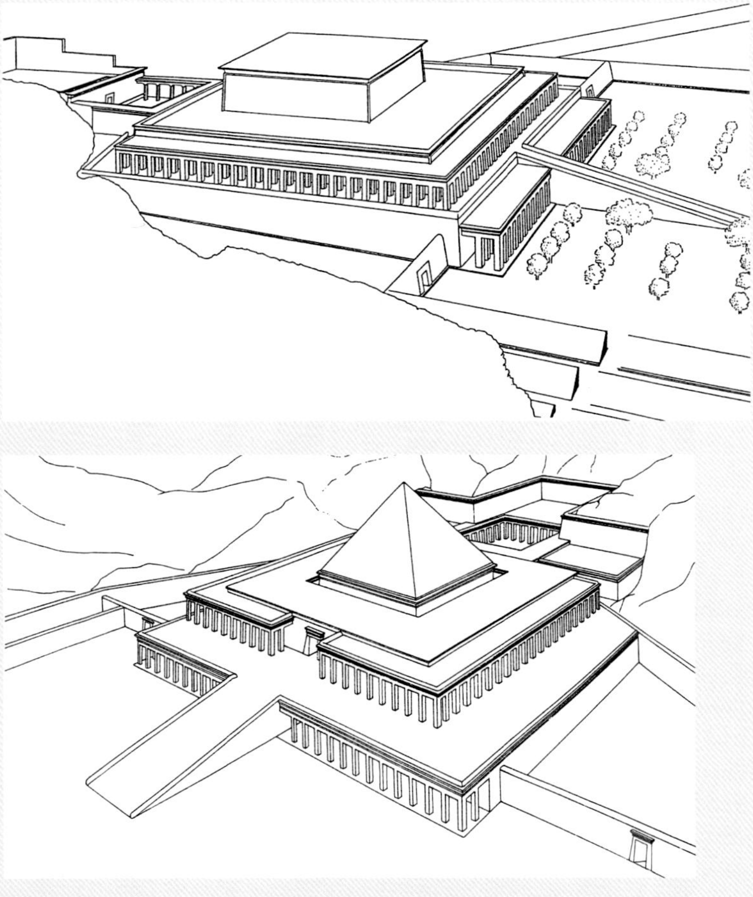

Reconstructions of the funerary monument of Mentuhotep II in Deir al-Bahri, according to Arnold (top) and Naville

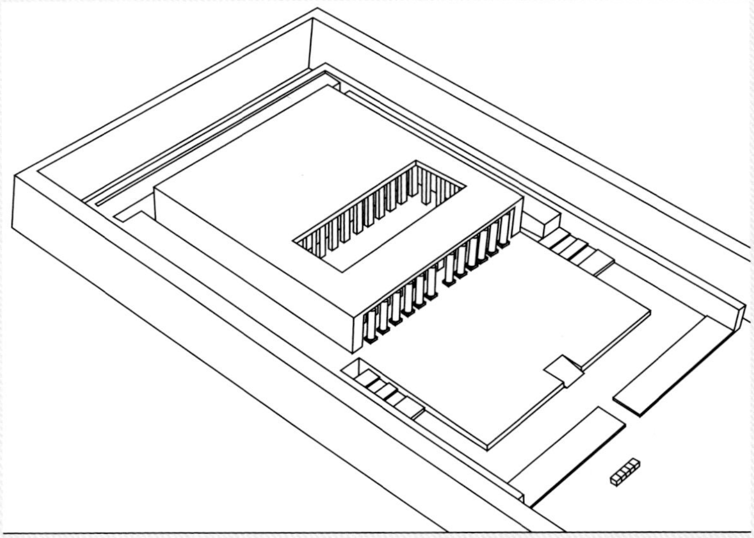

Reconstruction of the temple of Amun in Karnak under Senwosret I, drawn according to Charloux.

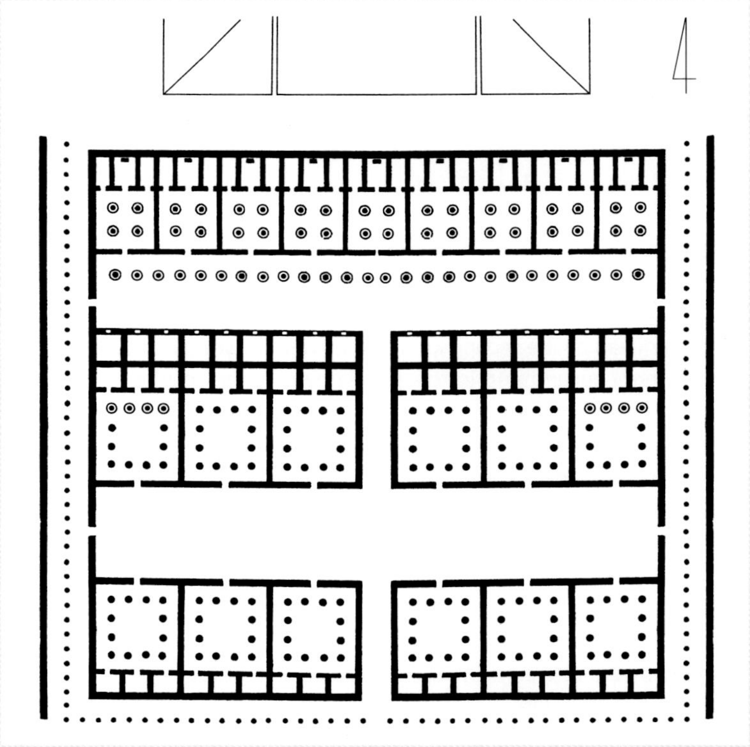

Plan of the northern part of the mortuary temple of Amenemhet III in Hawara, the 'labyrinth' of travelers in the ancient world.

The pyramid of Amenemhet III in Hawara.

which was probably the original setting of the White Chapel of Senwosret I—a new type of cult building conceived as a resting place for the barque with the statue of the god Amun that would be carried out in processions. This chapel—from a typological point of view, a small kiosk—was in the form of an open case, standing on a low base, and accessible by two low staircase ramps built on opposite sides. The edge of the roof was adorned with a concave cornice and supported by four pillars, together with another four pillars inside the chapel around the pedestal for the sacred barque; this ensured that the barque containing the statue of the god would be visible from all four sides. The whole temple may have been surrounded by a grove.

During the Twelfth Dynasty, temples of the gods were built on an increasingly large scale and interiors were ever more subdivided. One vivid example is the Temple of Montu built north of Karnak in Medamud by Senwosret III (see pp. 219–21) and progressively altered by kings of the Thirteenth Dynasty. It was built on the site of the Old Kingdom temple already mentioned. It likewise had a rectangular ground plan oriented roughly north–south and a double enclosure wall. It was constructed of mud brick except for limestone architectural features such as columns, lintels, doorjambs, and so on. There were hypostyle halls and courts in the northern part of the temple, rows of narrow storerooms in the central part, and cult rooms in the rear and southernmost part of the temple. A royal palace may have stood in the northwestern part of the complex. Blocks with scenes from the *sed* festival, Osiris columns, statues of Senwosret III, and other artifacts have been found in the ruins of the temple.

The trend during the Middle Kingdom toward greater subdivision of space affected not only temples of the gods but also royal mortuary temples. One example is the pyramid complex of the last great king of the Middle Kingdom, Amenemhet III, in Hawara in the Fayoum Oasis and his mortuary temple with its large hypostyle halls, identified by writers of antiquity with the legendary Labyrinth. If we consider the longer perspective of the evolution of the temple in the Middle Kingdom it is evident that the development initiated by Mentuhotep II, in whose buildings a series of new partially local elements of Upper Egyptian origin are identifiable, was later inhibited by the decision of the founder of the Twelfth Dynasty, Amenemhet I, to move the center of government of the country (in the interest of stability) from southern Egypt to the Lisht area, closer to the former capital Memphis and the ever more economically important Fayoum Oasis. Here, the Memphite architectural tradition deriving from the Old Kingdom was very strong and it substantially influenced the local architecture of the Middle Kingdom, especially the royal pyramid complexes. These conservative retro-inspirations were exhausted quite soon, however, and were succeeded by a period of exploration for new possibilities and ways forward.

The Second Intermediate Period and the New Kingdom

During the Thirteenth Dynasty the country experienced another period of economic and political decline and the central power was once again fractured. Local rulers gained the upper hand, with the onset of what is known as the Second Intermediate Period. Northern Egypt eventually fell under the sway of Semitic tribes from the Near East, the Hyksos—'the rulers of desert lands'—during this period. The Egyptians also lost control of Nubia. Once again, it was the rulers of Upper Egyptian Thebes who led the fight for reunification, eventually driving the Semitic interlopers out in pitiless battles at the end of the Seventeenth Dynasty; Ahmose I, founder of the Eighteenth Dynasty, sealed the victory over the Hyksos. Unlike the rulers of the Old and Middle Kingdoms, the kings of this dynasty adopted an imperial policy and embarked on a series of wars of conquest. In a short period, they built an empire without parallel in the history of Egypt, which during

The temple of Ramesses II in Wadi al-Sebua was one of the monuments in Nubia that were moved and saved during the UNESCO international rescue project.

the reign of Thutmose III reached from the Euphrates in the north to the Fourth Nile Cataract in the south.

Enormous wealth flowed into Egypt in the form of booty from the wars of conquest and the tributes paid by vassal states. The greatest part of the booty went to the Temple of Amun in Karnak, but other important temples, especially that of Re in Heliopolis and Ptah in Memphis, were hardly losers. Amenhotep I, the second king of the Eighteenth Dynasty, immediately embarked on the enlargement of the Temple of Amun, reconstructing the work of Senwosret I in the area known as the Middle Kingdom Court. Ever grander buildings followed in quick succession as each Eighteenth Dynasty king sought to outdo his predecessor. An immense temple complex grew up along the east–west axis of Karnak, with monumental pylon towers, obelisks, courts, hypostyle halls, and chapels (see chapter 5). Ambitious programs of renovation of older temples and construction of new temples dedicated to various gods were launched in many other places in Egypt, as well as in territories under Egyptian control, especially Nubia.

Temples maintained conceptual continuity with the buildings of the Middle Kingdom, but soon started to exceed them in size and internal complexity. The road to the entrance of the temple was now often an avenue of sphinxes with an apotropaic purpose (to ward off evil), the pylon's two massive towers guarded the entrance, and there was an array of poles with banners, obelisks, and colossal royal statues in front of the pylon. Temple areas and interiors previously built next to each other were sequenced (and further subdivided) in a fixed order during this period; that is, key cult interiors were arranged successively along the main axis of the temple.

The court beyond the entrance gate was the last area to which, on special festival occasions, the public would be admitted. The areas deeper into the temple's interior were reserved for priests and high-ranking dignitaries; access to the sanctuary was restricted to the king and a few initiated priests. A hypostyle hall leading off the open court symbolized the mythical marshy thicket in which life had been born and where the god Horus had been hidden from his pursuer Seth as a child. In the next interior, the 'offering hall,' sacrificial gifts would be assembled three times a day according to the temple ritual, while the interior beyond that, the 'hall of the Nine,' was the dwelling place of the gods accompanying and protecting the main temple god. The next room along the axis would be the 'hall of the barque,' immediately preceding the sanctuary, where the barque containing the statue of the god known as the 'noble god' in a wooden case would rest on a stone pedestal. The cult statue of the god known as the 'sacred' rested in a gilded sealed wooden shrine within a stone case within the sanctuary.

It should be stressed that this arrangement of the interiors along the main temple axis became wholly conventional from the New Kingdom onward. As visitors went deeper into a temple, they moved from the sun-drenched court to the half-illuminated hypostyle hall, to a dimmer hypostyle hall, and continued inward until—if they had been initiated—they reached the sanctuary, which was enshrouded in complete darkness. This progress would be accompanied by less noticeable changes, especially in the diminishing light: moving toward the interior of the temple, the floor of each room was a little higher and the ceiling a little lower. In this way, visitors were led to a sense of gradual withdrawal from the disruptive influence of the outside world and to cultivate an ever greater concentration and preparation for their meeting with the god.

The temple incorporated a pool, fed either by groundwater or by a canal from the flood, which was believed to spring from the primordial waters. The priests performed their daily ritual self-purification in the pool, but the pool also had a role in some festivals and ceremonies.

The terraced mortuary temple of Hatshepsut was not only harmoniously composed within the rock amphitheatre in Deir al-Bahri, but its east–west axis was aligned with the east–west axis of the temple of Amun in Karnak on the opposite bank of the Nile.

At the beginning of the New Kingdom there was a relatively brief fashion for columned or pillared frontage on all sides of the temple, but from the second half of the Eighteenth Dynasty (from the reign of Amenhotep III) only the façade on the main axis of the temple remained open, and so the great hypostyle hall was the temple's first interior space.

In the New Kingdom the solar shrine with a court open to the sky became a new and important component of temples. The earliest example is to be found in the Temple of Hatshepsut in Deir al-Bahri. In modified form this type of shrine briefly became central to the new concept of the temple associated with the dramatic religious reforms made by Amenhotep IV (Akhenaten). In a sharp break in continuity the existing concept of the divine temple was abandoned and replaced by another, which architecturally expressed the new religion of the one god Aten, manifest in the form of a solar disc. The dark, mysterious places were banished and the temple wholly opened up to the flood of sunlight (see chapter 6). Walls full of pictures of gods and mythical and ritual scenes gave way to great open courts full of altars for daily offerings to Aten. After Akhenaten's death and the rejection of his reforms, however, the architectural development of temples returned to its original track.

Ramesses II launched an ambitious program of architectural renovation of earlier temples and the construction of new ones in various places in Egypt. He also turned his attention to Nubia, as we can see from the great rock temples that he had built in Abu Simbel, Beit al-Wali, Gerf Hussein, Wadi al-Sebua, Derr, and Abu Simbel, and also a temple in Aksha south of Wadi Halfa on what is now Sudanese territory.

During the New Kingdom the new type of temple known as the 'temple of millions of years,' which combined the mortuary temple and divine temple, also developed to the full. Here, the central sanctuary was reserved for Amun and the royal cult had its place in the secondary interiors of the temple. Examples include not only the famous temples in western Thebes such as Hatshepsut's in Deir al-Bahri, Ramesses II's Ramesseum or the Temple of Ramesses III in Medinet Habu, and Ramesses II's rock temples, but also (according to some Egyptologists) individual buildings like Sethi I's Great

The entrance gate of the mortuary temple precinct of Ramesses III in Medinet Habu resembles a fortress tower.

Hypostyle Hall in Amun's temple complex in Karnak and Sethi I's temple in Abydos. It can be said that the developmental trends identifiable in temple building up to this point culminated in the Twentieth Dynasty, particularly in two of Ramesses III's buildings: the mortuary temple in Medinet Habu and the Temple of Khonsu in Karnak. In terms of their plans, both buildings were to provide inspiration for temple builders in the following period.

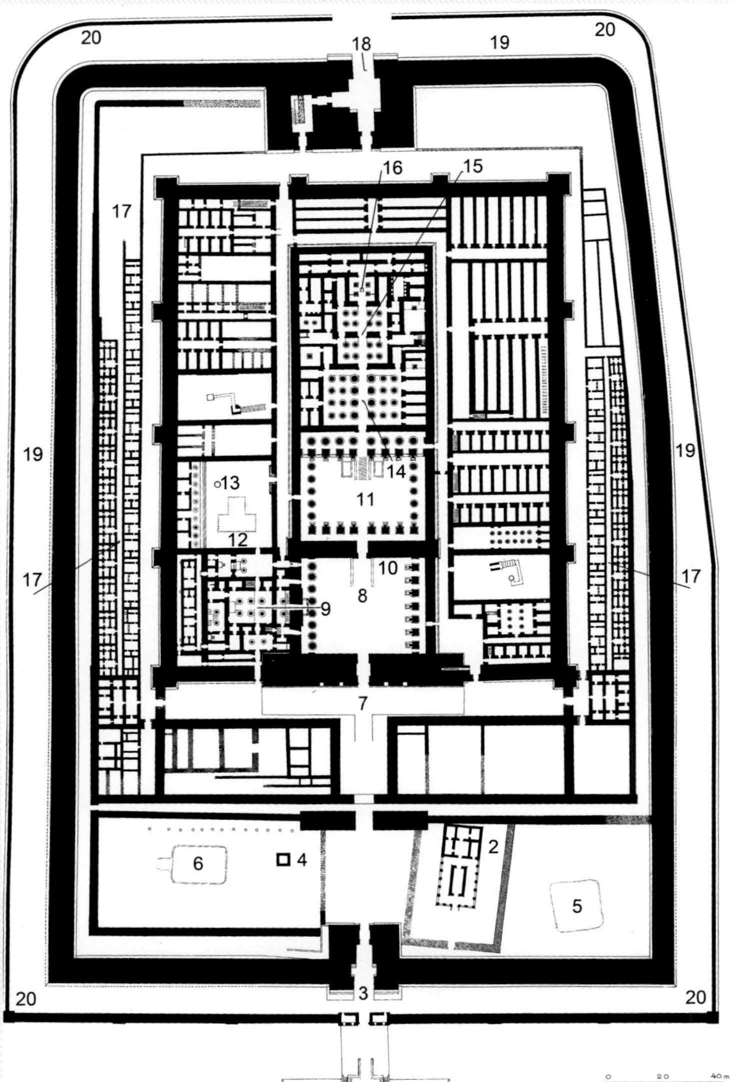

Plan of the temple district in Medinet Habu.
1. quay
2. small temple
3. entrance gate in the form of a fortress tower
4. Saite chapel of Amun's divine wives Amenardis and Nitokris
5. sacred pool
6. sacred pool
7. pylon I
8. first court
9. palace
10. pylon II
11. second court
12. palace court
13. wells
14. hypostyle hall
15. first and second columned antechambers
16. sanctuary
17. temple enclosure wall
18. western fortified gate
19. main enclosure wall of whole temple precinct
20. outer enclosure wall of temple precinct

Ramesses III's 'temple of millions of years' in Medinet Habu is an enormous and relatively complex building. The temple is entered through a monumental portico built on a landing, evoking a fortress—an impression intensified by the massive brick enclosure wall around the whole temple district. On the outer, facing wall of the tower of the pylon the king is depicted in high relief holding the kneeling chieftains of enemy nations by the hair and raising a stone mace to fulfill his mythical role and kill them with a single blow. The southwestern edge of the pylon is adorned with a superb scene showing the king hunting wild bulls. There are scenes from the king's military campaign against the Libyans on the interior wall of the pylon. There are two successive courts beyond the pylon, followed by the first great hypostyle hall, of basilica type (the ceiling is higher in the middle than at the sides), then two smaller columned halls, and the chapel of the barque. Behind the hall of the barque, at the end of the tract, there are eleven narrow chambers; one of them contained the cult statue of Amun. On the northern exterior wall of the temple there are scenes of battles with the Sea Peoples (see figure on p. 204), and a large calendar of temple festivals on the southern exterior wall. There are remains, by the outer south side of the temple, of a primarily mud-brick ceremonial palace, where the king would have stayed on his visits to the temple. To a certain extent, the design of the building was also inspired by the king's residential palace.

The tomb chapel of the adoratrice of Amun, Amenardis I, daughter of the Twenty-fifth Dynasty king Kashta, stands on the opposite, southern side of the court in front of the pylon and entrance to the temple. The chapel is considered to be the oldest example of a sacred building in which a passageway runs around a central cult room.

The Third Intermediate Period, the Late Period, and the Ptolemaic-Roman Period

With the decline of the mighty Egyptian empire built up during the New Kingdom and the Ramesside dynasty, state authority in Egypt once again fractured and the country fell apart into two parts governed from two centers: Upper Egypt was ruled by the priests in Thebes and Lower Egypt by kings from Tanis and Bubastis. The booty gleaned from wars of conquest ceased to flow into the country and building activities slackened off. The economic and political consequences of what has sometimes been called the 'final crisis' of the traditional Egyptian monarchy were momentous. Essentially, the king became the deputy for the real ruler: the god ruling the country from the temple. According to the German archaeologist Rolf Gundlach, the pharaonic state became a 'temple state.'

A major change connected with this process was the incorporation of royal tombs into the great temple complexes in Tanis, Sais, Mendes, and Sebennytus in the Third Intermediate Period and the Late Period. This was a time when large temples were built in a number of other places, for example, the Temple of Amun in Hibis in the Kharga founded by Psammetik II and dedicated to the Theban Triad and Seth. Amun's temple in Hibis is notable for the fact that the sanctuary and the hall of the barque were merged into one room with a circular corridor running around it.

In the Late Period we see the increasing adoption of this kind of a temple plan, in which the center is the *set weret* ('great throne')—a sanctuary with a case containing the cult statue of the god enclosed by a circular corridor, which the French Egyptologist François Daumas—the premier expert on temples from this period—terms the "mystery passage." The temple in Hibis, the Temple of Isis (Iseum) in Behbeit al-Hagar in the north of Egypt, and the Temple of Khnum on Elephantine Island are among the first to have this circular corridor around the sanctuary. Another new component to acquire a fixed place in the temple plan is the *wesekhet pesedjet* ('hall of the Nine'), which in this case means the sum of all the gods* of the land, forming a court of gods or retinue to the main god venerated in the temple. Viewed from the sanctuary, beyond the hall of the Nine was the *wesekhet wedenet* ('offering hall'), to which offerings were brought to the gods three times a day: in the morning, at noon, and in the evening. This hall could have other names, for example, *wesekhet khayet* ('the hall of appearance'). Behind it was the *wadjet* ('columned hall, hypostyle'). In Egyptological literature late Egyptian temples are sometimes subdivided into two parts, naos and pronaos: the pronaos is the hypostyle hall and the rest of the temple the naos. Columns with what are known as composite capitals formed of a bunch of leaves, flowers, and sometimes fruits became a characteristic feature of late Egyptian temples. The plant motifs symbolized the creative power of the god in nature.

In the Late Period we also witness the spread of a new form of kiosk—that is, a small, open, light-seeming building supported by columns with plant or composite capitals. This is a building type already encountered at the beginning of the Middle Kingdom in the form of Senwosret I's White Chapel in Karnak.

Crypts were among the elements that became characteristic of the plan of temples of gods in the Late Period. These were chambers, sometimes undecorated, set in the massive outer walls of the temples or sometimes underground. Their real meaning has never been fully explained, but to judge by inscriptions and scenes on the walls of some crypts, they may well have been used to store statues of the gods and symbols of the gods used

* Unlike the Heliopolitan Ennead, made up of nine particular gods, in the case of the 'hall of the Nine,' the ancient Egyptians understood the number nine as 3 × 3, where the number three (written with three counting strokes) meant plurality, so that nine, the tripling of the number three, is therefore total plurality—everything.

at certain festivals and in temple rites. On the feast of 'uniting with the sun disc,' the statues were taken up to the roof terrace of the temple so that the gods could recover and draw new strength from the first rays of the New Year sun.

At the end of the Late Period we also see the *wabet* ('pure place') appearing in the plan of the divine temple. This was a little set of rooms close to the staircase up to the roof terrace. As a rule, it consisted of no more than a small open courtyard separated by a pair of columns and low crosspiece from a cult room positioned a little higher. The *wabet*, also known as the 'place of the First Feast,' played an important role in the New Year rites for the regeneration of the statues of the gods. The predecessors of the *wabet* may have been the solar sanctuaries in the temples of the New Kingdom, which in contemporary inscriptions were called 'Re's shadow.'

≪The temple of Khnum on Elephantine, largely rebuilt by Nakhtnebef II, dominated the First Nile Cataract.

Variety of composite column capitals in the temple district on Philae.

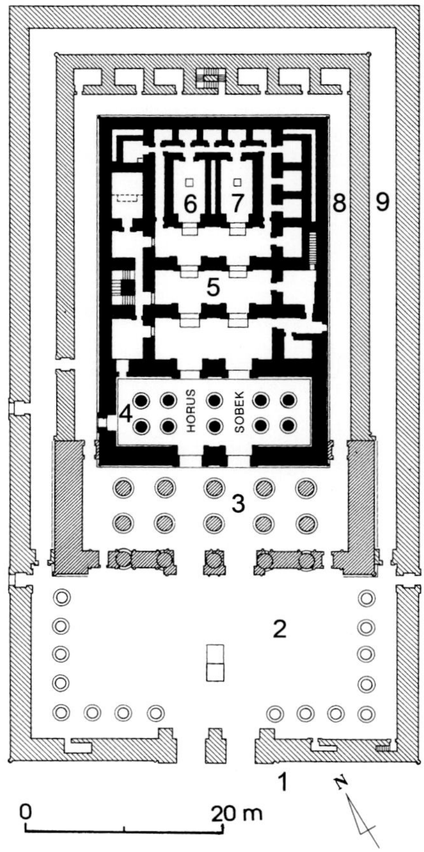

Plan of the temple of Harwer and Sobek in Kom Ombo.
1. pylon
2. columned court with altar
3. first columned hall
4. second columned hall
5. three antechambers between the columned hall and the sanctuary
6. chapel of Horus
7. chapel of Sobek
8. internal passage
9. external passage

The last great program of temple building in Egypt was initiated by the Ptolemies. Like the Roman emperors after them, they had good pragmatic reasons for the policy: ostentatious interest in Egyptian religion and support of the cults of the original ancient gods was intended to consolidate their power and establish mutually beneficial cooperative relationships with the Egyptians. During this period great temples were built, for example, in Dendera, Edfu, Esna, Kom Ombo, and on Philae in southern Egypt. Some of these have survived in a good state of preservation to this day, for example the temple in Dendera and the temple in Edfu (for detailed discussion of these temples see chapters 10 and 11), the latter considered to be the best preserved temple of ancient Egypt and perhaps all of antiquity.

The inscriptions and scenes covering the walls of the temples of the Ptolemaic and Roman Periods are helping us to form a better understanding of the religious ideas of the time and the important political and economic role played by temples in the life of the country at the time. Rapprochement between the ruling Greek cosmopolitan elite and the local Egyptian population was further encouraged by the creation of an artificial god—Serapis—who was a Greek interpretation of the Egyptian Osiris-Apis. His earliest shrine, the Serapeion or Serapeum (which should not be confused with the Saqqara cemetery of the sacred bulls of Apis), was built in Alexandria in Grecian style. Serapis temples, in which Isis was worshiped together with Serapis, were later built in other places in Egypt and beyond its borders. This attempt to create an artificial god did not ultimately succeed in its goals, however, and failed to stem the tide of history that eventually swept traditional Egyptian religion away.

This book opened with the words of Hermes Trismegistus from a speech to Asclepius, in which he described Egypt as the temple of the world, the place where the gods had resolved to make their earthly dwelling. Perhaps here is the right place to quote the final words of the prophecy of Hermes.

> *O Egypt, Egypt, of your reverent deeds only stories will survive, and they will be incredible to your children! Only words cut in stone will survive to tell your faithful works. For divinity goes back to heaven, and all the people will die, deserted, as Egypt will be widowed and deserted by god and human.* (Copenhaver, p. 81)

What can we add? Only that fortunately the fate of Egypt has not been as lamentable as Hermes Trismegistus prophesied. Furthermore, Jean-François Champollion managed to break the code and decipher Egyptian hieroglyphs, and since then the stones and papyri have been speaking to us and giving their testimony. The cultural and spiritual riches of Alexandria and ancient Egypt at large live on—uncovered, discovered, explored, and brought to a wider public by Egyptologists. It is simply up to us to learn from the wisdom and beauty of this inheritance.

Detail
the eas
the co
the ter

GLOSSARY

Abu al-Hol: 'The Father of Terror,' an Arab folk name for the Great Sphinx at Giza and also the colossus of Ramesses II in Mit Rahina

***akh*:** 1. 'illumination,' the climax of the initiation ritual; 2. 'spirit,' 'spiritual power'

***akhet*:** 'horizon'

Akh menu: 'Blessed through his monuments,' the name of the Temple of Thutmose III, cult center of the Temple of Amun in Karnak

***Amduat*:** "What Is in the Nether World," a set of religious texts from the New Kingdom relating to the journey of the deceased through the underworld

***ankh*:** 'life'

Ankh tawy: 'The Two Lands Are Living," name of the wider area of the Memphis necropolis

Anubeion: the Greek name for the district comprising cemeteries of dogs and jackals and the sanctuary of the god of the dead Anubis in Saqqara

Asclepion: the Greek name for the Temple of Imhotep in Saqqara

***atef*:** Upper Egyptian crown with two plumes and a solar disc

Aten tjehen: 'Dazzling Sun Disc,' attribute of Amenhotep III

***ba*:** 'soul,' 'spiritual power'

Bahr al-Libeini: 'The Libyan River,' a canal on the edge of the desert serving as a waterway for the pyramid builders

Ba neb Djed: 'Ram, lord of Djed,' name of the sacred ram and god in Busiris in Northern Egypt

***bat*:** symbol in the shape of a female face with cow ears and horns

The Beautiful Union: festival of Hathor involving the transport of the goddess's statue to Edfu

Bekh: known in Greek as Buchis, the earthly embodiment of the *ba* of the god Montu in Armant

***benben*:** stone fetish which was roughly conical in shape and worshiped as a form of the sun god

***benbenet*:** Egyptian term for the apex of a pyramid, the pyramidion

***benu*:** bird (ash grey kingfisher, *Ardea cinerea*), regarded as the embodiment of the spirit or *ba* of the sun god

***bes*:** 'induction,' Egyptian word for an initiation ceremony
blue crown: official royal crown relating to the coronation ritual
***Book of the Dead*:** a set of magical-religious incantations recorded mainly on papyrus scrolls (but also on other media), which was intended as a guide and document for the deceased on his posthumous journey to a blessed existence in the other world
***Book of Gates*:** a religious work describing the sun's night journey from the west to its morning 'resurrection,' which was divided into twelve sectors (hours) separated by gates; it was also supposed to secure the resurrection of the dead ruler.
***Book of the Night*:** a work containing pictures and descriptions of the night journey of the sun and other gods through the body of the sky goddess Nut from her mouth (the west) to her womb (the east).
***Book of Thoth*:** a legendary treatise supposed to contain all knowledge and magical power, which occurs in some late Egyptian stories as a literary motif
Bubasteion: the Greek name for the district with a cat cemetery and the sanctuary of Bastet in Saqqara
canopic jar: vessel where the internal organs removed during mummification were kept
Colossi of Memnon: colossal seated statues of Amenhotep III made of silificated sandstone, which adorned the first pylon of the king's mortuary temple in western Thebes
***djed*:** 'to endure'; pillar as a symbol of 'duration,' 'enduring'
Dodekaschoinos: Greek name of a territory measuring twelve schoins, the northern part of Nubia under Egyptian rule
dromos: corridor or ceremonial road to a cult site
Duat: the nether world
***duat netjer*:** 'adoratrice of the god,' high title of a priestess
Epaphos: another Greek name for the sacred bull Apis, born from the adulterous union of Zeus with Io
***heb tepy*:** 'the first festival,' the beginning of the ten-day celebrations at the end of the old and beginning of the New Year
***hemet netjer*:** 'female servant of the god,' title of priestess
***hemet netjer*:** 'woman of the god,' high title of priestess (written differently from 'female servant of the god')
hemispeos: Greek temple half-carved into a rock face
***hem netjer*:** 'servant of the god'; in the later Greek interpretation they were known as *prophetes* ('prophets')

***hem netjer tepy*:** 'first prophet of Amun,' the title of the high priest of Amun in Karnak

***henu*:** 1. ancient Egyptian hollow measure corresponding to approximately a half liter; 2. name of the barque of Sokar, which had a high raised prow decorated with the head of an oryx antelope

***heqa*:** royal scepter, possibly originally a shepherd's crook

***heret ib*:** 'she that is in the middle,' the name of the central part of the shrine Akh menu in Amun's temple in Karnak

Heri nefer: the name of the river harbor in Memphis

Hermaion: Greek term for a cult center of sacred ibises

***hetep*:** 'offering' or 'offering table (altar)'

Hetep Re: 'Re's offering table,' the name of Raneferef's solar temple

Hexapla ('Sixfold'): the Hebrew text of the Bible and its five different Greek translations, including the Septuagint, lined up in six columns beside one another

***hierogrammateis*:** the Greek term for highly educated priests, denoting their knowledge of sacred writings

***horologos*:** the Greek word for a priest who established the precise time according to the stars, the sun, or water clocks

***horoskopos*:** the Greek word for a priest knowledgeable about and able to interpret the constellations

***hu*:** 'the powerful word' mediated by the tongue

***hut nebu*:** the 'golden house,' the place where the ritual of the 'opening of the mouth' was carried out

***hut netjer*:** the 'abode of the god,' the most common term for an ancient Egyptian temple

Hyksos: the Grecized version of the Egyptian name *hekau khasut*, 'rulers of the mountainous desert lands'

***iaru* field:** 'field of rushes,' the ancient Egyptian paradise

***iat wabet*:** 'pure place,' in Greek Abaton; the term for the places where parts of Osiris's body fell

***ib*:** 'heart,' as the symbol of reason and emotion

Ibiotropheion: the Greek name for a farm where sacred ibises were bred

***id netjer*:** 'the hand of the god,' high title of a priestess, with sexual connotations

Iseion: 1. Greek name for the cemetery of the mothers of Apis in Saqqara; 2. Greek name for a temple of the goddess Isis (in Egyptian, Eset)

***ished*:** sacred tree, probably the 'sahel date,' *Balanites aegyptiaca*

***iteret Mehet*:** name of the land and coronation sanctuary of Lower Egypt

***iteret Shema*:** name of the land and coronation sanctuary of Upper Egypt

***Itinerarium Antonini: Itinerarium provinciarum Antonini Augusti*:** detailed account of the seventeen most important roads and many secondary roads of the Roman Empire, probably dating from the beginning of the third century

***it netjer*:** 'father of the god'; he walked at the head of processions sprinkling the route with ritually purified water and sometimes also carrying cult symbols

***iun*:** fetish in the shape of a wooden pillar (originally with bull's skull?) in Heliopolis

***khemen iten*:** 'union with the sun disc,' New Year temple ritual

Khemenu: '[City] of the Ogdoad,' in Greek Hermopolis Magna, 'Great Hermopolis'

Khemenu pa mek: the Egyptian name for the funerary temple district in Tuna al-Gebel

***khery hebet*:** 'he who is under the papyrus scroll,' lector-priest, in Greek *pteroforos* because of the feathers woven into his hair

Komasterion: 'house of processions,' Greek name for a building in Heropolis

Labyrinth: ancient name of the great mortuary Temple of Amenemhet III in Hawara

Lake of the Knife: sacred pool in the temple district of Hermopolis

***maa kheru*:** 'of truthful voice' or 'justified,' attribute of the deceased who had spoken the truth and passed final judgment

***maat*:** 'order' (but also 'law' and 'justice'), the order of the world established by the gods, fundamental idea of the ancient Egyptian state

***maa wer*:** 'He who looks on the Great One,' title of the high priest of Heliopolis

***mammisi*:** 'birth house,' specific type of Ptolemaic and Roman temple in Egypt

***mandjet*:** day barque of the sun god

Maru Aten: 'Summerhouse of Aten,' name of a building complex in Amarna

***medu shepsy*:** 'lofty staff,' the standard with ram head symbolising the *ka* of Amun

***menat*:** necklace, symbol of the goddess Hathor

Men nefer Pepi: 'Pepi's Beauty Endures,' name of the pyramid complex of Pepi I in Saqqara, which in shortened form replaced the name White Wall and from the Middle Kingdom onward gave the capital of Egypt the name Mennofer, later Grecized to 'Memphis'

Menta: Methydis in Greek, the sacred grove on the island of Biggeh

Mer wer: 'bull of Iunu,' in Greek Mnevis, the embodiment of the *ba* of the god Re; later also Men-ver

***meseketet*:** nocturnal barque of the sun god

***muu* dance:** funeral dance by dancers personifying spirits

Nebeh: sacred grove in Djedet (known in Greek as Busiris) in Northern Egypt, where Osiris's tomb was believed to be

***nekhakha*:** whip (cat-o'-nine-tails), insignia of royal power

Nekhen Re: 'Re's storeroom,' name of the sun Temple of Userkaf

***nemes*:** a type of cloth head covering

Nennisut: the political center of Northern Egypt in the First Intermediate Period, known in Greek as Herakleopolis

'opening of the mouth': a bringing-to-life ritual carried out on deceased persons and statues

***opet*:** very important festival at which the god Amun set out from his chief temple in Karnak to visit the Southern Harim, his temple in Luxor

Opet resyt: 'Southern Harim,' the name of Amun's temple in Luxor

ostrakon: shard of a clay vessel or chip of limestone; ostraka were used for short written records or artistic sketches

Pa lek: Coptic, 'Island of the End'; in Egyptian, Philae

***pastoforos*:** the Greek term for the priest who carried the case containing the statue of the god

Peqer: the name of the sacred district in Abydos containing the tombs of the earliest kings and the supposed tomb of the god Osiris

***per Amun*:** 'Amun's domain,' the term for the Temple of Amun including all its lands and assets

***per ankh*:** 'house of life,' the place in the temple where papyrus scrolls with religious and secular texts were compiled, copied, and kept

Per Bastet: the center of the cult of the cat goddess Bastet, close to the modern Zagazig in the Eastern Delta; in Greek, Bubastis

***per duat*:** 'Morning House,' the name of a temple chamber that served for the ritual symbolic morning purification of the king or priest representing the king in rituals

***per medjat*:** 'chamber of the book,' the name of the room in a temple where cases containing papyrus scrolls of religious, astronomical, medical, magical, and other texts were kept

***per meset*:** see *mammisi*

***per netjer*:** 'god's domain,' broader term for a temple, including its lands and other economic resources

***per nu*:** name of the Lower Egyptian type of sanctuary

Per Ramesse (Piramesse): 'City of Ramesses,' the new royal residence and government center founded by Ramesses II in the eastern Delta

Peru nefer: name of the river harbor in Memphis

***per wer*:** 'great house,' name of the Upper Egyptian type of sanctuary

***pesesh kaf*:** stone knife in the form of a swallow's tail used in the ritual of the 'opening of the mouth'

***phyle*:** 'watch,' organized unit of priests, but also boatmen and laborers in working shifts

***prophetes*:** 'prophets'; in the later Greek interpretation a term for *hem netjer* priests ('god's servants')

pylon: monumental entrance with two tower-like structures symbolizing the two hills on the horizon between which the sun rises

Pyramid Texts: the oldest set of religious texts, first recorded in the pyramid of Unas at the end of the Fifth Dynasty; they concern the fate of the king after death

***ra per*:** 'temple'

Ra setau: 'Mouth of the Underground Passages,' name originally of the seat of Sokar, later of Osiris

Red Chapel: a kiosk built by Hatshepsut in Karnak as a resting place for the sacred barque of Amun; archaeologists call it the Red Chapel because of the red-brown silificated sandstone from which it was built

Removal of Footprints: a magic ritual performed at the end of a ceremony

Re's Water: name of the easternmost, Pelusiac, or Bubastide branch of the Nile

***saqya*:** type of waterwheel that pumped irrigation water from the Nile

***sed*:** festival of the royal jubilee, ideally celebrated after thirty years of a king's rule; it was a reconfirmation of a king's capacity to govern

Sekhem: the center of the cult of the falcon god in Northern Egypt; in Greek, Letopolis; modern Ausim

***sekos*:** the Greek term for the precinct of the Temple of Apis in Memphis

***sem*:** priest who carried out burial rites; he wore the skin of a leopard or cheetah over his back and chest

Septuagint: Greek translation of the Hebrew scriptures, made in Alexandria by (traditionally) seventy Jewish scholars; the name comes from the Latin word for 'seventy.' The first five books, the Torah, are known as the Pentateuch.

Serapeion: 1. Greek term for the cemetery of sacred Apis bulls in Saqqara; 2. Greek term for a temple to the god Serapis. Latin, Serapeum.

shay**:** 'thinking,' 'thought,' considered by the Egyptians to have its seat in the heart

shetau**:** 'mystery,' being introduced to the mystery as part of an initiation ritual

shetayet**:** the name of Sokar's sanctuary

shut Re**:** 'Re's shadow,' a type of solar shrine

sistrum: small rattle, symbol of the goddess Hathor

Sothis cycle/period: a period of roughly 1,460 years when in ancient Egypt the beginning of the inundation coincided with the heliacal rising of the star Sirius

souls of Nekhen: the name of mythical royal ancestors from Upper Egypt

souls of Pe: the name of mythical royal ancestors from Lower Egypt

speos: Greek term for a temple carved into a rock face

stadion: Greek unit of length, roughly 180 meters

stela: 1. stone or wooden panel with inscription, usually also adorned with a painting or relief; 2. architectonic element in the form of so-called false doors often decorated with inscriptions and reliefs; 3. inscriptions and reliefs carved directly into rocks, for example the Amarna boundary stelae

stolistes**:** Greek term for the priests who undressed, dressed, and adorned a statue of the god

syntaxis: material support of priests from the state budget in the Ptolemaic Period

Tabula smaragdina: *The Emerald Tablet,* ancient literary work ascribed to Hermes Trismegistus; the text summarizes the metaphysical principles of the world, and connects events on earth to events in the heavens; it had considerable importance for alchemy

Ta dehnet: name of a rocky outcrop at Saqqara, around which was a cemetery of sacred animals

tekenu**:** a procession that was part of the funeral ritual

tep sepy**:** 'for the first time,' moment of the birth of the world, beginning of time

Tjeny: capital of Egypt in the Early Dynastic Period, not yet reliably located archaeologically. In Greek, Thinis or This.

Triakontaschoinos: territory of thirty schoins; northern part of Nubia briefly under Egyptian government

Via Nova Hadriana: Latin name for the road starting in Antinoopolis, running across the Eastern Desert, and connecting the ports on Egypt's Red Sea coast.

wab**:** 'pure,' term for member of the lower category of priests

***wabet*:** 'pure place'; sometimes also 'studio' as the place of mummification; in the Late and Ptolemaic Periods the term for a specific part of a temple

***wadjet*:** 'columned hall, hypostyle'

***was*:** 'power,' 'to be powerful'

Waset: city known in Greek as Thebes

Wenu: 'Hare [town],' administrative center of the fifteenth Upper Egyptian nome and older name of Hermopolis Magna

***wer diu*:** 'greatest of the Five,' title of the high priest of Hermopolis

***wer kherep hemut*:** 'greatest of the foremen of the craftsmen,' title of the high priest of Memphis

***wer maau*:** 'greatest of the seers,' title of the high priest of Heliopolis

***wesekhet pesedjet*:** 'hall of the Nine,' in this case meaning the sum of all gods

***wesekhet wedenet*:** 'hall of offering'

***wesheb*:** gold vessel for water used in the Osiris mysteries

Wetjes neferu: 'Extolled beauty,' name of the barque of Amun

White Chapel: a kiosk built by Senwosret I in Karnak as a resting place for Amun's sacred barque; the name given to it by archaeologists because it was built of fine white limestone

CHRONOLOGICAL TABLE

Reconstruction of the absolute chronology of ancient Egypt is extremely difficult and Egyptologists have conflicting views, especially on the earlier periods. There are major problems even with the reconstruction of a relative chronology, which in Egyptology traditionally involves the division of the Egyptian kings into thirty dynasties. This division was put forward by the Egyptian priest Manetho in his work *Aigyptiaka*, compiled at the request of King Ptolemy II Philadelphus. All that has survived of the *Aigyptiaka* has been some quite imprecise and unreliable excerpts (in Josephus Flavius's *Contra Apionem*) and extracts with some chronological information in the works of the church fathers Julius Africanus and Eusebius, later taken over by the Byzantine monk Georgios, called Synkellos. The original older Egyptian sources (for example, the Royal Canon of Turin) are likewise unfortunately incomplete, and so despite the sustained efforts of Egyptologists it has proved impossible even to compile a complete list of all the kings in some dynasties.

Despite modern scientific methods such as carbon-14 dating (which in any case have a margin of error of as much as several decades in the earlier periods of Egyptian history), reconstruction of the absolute chronology is complicated by other specific problems. One of these is the fact that until roughly the beginning of the second millenium BC the period of the reign of a king was counted not in calendar years but by the so-called census of cattle associated with the gathering of tax, and documentary evidence of these is often full of gaps. What is more, the census did not take place at consistent fixed intervals; it was mainly every two years but sometimes annual. This is why, for the period up to the middle of the second millennium BC (that is, up to the beginning of the New Kingdom), Egyptologists prefer to use a relative chronology and only outline chronological data for the epochs and individual dynasties into which the history of ancient Egypt at the time is divided. Only from the time of the New Kingdom do the sources become more precise and various (allowing cross-checking) and there is sometimes available evidence for comparison from surrounding countries of the ancient Near East. From this point onward, the reconstruction of an absolute chronology (see the following table) can be considered reliable except in a few obscure cases. The list of kings in the following chronological table is not complete, but contains only the names of the better-known rulers and, for the period up to the begining of the New Kingdom, only approximate framework dates for dynasties, not individual rulers. The information in the table is taken from the most recent fundamental work on the chronology of ancient Egypt: E. Hornung, R. Krauss, and D. Warburton, *Ancient Egyptian Chronology*. The chronological data for the period from Alexander the Great's conquest of Egypt to the conquest of Egypt by the Romans—that is, for the Greek and Ptolemaic dynasty—come from T. Schneider, *Lexikon der Pharaonen*.

Predynastic Era

(ca. 4500–2900 BC)
This era is usually subdivided into three main phases, sometimes defined in terms of archaeological cultures (such as Naqada I, II, and III), sometimes designated only as earlier, middle and later, with the latest overlapping with what is known as Dynasty 0.

Early Dynastic (Archaic) Era

(ca. 2900–2545 BC)
The precise dates of the reigns of individual rulers have not yet been established. Nor is the order or number of rulers, especially in the Second Dynasty, entirely certain.

First Dynasty

(ca. 2900–2730 BC)
Narmer
Aha
Djer
Wadj
Den
Adjib
Semerkhet
Qa‘a

Second Dynasty
(ca. 2730–2590 BC)
Hetepsekhemwy
Raneb
Ninetjer
Peribsen
Sekhemib
Sened
Khasekhememwy

Old Kingdom
(ca. 2592–2118 BC)
Egyptologists are not united in the definition of the Old Kingdom. Some consider that it ends with the Sixth Dynasty, while others, in accordance with the Royal Canon of Turin, include the Seventh and Eighth Dynasties.

Third Dynasty
(ca. 2592–2544 BC)
Djoser
Sekhemkhet
Khaba
Nebka
Huni

Fourth Dynasty
(ca. 2543–2436 BC)
Snofru
Khufu
Djedefre
Bikheris
Khafre
Menkaure
Shepseskaf

Fifth Dynasty
(ca. 2435–2306 BC)
Weserkaf
Sahure
Neferirkare

Shepseskare
Raneferef
Niuserre
Menkauhor
Djedkare
Wenis

Sixth Dynasty
(ca. 2305–2152 BC)
Teti
Weserkare
Pepi I
Merenre
Pepi II
Nemtyemsaf
Nitokris

Seventh Dynasty
A somewhat obscure period of internal political crisis, during which a large number of rulers probably reigned in quick succession.

Eighth Dynasty
(ca. 2150–2118 BC)
Neferkaure
Neferkauhor
Neferirkare

First Intermediate Period
(ca. 2118–1980 BC)

Ninth/Tenth Dynasty (Herakleopolitan)
(ca. 2118–1980 BC)
About eighteen rulers of relatively little importance, several of them having the name Khety.

Middle Kingdom
(ca. 1980–1760 BC)
Views on the precise beginning and end of the Middle Kingdom sometimes diverge. According to some scholars it starts with the reign of Metuhotep II, while others believe that it did not start until

Amenemhet I. Some consider that it ended at the end of the Twelfth Dynasty, while others believe that it included the Thirteenth and even the Fourteenth Dynasty.

Eleventh Dynasty
(ca. 2080–1940 BC)
Mentuhotep I
Antef I
Antef II
Antef III
Mentuhotep II
Mentuhotep III
Mentuhotep IV

Twelfth Dynasty
(ca. 1939–1760 BC)
Amenemhet I
Senwosret I
Amenemhet II
Senwosret II
Senwosret III
Amenemhet III
Amenemhet IV
Sebeknofru

Second Intermediate Period
(ca. 1759–1539 BC)

Thirteenth Dynasty
(ca. 1759–1630 BC)
This dynasty is marked by rulers of lesser importance reigning for comparatively short periods. Some had the names Amenhemhet, Mentuhotep, Senwosret, and Sebekhotep. Only three of them—Neferhotep I, Ibiya, and Ay—ruled for longer periods, of around ten years each.

Fourteenth Dynasty
(dates uncertain)
A few unimportant kings who reigned in the Delta. The best-known of them, Nehesey, reigned for less than a year.

Fifteenth Dynasty (Hyksos)
(ca. ?–1530 BC)
Khian
Apophis
Khamudi

Sixteenth Dynasty
(dates uncertain)
Vassals of the Hyksos.

Sixteenth and Seventeenth Dynasties
(ca ?–1540 BC)
The names and the length of reign of some of the rulers of these dynasties have not yet been precisely established. Some of the rulers had the name Antef. The last two rulers—Sekenenre Tao and Kamose—were particularly important.

New Kingdom
(ca. 1539–1077 BC)

Eighteenth Dynasty
(ca. 1539–1292 BC)
Ahmose I (ca. 1539–1515 BC)
Amenhotep I (1514–1494 BC)
Thutmose I (1493–1480 BC)
Thutmose II (1481–1479 BC)
Hatshepsut (1479–1457 BC)
Thutmose III (1479–1458 BC)
Amenhotep II (1425–1400 BC)
Thutmose IV (1400–1390 BC)
Amenhotep III (1390–1353 BC)
Amenhotep IV/Akhenaten (1353–1336 BC)
Semenkhkare (1336–1334 BC)
Tutankhaten/Tutankhamun (?–1324 BC)
Ay (1323–1320 BC)
Haremheb (ca. 1319–1292 BC)

Nineteenth Dynasty
(1292–1191 BC)
Ramesses I (1292–1291 BC)

Sethi I (ca. 1290–1279 BC)
Ramesses II (1279–1213 BC)
Merenptah (1213–1203 BC)
Sethi II (1202–1198 BC)
Amenmesses (1202–1200 BC)
Siptah (1197–1193 BC)
Tawosret (ca. 1192–1191 BC)

Twentieth Dynasty
(1190–1177 BC)
Sethnakht (1190–1188 BC)
Ramesses III (1187–1153 BC)
Ramesses IV (1156–1150 BC)
Ramesses V (1149–1146 BC)
Ramesses VI (1145–1139 BC)
Ramesses VII (1138–1131 BC)
Ramesses VIII (1130 BC)
Ramesses IX (ca. 1129–1111 BC)
Ramesses X (ca. 1110–1107 BC)
Ramesses XI (ca. 1106–1077 BC)

Third Intermediate Period
(ca. 1176–723 BC)

Twenty-first Dynasty
(ca. 1076–944 BC)
Nesbanebdjed (ca. 1076–1052 BC)
Pasbakhaenniut I (ca. 1051–1006 BC)
Amenemnisut (ca. 1005–1002 BC)
Amenemope (ca. 1002–993 BC)
Osorkon (ca. 992–987 BC)
Siamon (ca. 986–968 BC)
Pasbakhaenniut II (ca. 967–944 BC)

Twenty-second Dynasty
(943–ca. 746 BC)
Sheshonq I (943–923 BC)
Osorkon I (923–ca. 888 BC)
Takelot I (887–874 BC)
Sheshonq II (873 BC)

Osorkon II (872–842 BC)
Sheshonq III (841–803 BC)
Pami (789–784 BC)

Twenty-third Dynasty (Upper Egypt) and Rival Kings

(845–821 BC)
Takelot II (845–821 BC)
Iuput I (820–809 BC)
Osorkon III, Takelot III (780 ± 20 BC)
Petubast I, Sheshonq IV, Rudamon, Iny (834–812 BC)

Twenty-third Dynasty (Lower Egypt)

(ca. 730 BC)
Petubast II (?)
Osorkon IV

Twenty-fourth Dynasty

(ca. 736–723 BC)
Tefnakht (736–729 BC)
Bakenrenef (728–723 BC)

Late Period

(ca. 722–332 BC)

Twenty-fifth Dynasty

(722–ca. 655 BC)
Piye/Piankhy (ca. 753–723 BC)
Shabaka (ca. 722–707 BC)
Shabakata (ca. 706–690 BC)
Taharqa (690–664 BC)
Tanutamon (664–ca. 655 BC)

Twenty-sixth Dynasty

(664–525 BC)
Psammetik I (664–610 BC)
Neko II (610–595 BC)
Psammetik II (595–589 BC)
Haiebre (589–570 BC)
Ahmose II (570–526 BC)
Psammetik III (526–525 BC)

Twenty-seventh Dynasty (First Persian Occupation)

(525–404 BC)
Cambyses (525–522 BC)
Darius I (521–486 BC)
Xerxes (486–466 BC)
Artaxerxes I (465–424 BC)
Darius II (424–404 BC)

Twenty-eighth Dynasty

(404–399 BC)
Amenirdis (404–399 BC)

Twenty-ninth Dynasty

(399–380 BC)
Nefaarudj I (399–393 BC)
Pasherimut (393 BC)
Hakor (393–380 BC)
Nefaarudj II (380 BC)

Thirtieth Dynasty

(380–343 BC)
Nakhtnebef I (380–362 BC)
Djedhor (365–360 BC)
Nakhtnebef II (360–343 BC)

Thirty-first Dynasty (Second Persian Occupation)

(343–332 BC)
Artaxerxes III (343–338 BC)
Arses (338–336 BC)
Darius III (335–332 BC)

Greek Period

(332–305 BC)
Alexander the Great (332–323 BC)
Philip Arrhidaeus (323–317 BC)

Ptolemaic Period

(305–30 BC)
Ptolemy I Soter I (306/4–283/2 BC)
Ptolemy II Philadelphus (282–246 BC)

Ptolemy III Euergetes I (246–222/1 BC)
Ptolemy IV Philopator (221–204 BC)
Ptolemy V Epiphanes (204–180 BC)
Ptolemy VI Philometor (180–145 BC)
Ptolemy VII Neos Philopator (145–144 BC)
Ptolemy VIII Euergetes II (145–116 BC)
Ptolemy IX Soter II (116–107 BC)
Ptolemy X Alexander I (107–88 BC)
Ptolemy IX Soter II (restored) (88–81 BC)
Ptolemy XI Alexander II (80 BC)
Ptolemy XII Auletes (80–58 BC)
Ptolemy XII Neos Dionysos (80–58 BC)
Berenice IV (58–55 BC)
Cleopatra VII Philopator (51–30 BC)
Ptolemy XIII (51–47 BC)
Ptolemy XIV Philopator (51–44 BC)
Ptolemy XV Caesar (44–30 BC)

Roman Period
(30 BC–AD 337)

Byzantine Period
(337–641)

Arab Conquest
(642)

ABBREVIATIONS USED IN THE BIBLIOGRAPHIES AND ILLUSTRATION CREDITS

ÄA	Ägyptologische Abhandlungen
ÄAT	Ägypten und Altes Testament
ADAIK	Abhandlungen des Deutschen Archäologischen Instituts Kairo
ÄF	Ägyptologische Forschungen
ANES	Ancient Near Eastern Studies
Ä&L	*Ägypten und Levante/Egypt and Levant*
APAW	Abhandlungen der Preussischen Akademie der Wissenschaften
ASAE	*Annales du Service des antiquités de l'Égypte*
AV	Archäologische Veröffentlichungen, Deutsches Archäologisches Institut, Abteilung Kairo
BÄBA	*Beiträge zur ägyptischen Bauforschung und Altertumskunde*
BACE	*Bulletin of the Australian Centre for Egyptology*
BdÉ	Bibliothèque d'études, Institut français d'archéologie orientale
Beihefte TAVO	Beihefte zum Tübinger Atlas des Vorderen Orients
BIE	*Bulletin de l'Institut d'Égypte, Le Caire*
BIFAO	*Bulletin de l'Institut français d'archéologie orientale*
Cahiers de Karnak	*Cahiers de Karnak*, Institut français d'archéologie orientale
CU FA CzEgI	Czech Egyptological Institute of the Faculty of Arts of Charles University in Prague
DAWW	Denkschriften der Kaiserlichen Akademie der Wissenschaften
Description de l'Égypte	*Description de l'Égypte ou Receueil des observations et des recherches qui ont été faites en Égypte pendant l'expédition de l'armée française.* 2nd ed. Vol. 5. Paris: Imprimerie de C.L.F. Panckoucke, 1820

GM	*Göttinger Miszellen*
HÄB	Hildesheimer ägyptologische Beiträge
IFAO	Institut français d'archéologie orientale, Cairo
JARCE	*Journal of the American Research Center in Egypt*
JEA	*Journal of Egyptian Archaeology*
KMT	*KMT. A Modern Journal of Ancient Egypt*
LÄ	*Lexikon der Ägyptologie*
LD	Lepsius, K.R. *Denkmaeler aus Aegypten und Aethiopien: nach den Zeichnungen der von Seiner Majestaet dem Koenige von Preussen Friedrich Wilhelm IV nach diesen Laendern gesendeten und in den Jahren 1842–1845 ausgefuehrten wissenschaftlichen Expedition.* 12 vols. Berlin: Nicolaische Buchhandlung, 1849–59.
MÄS	Münchener ägyptologische Studien
MDAIK	*Mitteilungen des Deutschen archäologischen Instituts, Abteilung Kairo*
ÖAWD	Österreichische Akademie der Wissenschaften, Denkschrift
OBO	Orbis biblicus et orientalis
OEAE	*Oxford Encyclopedia of Ancient Egypt.* Vols. 1–3. Oxford: Oxford University Press, 2001.
OLA	Orientalia Lovanensia analecta
OrMon	*Orientalia Monspeliensia*
PÄ	Probleme der Ägyptologie
SAK	*Studien zur altägyptischen Kultur*
SPAW	Sitzungsberichte der Preussischen Akademie der Wissenschaften, Philosophy/History Group
UGAA	Untersuchungen zur Geschichte und Altertumskunde Ägyptens
ZÄS	*Zeitschrift für ägyptische Sprache und Altertumskunde*

BIBLIOGRAPHY

Selected General Studies on Ancient Egyptian Religion

Assmann, J. *Ma'at: Gerechtigkeit und Unsterblichkeit im Alten Ägypten.* Munich: C.H. Beck, 1990.

———. *Re und Amun.* OBO 51. Freiburg, Switzerland: Universitätsverlag; Göttingen: Vandenhoeck & Ruprecht, 1983.

Bonnet, H. *Reallexikon der ägyptischen Religionsgeschichte.* 3rd ed. Berlin and New York: De Gruyter, 2000.

Dunand, F., and Ch. Zivie-Coche. *Gods and Men in Egypt.* Ithaca, N.Y. and London: Cornell University Press, 2004.

Frankfort, H. *Kingship and the Gods: A Study of Ancient Near Eastern Religion as the Integration of Society and Nature.* 6th ed. Chicago and London: University of Chicago Press, 1969.

Frankfurter, D. *Religion in Roman Egypt: Assimilation and Resistance.* Princeton, N.J.: Princeton University Press, 1998.

Griffith, J.G. "Motivation in Early Egyptian Syncretism." In *Studies in Egyptian Religion Dedicated to Professor Jan Zandee,* edited by M.H. van Voss et al., 43–55. Leiden: E.J. Brill, 1982.

Hornung, E., R. Krauss, and D. Warburton. *Ancient Egyptian Chronology.* Leiden and Boston: Brill, 2006.

Kees, H. *Der Götterglaube im Alten Ägypten.* 2nd ed. Berlin: Akademie-Verlag, 1956.

———. *Totenglauben und Jenseitsvorstellungen der alten Ägypter: Grundlagen und Entwicklung bis zum Ende des Mittleren Reiches.* Berlin: Akademie-Verlag, 1956.

Koch, K. *Geschichte der ägyptischen Religion: Von den Pyramiden bis zu den Mysterien der Isis.* Stuttgart, Berlin, and Cologne: Kohlhammer, 1993.

Morenz, S. *Egyptian Religion.* 3rd ed. Ithaca, N.Y.: Cornell University Press, 1996.

Quirke, S. *Ancient Egyptian Religion.* London: British Museum Press, 1992.

Schneider, T. *Lexikon der Pharaonen: Die altägyptischen Könige von der Frühzeit bis zur Römerherrschaft.* Zurich: Artemis, 1994.

Shafer, B.E. *Religion in Ancient Egypt: Gods, Myths and Personal Practice.* Ithaca, N.Y. and London: Cornell University Press, 1991.

Wilkinson, R.H. *The Complete Gods and Goddesses of Ancient Egypt*. London: Thames and Hudson, 2003.

Editions of Egyptian Antiquities

Denon, V. *Voyage dans la Basse et la Haute Égypte*. 2nd ed. Paris: Henri Gaugain et Cie—Chaillou, Md d'Estampes, 1829.

Description de l'Égypte ou Recueilles des observations et des recherches qui ont été faites en Égypte pendant l'expédition de l'armée française. Antiquités 5. 2nd ed. Paris: Imprimerie de C.L.F. Panckoucke, 1823.

Lepsius, K.R. *Denkmaeler aus Aegypten und Aethiopien: nach den Zeichnungen der von Seiner Majestaet dem Koenige von Preussen Friedrich Wilhelm IV nach diesen Laendern gesendeten und in den Jahren 1842–1845 ausgefuehrten wissenschaftlichen Expedition*. 12 vols. Berlin: Nicolaische Buchhandlung, 1849–59.

Dedication

Copenhaver, B.P. *Hermetica: The Greek Corpus Hermeticum and the Latin Asclepius in a New English Translation with Notes and Introduction*. Cambridge, U.K.: Cambridge University Press, 2002.

1. The Temple of the World, and First Excursus

Altenmüller, H. *Texte zum Begräbnisritual in den Pyramiden des Alten Reiches*. ÄA 24. Wiesbaden: O. Harrassowitz, 1972.

Altenmüller, H. "Feste." *LÄ*, vol. 2, 171–91.

Altenmüller, H., and A.M. Moussa. "Die Inschrift Amenemhets II. aus dem Ptah-Tempel von Memphis: Vorbericht." *SAK* 18 (1991): 1–48.

Arnold, D. "Architektur des Mittleren Reiches." In *Das alte Ägypten*, edited by C. Vandersleyen, 150–70. Berlin: Propyläen Verlag, 1975.

Badawy, A. "Philological Evidence about Methods of Construction in Ancient Egypt." *ASAE* 54 (1957): 51–74.

Barta, W. "Zur Lokalisierung und Bedeutung der *mrt*–Bauten." *ZÄS* 110 (1983): 98–104.

Budge, E.A.W. *The Book of the Dead: Facsimiles of the Papyri of Hunefer, Ahai, Kerasher and Netchemet with Supplementary Text from the Papyrus of Nu*. London: British Museum, 1899.

Daumas, F. "Architektur der Spätzeit." In *Das alte Ägypten*, edited by C. Vandersleyen, 196–205. Berlin: Propyläen Verlag, 1975.

Edwards, A.B. *A Thousand Miles up the Nile*. London: G. Routledge, 1891.

Eigner, D. "Tell Ibrahim Awad: Divine Residence from Dynasty 0 until Dynasty 11." Ä&L 10 (2000): 17–36.

Gundlach, R. "Temples." *OEAE*, vol. 3, 363–79.

Haeny, G. "Architektur des Neuen Reiches." In *Das alte Ägypten*, edited by C. Vandersleyen, 170–78. Berlin: Propyläen Verlag, 1975.

Kaplony, P. "Ka-Haus." *LÄ*, vol. 3, 284–87.

Kemp, B. *Ancient Egypt: Anatomy of a Civilization*. New York: Routledge, 1989.

Kessler, D. "Tempelbesitz." *LÄ*, vol. 6, 365–76.

Kuhlmann, K.P. "Serif-style Architecture and the Design of the Archaic Egyptian Palace" ('Königszelt')." In *Haus und Palast im alten Ägypten/House and Palace in Ancient Egypt*, edited by M. Bietak, 117–37. ÖAWD 14. Vienna: Verlag der Österreichischen Akademie der Wissenschaften, 1996.

Lauer, J.-Ph. "Le triangle sacré dans les plans des monuments de l'Ancien Empire." *BIFAO* 77 (1977): 55–78.

Michailidis, G. "Moule illustrant un texte d'Hérodote relatif au bouc de Mendes." *BIFAO* 63 (1965): 139–60.

Niederberger, W. *Elephantine XX. Der Chnumtempel Nektanebos' II*. AV 96, 113–28. Mainz am Rhein: Verlag Philipp von Zabern, 1999.

O'Connor, D. "The Status of Early Egyptian Temples: An Alternative Theory." In *The Followers of Horus*, edited by R. Friedmann and B. Adams. Oxford: Oxbow Books, 1992.

Quibell, J.E. *Hierakonpolis*. Vol. 1. London: Bernard Quaritch, 1900.

Quibell, J.E., and F.W. Green. *Hierakonpolis*. Vol. 2. London: Bernard Quaritch, 1902.

Sauneron, S. *The Priests of Ancient Egypt*. New York: Cornell University Press, 2000.

Settgast, J. *Untersuchungen zu altägyptischen Bestattungsdarstellungen*. Glückstadt: J.J. Augustin, 1963.

Verner, M. *Abusir III: The Pyramid Complex of Khentkaus*. Prague: Czech Institute of Egyptology, 2001.

Wilkinson, A.H.T. *Royal Annals of Ancient Egypt: The Palermo Stone and Its Associated Fragments*. London and New York: Kegan Paul International, 2000.

Williams, B. "Narmer and the Coptos Colossi." *JARCE* 25 (1988): 35–59.

2. Heliopolis: The City of the Sun

Abd al-Gelil, M., A. Saadani, and D. Raue. "Some Inscriptions and Reliefs from Matariya." *MDAIK* 52 (1996): 143–56.

Arnold, D. *Die Tempel Ägyptens: Götterwohnungen, Kultstätten, Baudenkmäler*. Zürich: Artemis & Winkler, 1992.

Assmann, J. *Liturgische Lieder an den Sonnengott, Untersuchungen zur altägyptischen Hymnik. I.* MÄS 19. Berlin: B. Hessling, 1969.

Barsanti, A. "La nécropole des grands prêtres d'Héliopolis sous l'Ancien empire. 2. Rapports sur le déblaiment." *ASAE* 16 (1916): 213f.

Barta, W. *Untersuchungen zum Goetterkreis der Neunheit.* MÄS 28. Munich and Berlin: Deutscher Kunstverlag, 1973.

Borchardt, L. "Der Bau." In *Das Re-Heiligtum*, by F.W. von Bissing. Berlin: Verlag von Alexander Duncker, 1905.

Brunner-Traut, E. "Ichneumon." *LÄ*, vol. 3, 122f.

Budge, E.A.W. *The Book of the Dead: Facsimiles of the Papyri of Hunefer, Ahai, Kerasher and Netchemet with Supplementary Text from the Papyrus of Nu.* London: British Museum, 1899.

Corteggiani, J.P. "La 'butte de décolation' à Héliopolis." *BIFAO* 95 (1995): 141–51.

Daressy, G. "Graffiti de la Montagne Rouge." *ASAE* 13 (1913): 43–47.

———. "La nécropole des grands prêtres d'Héliopolis sous l'Ancien empire. 1. Inscriptions." *ASAE* 16 (1916): 193–212.

Debono, F. *The Predynastic Cemetery at Heliopolis.* Mainz am Rhein: Verlag Philipp von Zabern, 1988.

Görg, M. *Die Barke der Sonne: Religion im alten Ägypten.* Freiburg im Breisgau: Herder, 2001.

Goringe, H.G. *Egyptian Obelisks.* Page 70 and plate 32. New York: published by author, 1882.

Habachi, L. "Akhenaten in Heliopolis." *BÄBA* 12 (1971): 38–45.

Kahl, J. *'Ra is My Lord': Searching for the Rise of the Sun God at the Dawn of Egyptian History.* Menes 1. Wiesbaden: Harrassowitz, 2007.

Kákosy, L. "Heliopolis." *LÄ*, vol. 2, 1111–13.

———. "Ischedbaum." *LÄ*, vol. 3, 182f.

Lanzone, R.V. *Dizionario di mitologia egizia.* Vol. 3. Torino: Litografia fratelli Doyen, 1885, pl. 157.

Moursi, M. "Corpus der Mnevis-Stelen und Untersuchungen zum Kult der Mnevis-Stiere in Heliopolis." *SAK* 10 (1983): 247–67.

Petrie, W. M. F. *Heliopolis, Kafr Ammar and Shurafa.* London: School of Archaeology in Egypt: 1913.

Quirke, S. *The Cult of Ra: Sun-worship in Ancient Egypt.* London: Thames and Hudson, 2001.

Raue, D. *Heliopolis und das Haus des Re: Eine Prosopographie und ein Toponym im Neuen Reich.* ADAIK 16. Berlin: Achet-Verlag, 1999.

Ricke, H. "Der Hohe Sand in Heliopolis." *ZÄS* 71 (1935): 107–11.

———. "Eine Inventartafel aus Heliopolis im Turiner Museum." *ZÄS* 71 (1935): 111–33.

Saleh, A.A. *Excavations at Heliopolis: Ancient Egyptian Ounû I–II. The Site of Tell al-Hisn, Matarîiyah.* Cairo: Cairo University Faculty of Archaeology, 1981–83.

Schäfer, H. "Altägyptischer Bilder der auf- und untergehenden Sonne." *ZÄS* 71 (1935): 20, fig. 2.

Shaw, I., and P. Nicholson. *British Museum Dictionary of Ancient Egypt.* London: British Museum Press, 1995.

Stadelmann, R. "Swt-Raw als Kultstätte des Sonnengottes im Neuen Reich." *MDAIK* 25 (1969): 139–78.

Teeter, E. "Maat." *OEAE*, vol. 2, 135–45.

Velde, H. "Geb." *LÄ*, vol. 2, 427–29.

———. "Schu." *LÄ*, vol. 5, 735–37.

Verhoeven, U. "Tefnut." *LÄ*, vol. 6, 296–304.

3. Memphis: The White Wall

al-Amir, Mustafa. "The *sekos* of Apis in Memphis." *JEA* 34 (1948): 51–56.

Anthes, R., I.A. Aziz, H.S.K. Bakry, H.G. Fischer, L. Habachi, J. Jacquet, W.K. Simpson, and J. Yoyotte. *Mit Rahineh 1956.* Philadelphia: University Museum, University of Pennsylvania, 1965.

Anthes, R., H.S.K. Bakry, J.M. Dimick, H.G. Fischer, L. Habachi, and J. Jacquet. *Mit Rahineh 1955.* Philadelphia: University Museum, University of Pennsylvania, 1959.

Arnold, D. *Die Tempel Ägyptens: Götterwohnungen, Kultstätten, Baudenkmäler.* Zürich: Artemis & Winkler, 1992.

Aufrère, S.H. "Une nécropole de taureaux Apis visitée en 1716 par Paul Lucas et Claude Sicard?" In *Études sur l'Ancien empire et la nécropole de Saqqâra dédiées à Jean-Philippe Lauer*, edited by C. Berger and B. Mathieu. OrMon 9. Montpellier: Université Paul Valéry, 1997.

Borchardt, L. "Der Bau." In *Das Re-Heiligtum*, by F.W. von Bissing. Berlin: Verlag von Alexander Duncker, 1905.

———. *Das Grabdenkmal des Königs Ne-user-rê.* Leipzig: J.C. Hinrich-s'sche Buchhandlung, 1907.

Breasted, H. J. "The Philosophy of a Memphite Priest." *ZÄS* 39 (1901): 39–54.

Calverly, A.M., M.F. Broome, and A.H. Gardiner, eds. *The Temple of the King Sethos I at Abydos.* Vols.1–4. London: Egypt Exploration Society; Chicago: University of Chicago Press, 1933–58.

Daressy, G. "Le Temple de Mitrahineh." *ASAE* 3 (1902): 22–31.

Erman, A. *Ein Denkmal memphitischer Theologie.* SPAW 43, 916ff. Berlin: n.p., 1911.

———. "Adolf Erman: Bibliographie." *ZÄS* 71 (1935): 1–14.

Giddy, L.L. "Memphis, 1989: The Ptah Temple Complex." *BACE* 1 (1990): 38–41.

———. "Memphis and Saqqara during the Late Old Kingdom: Some Topographical Considerations." In *Hommages à Jean Leclant,* vol. 1, edited by C. Berger, G. Clerc, and N. Grimal. BdÉ 106, no. 1, 189–200. Cairo: IFAO, 1974.

Giddy, L.L., and D.G. Jeffrys. "Memphis, 1990." *JEA* 77 (1990): 1–6.

Helck, W. "Zu Ptah und Sokar." In *Religion und Philosophie im Alten Ägypten,* edited by U. Verhoeven and E. Graefe. OLA 39, 159–64. Leuven: Departement Oriëntalistiek, Uitgeverij Peeters, 1991.

Herodotus. *The Histories,* translated by G. Rawlinson, edited by H. Bowden. London: Everyman, 1992, reprinted 2000.

Hopfner, T. *Der Tierkult der alten Ägypter.* DAWW, Philosophy/History Group 57, Supp. 2. Vienna: Alfred Hölder, 1913.

Hornung, E. *Der ägyptische Mythos von der Himmelskuh: Eine Ätiologie des Unvollkommenen.* OBO 46. Freiburg, Switzerland: Universitätsverlag; Göttingen, Vandenhoeck & Ruprecht, 1982.

Hornung, G. *The Ancient Egyptian Books of the Afterlife.* Ithaca, N.Y. and London: Cornell University Press, 1999.

Jeffrys, D.G. *The Survey of Memphis.* Vol. 1. London: Egypt Exploration Society, 1985.

Junker, H. *Die Goetterlehre von Memphis.* APAW 23. Berlin: Verlag der Akademie der Wissenschaften, 1940.

———. *Die politische Lehre von Memphis.* APAW 6. Berlin: Verlag der Akademie der Wissenschaften, 1941.

Kaiser, W. "Die dekorierte Torfassade des spätzeitlichen Palastbezirkes von Memphis." *MDAIK* 43 (1986): 42–48.

Kees, H. "Die Grosse Festdarstellung." In *Das Re-Heiligtum,* edited by F.W. von Bissing. Leipzig: Hinrichs'sche Buchhandlung, 1928.

Kessler, D. *Die heiligen Tiere und der König.* Vol. 1. ÄAT 16. Wiesbaden: Otto Harrassowitz, 1989.

Lanzone, R. *Dizionario di mitologia egizia.* Vols. 1–3. Torino: Litografia Fratelli Doyan, 1881–85.

Lauer, J.Ph. "Les statues greques du *dromos* du Sérapeion à Saqqarah découvertes par Mariette en 1851." *BIE* 34 (1953): 207–27.

Leclère, F. *Les villes de Basse Égypte au Ier millénaire av. J.C.: Analyse archéologique et historique de la topographie urbaine*. Vol. 1. BdÉ 144, nos. 1–2. Cairo: IFAO, 2008.

Mariette, A. *Le Sérapéum de Memphis*, edited by G. Maspero. Paris: F. Vieweg, 1882.

Mélanges Mariette. BdÉ 32. Cairo: IFAO, 1961.

Newberry, P.E. "William Matthew Flinders Petrie, Kt., F.R.S., F.B.A." *JEA* 29 (1943): 67–70 and pl. 5.

Otto, E. *Beiträge zur Geschichte der Stierkulte in Aegypten*. UGAA 13, 11–34. Leipzig: J.C. Hinrichs Verlag, 1938.

Petrie, W. M. F. *Memphis*. Vol. 1. London: School of Archaeology in Egypt, 1909.

———. *Memphis*. Vol. 5. London: School of Archaeology in Egypt, 1913.

Porter, B., R.L.B. Moss, and J. Malek. *Topographical Bibliography*. Vol. 3: *Memphis*. Part 2, Fascicle 3. Oxford: Griffith Institute, Ashmolean Museum, 1981.

Ray, J. D. *The Archive of Hor*. London: Egypt Exploration Society, 1976.

Sandman Holmberg, M. *The God Ptah*. Lund: C.W.K. Gleerup, 1946.

Sayed Mahmud, A. *A New Temple for Hathor at Memphis*. *Egyptology Today*, vol. 1. Warminster: Aris and Phillips, 1978.

Sethe, K. *Dramatische Texte zu altägyptischen Mysterienspiele*. Leipzig: J.C. Hinrichs, 1928.

Shaw, I., and P. Nicholson. *British Museum Dictionary of Ancient Egypt*. London: British Museum Press, 1995.

Spiegelberg, W. "Ein Buchstück des Bestattungsrituals des Apisstieres." *ZÄS* 56 (1920): 1–33.

Steindorff, G. "Kurt Sethe †." *ZÄS* 70 (1934): 132–34.

Thompson, D. *Memphis under the Ptolemies*. Princeton, N.J.: Princeton University Press, 1988.

Verner, M., L. Bareš, and B. Vachala. *Ilustrovaná encyklopedie starého Egypta*. Prague: Karolinum, 1997.

4. Hermopolis: The City of the Eight

Arnold, D. *Die Tempel Ägyptens: Götterwohnungen: Kultstätten, Baudenkmäler*. Zürich: Artemis & Winkler, 1992.

Bailey, D. M. *Excavations at al-Ashmunein*. Vol. 4: *Hermopolis Magna. Buildings of the Roman Period*. London: British Museum Press, 1991.

Baraize, É. "Le 'Agora' d'Hermoupolis." *ASAE* 40 (1940): 741–60.

Bickerstaffe, D. "Death in the Nile: The Birth of Ancient Egypt's Last God." *KMT* 19, no. 2 (2008): 74–82.

Chlup, R. *Corpus Hermeticum*. Prague: Hermann and Synové, 2007.

Copenhaver, B. *Hermetica: The Greek Corpus Hermeticum and the Latin Asclepius*. Cambridge: Cambridge University Press, 1992.

Ebeling, F. *The Secret History of Hermes Trismegistus: Hermeticism from Ancient to Modern Times*. Ithaca, N.Y. and London: Cornell University Press, 2007.

Frankfurter, D. *Religion in Roman Egypt*. Princeton, N.J.: Princeton University Press, 2000.

Grieshammer, R. "Flammeninsel." *LÄ*, vol. 2, 258f.

Hanke, R. *Amarna: Reliefs aus Hermopolis*. HÄB 2. Hildesheim: Gerstenberg, 1978.

Hopfner, T. *Der Tierkult der alten Ägypter*. Vienna: A. Hölder, 1913.

Kamal, A. "Excavations of the Antiquities Department (1942) in the So-called 'Agora' of Hermopolis." *ASAE* 46 (1946): 289–309.

Kessler, D. *Die heiligen Tiere und der König*. Vol. 1. ÄAT 16. Wiesbaden: Otto Harrassowitz, 1989.

———. "Hermopolis." *OEAE*, vol. 2, 94–97.

———. "Tuna al-Gebel." *LÄ*, vol. 6, 797–804.

———. *Tuna al-Gebel II: Die Paviankultkammer G-C-C-2*. HÄB 43. Hildesheim: Gerstenberg, 1998.

Kurth, D. "Thot." *LÄ*, vol. 6, 497–523.

Oerter, W.B., and P. Pokorný. *Rukopisy z Nag Hammádí*. Vol. 1: *Kodex II/2–7*. Prague: Vyšehrad, 2008.

Petrie, W.M.F., and J.H. Walker. *The Palace of Apries (Memphis II)*. London: Bernard Quaritch, 1909.

Roberts, A. *My Heart My Mother: Death and Rebirth in Ancient Egypt*. Rottingdean: Northgate, 2000.

Roeder, G. *Hermopolis 1929–1939: Ausgrabungen der Deutschen Hermopolisexpedition in Hermopolis, Ober-Ägypten*. Hildesheim: Gerstenberg, 1959.

———. "Der Urzeit-Bezirk und die Urgottheiten von Hermopolis." *ZÄS* 67 (1931): 82–88.

Sethe, K. *Amun und die Acht Urgötter von Hermopolis: Eine Untersuchung über Ursprung und Wesen des Ägyptischen Götterkönigs*. APAW 4. Berlin: Verlag der Akademie der Wissenschaften, 1929.

Spencer, A.J. *Excavations at al-Ashmunein*. Vol. 2: *The Temple Area*. London: British Museum Press, 1989.

———. *Excavations at al-Ashmunein*. Vol. 3: *The Town*. London: British Museum Press, 1993.

Spiess, H. "Aufstieg eines Gottes: Untersuchungen zum Gott Thot bis zum Beginn des Neuen Reiches." PhD diss., Universität Hamburg, 1991.

Suys, É. *Vie de Petosiris, grand prêtre de Thot à Hermopolis-la-Grande*. Bruxelles: Fondation égyptologique reine Élisabeth, 1927.

Thissen, H.J. "Hermes: Hermetische Schriften." *LÄ*, vol. 2, 1133–37.

Wace, A.J.B., A.H.S. Megaw, and T.C. Skeat. *Hermopolis Magna, Ashmunein: The Ptolemaic Sanctuary and the Basilica*. Alexandria: Alexandria University Press, 1959.

Zivie, A.P. "Ibis." *LÄ*, vol. 3, 115–21.

5. The Kingdom of Amun, and Second Excursus

Arnold, D. *Die Tempel Ägyptens: Götterwohnungen, Kultstätten, Baudenkmäler*. Zürich: Artemis & Winkler, 1992.

Assmann, J. *Ägyptische Hymnen und Gebete*. 2nd ed. Freiburg, Switzerland: Universitätsverlag Freiburg; Göttingen: Vandenhoeck & Ruprecht, 1999.

———. *Liturgische Lieder an den Sonnengott: Untersuchungen zur altägyptischen Hymnik*. Vol. 1. MÄS 19. Berlin: Verlag Bruno Hessling, 1969.

Aufrère, S., J.C. Golvin, and J.C. Goyon. *L'Égypte restituée: Sites et temples de haute Égypte (1650 av. J.C.–300 ap. J.C.)*. Paris: Editions Errance, 1991.

Azim, M., and G. Réveillac. *Karnak dans l'objectif de Georges Legrain: Catalogue raisonné des archives photographiques du premier directeur des travaux de Karnak de 1895 à 1917*. Vols. 1–2. Paris: CNRS Editions 2004.

Barguet, P. *Le temple d'Amon-Re à Karnak: Essai d'exégèse*. Cairo: IFAO, 1962.

Behrens, P. "Karnak." *LÄ*, vol. 3, 341–52.

Bell, L. "The New Kingdom 'Divine' Temple: The Example of Luxor." In *Temples of Ancient Egypt*, edited by B.E. Shafer, 127–84. London and New York: I.B. Tauris, 1998.

Belzoni, G. *Plates Illustrative of the Researches and Operations of G. Belzoni in Egypt and Nubia*. London: John Murray, 1820.

Borghouts, J.F. "Month." *LÄ*, vol. 4, 200–204.

Burgos, F., F. Larché, and N. Grimal. *La chapelle Rouge: Le sanctuaire de barque d'Hatshepsout*. Vols. 1–2. Paris: Éditions Recherche sur les civilisations, 2008.

Carlotti, J.F. *L'Akh-menou de Thoutmosis III à Karnak: Étude architecturale*. Paris: Éditions Recherche sur les civilisations, 2000.

Charloux, G.Ch. "Karnak au Moyen Empire, l'enceinte et les fondations des magasins du temple d'Amon-Rê." In *Cahiers de Karnak*, vol. 12, fasc. 1, 191–226. Cairo: IFAO, 2007.

Daumas, F. "L'origine d'Amon de Karnak." *BIFAO* 65 (1967): 201–14.

Desroches-Noblecourt, Ch., ed. *Ramses le Grand*. Paris: Galeries nationales du Grand Palais, 1976.

Edwards, A.B. *A Thousand Miles up the Nile*. London, 1891.

Fakhry, A. "Recent Excavations at the Temple of the Oracle at Siwa Oasis." *BÄBA* 12 (1971): 17–33.

Goyon, J.C., Ch. Cardin, et al. *Trésors d'Égypte: La "cachette" de Karnak 1904–2004*. Grenoble: Musée dauphinois, 2004.

Gundlach, R. "Das Dekorationsprogramm der Tempel von Abu Simbel und ihre kultische und königsideologische Funktion." In *3. ägyptologische Tempeltagung: Systeme und Program der ägyptischen Tempeldekoration*, edited by D. Kurth. ÄAT 33, no. 1, 47–71. Wiesbaden: Otto Harrassowitz, 1995.

Habashi, L. *Features of the Deification of Ramesses III*. ADAIK 5, pls. 3 and 4. Berlin: Achet-Verlag, 1969.

Haeny, G. "New Kingdom 'Mortuary Temples' and 'Mansions of Millions of Years.'" In *Temples of Ancient Egypt*, edited by B.E. Shafer, 86–126. London and New York: I.B. Tauris, 1998.

Hawass, Z. *The Mysteries of Abu Simbel: Ramesses II and the Temples of the Rising Sun*. Cairo and New York: American University in Cairo Press, 2000.

Kitchen, K.A. *Pharaoh Triumphant: The Life and Times of Ramesses II*. Warminster: Aris & Phillips, 1982.

Lacau, P., and H. Chevrier. *Une chapelle de Sésostris Ier à Karnak*. Cairo: IFAO, 1956.

Lacau, P., H. Chevrier, M.-A. Bonhême, and M. Gitton. *Une chapelle d'Hatshepsout à Karnak*. Vol. 1. Cairo: IFAO: 1977.

Legrain, G. *Les temples de Karnak*. Bruxelles: Vromant, 1929.

Masse, D. *Burkhardt au coeur de l'Égypte*. Paris: Magellan, 2005.

Meeks, D. "Ipet." *LÄ*, vol. 3, 172–76.

Minutoli, H.K.M. von. *Reise zum Tempel des Jupiter Amon in der libyschen Wüste und nach Ober-Aegypten in den Jahren 1820 und 1821*. Berlin: n.p., 1824.

Murnane, W.J. "Opetfest." *LÄ*, vol. 4, 574–79.

Nelson, H.H. *The Great Hypostyle Hall in the Temple of Amun at Karnak*. Vol. 1.1. Chicago: Oriental Institute of the University of Chicago, 1981.

Ossian, C.R. "Karnak before the French Arrived: A Photographic and Literary Record." *KMT* 16, no. 4 (2005): 60–70.

Otto, E. "Amun." *LÄ*, vol. 1, 237–48.

Parker, R.A., J. Leclant, and J.C. Goyon. *The Edifice of Taharqa by the Sacred Lake at Karnak.* London: Lund Humphries, 1979.

Pécoil, J.F., and R. Baud. *L'Akh-menou de Thoutmosis III à Karnak: La Heret-ib et les chapelles attentantes. Relevés épigraphiques.* Paris: Éditions Recherche sur les civilisations, 2000.

Porter, B., and R.L.B. Moss. *Topographical Bibliography of Ancient Egyptian Hieroglyphic Texts, Reliefs, and Paintings.* Vol. 6: *Upper Egypt: Chief Temples (excluding Thebes).* Oxford: Clarendon Press, 1939.

Rilke, R.M. *Sämtliche Werke.* Vol. 2. Wiesbaden: Insel Verlag, 1957.

Saout, F., A.H. Ma'arouf, and Th. Zimmer. "Le Moyen Empire à Karnak: Varia I." In *Cahiers de Karnak 8 (1982–1985)*, 293–323. Paris: Éditions Recherche sur les civilisations, 1987.

Schwaller de Lubicz, R.A. *The Temples of Karnak.* London: Thames & Hudson, 1999.

Seton-Williams, V., and P. Stocks. *Egypt: Blue Guide.* London: A. and C. Black; New York: W.W. Norton, 1988.

Stadelmann, R. "Vierhundertjahrstele." *LÄ*, vol. 6, 1039–43.

Traunecker, C. "Une chapelle de magie guérisseuse sur le parvis du temple de Mout à Karnak." *JARCE* 20 (1983): 65–92.

Tyldesly, J. *Ramesses: Egypt's Greatest Pharaoh.* London: Penguin, 2000.

6. Amarna: City of the Heretic

Allen, J. "The Amarna Succession." In *Causing His Name to Live: Studies in Egyptian Epigraphy and History in Memory of William J. Murnane*, edited by P.J. Brand and L. Cooper, 9–20. Leiden: Brill Academic Publishers, 2009.

Anthes, R. *The Head of Queen Nofretete.* Berlin: Verlag Gebrüder Mann, 1954.

Arnold, D. *Die Tempel Ägyptens: Götterwohnungen, Kultstätten, Baudenkmäler.* Zürich: Artemis & Winkler, 1992.

Assmann, J. "Aten." *LÄ*, vol. 1, 526–46.

———. "Sonnengott." *LÄ*, vol. 5, 1087–94.

Callender, V.G. *In Hathor's Image.* Vol. 1: *The Wives and Mothers of Egyptian Kings from Dynasties I–VI.* Prague: Charles University Faculty of Arts, 2011.

Davies, N. de Garris. *The Rock Tombs of Amarna.* Vols. 1–6. London: Egypt Exploration Fund, 1903–1908.

Davis, T.M., G. Maspero, G.E. Smith, and E. Ayrton. *The Tomb of Queen Tîyi*. London: Constable & Co., 1910.

Glanville, S.R.K. "J.D.S. Pendlebury." *JEA* 28 (1942): 61–63 and pl. 8.

Hawass, Z. *Tutankhamun and the Golden Age of the Pharaohs*. Washington, D.C.: National Geographic Society, 2005.

Kemp, B.J. "Tell al-Amarna." *LA*, vol. 6, 310–19.

Kemp, B.J., and S. Garfi. *A Survey of the Ancient City of el-Amarna*. London: Egypt Exploration Society, 1993.

Kozloff, A.P., B.M. Bryan, and L.M. Berman. *Egypt's Dazzling Sun: Amenhotep III and His World*. Cleveland: Cleveland Museum of Art, 1992.

Krauss, R. "Why Nefertiti Went to Berlin." *KMT* 19, no. 3 (2008): 44–53.

Mallinson, M. "Akhetaten: Nothing Comes from Nowhere." In *Beyond the Horizon: Studies in Egyptian Art, Archaeology and History in Honour of Barry J. Kemp*, edited by S. Ikram and A. Dodson, vol. 1, 223–40. Cairo: American University in Cairo Press, 2009.

Martin, G.T. *The Royal Tomb at El-Amarna*. Vol. 1: *The Objects*. London: Egypt Exploration Society, 1974.

Peet, T.E., C.L. Wooley, B. Gunn, P.L.O. Guy, and F.G. Newton. *The City of Akhenaten*. Vol. 1: *Excavations of 1921 and 1922 at Tell el-'Amarneh*. London: Egypt Exploration Society, 1923.

Pendlebury, J.D.S. *Tell al-Amarna*. London: Dickson & Thompson, 1935.

Pendlebury, J.D.S., et al. *The City of Akhenaten*. Vol. 3: *The Central City and the Official Quarters. The Excavations at Tell el-Amarna during Seasons 1926–1927 and 1931–1936*. London: Egypt Exploration Society and Oxford University Press, 1951.

Petrie, W.M.F. *Tell al-Amarna*. London: Methuen, 1894.

Pritchard, J.B., ed. *The Ancient Near East*. Vol. 1: *An Anthology of Texts and Pictures*. Princeton, N.J.: Princeton University Press, 1958.

Redford, D.B. *Akhenaten: The Heretic King*. Princeton, N.J.: Princeton University Press, 1984.

Redford, D.B., A. Spalinger, J.K. Hoffmeier, R.J. Leprohon, A.R. Schulman, and E.S. Meltzer. *The Akhenaten Temple Project*. Vol. 2: *Rwd-mnw, Foreigners and Inscriptions*. Toronto: University of Toronto Press, 1988.

Reeves, N. *Akhenaten: Egypt's False Prophet*. London: Thames & Hudson, 2001.

Reeves, N., and R.H. Wilkinson. *The Complete Valley of the Kings*. London: Thames & Hudson, 1996.

Smith, R.W., D.B. Redford, S. Tawfik, R. Saad, and J. Gohary. *The Akhenaten Temple Project*. Vol. 1: *Initial Discoveries*. Warminster: Aris & Phillips, 1976.

Stevens, A. *Private Religion at Amarna: The Material Evidence*. Oxford: Archaeopress, 2006.

Tietze, Ch., ed. *Amarna: Lebensräume, Lebensbilder, Weltbilder*. Potsdam: Arcus-Verlag, 2008.

Vachala, B. *Milostné písně starého Egypta* [Love Songs of Ancient Egypt]. Prague: Setout, 2003.

7. Tanis: The Thebes of the North

Beckerath, J. von. *Tanis und Theben: Historische Grundlagen der Ramessidenzeit*. ÄF 16. Glückstadt, Hamburg, and New York: J.J. Augustin, 1951.

Brissaud, Ph., and Ch. Zivie-Coche. *Tanis: Travaux récents sur le Tell Sân al-Hagar. Mission française des fouilles de Tanis 1987–1997*. Paris: Éditions Noesis, 1998.

Dawson, W.R., E.P. Uphill, and M.L. Bierbrier. *Who Was Who in Egyptology*. 3rd ed. London: Egypt Exploration Society, 1995.

Goyon, G. *La découverte des trésors de Tanis: Aventures archéologiques en Égypte*. Paris: Perséa, 1987.

Griffith, F.Ll., and W.M.F. Petrie. *Two Hieroglyphic Papyri from Tanis*. London: Trübner, 1889.

Leclant, J. *Tanis: L'or des pharaons*. Paris: Galeries nationales du Grand Palais, 1987.

Montet, P. *Douze années de fouilles dans une capitale oubliée du delta égyptien*. Paris: Payot, 1942.

———. "La stèle de l'an 400 retrouvée." *Kêmi* 4 (1931): 191–215.

———. "Le temple du nord à Tanis." *Kêmi* 11 (1950): 46–58.

Petrie, W.M.F. *Tanis I, 1883–1884*. 2nd ed. London: Trübner, 1889.

Petrie, W.M.F., A.S. Murray, and F. Ll. Griffith. *Tanis II, Nebesheh and Defenneh (Tahpanhes)*. London: Trübner, 1888.

Römer, M. "Tanis." *LÄ*, vol. 6, 194–209.

Stadelmann, R. *Syrisch-palästinensische Gottheiten in Ägypten*. PÄ 5. Leiden: E.J. Brill, 1967.

8. Abydos: The Sacred Land, and Third Excursus

Altenmüller, H. "Djed-Pfeiler." *LÄ*, vol. 1, 1100–1105.

Amélineau, É.C. *Les nouvelles fouilles d'Abydos 1985–1898*. Paris: Leroux, 1902–1905.

Arnold, D. *The Encyclopedia of Ancient Egyptian Architecture*. Cairo: American University in Cairo Press, 2003.

———. *The Pyramid Complex of Senwosret III at Dahshur: Architectural Studies*. New York: Metropolitan Museum of Art, 2002.

Assmann, J. "Stundenwachen." *LA*, vol. 6, 104–106.

Ayrton, E.R., C.T. Currelly, A.E.P. Weigall, and A.H. Gardiner. *Abydos III*. London: Egypt Exploration Fund, 1904.

Begelsbacher-Fischer, B.L. *Untersuchungen zur Götterwelt des Alten Reiches im Spiegel der Privatgräber der IV. und V. Dynastie*. OBO 37. Freiburg, Switzerland: Universitätsverlag Freiburg, 1981.

Budge, E.A.W. *The Book of the Dead: Facsimiles of the Papyri of Hunefer, Ahai, Kerasher and Netchemet with Supplementary Text from the Papyrus of Nu*. London: British Museum, 1899.

Calverly, A., and A.H. Gardiner. *The Temple of King Sethos I at Abydos*. Vols. 1–4. London: Egypt Exploration Society; Chicago: University of Chicago Press, 1933–58.

Chassinat, É. *Le mystère d'Osiris au mois de Khoiak I–II*. Cairo: IFAO, 1966–68.

Cott, J. *The Search for Omm Sety*. New York: Doubleday, 1987.

David, R. *A Guide to Religious Ritual at Abydos*. Warminster: Aris & Phillips, 1981.

Dreyer, G. "Neue Forschungen in Abydos." *Sokar* 18 (2009): 6–7.

———. *Umm el-Qaab*. Vol. 1: *Das prädynastische Königsgrab U-j und seine frühen Schriftzeugnisse*. Mainz am Rhein: Verlag Philipp von Zabern, 1998.

Eady, D.L. *Omm Sety's Abydos*. Mississauga: Society for the Study of Egyptian Antiquities Publications, Benben Publications, 1983.

Frankfort, H. *The Cenotaph of Seti I at Abydos*. Vols. 1–2. London: Egypt Exploration Society, 1933.

Griffith, F.Ll. *Plutarch's* De Iside et Osiride. Cardiff: University of Wales, 1970.

Griffith, J.G. *The Origins of Osiris and His Cult*. Leiden: Brill, 1980.

———. "Osiris." *LÄ*, vol. 4, 624–33.

Helck, W. "Bemerkungen zum Ritual des Dramatischen Ramesseums-Papyrus." *Orientalia* 23 (1954): 408f.

Hopfner, T. *Plutarch über Isis und Osiris*. Vols. 1–2. Prague: Oriental Institute, 1940.

Ikram, S. "Animals in the Ritual Landscape at Abydos: A Synopsis." In *The Archaeology and Art of Ancient Egypt*, edited by Z. Hawass and J. Richards, vol. 1, 417–32. Cairo: Supreme Council of Antiquities of Egypt, 2007.

Junker, H. *Das Götterdekret über das Abaton*. DAWW 56. Vienna: A. Hölder, 1913.

———. *Die Stundenwachen in den Osirismysterien*. DAWW 54. Vienna: A. Hölder, 1910

Kemp, B. "The Osiris Temple at Abydos." *MDAIK* 23 (1968): 138–55.

Leitz, Ch., ed. *Lexikon der ägyptischen Götter und Götterbezeichnungen*. Vols. 1–7. OLA 111–17. Leuven, Paris, and Dudley, Mass.: Peeters, 2002.

Mariette, A. *Abydos: Description des fouilles exécutées sur l'emplacement de cette ville*. Vols. 1–2. Paris: A. Franck, 1868–80.

Marlar, M. "Sex as a Votive Offering at the Osiris Temple." In *The Archaeology and Art of Ancient Egypt*, edited by Z. Hawass and J. Richards, vol. 2, 111–20. Cairo: Supreme Council of Antiquities of Egypt, 2007.

Mojsov, B. *Osiris: Death and Afterlife of a God*. Malden, Md., Oxford, and Carlton, Victoria: Blackwell Publishing, 2005.

Murray, M.A., J. Grafton Milne, and W.E. Crum. *The Osireion at Abydos*. London: Quaritch, 1903.

Naville, E., T.E. Peet, H.R. Hall, and K. Haddon. *The Cemeteries of Abydos*. Vol. 1: *The Mixed Cemetery and Umm al-Ga'ab*. London: Egypt Exploration Fund, 1914.

O'Connor, D. *Abydos: Egypt's First Pharaohs and the Cult of Osiris*. Cairo: American University in Cairo Press, 2009.

———. "The 'Cenotaphs' of the Middle Kingdom in Abydos." In *Mélanges Gamal Mokhtar*, edited by P. Posener-Kriéger, vol. 2, 161–77. Cairo: IFAO, 1985.

———. "The Status of Early Egyptian Temples: An Alternative Theory." In *The Followers of Horus: Studies Dedicated to Michael Allen Hoffmann 1944–1990*, edited by R. Friedman and B. Adams, 83–98. Oxford: Oxbow Books, 1992.

Peet, E. *The Cemeteries of Abydos*. Vol. 2: *1911–1912*. London: Egypt Exploration Fund, 1914.

Petrie, W.M.F. *Abydos I–II*. London: Egypt Exploration Fund, 1902–1903.

Roberts, A. *My Heart My Mother: Death and Rebirth in Ancient Egypt*. Rottingdean: Northgate, 2000.

Simpson, W.K.S. *The Terrace of the Great God at Abydos: The Offering Chapels of Dynasties 12 and 13*. New Haven, Conn.: Peabody Museum of Natural History of Yale University; Philadelphia: University Museum of the University of Pennsylvania, 1974.

Stock, H. "Hermann Junker." *MDAIK* 18 (1962): 1–2.

Wegner, J. *The Mortuary Temple of Senwosret III at Abydos*. New Haven, Conn.: Peabody Museum of Natural History of Yale University; Philadelphia: University of Pennsylvania Museum of Archaeology and Anthropology, 2007.

Wilkinson, R.H. *The Complete Temples of Ancient Egypt*. London: Thames & Hudson, 2000.

Winlock, H. *The Temple of Ramesses I at Abydos*. New York: Metropolitan Museum of Art, 1937.

9. Philae: The Pearl of Egypt

Brunner-Traut, E., and V. Hell. *Ägypten: Studienreiseführer mit Landeskunde*. Stuttgart: Hans E. Günther Verlag, 1962.

Curzon, R. *Visits to the Monasteries of the Levant*. London: J. Murray, 1849.

Edwards, A.B. *A Thousand Miles up the Nile*. London: G. Routledge, 1891.

Junker, H. *Das Götterdekret über das Abaton*. Denkschriften KAWW 4. Vienna: A. Hölder, 1914.

Lloyd, A.B. "Philae." *OEAE*, vol. 3, 40–44.

Säve-Söderbergh, T. *Temples and Tombs of Ancient Nubia: The International Rescue Campaign at Abu Simbel, Philae, and Other Sites*. London: Thames & Hudson, 1987.

Seton-Williams, V., and P. Stocks. *Egypt: Blue Guide*. London: A. & C. Black; New York: W.W. Norton, 1988.

Stock, H. "Hermann Junker." *MDAIK* 18 (1962): 1–2.

Vassilika, E. *Ptolemaic Philae*. OLA 34. Leuven: Peeters, 1989.

Winter, E. "Philae." *LÄ*, vol. 4, 1022–27.

Zaki, G. *Le premier nome de Haute-Égypte du IIIe siècle avant J.C. au VIIe siècle après J.C. d'après les sources hiéroglyphiques des temples ptolémaïques et romaines*. Turnhout: Brépols, 2009.

10. Edfu: The Throne of Horus

Alliot, M. *Rapport sur les fouilles de Tell Edfou (1932)*. Cairo: IFAO, 1933.

———. *Rapport sur les fouilles de Tell Edfou (1933)*. Cairo: IFAO, 1935.

———. *Le temple d'Edfou*. Vols. 1–2. Cairo: IFAO, 1984–90.

Aufrère, S., J.C. Golvin, and J.C. Goyon. *L'Égypte restituée: Sites et temples de haute Égypte (1650 av. J.C.–300 ap. J.C.)*. Paris: Éditions Errance, 1991.

Blackman, A.M., and H.W. Fairman. "The Myth of Horus at Edfu II." *JEA* 28 (1942): 34.

Cauville, S. *Edfou*. Bibliothèque générale 6. Cairo: IFAO, 1984.

———. *Essai sur la théologie du temple d'Horus à Edfou*. BdÉ 102. Cairo: IFAO, 1987.

Chassinat, É. *Le mammisi d'Edfou*. Cairo: IFAO, 1939.

Fairman, H.W. *The Triumph of Horus: An Ancient Egyptian Sacred Drama*. Berkeley and Los Angeles: University of California Press, 1974.

Helck, W. *Die ägyptischen Gaue*. Beihefte TAVO, Series B, no. 5. Wiesbaden: Reichert, 1974.

Kurth, D. *Treffpunkt der Götter: Inschrfiten aus dem Tempel des Horus von Edfu*. Munich: Artemis, 1994.

Montet, P. *Géographie de l'Égypte ancienne*. Vol. 2: *La Haute Égypte*. Paris: Librairie C. Klincksieck, 1961.

Porter, B., and R.L.B. Moss. *Topographical Bibliography of Ancient Egyptian Hieroglyphic Texts, Reliefs, and Paintings*. Vol. 6: *Upper Egypt: Chief Temples (excluding Thebes)*. Oxford: Clarendon Press, 1939.

Rochemontieux, M. de, and É. Chassinat. *Le temple d'Edfou*. Vols. 1–14. Cairo: IFAO, 1897–1934.

Simpson, W.K., ed. *The Literature of Ancient Egypt: An Anthology of Stories, Instructions, Stelae, Autobiographies, and Poetry*. New Haven, Conn. and London: Yale University Press, 2003.

Vernus, P. "Tell Edfu." *LÄ*, vol. 6, 323–31.

11. Dendera: The Heliopolis of Hathor, and Fourth Excursus

Albright, W.F. *The Protosinaitic Inscriptions and Their Decipherment*. Cambridge: n.p., 1966.

Aufrère, S., J.-Cl. Golvin, and J.-Cl. Goyon. *L'Égypte restituée. Sites et temples de Haute Égypte*. Paris: Errance, 1991.

Bonnet, Ch., and D. Valbelle. "The Middle Kingdom Temple of Hathor at Serabit al-Khadim." In *The Temple in Ancient Egypt*, edited by S. Quirke, 82–89. London: British Museum Press, 1997.

Borchardt, L. *Das Grabdenkmal des Königs Sahure*. Vols. 1–2. Leipzig: J.C. Hinrichs'sche Buchhandlung, 1910–13.

Butin, R.F. "The Protosinaitic Inscriptions." *Harvard Theological Review* 25, no. 2 (1932): 130–203.

Cauville, S. *Dendera: Guide archéologique*. Cairo: IFAO, 1990.

———. *Essai sur la théologie du temple d'Horus à Edfou*. BdÉ 102. Cairo: IFAO, 1987.

Chassinat, É. *Le temple de Dendera*. Vols. 1–6. Cairo: IFAO, 1934–65.

Daumas, F. "Dendera." *LÄ*, vol. 1, 1060–63.

———. *Dendera et le temple d'Hathor*. CAIRO: IFAO, 1969.

———. "Le sanatorium de Dendera." *BIFAO* 56 (1957): 35–58.

Desroches-Noblecourt, Ch. *Amours et fureurs de La Lointaine: Clés pour la compréhension des symboles égyptiens*. Paris: Stock/Pernoud, 1995.

Fischer, H.G. *Dendera in the Third Millenium* BC. New York: J.J. Augustin, 1968.

Giveon, R. "Protosinaitische Inschriften." *LÄ*, vol. 4, 1156–59.

———. "Serabit al-Chadim." *LÄ*, vol. 5, 866–68.

Kemp, J.J. "The Location of the Early Town at Dendera." *MDAIK* 41 (1985): 89–95.

Landgráfová, R., and H. Navrátilová. *Sex and the Golden Goddess*. Vol. 1: *Ancient Egyptian Love Songs in Context*. Prague: Agama, 2009.

Petrie, W.M.F. *Denderah*. London: Egypt Exploration Fund, 1900.

Porter, B., and R.L.B. Moss. *Topographical Bibliography*. Vol. 6: *Upper Egypt: Chief Temples*. Oxford: Clarendon Press, 1939.

Watterson, B. *Gods of Ancient Egypt*. 3rd ed. Phoenix Mill: Sutton, 2003.

12. Alexander's City by Egypt

Bernard, A. *Alexandrie la Grande*. Paris: Hachette, 1996.

Bowman, A.K., R.A. Coles, N. Gonis, D. Obbink, and P.J. Parsons, eds. *Oxyrhynchus: A City and Its Texts*. London: Egypt Exploration Society, 2007.

Duell, L. *Svědkové času*. Prague: Odeon, 1974. Published in English as *Testament of Time*, 1965.

Empereur, J.Y. *Alexandria Rediscovered*. London: British Museum Press. 1998.

Frankfurter, D. *Religion in Roman Egypt: Assimilation and Resistance*. Princeton, N.J.: Princeton University Press, 1998.

Fraser, P.M. *Ptolemaic Alexandria*.Vols. 1–3. Oxford: Clarendon Press, 1972.

Grenfell, B.P., and A.S. Hunt. *The Oxyrhynchus Papyri*. Vol. 11. London: Egypt Exploration Fund, 1915.

Grimm, G. *Alexandria: Die erste Königsstadt der hellenistischen Welt*. Mainz am Rhein: Verlag Philipp von Zabern, 1998.

Jacob, Ch., and F. de Polignac, eds. *Alexandria, Third Century* BC: *The Knowledge of the World in a Single City*. Alexandria: Harpocrates, 2000.

McKenzie, J. *The Architecture of Alexandria and Egypt c. 300* BC *to* AD *700*. New Haven, Conn. and London: Yale University Press, 2007.

Rowe, A. *Discovery of the Famous Temple and Enclosure of Serapis at Alexandria. ASAE,* supplement 2. Cairo: IFAO, 1946.

Sabottka, M. *Das Serapeum in Alexandria: Untersuchungen zur Architektur und Baugeschichte des Heiligtums von der frühen ptolemäischen Zeit bis zur Zerstörung 391 n. Chr.* Études alexandrines 15. Cairo: IFAO, 2008.

Thiersch, H. *Pharos, Antike Islam und Occident: Ein Beitrag zur Architekturgeschichte.* Leipzig and Berlin: B.G. Teubner, 1909.

Tkaczow, B. *The Topography of Ancient Alexandria: An Archaeological Map.* Warsaw: Polish Academy, 1993.

Zandee, J. "Religion und Philosophie in der alexandrinischen Theologie, besonders in Justinus Martyr, Klemens von Alexandria, Origenes und 'Die Lehren des Silvanus.'" In *Religion und Philosophie im Alten Ägypten,* edited by U. Verhoeven and E. Graefe, 375–97. OLA 39. Leuven: Peeters, 1991.

Final Excursus: A Brief Outline of the Overall Architectural History of the Ancient Egyptian Temple

Arnold, D. *Die Tempel Ägyptens: Götterwohnungen, Kultstätten, Baudenkmäler.* Zürich: Artemis & Winkler, 1992.

———. *Temples of the Last Pharaohs.* New York and Oxford: Oxford University Press, 1999.

Badawi, A. *Le dessin architectural chez les anciens Égyptiens: Étude comparative des représentations égyptiennes de constructions.* Cairo: Imprimerie nationale, 1948.

Bárta, M., and M. Frouz. *Swimmers in the Sand.* Prague: Dryad, 2010.

Charloux, G.Ch. "Karnak à Moyen Empire: L'enceinte et les fondations des magasins du temple d'Amon-Rê." In *Cahiers de Karnak,* vol. 12, fasc. 1, 191–226. Cairo: IFAO, 2007.

Eigner, D. "Tell Ibrahim Awad: Divine Residence from Dynasty 0 until Dynasty 11." *Ä&L* 10 (2000): 17–36.

Hölscher. U. *The Excavation of Medinet Habu.* Vol. 1: *General Plans and Views.* Chicago: University of Chicago Press, 1934.

Hornung, E. *Geschichte als Fest.* Darmstadt: Wissenschaftliche Buchgesellschaft, 1966.

Munro, I. *Das Zelt-Heiligtum des Min: Rekonstruktion und Deutung eines fragmentarischen Modells (Kestner-Museum 1935.200.250).* MÄS 41. Munich and Berlin: Deutscher Kunstverlag, 1983.

Naville, E. *The Eleventh Dynasty Temple at Deir el-Bahari.* Vol. 2. London: Egypt Exploration Fund, 1910.

Petrie, W.M.F. *Hawara, Biahmu and Arsinoe.* London: Field & Tuer, The Leadenhall Press, 1889.

Quibell, J.E., and F.W. Green. *Hierakonpolis*. Vol. 2. London: Bernard Quaritch, 1902.

Ricke, H. "Bemerkungen zur ägyptischen Baukunst des Alten Reiches." *BÄBA* 5 (1950): 3–128.

Shaefer, R., ed. *Temples of Ancient Egypt*. Ithaca, N.Y.: Cornell University Press, 1997.

Shehata Adam. "Report on the Excavations of the Department of Antiquities at Ezbet Rushdi." *ASAE* 56 (1959): 207–26.

Spencer, P. *The Egyptian Temple: A Lexicographical Study*. London, Boston, and Melbourne: Kegan Paul International, 1984.

Vandier, J. *Manuel d'archéologie égyptienne*. Vol. 2. Paris: Picard, 1955.

Varille, A., and C. Robichon. *Description sommaire du temple primitif de Médamoud*. Cairo: IFAO, 1940.

Vörös, G. *Egyptian Temple Architecture: 100 Years of Hungarian Excavations in Egypt, 1907–2007*. Budapest: Kairosz Press, 2007.

Wightman, G.J. *Sacred Spaces: Religious Architecture in the Ancient World*. ANES, Supplement 22. Leuven, Paris, and Dudley, Mass.: Peeters, 2007.

Wilkinson, R.H. *The Complete Temples of Ancient Egypt*. London: Thames & Hudson, 2000.

ILLUSTRATION CREDITS

Only abbreviated bibliographical references are used in this section; for a full citation of the reference, consult the chapter bibliographies.

Other abbreviations are as follows:

CU FA CzEgl	Czech Egyptological Institute of the Faculty of Arts of Charles University, Prague
b	below/bottom
c	center
l	left
r	right
t	top

Cover CU FA CzEgI: Martin Frouz. **ii–iii** *LD,* Part 1, fig. 71, Berlin 1849–59. **iv** CU FA CzEgI: Milan Zemina. **v** *Description de l'Égypte,* pl. 53,5. **x** CU FA CzEgI: Jaromír Krejčí. **1** *Description de l'Égypte,* A, vol. 3, pl. 45. **2** *LD,* part 1, pl. 106. **4** *Description de l'Égypte* A, vol. 3, pl. 19. **5** CU FA CzEgI: Milan Zemina. **7** Drawing by Miroslav Ottmar after Lauer, "Le triangle sacré," 64 fig. 8. **8** CU FA CzEgI: Milan Zemina. **10** *Description de l'Égypte,* A, vol. 1, pl. 50. **12** CU FA CzEgI: Jolana Malátková. **13** CU FA CzEgI: Milan Zemina. **15** CU FA CzEgI: Milan Zemina. **16** CU FA CzEgI: Jolana Malátková. **19** CU FA CzEgI: Milan Zemina. **20** Quibell, *Hierakonpolis,* vol. 1, pl. 26 (t); CU FA CzEgI: Jolana Malátková (b). **23** Budge, *The Book of the Dead,* pl. 7. **24** CU FA CzEgI: Milan Zemina. **25** CU FA CzEgI: Jolana Malátková. **30** Verner, *Abusir III. The Pyramid Complex of Khentkaus,* fig. 86 no. 90/A/78. **31** CU FA CzEgI: Milan Zemina. **33** Drawing by Jolana Malátková after Michailidis, "Moule illustrant un text d'Hérodote," 63 pl. 7. **36–37** CU FA CzEgI: Milan Zemina. **39** CU FA CzEgI: Kamil Voděra. **41** CU FA CzEgI: Milan Zemina. **43** CU FA CzEgI: Jolana Malátková. **44–45** Aus d. Kunstanst. d. Bibliogr. Inst. in Hildbk. **46** CU FA CzEgI: Jaromír Krejčí. **48** CU FA CzEgI: Jaromír Krejčí. **49** CU FA CzEgI: Milan Zemina. **50** CU FA CzEgI: Miroslav Ottmar. **51** Drawing by Jolana Malátková after Daressy, "Graffiti," 46 fig. 1. **52** Budge, *The Book of the Dead,* pl. 8. **53** CU FA CzEgI: Jolana Malátková. **54** CU FA CzEgI: Jolana Malátková. **56** Drawing by Luděk Wellner after Ricke, "Der Hohe Sand," 116 fig. 3. **57** Drawing by Luděk Wellner after Ricke, "Eine Inventartafel," 130 fig. 6. **58** Arnold, *Die Tempel Ägyptens,* p. 205; reproduced by author's permission. **59** CU FA CzEgI: Jolana Malátková. **60** CU

FA CzEgI: Milan Zemina. **63** CU FA CzEgI: Milan Zemina. **64** CU FA CzEgI: Jaromír Krejčí. **65** CU FA CzEgI: Kamil Voděra. **67** Borchardt, "Der Bau," pl. 1. **73** Drawing by Jolana Malátková after Schäfer, "Altägyptische Bilder," 20 fig. 2. **74** CU FA CzEgI: Milan Zemina. **75** Drawing by Jolana Malátková after Lanzone, *Dizionario*, pl. 155. **77** CU FA CzEgI: Milan Zemina. **80** Budge, *The Book of the Dead*, pl. 11. **81** CU FA CzEgI: Milan Zemina. **82** CU FA CzEgI: Milan Zemina. **85** CU FA CzEgI: Jolana Malátková. **88–89** *Description de l'Égypte* A, vol. 5, pl. 12. **90** CU FA CzEgI: Milan Zemina. **92** CU FA CzEgI: Jolana Malátková. **93** CU FA CzEgI: Jolana Malátková. **94** Newberry, "William Matthew Flinders Petrie," pl. 5. **96** CU FA CzEgI: Milan Zemina. **97** Drawing by Luděk Wellner after Petrie, *Memphis*, vol. 1, pl. 1 and Porter, Moss, and Malek, *Topographical Bibliography*, pl. 71. **98** *Description de l'Égypte*, A, vol. 5, pl. 1. **99** *Description de l'Égypte*, A, vol. 5, pl. 3. **100** CU FA CzEgI: Milan Zemina. **102** CU FA CzEgI: Milan Zemina. **103** After Kaiser, "Die dekorierte Torfassade," fig. 2. **104** CU FA CzEgI: Milan Zemina. **105** CU FA CzEgI: Milan Zemina. **106** CU FA CzEgI: Jolana Malátková. **107** After Arnold, *Die Tempel Ägyptens*, p. 193; reproduced by author's permission. **108** Petrie, *Memphis*, vol. 1, pl. 9. **109** CU FA CzEgI: Milan Zemina. **111** CU FA CzEgI: Milan Zemina. **112** CU FA CzEgI: Milan Zemina. **115** CU FA CzEgI: Jolana Malátková. **116** CU FA CzEgI: Drawing by Jolana Malátková. **118** Borchardt, *Das Grabdenkmal*, 41 fig. 23. **119** CU FA CzEgI: Milan Zemina. **121** Breasted, "The Philosophy," pls. 1–2 (t); after Steindorff, "Kurt Sethe," fig. p. 132 (l, b); Erman, "Bibliographie," fig. p. 1 (r, b). **125** CU FA CzEgI: Milan Zemina. **127** CU FA CzEgI: Milan Zemina. **128** Kees, "Die Grosse Festdarstellung," in F.W. von Bissing, pl. 15, 251. **129** After Lauer, "Les statues grecques," fig. p. 218. **130** After Mariette, *Le Sérapéum*, 199, fig. 3. **131** After Mariette, *Le Sérapéum*. **133** After Mariette, *Le Sérapéum*. **134** *Mélanges Mariette*, pl. 1. **135** CU FA CzEgI: Milan Zemina. **136** CU FA CzEgI: Jolana Malátková. **138** CU FA CzEgI: Milan Zemina. **140** CU FA CzEgI: Milan Zemina. **141** Mariette, *Le Sérapéum*, vol. 3, pl. 8. **142–143** *Description de l'Égypte*, vol. 4, pl. 51. **144** CU FA CzEgI: Milan Zemina. **146** CU FA CzEgI: Milan Zemina. **147** Arnold, *Die Tempel Ägyptens*, fig. on p. 182; reproduced by author's permission. **148** CU FA CzEgI: Milan Zemina. **149** *Description de l'Égypte*, vol. 4, pl. 54. **150** CU FA CzEgI: Milan Zemina. **151** After Kessler, *Die heiligen Tiere*, vol. 1, 207 fig. 14; reproduced by author's permission. **152** Petrie and Walker, *The Palace of Apries*, pl. 15 (u). **153** CU FA CzEgI: Jolana Malátková (t, b). **156** CU FA CzEgI: Jolana Malátková. **159** CU FA CzEgI: Jolana Malátková. **166–167** *Description de l'Égypte*, vol. 3, pl. 3. **168** Daniel Malátek. **170** CU FA CzEgl: Milan Zemina. **171** CU FA CzEgl: Jolana Malátková. **172** *LD*, part 1, pl. 126. **174** CU FA CzEgl: Jolana Malátková. **176** Denon, *Voyage*, pl. 43, 2 and 3 (t, b). **177** Arnold, *Die Tempel Ägyptens*, fig. p. 112–13; reproduced by author's permission. **178**

CU FA CzEgl: Milan Zemina. **179** CU FA CzEgl: Jolana Malátková. **180** CU FA CzEgl: Miroslav Ottmar. **181** Drawing by Jolana Malátková after Saout, Ma'arouf, and Zimmer, *Karnak 8*, 314, pl. I. **182** CU FA CzEgl: Jaromír Krejčí. **183** CU FA CzEgl: Milan Zemina. **184** CU FA CzEgl: Milan Zemina. **186** After Arnold, *Die Tempel Ägyptens*, fig. p. 113; reproduced by author's permission. **187** CU FA CzEgl: Milan Zemina. **188** CU FA CzEgl: Daniel Malátek. **190** *LD*, part 1, pl. 81. **191** CU FA CzEgl: Jolana Malátková. **192** CU FA CzEgl: Jolana Malátková. **194** CU FA CzEgl: Jaromír Krejčí. **196** CU FA CzEgl: Milan Zemina. **198** *LD*, part 1, pl. 77. **199** CU FA CzEgl: Milan Zemina. **200** CU FA CzEgl: Milan Zemina. **201** Legrain, *Les temples de Karnak*, fig. 13. **204** CU FA CzEgl: Drawing by Jolana Malátková after photo by Milan Zemina. **205** CU FA CzEgl: Milan Zemina. **206** CU FA CzEgl: Milan Zemina. **208** CU FA CzEgl: Milan Zemina. **210** CU FA CzEgl: Martin Frouz. **211** CU FA CzEgl: Jolana Malátková. **213** CU FA CzEgl: Milan Zemina. **215** CU FA CzEgl: Jaromír Krejčí. **217** Courtesy Dr. Hourig Sourouzian, Memnon Colossi Conservation and Preservation Project: Jolana Malátková. **218** CU FA CzEgl: Jolana Malátková. **219** CU FA CzEgl: Jaromír Krejčí. **221** Denon, *Voyage*, pl. 49, 2. **222** CU FA CzEgl: Milan Zemina. **224** Arnold, *Die Tempel Ägyptens*, fig. p. 128; reproduced by author's permission. **225** CU FA CzEgI: Milan Zemina. **226** CU FA CzEgl: Milan Zemina. **228** CU FA CzEgl: Miroslav Verner. **229** CU FA CzEgl: Milan Zemina. **230** CU FA CzEgl: Milan Zemina. **231** CU FA CzEgl: Milan Zemina. **234** CU FA CzEgl: Jolana Malátková. **235** CU FA CzEgl: Milan Zemina. **238** CU FA CzEgl: Milan Zemina. **239** *LD*, part 1, pl. 109. **240** CU FA CzEgl: Milan Zemina. **241** CU FA CzEgl: Jaromír Krejčí. **242** Belzoni, *Plates Illustrative*, frontispiece. **244** Arnold, *Die Tempel Ägyptens*, fig. on p. 78; reproduced by author's permission. **246** CU FA CzEgl: Milan Zemina (t); drawing by Jolana Malátková after Desroches-Noblecourt, *Ramses le Grand*, 42 (b). **247** CU FA CzEgl: Milan Zemina. **248** CU FA CzEgl: Jaromír Krejčí. **249** CU FA CzEgl: Miroslav Verner. **251** CU FA CzEgl: Milan Zemina. **254** CU FA CzEgl: Jolana Malátková. **256** Drawing by Miroslav Ottmar after Fakhry, *Recent Excavations*, 24, fig. 13. **257** CU FA CzEgl: Jolana Malátková. **260–261** CU FA CzEgl: Jolana Malátková. **262** CU FA CzEgl: Luděk Wellner. **264** CU FA CzEgl: Jolana Malátková. **266** CU FA CzEgl: Jolana Malátková. **268** CU FA CzEgl: Jolana Malátková. **270** CU FA CzEgl: Milan Zemina. **272–273** After *Description de l'Égypte*, vol. 4, pl. 63. **274** CU FA CzEgI: Jolana Malátková. **276** CU FA CzEgI: Milan Zemina (t); after Glanville, "J.S. Pendlebury," pl. 8 (b). **278** CU FA CzEgI: Milan Zemina. **281** CU FA CzEgI: Milan Zemina. **282** Petrie, *Tell el-Amarna*, pl. 3 no. 3. **284** Courtesy Dr. Hourig Sourouzian, Memnon Colossi Conservation and Preservation Project: Jolana Malátková. **285** W.R. Johnson in Kozloff, Bryan, and Berman, *Egypt's Dazzling Sun*, 72, fig. 2a; reproduced by author's permission. **287** CU FA CzEgI: Milan Zemina. **288** Pendlebury, *The City of Akhenaten* 3, pl. 59, no. 1. **289** CU FA CzEgI: Jaromír Krejčí. **291** CU FA CzEgI: Milan Zemina. **292** Drawing by Luděk Wellner after Pendlebury, *Tell al-Amarna*, 36. **293** CU FA CzEgI: Jolana Malátková. **294** Pendlebury et al., *The City of Akhenaten*, pl. 4. **295** CU FA CzEgI: Jolana Malátková. **296** Arnold, *Die Tempel Ägyptens*, fig. on p. 180. **297** After Pendlebury, *The City of Akhenaten*, pl. 2. **298** After Peet, Wooley, Gunn, Guy, and Newton, *The City of Akhenaten*, pl. 39. **299** CU FA CzEgI: Jolana Malátková. **301** CU FA CzEgI: Jolana Malátková. **303** CU FA CzEgI: Jolana Malátková. **305** CU FA CzEgI: Milan Zemina. **306** CU FA CzEgI: Milan Zemina. **309** CU FA CzEgI: Jolana Malátková. **314** Bildarchiv Preussischer Kulturbesitz/Ägyptisches Museum und Papyrussammlung, Staatliche Museen zu Berlin/Margarete Büsing. **318–319** *Description de ⊠Égypte*, vol. 5, pl. 28. **320** CU FA CzEgI: Jolana Malátková. **322** CU FA CzEgI: Jolana Malátková. **323** CU FA CzEgI: Jaromír Krejčí. **324** Dawson, Uphill, and Bierbrier, *Who Was Who in Egyptology*, 293. **325** Drawing by Miroslav Ottmar after Brissaud and Zivie-Coche, *Tanis*, 15 (l); drawing by Jolana Malátková after Montet, "La stèle de l'an 400 retrouvée," pl. 11 (r). **327** CU FA CzEgI: Jolana Malátková. **328** CU FA CzEgI: Jolana Malátková (t); Arnold, *Encyclopedia*, fig. p. 238; reproduced by author's permission (b). **329** CU FA CzEgI: Jolana Malátková. **330** CU FA CzEgI: Jolana Malátková. **332** CU FA CzEgI: Jolana Malátková. **333** CU FA CzEgI: Jolana Malátková. **335** CU FA CzEgI: Jolana Malátková. **336** Drawing by Miroslav Ottmar after Montet, *Douze années de fouilles*, 133 fig. 37. **337** CU FA CzEgI: Milan Zemina. **339** CU FA CzEgI: Jolana Malátková. **342–343** *LD*, part 1, pl. 65. **344** CU FA CzEgI: Jolana Malátková. **346** CU FA CzEgI: Jolana Malátková. **347** Plan by Felix Arnold published in Dreyer, *Umm el-Qaab*, fig. 1; reproduced by author's permission. **348** CU FA CzEgI: Milan Zemina. **349** CU FA CzEgI: Milan Zemina. **350** CU FA CzEgI: Milan Zemina. **351** CU FA CzEgI: Jolana Malátková. **352** CU FA CzEgI: Milan Zemina. **353** *Description de l'Égypte*, vol. 4, pl. 35. **354** CU FA CzEgI: Jolana Malátková. **355** Junker, *Das Götterdekret*, 51 fig. 15. **356** CU FA CzEgI: Jolana Malátková. **358** Arnold, *Encyclopedia*, 196; reproduced with author's permission. **359** Arnold, *The Pyramid Complex of Senwosret III*, plan VI (t), reproduced by author's permission; drawing by Jolana Malátková after Ayrton, Currelly, Weigall, and Gardiner, *Abydos III*, pl. 36 (b). **361** CU FA CzEgI: Milan Zemina. **362** CU FA CzEgI: Milan Zemina. **364** Arnold, *Die Tempel Ägyptens*, fig. on p. 170; reproduced by author's permission. **365** CU FA CzEgI: Jolana Malátková. **366** CU FA CzEgI: Jolana Malátková. **368** CU FA CzEgI: Jolana Malátková. **369** Murray, Milne, and Crum, *The Osireion*, pl. 26. **370** CU FA CzEgI: Jolana Malátková. **374** Budge, *Book of the Dead*, pl. 5. **377** Junker, *Das Götterdekret*, 40 fig. 9. **379** CU FA CzEgI: Jolana Malátková. **381** Drawing by Jolana Malátková after Calverly, Broome, and Gardiner, *Abydos*, vol. 3, pl. 8. **383** CU

FA CzEgI. **384–385** CU FA CzEgI: Milan Zemina. **387** Junker, *Das Götterdekret*, 67 fig. 24. **388** CU FA CzEgI: Martin Frouz. **391** CU FA CzEgI: Milan Zemina. **394** Courtesy Roemer-Pelizeus Museum in Hildesheim (inv. no. 4550). **397** Stock, "Hermann Junker," fig. p. 1. **400–401** After *Description de l'Égypte*, vol. 1, pl. 4. **402** CU FA CzEgI: Martin Frouz. **404** CU FA CzEgI: Jolana Malátková (t); *LD*, part 1, pl. 105 (b). **405** CU FA CzEgI: Milan Zemina. **406** CU FA CzEgI: Milan Zemina. **407** After Brunner-Traut and Hell, *Ägypten*, 528. **408** CU FA CzEgI: Milan Zemina. **409** CU FA CzEgI: Jolana Malátková. **410** CU FA CzEgI: Milan Zemina. **412** *Description de l'Égypte*, vol. 1, pl. 4. **413** CU FA CzEgI: Jolana Malátková. **414** *LD*, part 1, pl. 103 (b). **415** Drawing by Jolana Malátková after Junker, *Das Götterdekret*, 42 fig. 10b. **417** CU FA CzEgI: Jolana Malátková. **420–421** Denon, *Voyage*, pl. 57 (t). **422** CU FA CzEgI: Jolana Malátková. **424** CU FA CzEgI: Jolana Malátková (t); Denon, *Voyage*, pl. 58 (b). **425** Montet, *Géographie de l'Égypte ancienne*, 32 fig. 2. **427** CU FA CzEgI: Milan Zemina. **428** *Description de l'Égypte*, vol. 1, pl. 55. **429** CU FA CzEgI: Milan Zemina. **430** Arnold, *Die Tempel Ägyptens*, fig. p. 100 (t); reproduced by author's permission. **432** CU FA CzEgI: Jolana Malátková. **434** CU FA CzEgI: Jolana Malátková. **435** *Description de l'Égypte*, vol. 1, pl. 65. **436** CU FA CzEgI: Jolana Malátková. **438** CU FA CzEgI: Jolana Malátková. **442–443** *Description de l'Égypte*, vol. 4, pl. 9. **444** CU FA CzEgI: Jolana Malátková. **446** Denon, *Voyage*, pl. 38, 4–5. **447** CU FA CzEgI: Jolana Malátková (t); *Description de l'Égypte*, vol. 4, pl. 4 (b). **449** *Description de l'Égypte*, vol. 4, pl. 9 (t); Arnold, *Die Tempel Ägyptens*, fig. p. 100 (b); reproduced by author's permission. **451** CU FA CzEgI: Jolana Malátková. **453** *Description de l'Égypte*, vol. 4, pl. 12 (b). **454** Drawing by Jolana Malátková after photo in Cauville, *Dendera*, fig. p. 51. **455** CU FA CzEgI: Jolana Malátková. **456** CU FA CzEgI: Jolana Malátková. **457** *Description de l'Égypte*, vol. 4, pl. 21. **458** CU FA CzEgI: Jolana Malátková. **459** Drawing by Miroslav Ottmar after Aufrère, Golvin, and Goyon, *L'Égypte Restituée. Haute Égypte*, fig. p. 228. **461** CU FA CzEgI: Jolana Malátková. **463** CU FA CzEgI: Milan Zemina (t); CU FA CzEgI: Jolana Malátková (b). **464** CU FA CzEgI: Jolana Malátková. **465** CU FA CzEgI: Jolana Malátková. **467** CU FA CzEgI: Jolana Malátková. **470** CU FA CzEgI: Drawing by Jolana Malátková after Cauville, *Dendera*, fig. p. 59. **472–473** CU FA CzEgI: Milan Zemina. **474** CU FA CzEgI: Milan Zemina. **475** Sketch plan of Sinai, CU FA CzEgI. **476** CU FA CzEgI: Miroslav Bárta (t); after Arnold, *Die Tempel Ägyptens*, fig. on p. 224 (c); reproduced by author's permission. **477** CU FA CzEgI: Milan Zemina. **478** Borchardt, *Das Grabdenkmal des Königs Sahure*, pl. 5. **480** Butin, "The Protosinaitic Inscriptions," fig. p. 177. **482–483** *Description de l'Égypte*, vol. 5, pl. 32. **484** CU FA CzEgI: Jaromír Krejčí. **486** Private collection (t); CU FA CzEgI: Jolana Malátková (b). **487** CU FA CzEgI: Jolana Malátková. **489** CU FA CzEgI: Drawing by Jolana Malátková after

Thiersch, *Pharos,* frontispiece. **490** CU FA CzEgI: Jaromír Krejčí. **491** CU FA CzEgI: Jolana Malátková. **493** CU FA CzEgI: Milan Zemina. **494** CU FA CzEgI: Jolana Malátková. **495** *Description de l'Égypte,* vol. 5, pl. 34. **496** CU FA CzEgI: Jolana Malátková. **498** CU FA CzEgI: Jolana Malátková. **501** CU FA CzEgI: Milan Zemina. **502** Denon, *Voyage,* pl. 31. **503** CU FA CzEgI: Milan Zemina. **504** Grenfell and Hunt, *The Oxyrhynchus Papyri,* pl. 2. **506–507** CU FA CzEgI: Milan Zemina. **509** CU FA CzEgI: Miroslav Verner. **510** CU FA CzEgI: Miroslav Bárta. **511** Drawing by Jolana Malátková after Badawi, *Le dessin architectural,* 13 fig. 11. **512** Quibell and Green, *Hierakonpolis II,* pl. 73. **513** Drawing by Jolana Malátková after Badawi, *Le dessin architectural,* 159 fig. 197. **514** CU FA CzEgI: Milan Zemina. **515** Drawing by Jolana Malátková after Badawi, *Le dessin architectural,* 48 fig 48,12 and 49 fig. 49,9. **516** CU FA CzEgI: Jolana Malátková. **517** CU FA CzEgI: Jolana Malátková. **518** CU FA CzEgI: Jolana Malátková (t); Arnold, *Die Tempel Ägyptens,* 161 A, B (b); reproduced by author's permission. **520** Eigner, "Tell Ibrahim Awad," 26 fig. 5; reproduced by author's permission. **521** CU FA CzEgI: Milan Zemina. **522** Drawing by Jolana Malátková after Ricke, "Bemerkungen zur ägyptischen Baukunst," 72 fig. 28. **523** CU FA CzEgI: Jaromír Krejčí. **525** Arnold, *Die Tempel Ägyptens,* fig. on p. 141 (t), reproduced by author's permission; Naville, *The Eleventh Dynasty Temple,* pl. 23 (b). **526** Vörös, *Egyptian Temple Architecture,* 85 fig. 49 (l); drawing by Miroslav Ottmar after Shehata Adam, "Report on the Excavations," pl. 2 (r). **528** Charloux, "Karnak à Moyen Empire," pl. 20 (t), reproduced by author's permission; Petrie, *Hawara, Biahmu, and Arsinoe,* pl. 25 (b). **529** CU FA CzEgI: Milan Zemina. **531** CU FA CzEgI: Milan Zemina. **533** Daniel Malátek. **534** CU FA CzEgI: Milan Zemina. **535** After Hölscher, *The Excavation of Medinet Habu,* pl. 2. **538** CU FA CzEgI: Milan Zemina. **539** *LD,* part 1, pl. 108. **540** CU FA CzEgI: Milan Zemina. **541** CU FA CzEgI: Jolana Malátková. **542** Arnold, *Die Tempel Ägyptens,* fig. p. 97; reproduced by author's permission. **545** CU FA CzEgI: Milan Zemina.